34 ⁹⁵

D1500278

CLASS AND IDOL IN THE ENGLISH HYMN

Class and Idol in the English Hymn completes Lionel Adey's study of English hymnody which began with *Hymns and Christian "Myth"* (1986). In his new book Adey surveys the contents of English hymnody, primarily between 1700 and 1939, investigating the social context in which the hymns were sung and their influence on the singers.

Adey describes the nature of hymns written in the "Learned" and "Popular" styles and links them to particular denominations and sects. (This is inferred from a computer survey that identifies which hymns were sung most frequently and by which worshippers.) The traditions grew increasingly separate during the English evangelical revival but converged in the late Victorian period, preparing the way for the ecumenical movement of this century.

Two kinds of hymn books instilled different ethics: one applicable to the "order-givers" of the world, the other to the "order-receivers." Different religious codes are perceived in hymnals for "submerged" children in English charity schools and orphanages, "average" children in day and Sunday-schools, and "privileged" youth in boarding schools. (The parallel division within North American hymnody and worship Adey finds more a matter of race than of class.) In the hymns he detects a shift in emphasis from the awefulness of God to identification with Jesus as a human figure, a consecration of nature and childhood and, eventually, the attribution of religious value to the nation-state. These themes reached a climax in late Victorian and Edwardian hymnody for children but their conditioning, Adey concludes, played a part in preparing young people to fight in the First World War and disillusioned many with religion.

In his closing chapters Adey examines the effect of the war upon hymns and hymn-singing, the subsequent reaction against idolatry and sentimental-ism, and the improving literary quality of post-war hymnals—notably for children. He considers briefly the recent torrent of new hymns and the prospects for their use and performance in an age of pluralism and widespread unbelief or, at best, indifference.

Class and Idol in the English Hymn is pertinent not only to academics in fields of literature, religion, history, and psychology but also to hymn lovers, hymn writers, and clergy.

LIONEL ADEY is a professor in the department of English at the University of Victoria.

CLASS and IDOL
in the
ENGLISH HYMN

LIONEL ADEY

University of British Columbia Press
Vancouver 1988

This book has been published with the help of a grant
from the Canadian Federation for the Humanities, using
funds provided by the Social Sciences and Humanities
Research Council of Canada.

Canadian Cataloguing in Publication Data
Adey, Lionel.
    Class and idol in the English hymn

    Bibliography: p.
    Includes index.
    ISBN 0-7748-0304-5
    1. Hymns, English—History and criticism.
I. Title.
BV312.A33 1988   264'.2'0942   C88-091616-8

ISBN 0-7748-0304-5
Printed in Canada

To my wife

CONTENTS

PREFACE

The research for this book began in 1976, in preparation for a conference paper on Victorian hymnody. I cannot better describe how images in mind since childhood combined with long experience of thumbing through hymn-books in choir-stalls to form the underlying realization than from the preface to my preceding volume, *Hymns and the Christian "Myth"* (1986). There I described how a great-aunt recalled the long defunct family prayers and Sunday evening performances of "beautiful 'ymns," then how my mother recollected that in her girlhood gentlemen choristers from the parish church would process after Evensong to her uncle's public house, "seat themselves round the specially polished mahogany table" in the front parlour, "lay down their top-hats, and, for the edification of the erring sheep in the public bar, sing a hymn." Whereas my great-aunt's family prayed and sang at home in the 1870s, by the 1890s many customers in the pub "prayed only to the barman," for "to request and hear a hymn was their only form of Sunday observance."

When Matthew Arnold prophesied in 1880 that poetry would usurp the functions of religion, "to interpret life . . . console . . . and sustain" mankind, that "most of what now passes . . . for religion and philosophy would be replaced by poetry,"[1] he was prophesying after the event. He had failed to take account of Christian folk-poems for the same reason that critics of former generations had overlooked the secular folk-poems, such as ballads, that were still passed down orally among country people. He belonged to the professional class, they and townsfolk to the populace that, in *Culture and Anarchy* (1871), he had not credited with any form of mass expression beyond "bawling, hustling and smashing" or else "beer."[2] Since the populace evidently enjoyed hymns, did they enjoy a different kind from those sung by such as Arnold, who thought "When I survey the wondrous Cross" the finest hymn in the language? Did this difference extend to the hymn-books at the chapels where miners, mill-hands, and their wives had formerly worshipped, as distinct from public school and college chapels or fashionable churches?

At the conference I spoke of a "university" and "back-street chapel" tradition of hymnody, the one sanctifying the ethos of a ruling class, the other that of people condemned to daily drudgery and privation in this life, their hope being fixed on the next. In time "Learned" and "Popular" replaced these more limited terms, but failed to meet the objection that the Wesleys, from whom stemmed the whole of Methodist hymnody, manifestly belonged to the same class as Arnold and Cowper, authors of that paradigm of Popular hymnody "There is a fountain filled with blood." Light came via R.L. Greene's distinction between medieval carols that were "popular by origin" and "popular by destination."[3] At once the differences became clear between the Learned tradition originating in monastic hymnody and continuing in that of churches largely attended by the educated, the Wesleyan hymns that were Popular by destination, and the Primitive Methodist hymns that were, like the negro spirituals, Popular by origin.

The detachment of hymns from their liturgical context, illustrated at an early stage in my mother's recollection of choristers singing in a pub, and at a later one in the singing of "Abide with me" at English soccer Cup finals, sheds light on a Remembrance Day ritual observed in my schooldays. Each year we lined up before a gilded list of Old Boys killed in the First World War and sang "For all the saints." As remarked in my earlier preface, no boy ever seemed to notice "that junior officers and soldiers did not . . . become Christian martyrs by dying in battle," or that Bishop How had composed the hymn for All Saints' Day, a feast of which few boys had heard. "The solemn ritual and Vaughan Williams' splendid tune, admiration and pity for our elder brethren, and sometimes parental reminiscences of dead or maimed relatives compelled respectful assent to this diversion of religious imagery and emotion to a secular object." For that day, the "supreme sacrifice" meant death not on the Cross but in battle.

My three objects in this book are to show how the Learned and Popular traditions bifurcated during the late eighteenth century and came together during the late nineteenth, to show how hymns transmitted class conditioning to children, and to trace the intrusion of other secular concerns, such as nationalism, into the sacred domain of hymnody. These secular interests caused hymn-texts to change their meaning according to the time and circumstances in which they were sung. My earlier book traced changing representations in hymns of the basic Christian beliefs, especially in the Middle Ages and since the Reformation. The two books were conceived as one, under the general title "Myth, Class and Idol in the English Hymn," but had to be separated when the proposed preliminary chapters on the "Myth" grew into a book-length manuscript.

Like the earlier one, this book is not a history. It owes much to three great historians of the hymn, Louis F. Benson, John Julian, and the late Erik Routley, whose last work, *Christian Hymns Observed*, seen since the time of writing, has a wealth of detail that would have improved my Chapter 16. It also draws heavily upon standard biographies and works of ecclesiastical and social history. Its originality resides in its material drawn from long-disused hymnals for adults and children in the many collections listed in the Acknowledgments, and in its aim of explaining not the circumstances under which hymns were written but what they are likely to have conveyed within the interpretive contexts in which they were sung. To my knowledge, no one has attempted such explanation on this scale before. It is intended to interest any open-minded student not only of religion but of related disciplines: literature, psychology, history, and sociology. As contended in my earlier preface, "The past and future direction of Christianity in English-speaking countries and the effects upon the individual or collective psyche of Christian folk poems ceaselessly reiterated, especially in childhood . . . will, I hope, repay the attention of all who have not arrived at unchangeable certainties concerning the human condition, and even more, perhaps, of those who have."

ACKNOWLEDGMENTS

To the Victorian Studies Association of Western Canada for my first opportunity to pursue this topic; to the Hymn Society of Great Britain and Ireland and the editors of *Essays in Criticism*, *The Hymn*, *Mosaic*, and *Wascana Review* for further opportunities to develop it in articles or reviews. To the late Erik Routley for encouragement and advice on sources; to Drs. Routley, the late George Whalley, and the happily surviving Georg Tennyson for assistance in securing grants. To the Social Sciences and Humanities Research Council of Canada for funding not only my research but the indispensable services of John Duber and Maria Abbott as my research assistants, and a long leave that enabled me to write this and the preceding book. To the assessors of the Canadian Federation for the Humanities for much good advice. To the University of Victoria for funding short-term research, computer work and storage, and the typing carried out with inexhaustible patience by Colleen Donnelly and Tracey Czop, and the checking of notes by Kirsty Barclay-Estrup.

To the librarians of the universities of Victoria and British Columbia; Vancouver School of Theology; Princeton Seminary; the Bodleian Library, Oxford; the British Library; the Evangelical Library, London; King's College, London; New College, Edinburgh; Westminster College, Cambridge; Dr. Williams' Library, London; John Ryland's Library, Manchester; the National Library of Scotland; and the Public Libraries of Edinburgh, Birmingham, and Manchester.

To countless Directors of Education, Records Office librarians, school head teachers, and archivists whom space does not permit me to list, but who have spared valuable time to answer questionnaires and enquiries and often to send photocopies of hymn texts. To the following who, gave help, hospitality, and in many cases hymnals or other printed materials: Ms. S. Cleary of Cheltenham Ladies' College; Mr. A.D.K. Hawkyard and Mrs.

R. Hudson of Harrow School; Mr. K. Howard of Queen Mary's School, Walsall; Sister Mary Edward of St. Dominic's School, Stoke-on-Trent; Mrs. H. Brigstocke of St. Paul's Girls' School; Mr. D. Burrell of Truro School; Mr. Bryan Matthews of Uppingham School; Mrs. S. Waine of Rugby School; the Rector of Edinburgh Academy; J.R. Avery, J. Mackay and G.J. Weaver of Bristol Grammar School; and the staffs of Bristol, Leicestershire, and Surrey Records Office.

To colleagues in the University of Victoria: John Money, historian, for valuable suggestions regarding the historical introduction; David Campbell and Gordon Shrimpton, classicists, for advice on a Greek quotation; to Drs. A. Tweedale and A. Brett, Ms. Moira Glen, Ms. Laura Proctor, and others who assisted with computer programs; to Ian Adam, University of Calgary, for a George Eliot reference; and to Dr. Gordon Spaulding, formerly of the University of British Columbia, for advice on computer surveying and information and texts pertaining to American evangelical hymnody.

Finally, to Jane Fredeman and Jean Wilson of UBC Press, for acquisition and editing respectively, and to Elizabeth Hart, of Vancouver School of Theology, for kindly reading the galley proofs and suggesting many improvements.

1

CLASS, CONTEXT, AND ALLEGIANCE

Chapel-folk be more hand-in-glove with them above than we.

We know very well that if anybody do go to heaven, they will. They've worked hard for it, and they deserve to have it, such as 'tis. I bain't such a fool as to pretend that we who stick to the Church have the same chance as they, because we know we have not. But I hate a feller who'll change his old ancient doctrines for the sake of getting to heaven.[1]

In my preceding book, *Hymns and the Christian "Myth,"*[2] the changing representation in hymns of the *mythos*, or sacred story, of fallen man's redemption, inspiration, judgment, and final state was traced through two millennia, a speck in the geologist's eye but an immense tract of time to the cultural historian. A quest for images of the divine nature and human prospect transported us from secret gatherings in the Holy Land to sumptuous processions before the Emperor at Hagia Sophia, the daily offices of monks and missions by friars, thanksgivings in the lands of Luther and the Pilgrim Fathers, Methodist open air meetings, and the quieter services of country churches and Dissenting chapels. In the English-speaking countries hymnody has undergone changes in the last quarter of the Christian era no less marvellous than those that occurred throughout Christendom in the first. God the Father, who had earlier yielded his throne to Christ the Victor and Lover reborn as Christ the Judge, and his place in the human heart to the Virgin Mother, has reappeared as the "terrible God"[3] of thunder and wrath, while the Spirit who once descended in the whirlwind and tongues of flame has reappeared as the inner Light of church and believing heart. The just who earlier slept in hope of joyful resurrection, then trembled in fear of the Judgment, have in latter centuries gathered at the River to meet their loved ones gone before, and finally joined the unjust in the hospital's most remote and silent corridor. The unjust, who earlier bequeathed ill-gotten riches to endow masses in amendment as their misdeeds flashed before their closing eyes, once shrieked and groaned before an angry God and flaming pit, but now pay for their morphine in laundered funds. Heaven has appeared before longing eyes as the golden city where rust corrupts not, nor thieves break through and steal; as an unfading garden watered by the springs of grace; as a palace where the hungry dine forever at the Lord's table, and the naked and unloved put on wedding garments for the Bridegroom; as home for exiles led there through the wilderness; and finally as a gathering of long-lost friends and relatives.

Constrained by the Calvinist taboo, hymns of "human composure"[4] became a social influence only in the age of Watts and the Wesleys, yet within the following two centuries penetrated to the roots of English life and consciousness. Even now, the mention of "Abide with me" evokes in the unbeliever an image of the funeral—or the Cup Final crowd. Conversely, he dismisses the life to come in clichés of pearly gates or golden harps drawn from forgotten Sunday-school hymns.

HYMNODY: LEARNED AND POPULAR

The findings of sociologists and ecclesiastical historians—in particular Charles Booth, Hugh MacLeod, Desmond Bowen, Horton Davies, and Owen Chadwick—confirm a hypothesis formed from reading hymn texts in church and developed by extensive study of adult and school hymnals in several famous library collections, that from the time of the Wesleys until the First World War a Learned and a Popular tradition of hymnody can be distinguished. The educated congregation, which learned its religion at boarding-school and university rather than Sunday-school or back-street chapel, sang more of social and national service, perceiving work as vocation or fulfilment. While professing the same beliefs as the uneducated, it sang of death and the Second Coming in less dramatic and personal vein, attending more to nature and to its responsibilities within this world. Ultimately, it took over domestic affection from the Popular tradition, while passing down its own patriotism.

The distinction between the two traditions cuts across theological boundaries, for the strongly Evangelical *Hymnal Companion to the Book of Common Prayer* catered as much for the educated worshipper as the High Church *Hymns Ancient and Modern*. As compared with contemporary Baptist or Primitive Methodist hymnals, the *New Congregational Hymnbook* of 1859 and its successor of 1874 reflect superior literary judgment and a wider historical perspective wherein to place religious experience. The "Popular" hymnals of Baptists and Primitive Methodists convey feelings ranging from crude apprehension of Judgment and hell-fire to Dionysian jubilation at the prospect of deliverance from the wilderness, an ethos befitting those who cannot choose their path in life and in hard times are blown about on the world's tempestuous sea. Even as the two traditions converged, in the prosperous late Victorian era, hymnals for secular schools continued to imbue the young with contrasting class attitudes: young patricians with patriotism and the ideal of service; future mill-hands with domestic love and the hope of heaven.[5] After following the traditions in their bifurcation and convergence, I shall pursue the elusive quest for the hymns people actually sang (as distinct from those editors provided), and which therefore influenced national attitudes on both sides of the Atlantic.

DENOMINATIONS OF THE LEARNED TRADITION

First we need to define social class as related to denominational allegiance. Despite its prayer for "all sorts and conditions of men," the Established Church had by the time of Wesley identified itself with the social hierarchy. Its divines, High or Low, had supported Stuart, then Hanoverian monarchs; its bishops sat in the House of Lords; its rectors often served as justices. One early Victorian clerical magistrate took a fiendish delight in committing applicants for outdoor relief to the notorious Andover workhouse.[6] Well into the Victorian era, the Church remained the spiritual arm of monarch and squire. Only in the time of Dickens did "gentleman" and "respectable" acquire moral rather than social connotations. A late Victorian bishop lamented without moral aspersion that his clergy were no longer "gentlemen."[7] Back in the 1820s, Whigs had found the parson a "black recruiting-sergeant for the Tories," and the Benthamite John Wade found him a minister of the government "exerting all his influence to promote tyranny."[8] Few authors employed terms so extreme, but farmers and labourers alike had little reason to love the parson-magistrate so reluctant to dole out relief, so relentless in exacting tithes. The rector who humbly did his duty by all, and his sometimes miserable living, received far less attention than the overendowed absentee deputing his duty to an underpaid curate. Not until the 1840s did the Ecclesiastical Commissioners iron out the worst inequalities and endow livings in desperately underchurched industrial towns.

Devoted Evangelical Sunday-school teachers had been teaching more and more children to read the Bible in villages and city slums since the 1780s, while in 1817 the High Church National Society began to provide day-schools for poor children. Yet the Evangelical Hannah More, together with the neo-conservative Methodist Conference, forbade Sunday-schools to teach writing lest they make children discontented with their station.[9] Even Wilberforce, who for what he did to end the vile commerce in slaves should receive nothing but honour, has been accused of mounting his crusade to distract attention from the plight of industrial workers.[10] Certainly some leaders of the Oxford Movement offered the poor little hope. Newman asked what truck "private Christians" could have with "schemes of change, or dreams of reform.'' A disciple, Frederick Oakeley, urged the poor to ''submit with cheerfulness,'' while another, Thomas Mozley, claimed that ''nothing but the deepest and bitterest poverty will subdue the uneducated classes.''[11] Pusey, to his credit, espoused reform and gave generously to slum parishes. For all the new sense of vocation aroused in the clergy by the Evangelical and Oxford movements, in particular the heroic sanctity of East End clergy, the ill educated still feel more at home in ''chapel'' than ''church.'' As late as 1873 a clergyman confessed that the man he would most fear to meet at the Judgment was the labourer.[12] If Thomas Hardy's rustics recall with gratitude the generosity of Parson Thirdly,[13] Flora Thompson complains bitterly of sermons in her late Victorian childhood that urged villagers to submit to their masters.[14]

In the early nineteenth century the Independents, who formed the Congregational Union, were the best-educated heirs to the Puritan tradition. Their preaching retained a fierceness exemplified in the attacks of the young Rowland Hill upon Wesley,[15] and later in power struggles between old-line Calvinists and liberal-evangelical reformers which led to the expulsion of George Macdonald for denying eternal punishment and to savage criticism of the nature imagery in T.T. Lynch's hymns.[16] Donald Davie has memorably recorded the dwindling of victorious liberalism into the ''vague, hymn-singing pietism''[17] of the chapel attended by the young D.H. Lawrence in the 1890s. The very charge of bloodless intellectualism levied by that novelist against Christianity, however, says something for the Congregational sermons of his boyhood. An earlier Congregational novelist, ''Mark Rutherford,'' remarks how the sermons of a fictive preacher modelled on Thomas Binney ''taxed the whole mental powers of his audience . . . utterly unlike the simple stuff which became fashionable with the Evangelical movement.''[18]

The Independents had a tradition of monarchical patriotism combined with social concern. Isaac Watts, though no jingoist, proclaims in one hymn that the Redeemer ''scatters . . . His choicest favours here,'' while ''creation's utmost bound / Shall see, adore, and fear.'' Such was his continuing influence upon hymnal editors that a century later Independent congregations were still singing this hymn, ''Shine, mighty God, on Britain shine / With beams of heavenly grace''[19] with its petition for God to surround ''like a wall of guardian fire'' His ''favourite land,'' its confidence that the Deity will ''crown his chosen isle / With fruitfulness and peace.''

Watts, as a biographer remarks, moved in a ''stately and learned society'' that had little of the lower-class Bunyan's ''bibliolatry and intolerance,'' and would have been appalled by the evangelical Dissent of a later day, with its ''emotional appeal to the multitude.'' Harry Escott traces to its memories of Commonwealth leaders the ''almost arrogant patriotism'' of Watts' verse.

Unlike Baptists or Methodists, these men conceived "wealth, rank and learning" as "signs and seals" of divine favour.[20] Until our own day, Congregationalism has been the first choice of nonconformists from the mercantile and professional classes.

The logic of Calvinism, as of Catholicism, has always appealed to a certain cast of mind. The Scottish Kirk and English Independent chapel attracted lawyers, scholars, and merchants. Even the Baptist Robert Hall produced a journal far excelling the *Evangelical Magazine* in quality and range of ideas.[21] Both the early spread of education in America and the traditional excellence of Scottish schooling owed much to Calvinist logic and insistence on Bible-reading.

The Anglican, Congregational, and Unitarian denominations made up that "clerisy" that Coleridge (an ex-Unitarian) envisaged as preserving the national culture and exercising social responsibilities, and that Thomas Arnold saw as the basis of a national church.

It will be useful here to introduce the class division of Hugh McLeod, based on that of Charles Booth's survey of cultures in London at the end of the century:[22]

Class 1: the poor, including casual workers in the East End docks;
Class 2: manual workers in steady employment;
Class 3: skilled workers, the elite in London being printers;
Class 4: lower middle class, eg, clerks and shopkeepers;
Class 5: middle class proper, eg, doctors, teachers, businessmen;
Class 6: wealthy manufacturers, merchants, professional men living in
        select suburbs;
Class 7: the aristocracy living in West End squares.

According to Booth, the Congregational Union drew largely from classes 5 and 6, the Wesleyan church from classes 3-5, the Baptists from 3 and 4, the Primitive Methodists alone from 1 and 2.

DENOMINATIONS OF THE POPULAR TRADITION

Although Booth drew his conclusions from research at the end of the nineteenth century, they show how a distinction between hymnody "popular by destination" and "popular by origin" would hold good from its beginning. During the age of repression after the French Revolution, internal divisions caused the Methodist Connexion, once the Church's ginger-group but now its most serious rival, to take up an ambivalent position in the class war. Wesley had taught the duty of submission to higher powers and the spiritual equality of all classes, yet his system of lay preachers and class meetings would ultimately create a literate working class.[23] Even during the reaction following his death a radical wing of Methodists fought for a democratic alternative to the rule of ministers and wealthy trustees.[24] In general, the Methodists campaigned with Anglican Evangelicals against drink and Sunday trading, and likewise disapproved of arts and entertainments. If less pilloried by novelists and poets than the Evangelicals, who spread gloom in aristocratic households, they drew similar charges of bigotry on account of their apartness from "the world," their separate schools, books, or journals, their unwillingness to marry their children to the unconverted.

Ironically, that very separation originated in a social bond John Wesley had endeavoured to forge after observing how Moravian missionaries kept their heads in a storm at sea while his fellow Englishmen were losing theirs. Later, on Count Zinzendorf's estate at Herrnhut, he noted how this uncelibate religious order regulated even family life. From this model, he designed communities of "real Christians" within the Established Church, whose members would dress with "Quaker plainness," deal at each other's shops, and send their children to schools run by fellow members.[25] In the end he failed to induce adult Methodists to let the Societies run their lives in the manner of modern Japanese companies, just as he failed to make the boys of Kingswood School totally religious. When the Societies broke down, the system of class meetings continued to draw together Methodist families. It enabled parents, moreover, to bring up their children in a quasi-monastic environment of family prayer, Bible study, chapel-going, and both domestic and collective hymn-singing that was calculated to induce a saving "experience." As their apartness diminished, Methodists became difficult to distinguish from Evangelicals. No longer confined (if it ever was)[26] to the poor for whom Wesley designed his famous *Collection . . . for People Called Methodists*, the new denomination imposed on its members a discipline of work and abstinence that enabled many to rise in the economic scale. If unable to make all classes one in Christ, the Wesleys played a part in the still incomplete evolution of their nation from a hierarchical to an organic society.

The sect of Primitive Methodists, known as "Ranters," originated in outdoor missions held in imitation of the camp meetings already popular in the United States. Such gatherings in rural areas in the early nineteenth century were as much Dionysian orgies as our rock festivals, but involved an unlettered class instead of a cross-section of the young. They frightened authorities with no less reason. In the turbulent years after the Napoleonic War magistrates at Burton-on-Trent urged the Home Office to suppress the "Ranters," whose gatherings of "thousands of the lower orders" had "so much increased that we cannot but be apprehensive of the consequences."

During the same summer (1817), the Sheriff of Nottingham complained of villages being "disturbed by this new sect . . . praying, singing and making other noises" until "near midnight."[27]

Both that officer's title and the occupation of the founder, the carpenter Hugh Bourne, were peculiarly appropriate for this mushrooming sect. Bourne began to evangelize about 1800 at Mow Cop, in the Potteries. In 1807 the American Lorenzo Dow held the first English Camp Meeting. In 1810, after condemning such meetings, the Wesleyan Conference expelled Bourne and his comrade William Clowes, who the following year launched the new sect, "Primitive" because apostolic. Mainstream Methodism having become largely middle class, the Primitives grew by 1850 into a denomination of 100,000 consisting still, to cite George Borrow, "entirely of the lower class, labourers and mechanics and their wives and children."

Recently Julia Werner has with some reservations confirmed its lower-class composition and ascribed its popularity to nostalgia on the part of rural labourers and "uprooted newcomers who had yet to find a place in the grimy factory towns of industrial England," and to the strong emphasis of its leaders on participation by uneducated lay members—male and female, adolescent and adult—who in the older churches would have remained passive in deference to their "betters."[28]

In his preface to the 1841 edition of the *Large Hymn-book*, originally published in 1824 together with his less successful *Small Hymn-book* of 1809,[29] Bourne explains the structure and purpose of the day-long camp meetings. Each exercise—praying, preaching, or "praying in companies"—must be short, for "long exercises are especially injurious." He so organizes the day that "attention and energy" may keep "rising and increasing to the last." Groups can extend their prayers if "pious praying labourers are engaged with mourners." Sometimes, when "the work breaks out powerfully under preaching, it is found necessary" for the whole meeting to remain together. In this case preachers should "make a ring or opening and call up the mourners to be prayed for." Here Bourne follows the precepts of the American evangelist Charles Finney.[30]

Clearly "work" has the Wesleyan sense of emotional ferment among penitents or "mourners" convinced by the preachers of "sin," that is of their self-alienation from God. In these as in some instructions for conventional Methodist prayer and preaching services, class meetings and "love-feasts," Bourne takes into account the short attention span of the subliterate.

Like the original Methodists, the "Ranters" used other means of making converts: street conversations; teaching illiterates to read the Bible; above all, subliminal suggestion. Children attracted by the popular song tunes attached to hymns would pick up first the jingling refrain, then whole verses.

These they would introduce to their parents. The families most probably lived in northern and midland industrial areas during the Luddite era of machine-breaking, or else in rural East Anglia and the southern counties during the "Captain Swing" epidemic of thresher-breaking and rick-burning.[31] For this reason J.F.C. Harrison, like E.P. Thompson, sees in this and other millenarian sects an expression of lower-class radicalism.[32] Certainly it included several of the Tolpuddle Martyrs, and in his *Memories of an Old Potter*, C. Shaw recalls arrests of Primitive Methodist preachers during the food riots of the early forties, but Werner finds the evidence for this association inconsistent and the success of revivals much more dependent on preachers and organizers.[33]

Having grown by leaps and bounds during the thirties and "hungry forties," "Ranters" had foregone lusty street-singing for more ordered worship in "tin tabernacles." While doing much to improve the behaviour of adults and teach children to read in poor districts, they no longer preached the millennium to the desperate.[34] In 1865 they opened a seminary to train full-time clergy and in 1887 produced a hymnal yielding to no Methodist collection for taste and catholicity. By now, the Primitive Methodist denomination inculcated middle-class values.

In the eighteenth century, despite being the heirs of John Bunyan, neither the sternly Calvinistic Particular Baptists nor the Arminian General Baptists had sought to win the masses. In the nineteenth century, while the Particular Baptist shopkeeper or craftsman kept to his conventicle, knowing his trade, his Bible, his *Pilgrim's Progress* and very little else, the General Baptist, if a Londoner, would join the throng that filled a vast new chapel, or even a theatre, to hear Charles Haddon Spurgeon preach a world-denying fundamentalism that has remained the essence of popular Evangelicalism from his era to that of Billy Graham. It had not then acquired right-wing, or indeed any, political overtones. As much as his Roman Catholic contemporaries, Spurgeon taught the believer to regard the attainment of salvation as man's sole purpose in life.

THE BACKLASH AGAINST EVANGELICALS

To this dichotomy between religion Learned, Popular by origin, and Popular by destination, we may in part ascribe the animus against Evangelicals by English novelists and cultural historians that has continued from the mid-nineteenth century to the present day. But another cause lay in the Evangelical temper itself. For the venom of their attacks upon the Arminian Wesley, the Calvinistic Evangelicals of the first generation—Venn, Romaine, and especially Toplady— deserved whatever tongue-lashings they have incurred.[35] Yet the savaging of later Evangelicals by critics, novelists, and social historians appears as ungrateful as anti-Americanism in countries once glad of Marshall Plan Aid, for had they not fought to abolish slavery and pass the first Factory Acts?

As with American aid, the attitude was at fault. From the gentle peremptoriness of Lady Huntingdon to the loving zeal of Newton in urging hymnography upon Cowper as a distraction from melancholy, from the Evangelicals who bought up clerical livings to the coldly benevolent Shaftesbury, whose Bill to suppress Sunday amusements provoked riots in London, the pious intention barely concealed the power urge.[36] The Methodists showed this too—witness the rules for Kingswood School[37]—but never so attracted the satirist. Whereas in Wesleyan meetings and hymns, Dionysian fervour supplanted Old Dissenting self-abasement, your stock Evangelical clergyman, arrayed from head to foot in black, would seat himself in some mournful early nineteenth-century drawing-room to enquire of her ladyship "Shall we engage?" And engage the Evangelicals did, from Cowper endlessly discussing salvation with Mrs. Unwin to the families that prayed, attended church, and read the Scriptures to fill—or almost fill—the long hours of the early Victorian Sabbath.

Although the former Oxford don Wesley had preached largely ethical sermons in restrained style, while the lower-middle class Whitefield had delivered some of the most theatrical in the history of the Established Church, Calvinist Evangelicalism appealed mainly to the educated. Its clerical proponents ministered more willingly than the Wesleyans to those born into wealth and rank. Conversely, "the more socially select Evangelicals" espoused Calvinism in preference to Arminianism. The servilities addressed to Lady Huntingdon by those whom Wesley dubbed "my lady's ministers"[38] could have come from the pen of Thackeray.

To be fair, the hymnists Newton and Joseph Irons preached to the poor as fervently as Wesley. Neither their power urge, obsessive religiosity, anti-intellectualism, nor philistine disapproval of artist and actor can entirely account for the bile poured over the Evangelicals by Blake, Dickens, Thackeray, and the Brontës.[39] Those who create images of life have a vested interest in combatting world-denial, but the element common to Blake's parent figures, to the Murdstones, and to Mr. Brocklehurst, who dressed his charity school girls in sackcloth and his daughters in fine raiment, was a propensity for doublethink inherent in the Evangelical class ethos and pietism. Evangelical aristocrats and businessmen denounced the world while enjoying divinely bestowed prosperity. No Christians strove harder to improve the lot of slaves and child-workers, yet their effort to reform the nobility rather than the poor to whom Wesley had preached, their religious argot and their combination of puritanism with politicking and money-making drowned their prayers and exhortations. George Eliot put her finger on the spot in her Mr. Bulstrode, who had tried to be "a better man than he was."[40] In any case, people resent those who would reform them from above. Before the felon will listen, a Wesley must enter his stinking cell.

RELIGIOUS CONSENSUS AND ITS LIMITS

An epigram describing Old Dissent as the religion of the state, Methodism as that of the heart, Evangelicalism as that of the home, and Tractarianism as that of the church oversimplifies the facts.[41] The Wesleyans did teach working people to read, work regular hours, stay sober, wash, and, above all, organize. The Calvinist Evangelicals, mainly Anglican, did reform laws and lawmakers. But early Victorian Evangelicals combined the Puritan sense of the family as a religious community with the inward-looking piety of the Methodists. Their hymns, like those of Wesley, direct attention to the inward drama of conversion, temptation, and daily renewal rather than the war of the angels and Fall of man. Where the Wesleyan hymns had brought hope, drama, and meaning into drab lives, those of the Evangelicals brought also a keener sense of guilt and a livelier fear of God's all-seeing Eye. As Donald Davie has shown, in the early nineteenth century the Baptist intelligentsia, or at least their journal, fitted Coleridge's model of the clerisy much better than did the Evangelicals of the Established Church. That model itself fitted Coleridge's society better than Queen Victoria's, for as Davie points out, philistine indifference to standards of taste in architecture, art, and literature was at least as characteristic of Anglican Evangelicals as of the Nonconformists whom Matthew Arnold attacked in *Culture and Anarchy*.[42]

Nevertheless, the more prosperous era after the Great Exhibition saw the formation of a shared understanding that endured until the Second World War, a largely undeclared religion of nation, church, home, and heart. For three or four generations, the middle and upper classes felt obliged for the most part to attend church, avoid recreations on Sundays, and maintain strict financial and sexual probity.[43] This mainly Protestant tradition, whether Evangelical, Broad Church, High Church, or Nonconformist, had its variations. The upper-class Victorian family might hold formal daily prayers with servants who filed in according to rank; the middle or superior working-class Victorian family might pray together informally or sing hymns round the piano on Sunday evenings. Both at home and "public" school, the upper-class boy learned to serve society and his country, while the middle-class boy heard more about the need to "get on." The Anglican mother would pass on the creed and tribal ethos, the Methodist a religion centred more on personal experience. But on the broad essentials— Providence and the sanctity of family life; sexual and other restraints; the work ethic and the Commandments; the social system and their places within it—these groups remained for generations in tacit agreement.

Nostalgia can mislead us into exaggerating the degree of consensus. On popular education Nonconformists and Anglicans fought each other even after the 1870 Act had ensured elementary instruction for all. While Carlyle, Dickens, and Disraeli were drumming the realities of lower-class life into middle- and upper-class heads, a census in the very year of the Great Exhibition showed less than 40 per cent of the population at any place of worship, the very poor and the industrial workers being "as utter strangers to religion's ordinances as people in a heathen country."[44] While this makes nonsense of the Marxist charge that religion was the "opium of the people," it shocked the Established Church even more than the revelation that there were almost as many Nonconformists as Anglicans. Unfortunately no such poll was taken in the 1870s, by which time, under pressure from the census, the Oxford Movement and the Darwinian theory, Anglican clergy such as Bishop Blomfield of London and Dean Hook of Leeds had striven harder to reach the industrial working class than ever before or since.[45] By this time also a second Evangelical revival was under way, fuelled by the "sacred songs" of Moody and Sankey.

The proportion of the working class that found the teachings of the Established Church irrelevant to life may raise doubts about the influence of the Primitive Methodist and, increasingly, Baptist denominations, that drew their members mainly from the lower classes. The Primitive Methodist Connexion originated in agricultural areas, then spread to East Midland, Black Country, and Yorkshire industrial towns.[46] Traditionally, the Baptists had flourished in small towns. According to the 1851 census, the Established Church was strongest in the Home and Eastern counties, the Nonconformists in Northern and Midland industrial areas and Welsh mining valleys.[47]

During the third quarter of the century other bodies than the "Ranters" reached the lower classes. The Anglican church, which always enjoyed more rapport with agricultural than with town labourers, had by the 1860s made some headway in the East End. In the year of the census and Exhibition, Henry Mayhew provided a further stimulus with his *London Life and Labour*. Dickens, meantime, continued to paint in their darkest colours the slums of the metropolis, and Mrs. Gaskell those of Manchester.[48] As early as 1816 Jane Austen had delineated an upper-class ethos of social service[49] but the efforts of reformers did not always meet with the gratitude they deserved. As a school inspector sagely remarked in 1845, "The . . . inner life of the classes below us . . . is never penetrated. . . . We are profoundly ignorant of the springs of public opinion. . . . "[50] Only such rare outbreaks as the demonstrations against Shaftesbury's Sunday closing bill would lift the curtain on the anger of working people at this attempt to restrict their recreation on their only free day. By the end of the century, the popular press had lifted the curtain for good.

The social service ethic spread to the "merchant princes" and middle class, the backbone of the now evangelical Congregational Union, and to Quaker and Unitarian employers who owed their wealth to the puritan virtues of thrift, honesty, and diligence. The latter sect, in decline after Priestley and Mrs. Barbauld, had been restored to prominence by distinguished preachers like James Martineau. In local government it wielded an influence out of all proportion to its numbers.[51]

Coleridge and Thomas Arnold hoped the clerisy would supply the needs of the underfed, ill-housed, and uneducated lower class. *Tom Brown's Schooldays* exaggerated the social thrust of Arnold's teaching, but this Christian socialist *roman à clef* demonstrates the spread of the service ethic among the landowning and professional classes. As Bowen remarks, acceptance of this ethic, "the great accomplishment of the Church in the nineteenth century," did more than utopian or secular measures to abate class conflict after the demise of Chartism and to prevent the middle class from becoming "an urban bourgeoisie at war with the proletariat."[52] Whether or not they attended church, many in Booth's classes 2 and 3 accepted the middle-class ethic of respectability, work, and restraint. The thousands of young men and women who taught in ragged-schools and Sunday-schools, or manned soup kitchens in hard times, and the minority of public schoolboys who helped at slum settlements, had not laboured in vain.[53]

In 1881 a Nonconformist head count found chapel better attended in Southern than Northern or Midland towns, with twice as large a percentage attending in the naval base of Portsmouth as in the dock city of Liverpool.[54] In the same year, a Bristol newspaper found a quarter of its readers nominally Anglican, with Congregationalists far behind at 6 per cent, followed closely by those attending Salvation Army, Baptist, and Methodist services,[55] though Bristol had been the city most responsive to Wesley. This survey shows also that only the Army and the Baptists made any impact in the dockside area. Five years later, an Anglican enquirer found that since 1875 Congregational and Wesleyan membership had kept pace with the increase in population, and Methodist offshoots and the Baptists had done better, but the Primitive Methodists had fallen off.[56] This change reflects either economic improvement or, more probably, the dying off of older "Ranters." In the last twenty years of Victoria's reign, chapel and marriage rolls at Bethnal Green (London) showed a little over half of Wesleyan and Baptist bridegrooms in manual occupations as against about 39 per cent of Congregationalists. Of the latter, a further 35 per cent were clerical workers, as against 24 per cent of Baptists. In the middle-class suburb of Lewisham, a "significantly higher" proportion of professional men belonged to the Congregational than to any other denomination. Since McLeod regards the differences at working-class Bethnal Green as "matters of detail," the Congregational figure at Lewisham must have far exceeded the others. He concludes, however, that the Congregational and Baptist denominations "drew their support from the same sections . . . lower middle-class and respectable artisans."[57]

Further surveys by Booth in 1900, the Rowntrees and the Cadburys in 1901-2 showed church attendance declining after its long boom,[58] but how far this reflects a change in belief is open to question. London being the area most surveyed, a fall of one-third there might mean only that more could afford week-end excursions, were it not that the poorer the area, the fewer attended the church. C.F.G. Masterman's conclusion with regard to South London presumably had some validity for the country as a whole. The poor, unless Roman Catholic, Primitive Methodist, Baptist, or Salvation Army did not go to church, nor did working men in general. Tradesmen and middle class people of the poorer boroughs were active in Nonconformist chapels, especially Baptists, and residents in suburbs supported all forms of organized religion.[59] So much for the "opium of the people." Working-class families, moreover, often began to attend after moving into middle-class suburbs,[60] and until the mid-twentieth century sent their children to Sunday-schools.

Booth's findings on class distribution in London must again have some validity for the whole country. Attendance rose sharply between classes 1 and 4 (middle class), more steeply to class 5, even more so to the wealthy class 6, then fell off among the West End aristocracy (class 7). Relatively speaking, three times as many of the wealthy as of the poorest went to church. Again, so much for the "opium." In all classes save 7 (where many went to boarding-schools), children were sent to Sunday-schools in the belief that these made them more obedient and easier to live with.[61]

Booth showed that aristocratic and wealthy professional people were mainly Anglicans, the remainder being Congregational; and that teachers, clerks, and shopkeepers attended Congregational, Methodist, or Salvation Army services. The last denomination, he contended, had never flourished among the poor as much as had been supposed. On the appeal of Baptist world-and-life-denial to artisans and shopkeepers, Booth comments amusingly that "the life circumstances of that class, acting on a not uncommon type of mind," one "unable to take sin, or anything else, lightly," conduce to "those stern opinions."[62] Booth, Bernard Shaw (in *Major Barbara*), and in our own day MacLeod all maintain that the lowest classes were so blinkered by circumstance that they practised at best a humanistic cult of comradeship and family, leaving agapé, strict principle, and patriotism to those who could afford them.[63] Thanks to the social service ethic of the bourgeoisie,[64] the home missionary could expect a politer reception than in Wesley's time, but would have found it easier to convert East Africans than East Londoners.

Most people observed one of four moralities: the poorest, mutual aid in the daily struggle; skilled workers, pride in craftsmanship and devotion to family and later to a soccer team; business and professional people, the work ethic with more or less of the puritan insistence on integrity and propriety; and the upper class what Alasdair MacIntyre calls a "tribal" morality.[65] In the late nineteenth century, the last involved loyalty to house and school, followed by submission to tribal mores whether among officers, civil administrators, or college dons and public school masters. By reason of a common educational background, speech, and code of dress, and a more or less religious upbringing and home background, members of the upper classes respected the same conventions and owed fealty to the overarching tribes of Church and Nation. As David Newsome has shown, the shift of emphasis from "godliness and good learning" in the first half of the century to "manliness," character building, and team spirit in the second diminished the supply of eccentric geniuses and distinguished scholars.[66] The best day-schools, such as King Edward's, Birmingham, or Manchester Grammar School, have always had more in common with academically distinguished public schools like Winchester and Rugby than with the average boarding-school content to turn out its quota of junior officers and business executives. If often aping the public school, the average town grammar school has had to concentrate more on examination results. Until the recent creation of North American-style comprehensive schools, the grammar and public schools have for a century imbued a clerisy of professional men and executives with an ideal of service rather than acquisition, and bound it loosely by a liberal Anglican or other form of Christianity, more tightly by common accent, dress, manners, and morality. If exasperating to the talented who lack the "right" accent and "background," the clerisy has proved far more penetrable than the ruling classes of other empires that collapsed in revolution, and has earned for its country a name for humane government.

IDOLS: THE NATION

Conventions were readily transferred from one occupation to another, hence the formation of quasi-military religious organizations like the Church Army, Boys' Brigade, and Boy Scouts. In the early twentieth century, the German menace that brought patriotism and military training to the fore led to the formation of the Territorial Army and of officer cadet units in public schools. In his autobiography published in 1918, E.B. Bax comments that "Patriotism" had "undoubtedly taken the place formerly occupied by Christian sentiment and aspiration in the mind of the average man."[67]

This identification of religion goes back—as I have argued in *Hymns and the Christian "Myth"*—not merely to the Puritan Commonwealth but to the Old Testament concept of the holy nation, loved yet chastened of the Lord. Watts' early "Hymn of Praise for Three Great Salvations" (5 November 1695)[68] showed his patriotism as rooted in relief at the deposition of James II. In "The beauty of my native land / Immortal love inspires"[69] he refers, like his model the Polish-Latin poet Cassimir Sarbiewski, to the heavenly homeland, which in "There is a land of pure delight"[70] he depicts as an English scene.

Patriotic and social zeal combine in two missionary hymns of Watts: "Jesus shall reign where'er the sun" (entitled "Christ's Kingdom among the Gentiles"), based on the second part of Psalm 72, and his less famous version of the first part, on divine justice, which will "avenge the poor," disarm the proud, vindicate the just, and "tread the oppressor in the dust." In now unused stanzas of "Jesus shall reign" he imagines the Kingdom restoring "heathen lands" and "deserts" not by conquest but by voluntary submission. At this point his vision falls apart, for while the first hymn ends: "Peace like a river from his throne / Shall flow to nations yet unknown," two stanzas of the second envisage the divine *imperium* with just that hauteur of which British rulers and missionaries have often been accused:

> Behold the islands with their kings,
> And Europe her best tribute brings;
> From north to south the princes meet
> To pay their homage at his feet.
>
> There Persia glorious to behold,
> There India shines in eastern gold;
> And barbarous nations at his word
> Submit, and bow, and own their Lord.[71]

Doddridge surpassed even the kindly Watts in his concern for the poor,[72] but his patriotism had more of religious humility. In entreating God to "make the British Isles" His care "when angry Nations" threatened them, he owned that "the Land thine Arm hath sav'd / That Arm most impiously hath brav'd" and God's beloved land "a Rebel to that Love hath prov'd." Since God loved and chastened Britain as a second Israel, its people should prepare humbly to meet Him rather than "In mad Rebellion . . . arise."[73]

Hymn collections, especially for the young, may be expected to tell us whether patriotic and military conditioning figures significantly in public school life and whether before the First World War it had spread to schools attended by the mass of the population. They should also indicate whether more of it took place in Sunday-schools and churches attended by the clerisy than by the lower orders. In McLeod's view, during the Boer War patriotism was most in evidence among Anglican clergy, pacifism among Nonconformist ministers.[74] Did hymns in any significant way help to prepare the young minds to make war in 1914? Most importantly, do they confirm the view of Bax that the nation had replaced God as object of heartfelt devotion?

IDOLS: HOME AND SOCIETY

In his study of the Puritan family in the seventeenth century, Levin Schücking first drew the parallel with the monastic community. Calling the Puritan way of life a "family theocracy," he continues: "the family became the very centre of life to a degree without parallel in previous ages . . . the whole Puritan movement has its roots in the family. . . . Religion is for the Puritan family religion. Divine worship is . . . primarily, family worship." With Baxter and Bunyan as his authorities, he expounds the Puritan attempt to inject in "practical activities," public or private, an "ethico-religious content" the effects of which "penetrated to the very core of personality and permeated the whole man." This he calls an attempt to create, "cell by cell," a new social structure, a "great religious bee-hive."

> The principal duty fell upon the head of the family. His thorough knowledge of the characters of its members made him better fitted for this task than the clergyman. Moreover, it was more fitting that he should undertake the task because he himself was responsible for bringing children into the world bearing the stain of original sin. Also the practical results of their being born again affected nobody so strongly as himself. Thus the home was deliberately and not illogically transformed into a church.[75]

In both monastery and home a parent figure or surrogate Reverend Father or Mother Superior assumes responsibility for the common well-being, under general oversight by church elders or superiors of the order. As Philippe Ariès notes, in Roman Catholic France the nuclear family took precedence over the line or clan as children became important in their own right.[76] In eighteenth-century England, the rise of the middle class further strengthened the family unit.

We may expect suffering and death to loom large in all service-books compiled before the advent of chloroform and the germ theory. As a rule, the short and poorer the life expected here, the greater the emphasis upon the life hereafter and the more radical its difference from this. Singers of early Evangelical hymns expected an eternal life wholly other than the temporal; their longer-lived descendants who gathered at the river with Moody and Sankey expected to renew their home life and friendships. By this token, the home life that middle-class Christians took for granted would to slaves appear a celestial vision, hence the preoccupation of spirituals with the Promised Land rather than the golden city.

Evangelical hymns sung to compelling tunes, for instance "Rock of Ages," having survived long after the Revival, we may expect the themes of sin, death, and Atonement to persist in Evangelical hymnals. In any case, owing to the time-lag between text and melody, and between editions, hymn-books often appear behind their times. Further conservative influences are the tendency noted by Ariès for cultures to hand on obsolescent customs or artefacts to children,[77] and that of teachers to prescribe poems they learned in youth. That we so often think of Christmas and royal visits as peculiarly suitable for children bodes ill for the future of these occasions.

As regards class differences, hymnals used by order-giving members of classes 5 to 7, that is Anglican, Congregational, and Presbyterian ones, ought to teach an ethos compounded of social service and the struggle to achieve a personal and social ideal. For two reasons, the doubts raised about the Christian mythos by biblical criticism and science intensified this shift of emphasis from salvation to service. In the words of Horton Davies, "strong energies of devotion and compassion" are released because "Christ as Exemplar shines most clearly when attention is withdrawn from Christ as Second Person of the Trinity." Further, the liberal-Protestant focus on Christ as Son of Man led to a "saccharine religious sentimentality" and to "impressive social service."[78] Being for collective use, hymnals usually adhere to the norms among their intended users. Social activism often predominates in those for worshippers accustomed to strenuous competition in education or business. Conversely, in those for worshippers with less control over their terrestrial future, an ethos of patient resignation prevails.[79] The term "work" in hymns can mislead us, for it often refers to the work of clergymen or missionaries. The era between 1870 to 1914 is regarded by ecclesiastical historians as "the most clerical . . . in English history" and "the golden age of parochial work."[80] Even half a century earlier, the Primitive Methodist "labourer" performs a "work" of conversion, as did preachers at Kingswood, the first Wesleyan public school.[81] On the toil of countless multitudes in mine or mill, hymnists say little before the twentieth century.

IDOLS: CHILDHOOD

Not only did Wesley's famous preface to his *Collection* in several ways anticipate that of Wordsworth to the *Lyrical Ballads*, but that poet, Blake, and Coleridge, who all composed their major works before hymn-singing became legal in Anglican churches (1822),[82] influenced the content of hymnals. Their consecration of childhood extends into almost every area of Victorian culture. With it may be associated that of ordinary home and family. At best, the beatification of the child gave rise to a host of carols and hymns on Jesus as the child's exemplar, at worst to nostalgic verse by Lewis Carroll, or nostalgic prose by Sir James Barrie or Forrest Reid.[83] In the hymnist, it may be expected to induce child-like attitudes of trust and unquestioning belief, moral rigidity and black-and-white judgments, together with that nostalgia for a pre-scientific style of life so evident in Wordsworth and Shelley. This cultural regression forms part of a matrix that includes the theological and historical regression underlying the Oxford Movement and Victorian medievalism in general. To the Anglo-Catholic, the "objective and mythological" hymns of Prudentius or Bernard, like the hymns sacred to Evangelicals, evoke the untroubled faith of an older or simpler culture.

This consecration of childhood prevailed over the Evangelical conditioning of children during what has been called the "Age of Admonition." Charles Simeon, the model for Samuel Butler's Mr. Hawke, was counselled by Berridge to begin his sermons by "ripping up" his audience, laying open the "universal sinfulness of nature, the darkness of the mind, forwardness of the tempers," and "earthliness of the affections." The preacher should declare "Man's utter helplessness to change his nature, or make his peace," and acquaint his hearers with "the searching Eye of God . . . spying at every thought, word and action, noting them down in the Book of His remembrance, bringing every secret work into judgment." Only then should he "lay open the Saviour's Almighty Power" to bring "repentance, pardon, holiness and faith."[84] The shock-and-relief formula, when practised even by the mild-mannered John Wesley, could produce fainting fits. Without his power to arouse an equal conviction of forgiveness, the Evangelical preacher could, as Butler's parody shows, be desolating in the extreme.[85] Some Evangelical hymns for children suggest a celestial telescreen in a Christian *Nineteen Eighty-Four*.

AN IDOL?: NATURE

In hymnody, the Romantic attribution of sacredness to Nature took a complex form. Despite the love of Christ for the lilies and the fowls of the air, the more firmly the medieval or post-Reformation hymnist fixed his eyes upon divine transcendence and the prospect of heaven that makes death easy, the less he attended to the natural world, save by way of metaphor or analogy. In the *Christian Year*, dubbed by Chadwick the *Pilgrim's Progress* of the Anglican middle class,[86] Keble shows a devotion to nature exceeded only by that of Hopkins or Whitman. He thus appears to invalidate this rule as clearly as the increasingly popular Harvest Festival confirms it. In "There is a book, who runs may read," however, Keble, who at Oxford lectured on the principle of analogy, treats of Nature as an emblem or type of the divine nature.[87]

Some hymns express reactions against pollution and overcrowding similar to those of Cowper in "God made the country, and man made the town" (*The Task* I, 749), the Quaker hymnist Whittier in "God is most where man is least,"[88] or Hopkins in "God's Grandeur." The famines of the "Hungry Forties," due less to overpopulation than to bad weather and the Corn Laws, helped to popularize the Harvest Festival, which was sanctioned by the archbishops after the good harvest of 1842.[89] That festival stimulated not only the singing of a great German hymn, "Wir pflügen" ("We plough the fields and scatter"), but the composition of some good native hymns. In the latter half of the century congregations enjoying a longer life-span, with more secure employment and cheap imported food, and hence a more optimistic view of life, sang nature hymns in praise of a benign Creator rather than the inscrutable thunder-God feared and adored in harsher times.

In that case, what about evolution? Had Darwin not proved Nature more ruthless and capricious than the God of the Old Testament? Not to Kingsley, Alford, or Whittier, at least. Even Tennyson, so aware that "Nature red in tooth and claw" shrieked against a religion of love, came to see evolution as a slow-moving Providence.[90] His view was borne out in letters submitted in response to an enquiry by the *Daily Telegraph* ("Do we believe?") in 1904. While many disowned religion in favour of science, the majority described evolution as "metaphysical," that is, purposive. While accepting the concept they denied the randomness that Darwin had demonstrated, using, as McLeod says, "A garbled version of Darwinism . . . to reinforce existing ideas." The idea of purposive evolution pervades, among others, a hymn-book brought out in 1892 for Cheltenham Ladies' College and may be found in an Uppingham School Commemoration hymn.[91]

"SYNCHRONOUS CHANGE"

With like optimism, the late Victorian contributors to Charles Gore's *Lux Mundi* (1889) treated the Incarnation rather than the Passion as the central Christian dogma. Near the end of the century, rising standards of living and

education spread this optimistic temper among all classes. Class differences
between hymnals and barriers between denominations crumbled as more
and more they sang the same hymns. Death and hell-fire retreated from
consciousness until violently reintroduced by the war in France.

As the apogee of Evangelical hymnody on the Passion coincided with the
Catholic cult of the Precious Blood, so did the uniform "chronology of
change" in belief and morality cause Great Awakenings and temperance
movements, together with "scientific" attacks on Christianity, declines in
church-going and liberal movements in theology to take place concurrently
in different countries.[92] From their different perspectives, a biologist may
trace religious decline to Darwinism, a theologian or literary scholar to
German biblical criticism, a social or economic historian to changes from a
hierarchical and pastoral to a democratic and capitalist system. But McLeod
is surely right to reject a purely materialist explanation in favour of a
movement of ideas that everywhere proved irrepressible. If American
fundamentalists are still trying to put the genie of evolution back in the
bottle, so long as Western countries permit free movement of ideas their
citizens will decide for themselves what, if anything, to believe. Before the
spread of universal education, ideas spread horizontally, but not vertically,
so that the lower classes, notably children, sang many hymns embodying
beliefs only nominally held by their "betters."

Finally, the ugly word "secularization," though indispensable for
discussion of idols in late Victorian hymns, can as McLeod warns become a
vehicle for another "mechanical theory" in which "human thoughts and
actions merely reflect . . . those aspects of the environment that the
historian chooses to select."[93] In this context it means that in the nineteenth
and early twentieth centuries hymns were composed or sung increasingly for
secular purposes: in praise of human rather than divine actions; in devotion
to a country rather than to its Creator; for entertainment rather than
worship. Whether Nature constitutes an idol depends upon whether God be
regarded as immanent within the cosmos or as its transcendent Creator. But
secularization has in this century taken forms more sinister than nature
hymns, or even hymn-tune ditties that hail soccer teams as "saints."

2

REVIVAL HYMNODY AND THE PEOPLE

Would God that our minstrels had none other thing to play upon, neither our carters and ploughmen other thing to whistle upon, save psalms, hymns and such godly songs as David is occupied withal!
                                                              Miles Coverdale

Religion is the sigh of the oppressed, the heart of a heartless world, the spirit of spiritless conditions.
It is the opium of the people.[1]
                                                              Karl Marx

In her *Protestant Poetics and the Seventeenth-Century Religious Lyric*, Barbara Lewalski expounds a number of biblical tropes for the Christian life, most of which figure largely in the hymnody of the Evangelical Revival.[2] Some of these, taken either directly from scripture or via *The Pilgrim's Progress*, appear in those *Olney Hymns* that were composed by the unlearned Newton. Of four denoting sin, one supplies the theme for "Physician of my *sin-sick* soul" and some lines elsewhere on the divine Word as the soul's "Food and Medicine"; another a line in "Amazing Grace," "Was *blind*, but now I see"; and another a whole hymn on hell as debtor's *prison*. In addition the trope on the Christian as *child* of God appears in "Quiet, Lord, my froward heart," that of the *Bridegroom* or "Husbandry" in "How sweet the Name of Jesus sounds."[3]

The indebtedness of the Wesleys to seventeenth-century poets has been fully recorded. Tropes for the stages of the Christian life, such as warfare and the pilgrim's journey, appear in Wesley's "Soldiers of Christ, arise" and "Leader of faithful souls, and Guide."

As Professor Lewalski shows, the fourfold interpretation of biblical narrative—literal, typological, moral, and eschatalogical—that is, as history, as foreshadowing of Christ, of conversion and of the Last Things, continued to influence Cavalier and Puritan poets.[4] In revival hymns, though no longer expounded systematically, it can be discerned fitfully and in peculiar modes. Thus in "Guide me, O Thou great Jehovah" the Exodus foreshadows not the coming of Christ but the soul's journey through the desert of this world. The lower-class believer, in particular, learned from his hymn-book to apply this typology directly to his own life. It is easy to confuse the hunger and thirst of the Israelites for God, or of the blessed for righteousness, with literal poverty. To read the lyrics out of their context of scriptural reading and exposition is often to misread them as "pie-in-the-sky" or "opium of the people." So steeped were the hymnists in the Scriptures that only careful reading can establish whether harvest images refer to earthly crops or the Judgment, food images to literal or eucharistic bread or to manna. But increasingly during the nineteenth century hymns were sung apart from their context of Wesleyan or Olney hymn-books, with resultant shifts of meaning. Before tracing the course of the Popular tradition, therefore, we should consider the original collections.

A COLLECTION OF HYMNS FOR . . . PEOPLE CALLED METHODISTS

Without doubt, the hymns of Watts that for so long dominated Dissenting hymnals belong to the Learned tradition. The same can be said of those by Doddridge, Ann Steele, and other Dissenting poets that were compiled by Watts' editor George Burder.[5] With these stand many Anglican hymns by Toplady, Cowper, and Wesley to be distinguished from hymns of the Popular tradition by superior diction and restraint from the extremes of egoism. John Wesley, a lesser scholar than Watts but no less a gentleman, intent on keeping poor converts within the Established Church, provided for them a *Collection*, to be read as well as sung, that amounts to a poor man's breviary and guide to life.[6] Where the Roman breviary directed the monk's attention to the acts of God and his saints, to celebrate which was the Church's "work," and Reformed service-books followed the scheme of salvation, the *Collection* would accompany the layman from morning to evening and from his first invitation to believe until his entry to Paradise. Read in sequence, its hymns teach the very opposite of that egocentric withdrawal into devotional life so often associated with Evangelical conversion. Charles being the poet, and John the editor, to read it is to travel by coach along a highway fed by tracks coming in from the Bible, Latin and German hymns, John Milton and George Herbert, and the Psalms of Watts. Curtained within, the passenger cannot see just where the road leads. Up front, John the driver, in full control, sometimes muffles the voice of his too enthusiastic co-driver Charles.[7] But first, he persuades the wanderer to come aboard:

O for a thousand tongues to sing / My great Redeemer's praise (1)
Come, sinners, to the gospel feast (2)

O all that pass by, / To Jesus draw near (3)
Ho, every one that thirsts, draw nigh (4).

The next subsection, "On the Pleasantness of Religion,"[8] conveys the jubilation of co-driver and passengers intoxicated with love of their lifelong journey:

Come, ye that love the Lord, / And let your joys be known (12)

Happy the man that finds the grace (14)

Happy soul that, free from harms, / Rests within his shepherd's arms (13)

Happy the souls to Jesus join'd. (15)

The next subsection, on the "Goodness of God," displays the fusion of Moravian missionary zeal with Pietist inwardness that distinguishes new Methodist from old Puritan. On every side the Saviour's love invites all mankind: the "weary," "burden'd," and "reprobate" find pardon; the blind see, the lame walk, the deaf hear, and the dumb speak, for "Heaven / Springs up in their heart." Let Christ "teach" His "new song" to "every nation . . . people and tongue." The mission hymns of Watts have the fervour and universalism but not the inward application of Gospel miracles.

Not until the convert has discerned the "Goodness" in the Sacrifice on Calvary does he read those hymns on the Last Things that so terrifyingly begin some Victorian children's collections. Admittedly "And am I born to die?" (43) and "Am I only born to die?" (44) depict death in colours too harsh for modern adults, let alone the children for whom they were reprehensibly designed. In what child should parents have implanted fear of "dreary regions" and "Flaming skies," or of being dragged away by devils, or the self-preoccupation of:

My sole concern, my single care,
To watch, and tremble, and prepare
Against the fatal day!

Their inclusion can be explained, though not justified, on the ground that in forty years of riding through Godforsaken villages and new towns, John has seen many children die and noted how many adults have died singing his brother's hymns. In 1748 a felon mounted the scaffold singing "Lamb of God, whose bleeding love." In 1766 a woman cried "Glory!" after singing "Nature's last agony is o'er." The following year, another died "overwhelmed with peace and joy unspeakable" after singing "I the chief of sinners am, / But Jesus died for me."[9] An immeasurable gulf is fixed between their prison cells or cottages and our modern camps or shanty towns. To contrast the records of Wesley with those of Anne Frank and Alexander Solzhenitsyn[10] is to realize not merely the horror of godless totalitarianism but the power of the Wesleys to persuade the old, the sick, and the downtrodden that God loved and awaited each one of them.

When reading the *Journal* it is difficult to acquit John Wesley of a fascination with death, but the hymn-singer who must "soon resign this fleeting breath" (45) cannot have found the notorious "Ah, lovely appearance of death" (48) so morbid as we who read it out of context. The first readers could testify how death smoothed out lines of pain and restored the youthful appearance. More assuredly than we of little faith, they could rejoice that a "brother deceased" had secured lodging in the "Eden of love" (49), or a widow's soul "o'ertaken her mate" (53). The "midnight cry" of impending Judgment need hold no terror for those who waited "in patient hope." The ubiquity of death among the poor compelled the "half-awaken'd" readers on their "narrow neck of land" betwixt heaven and hell to make their choice that instant.

> Be this my one great business here,
> With serious industry and fear
> Eternal bliss t'ensure. . . .

Despite these commercial metaphors, the sincere convert strove not to attain salvation at the expense of others, but to enjoy their "everlasting love."

Yet the pilgrim's journey begins, not ends, in anxiety and self-concern. How happy one who, owning nothing and a "stranger, to the world unknown," despising its goods, seeks those of a "country out of sight" (68), journeys not alone, but with other "strangers and pilgrims" under their "Leader of faithful souls, and Guide." Beside their prospect, the "city above" and "palace" of their "glorious King" (71), what matter the vexations of this toilsome exile from their "home" (73)?

Before accusing the Wesleys of fobbing off the poor with pie in the sky, we should note how, like the *Lyrical Ballads* of Wordsworth, their hymns owned the importance of those the world knew not. The faith of the Wesleys, their imitation of the divine descent among the poor and outcast, must weigh in the scale against their support of the established order. It was Wordsworth who deplored the common people seeking their happiness "in ways that cannot lead to it," but John Wesley whose addresses showed them ways that could: work, thrift, sobriety, cleanliness, perseverance in an examined life.

The hymns of his Part Second demonstrate how by progressing from "Formal" to "real" and scriptural religion converts can find the "fountain" that will quench their thirst, as debauchery will not. But first must come, in

Part Third, repentance and recovery from the "backsliding" that often followed an emotional conversion. Here "mourners" lament not physical death but their relapses into sin brought home to them by the preacher. As "Believers," in the fourth and longest part, they sing hymns on Rejoicing, Fighting, Praying, Watching, Working (in the special Wesleyan sense),[11] Suffering, Seeking [full] Redemption, being Saved, and, no longer self-centred, "Interceding for the World."[12]

In the fifth and last, no longer "I" but "we," they sing on behalf of the "Society" that offers collective thanks and prayer. The *Collection* began with "O for a thousand tongues," a proclamation of the Saviour whose "blood avail'd for *me*." Its final part begins with a corporate song as meaningful when first sung at meetings of the Societies as today at the annual Methodist Conference:

> And are we yet alive,
> And see each other's face?
> . . .
> What troubles have we seen,
> What conflicts have we past,
> Fightings without, and fears within,
> Since we assembled last!
> But out of all the Lord
> Hath brought us by his love;
> And still he doth his help afford,
> And hides our life above.

However steeped this soul-stirring avowal in the teaching of St. Paul, it is in such corporate Christianity that the danger of secularization lurks. The institution miraculously preserved from intolerant landlords and howling mobs can become an end in itself, and so fall into idolatry. Who that first read through this manual, which has been overpraised as "perfect,"[13] could have dreamed that within little more than a century a Methodist hymnal would incite patriotic fervour in children as strongly as this hymn does corporate piety?[14]

Though early Methodists and Evangelicals would irritate the unconverted by discerning Providence in everyday events, Moravian quietism was not for them. The convert must "work" for his salvation. Only the context of a Wesleyan hymn enables us to distinguish the literal from the more common metaphorical use of this terminology. Thus in "Forth in thy name, O Lord, I go" still the best hymn on work in English, there can be no mistaking the injunction to treat all honest toil as sacred:

> The task thy wisdom hath assign'd
> O let me cheerfully fulfil!
> In all my works thy presence find,
> And prove thine acceptable will.

Lest we wonder how a clergyman dare describe twelve hours or more, six days a week, in mine or mill as "an easy yoke," Wesley was writing in 1749, somewhat before the Industrial Revolution got into full swing. John had the sense to omit the objectionable verse "Preserve me from my calling's snare . . . The gilded baits of worldly love."[15] No doubt Charles was inspired by Herbert's "Teach me, my God and King," as well as the text "My yoke is easy and my burden is light," but the Methodist believer's attitude transfigured whatever task lay before him; he did not, like the Victorian gentleman, seek to develop his God-given talent or to perform high service to the community. The Wesleys wrote not for artists or rulers but for those powerless to choose their role in life. In their hymns, at least, they erred not by cheating workers into submission to the factory system,[16] but by demanding their own total commitment and overdramatizing ordinary life. When Charles rejoiced in the pilgrim's lot: "No foot of land do I possess, / No cottage in the wilderness"; when John expected schoolboys to pray from four in the morning and never play or be alone, they violated human nature as surely as any communist government that herds peasants into collective farms. However beneficial to the drunkard, whore, or felon, a dramatic conversion simply does not happen to many of more stable temperament, nor can the majority endure a life wholly given up to religion.

EVANGELICAL AND BAPTIST HYMNODY

A detailed picture of the Evangelical attitude to working-class life emerges from some long-forgotten items in the *Olney Hymns* and other collections. The following selection of first lines from Baptist hymnals between the Ash and Evans collection of 1769 and the "Comprehensive Rippon" (1844) raises an important question:

> A beggar poor at mercy's door
> Come, ye sinners, poor and wretched
> Hungry and faint and poor
> Ye wretched, hungry, starving poor
> Another six days' work is done
> For weary spirits, rest remains
> O where shall rest be found
> Let worldly minds the world pursue
> We travel through a barren land[17]

Being literate, hence not below Booth's Class 4 (clerical), were the authors propounding the Christian hope as the divine consolation for the miseries of the poor in this life, or were they using metaphors of hunger and thirst to symbolize the operations of grace? Since both Particular (ie, Calvinist) and General (Arminian) Baptists held Communion services more frequently than most Anglican clergy, and since, anomalously, the "Particulars" sang hymns in chapel, the above examples could have represented mankind as beggars in need of spiritual sustenance.[18] Occasionally a text supplies its own explanation. As unequivocally as St. Augustine and the early Christian hymnist "Solomon," Montgomery, author of "O where shall rest be found" refers to immortality as the "rest" that "The world can never give."[19] Whether the symbolism was understood depended on the singer, yet a whole cluster of metaphors of hunger, thirst, disease, and poverty surely indicates what was uppermost in the minds of poet, editor, and singer alike.

For instance, in 1795, during the ferment stirred up by declaration of war on France, John Agg published a collection of 275 "Psalms and Hymns"[20] of which at least fifty prominently mention the blood of Christ, who "spreads" for our gaze "bleeding hands" (129) and limbs (8), sprinkles (134), washes (32), or refreshes (113) us with his blood, seals our pardon therewith (133), and displays his mangled corpse for our edification (186). In such company, "There is a fountain filled with blood" (103) appears restrained. About half of its first hundred texts being subjective and first-person, and forty-three being objective, Agg's collection, which includes some classics, fairly represents Evangelical hymnody at that time. The fifty blood-spattered lyrics clearly evince a preoccupation with violence and death that appears also in Gothic novels and in Wordsworth's allusions to "gross and violent stimulants" in contemporary literature.[21]

As regards images of poverty and disease, Newton, who was less liable than Cowper to intrude personal delusions, employs bankruptcy as a metaphor for the need of *redemption* (itself a dead metaphor of being bought out from slavery):

> I owe a vast debt,
> And nothing can pay;
> I must go to prison,
> Unless that dear Lord,
> Who died and is risen,
> His pity afford. (OH III, 9)

Admittedly, more than twenty of the *Olney Hymns* develop the image of exile and homecoming familiar from "Amazing grace" (I, 41). Into three, however, Newton sweeps the other stock metaphors at the heart of the Evangelical world-view. In "Precious Bible! what a treasure" (II, 63) he finds the divine Word all-sufficient "Food and Med'cine." What would nowadays be perceived as eucharistic symbols, "Food to which the world's a stranger" and "cordials" of grace reviving "faint and sickly" faith, here denote Bible-reading.

In his oft-reprinted "Physician of my sin-sick soul" (I, 62), Newton works out the metaphor of sin and "evil thoughts" as a "raging malady" and "burning fever" of the heart. In another once popular text, "Poor, weak and worthless as I am, / I have a rich Almighty Friend," he reproaches the backslider with a scriptural quotation "Is this thy kindness to a friend?"[22] His line "Oh! what a Friend is Christ to me!" doubtless inspired a famous gospel hymn of the Second Evangelical Revival.

In letters of advice that Dickens would have guyed as humbug, Newton lists the following "advantages" of poverty: apostolic dependence on Providence, a lessening of self-importance and "idolatrous cleaving" to this world's goods, an increase in "consolation and refreshment, and remission of many temptations." In concluding "You are not poor but rich," he misapplies an old argument for monasticism to the involuntary poverty of his correspondent.[23] Yet Newton was no hypocrite, for he had himself sojourned with Lady Poverty and had met her daily among the depressed lacemakers of Olney.

To the Evangelical, as to the monk, religion was the whole of life, but whereas the monk had renounced family and secular calling for his life of poverty, chastity, and obedience, the Evangelical incorporated into his self-image a spiritual poverty and obedience to conscience, exulting in his hunger and thirst after grace, his homesickness for heaven and alienation from "the world." "Hungry, and faint, and poor," implores Newton, "Behold us, Lord, . . . at Thy mercy's door," by invitation of the Word without which "we must starve indeed," having neither "money" to buy nor "righteousness to plead" for the "good our spirits want." The soul's hunger and thirst, its poverty and nakedness, form the self-image of the "real Christian" who beholds himself and his world in the eternal perspective. Did the poor believer, despised and rejected of men, sustain himself with a fantasy of being chosen to enjoy eternal riches, as a lyric by Newton on "The Lord's Day" (II, 45) seems to imply? The "saints," wearied with "six days' noise, and care, and toil," "pinched with poverty at home," with "sharp afflictions daily fed," find solace at "God's own house" in "heavenly bread." In context, these lines bear a quite different sense. At church, the poor "breathe a different air," for the Gospel "renews their strength, and heals their wounds." An age-old Christian equivoque underlies Newton's image of "manna" bestowed as earnest of "joys above," for "Word" implies both the Gospel and Christ himself, who was encountered in the Lessons and Communion. Both literally and metaphorically, "manna" signifies the exile's sustenance in the desert of this world. Among texts framed in Newton's study stood one on the bondsman in the house of Egypt who was precious in the Lord's sight.[24] In this undistinguished lyric, he brings before us the unbridgeable chasm between the religious and the materialistic view of life, for no Marxist can discredit the testimony of believers who had found spiritual resources to plod through the wasteland of the life they knew. For all the needless inhumanity of laissez-faire economics, the examples of France and Russia scarcely demonstrate that revolution would have improved the lot of the poor. Yet if Marxist historians seem wilfully to misapply Evangelical metaphors, some by Newton and the Baptists seem to cross the line between spiritual and literal reference. The most literal-minded devotees surely cultivated "enthusiasm" to compensate themselves for being poor.

Newton himself, however, spans the inner worlds of Bunyan and Wesley in a text used well into this century, "Come, my soul, thy suit prepare" (I, 31). The soul, having petitioned its King to remove its "burden" of sin, urges him to

> Take possession of my breast;
> There thy blood-bought right maintain
> And without a rival reign.

More naïvely than Wesley, Newton here (I, 82) portrays Christ as "formed in sinners' hearts" by applying Christ's healing of leprosy to his own (II, 26).

The Evangelicals of the Revival impoverished middle- and lower-class culture, for by proscribing drama (the sin of posing as someone else), fiction, secular verse, and even non-liturgical music, they deprived believers of recreation and something more. To see religion as the whole of life need not inhibit the monk from enjoying music and art, since religion had saturated the medieval environment to a degree no longer possible in the eighteenth century. In the 1914-18 war, English soldiers expressed amazement at the carved crucifixes they saw everywhere in Flanders.[25] In England, the Evangelicals could restore the identity of religion and culture only by imposing censorship. Fortunately few went so far as Newton, for what would Victorian provincial music have been without the *Messiah*, which he condemned?[26]

Where the Marxist historian traces the egocentricity of some texts to the smashing of ancient communities by enclosures and industrialism,[27] the literary historian scents Romantic self-consciousness. In "Quiet, Lord, my froward heart" and in a pivotal but now disused stanza of "How sweet the name" (I, 57), we cannot miss the anticipations of Wordsworth and Blake.

In the former, the sinner would be "owned a child," while in the latter, as the infant relies on a "care beyond his own," so let the adult abide with God as "Father, Guard and Guide."

In different ways Cowper and the Romantics rejected the "world": Cowper by regarding as an "idol" any love object not specifically religious; Wordsworth by rejecting commercial "getting and spending"; Blake, Byron, and Shelley by rejecting the decorum and conventional religion of polite society. Unlike Newton, Cowper could not reject secular learning, and might even have influenced his mentor by his own delight in flora, fauna, and the changing seasons. The hymns of both bridge the gap between the medieval and romantic views of Nature. A beautiful example of analogy in Cowper's "Sometimes a light surprises" was anticipated in "O sol salutis intimis," in which Christ the heavenly Sun makes the world blossom anew, "Aurora caelum purpura,"[28] in which the roseate dawn typifies the Resurrection, and Wesley's "Christ, whose glory fills the skies." The Lord rising anew within the desolate soul grants "A season of clear shining / To cheer it after rain." He then employs Dominical nature images to illustrate dependence on Providence:

> Who gives the lilies clothing
> Will clothe his people too;
> Beneath the spreading heavens
> No creature but is fed;
> And he who feeds the ravens
> Will give his children bread.

The seven hymns of Newton on the seasons (II, 30-6) range from analogy to literal portrayal. In "See how rude Winter's icy hand" (II, 30), his barren soul mourns until Jesus its "glorious sun" rises to thaw it. Similarly, in "Waiting for Spring" (II, 31), after "winters" kill the "weeds" in the hearts of believers, spring can make their "graces grow." In the next lyric, "Spring" (32), Newton slips into the naturalistic mode, exulting that blossom, "clustering flowers" and "artless birds" invite the heart to sing. After retreating into analogy, he hovers between that and naturalism, for until the Saviour break through no "warbling thrush" nor "cowslip's sweet perfume" can dissipate his gloom, any more than the blooms of Eden could console the fallen Adam. In "Pleasing Spring is here again" (33) (as "kindly spring" used in a 1905 hymnal), he returns to analogy by treating spring as the state of grace within Christ's garden, the soul. Despite some descriptive detail, he likewise treats "Summer Storms" (34) as emblematic of the spiritual life, the forgiven convert's "summer morning" being spoiled by storm clouds until the "sun" dissipate them. Though intended to show that all flesh is grass, "Hay-time" (35) shows a genuine if ineptly conveyed feeling for the grass and flowers that "clothe the field" until they yield "defenceless" to the scythe.

In his final nature lyric, "Harvest" (36), Newton crosses over to literalism. On seeing fields and valleys smile with "corn again in ear" he prays God "secure the crop," repay the farmer's toil and "satisfy the poor with bread." Just as he seems about to return to analogy, in adducing the parallel between the corn's growth and the soul's, he fixes his eye again on the object, the "eastern storms" (noticeable in the south midland plain) and frosts that threatened the young corn, the "kindly heat and gentle showers" that have caused it to wave over "furrowed lands." His application, on God sowing seeds of "heavenly joy" in "barren hearts" and ripening them for harvesting by "death the reaper," comes unforced. Thus although Cowper's finest verse on Nature and society was yet to come, even the obsessed Newton can give thanks that the poor labourers of Olney will be supplied with earthly as well as heavenly bread.

In some later Evangelical collections for orphanages and ragged-schools, the discerning of providence or judgment in daily events could intensify the natural self-blame of the deprived and outcast. In the convert of a higher class, it could induce new guilt feelings and superstitions to replace those he had shed. Cowper's conviction of being damned was a special case, but Newton uses shock-and-relief to remind converts of their common guilt for the Fall and of the abyss that yawned before the backslider.[29]

George Eliot's Evangelical upbringing underlies Dinah Morris's practice of seeking guidance from a scriptural verse picked at random.[30] Like many others, such as Blake, the Evangelicals saw divine judgment at work in political upheavals. Collective guilt over the American War of Independence and the apocalyptic convictions of Primitive Methodists will concern us in later chapters. In this it remains to consider whether, if at all, the Revival averted revolution.

THE REVIVAL AND THE WORKING CLASS

English support for the French Revolution came mainly from Unitarians and Deists—such as Joseph Priestley or Tom Paine—who comprised the membership of Jacobin clubs and Corresponding Societies. Revolutions have always been led from above. But as E.P. Thompson has shown, the Methodist societies in the 1790s had nothing like enough members to have brought about a popular revolution.[31] Elie Halevy's famous dictum that the Methodist movement averted revolution therefore needs, as R.F. Wearmouth has shown,[32] to be amended to a statement that by teaching intelligent workmen to read, by providing incentives for them to speak and help run

Methodist Societies and class meetings, Wesley made possible the growth of the trade unions that he would certainly have condemned. Having so far overcome class prejudice as to love and teach the ragged and malodorous poor, who felt so unwelcome in church, he relieved their distress whenever he encountered it (as did Wilberforce), yet remained at best indifferent to reform.[33] It was for the future utilitarians and Evangelicals to improve working conditions and wages in the teeth of opposition from many a self-made ironmaster or mill-owner who had learned to read in a Methodist Bible class. Such reforms enabled the English working class to enjoy the fruits of revolution without the pillage and massacre. In the meantime, there were Methodists among the martyrs of Peterloo and Tolpuddle.

The Marxist indictment of Evangelical religion as an opiate ignores not merely the distinction between literal and metaphorical treatment of hunger, poverty, or disease but the failure of middle-class poets and preachers, often clergymen, to imagine industrial conditions. It ignores the benefit to workers of learning to read, keep sober, and keep clean. Those poor converts who indeed experienced life as a mercifully short journey across a desert learned how divine love could transfigure their inner lives and homes. To contrast their examined lives with the existential chaos of the alcoholic or drug addict is to discover the limitations of Marx's metaphor. Neither inner nor outer reality can be dismissed as illusion.

Undeniably, converts can still become addicted to hymn-singing or Bible-reading as others can to drugs, to rock music, or to reading romances. The moment passivity turns into active reflection on scriptural symbols or events, the narcotic turns into a stimulant. When, after Wesley's death, the classes he had desired to keep together flew apart, to form the Learned and Popular traditions of hymn-book religion, both narcotic and stimulant were abundantly in evidence.

3

THE TRADITIONS DIVERGE

A home in heaven, what a joyful thought,
As the poor man toils in his weary lot.''[1]

The evidence for the evolution of Christianity as a mythos emerged from the greater hymn-texts; that for its division along class lines will come from collections. Selection and ordering of hymns betray the special emphases of a denomination, the more so if done by a committee. The compilers alone have read all the texts, and know on what principle they have chosen and grouped them. Inevitably their choice reflects the prevailing tone, doctrinal emphasis, and social level of the denomination. Conversely, even words unremarked but sung year in and year out leave their imprint on singers at the conscious and the unconscious levels.

To apply a term used of Franciscan carols, the Wesleyan and Olney hymns were "popular by destination,''[2] yet in their richness of scriptural and poetic allusion the former and those of Cowper belong also to the Learned tradition. In regard to those of the half-educated Newton, the distinction breaks down, for in their unevenness and restriction to biblical sources his hymns approach the category "popular by origin" although as an Anglican priest he belonged in principle to the Learned tradition. In truth, the distinction holds only for hymnals published between about 1800 and 1880. Before then, all collections save those of fringe groups, such as the Muggletonians, were compiled if not composed by men of learning even if destined for popular use. Thereafter substantially the same texts appeared in hymnals of all denominations.

Within that period, British hymnals fell into two broad groups:

Learned: Anglican, Congregational, Presbyterian, Unitarian

> *Popular*: Primitive Methodist, Baptist, Salvation Army; American
> gospel songs and spirituals; compilations for groups within
> the working or lower middle class.

In the United States the distinction, where not racial, was less clear-cut.

The now separate Methodist denomination has been omitted from the following survey on account of its reliance upon the Wesleyan *Collection* and upward mobility. Wesleyan hymns bawled lustily by miners in the eighteenth century came to be sung decorously by schoolmistresses and small businessmen in the nineteenth. Because the *Collection* had originally been used alongside the Prayer Book, after the separation it was expanded by the addition of hymns for seasons of the Christian year.[3]

For several reasons Roman Catholic collections also will not fit into these categories. The class of members varied according to region and ethnic origin. Moreover, the upper-class converts who followed Newman out of the Anglican Church produced most of the translations and new Catholic hymns, but usually for lower-class congregations with no tradition of hymn-singing.[4]

LEARNED, 1800-50

Before 1822, Anglican clergy could not legally use hymns during services. Nevertheless, "not less than fifty"[5] Anglican hymnals had come out since 1800. This unofficial hymnody must therefore have been in a more volatile state than that for Dissenters, who had mostly sung hymns since the time of Watts. Anglican clergymen went on producing their own hymnals until *Hymns Ancient and Modern* and its rivals *Church Hymns* and the *Hymnal Companion* (to the Prayer Book) cornered the market.

In the first quarter of the century, the best-known Anglican hymnals, those of Cotterill (1810), Heber, and Keble (both 1827), all assume familiarity with the Church calendar. From the very title of Cotterill's oft-reprinted *Psalms and Hymns for Public and Private Use, Adapted to the Festivals of the Church of England* we may infer a body of worshippers who read devotional verse at home, and knew their way about the *Book of Common Prayer*. Furthermore, Cotterill notes the declining use of the "cold and unimpressive" metrical psalters, lists some ancient hymnists, and knows why hymnody withered on the vine after the English Reformation, notwithstanding its endorsement by Queen Elizabeth.[6] A further mark of the Learned tradition is Cotterill's focus not upon the believer's experience but upon its objective correlative, the nativity, life, and death of Christ. Like the editors of *Hymns Ancient and Modern*, he feels free to alter texts even by Watts, Wesley, Newton, or Cowper in the interests of taste and moderation.

"There is a fountain filled with blood" becomes "Behold a fountain freely flows" (7);[7] "How sweet the name of Jesus sounds" (20), "How blest," and every "I" a "we" (despite the anomaly of "Weak is the effort of our heart"). The great Jehovah, again, guides "us" (109), but Cotterill's most radical alteration is that of Wesley's famous lyric into "Jesus! Refuge of the soul" to *whom* (not whose "bosom") "we" fly (185). Where he does retain the "I," he makes Addison's evaluation of the Judgment conditional in "*If* rising from the bed of death" (166) and omits the lines on physical torments.

For having followed the ecclesiastical year to the red letter, Heber's earthly reward was an order from Lambeth Palace never to publish his hymns.[8] His "Seasons" are the Sundays of that year, his "occasions" days of public thanksgiving or penitence, or the funeral and sickness provided for in the Prayer Book. His hymnal suits the Learned tradition not merely in its churchiness but its pervading spirit of noblesse oblige rather than abject dependence. A verse for Advent (traditionally apportioned to the Judgment) begins "Go, tyrant, to the rocks complain," while another, predicting that "evil thoughts . . . racking doubt" and "restless fear" will shake the proud, affirms the duty of prophet and minister to instruct the poor.[9]

Even Heber's puritanism is that of an order-giving class. A Byronic Advent hymn "The world is grown old," lamenting pleasures "past" (before the Fall), urges the young to use well their "morning light of hope" or else lament for "endless years. . . . moments lost and wasted." Likewise, the "pilgrim" journeys not through a desert but along "the world's highway."[10] Even "From Greenland's icy mountains" implies the activism of a decisionmaking class. Logically, "we whose souls are lighted" with divine wisdom are not denying the "lamp of life" to "men benighted" by staying at home, but to stand by inactive is to fail in our duty.

The Christian must combat foes that devour his own land, too: "lust of power," "wild sedition," the "yoke of slavery," and "blinded zeal by faction fed." The "lords of hell" await the proud nobleman who "mock'd at poverty." God forbids not pleasures pure, lovely, or of good report, but those that destroy order in society or the soul: the heedlessness of youth, the selfishness of age, the miser's lust and "drunkard's jest obscene," the "whirlwind of passion" that raises "hell in the heart."[11] Heber, like his contemporary Jane Austen or her beloved Dr. Johnson, preaches an ethic not of life-denial but of restraint and social duty. He was a Romantic only in his predilection for faraway scenes. The devotional passion of his eucharistic hymn "Bread of the world in mercy broken . . . " was more baroque than romantic.[12]

To call Keble a Romantic may seem unhistorical for is not his name forever linked with the Oxford Movement and *Hymns Ancient and Modern*? In fact, his hymns, like Heber's, appeared in 1827. During the next half-century, to cite even the unsympathetic James Martineau, the "tender music" of the *Christian Year* (published to raise funds for Keble's parish church), was found side by side with the Bible "in the boudoirs of innumerable English homes," and "reached the soul of our time."[13] The *Christian Year* is a manual of devotional verse.[14] Eleven of its poems, nevertheless, were included in *Hymns Ancient and Modern* (1889) and some half-dozen in *Hymns Ancient and Modern Revised* (1950).[15] To divide them into groups seasonal, mythic, and moral is to overcategorize, for the Christian ethic was never absent from Keble's ministry or his verse.

In its entirety, "Oh! timely happy, timely wise," better known as "New every morning is the love," teaches the ethic of duty and restraint.[16] Too opaque for singing, its original opening converts the text "Behold, I make all things new" (Rev. 21.5) into an encomium on those who rise with the sun. What God perpetually renews is a consciousness of the moral life not as an exile's march through the desert but as a "daily course" wherein the devotee's mind sheds sanctity upon the "Old friends" and scenes it beholds. As if to adopt Wordsworth's dictum that man must find happiness here or not at all,[17] Keble presents life not as apocalyptic drama, nor as an ascetic's quest for perfection, but as "trivial round" and "common task" within a social setting: "We need not bid, for cloistered cell, / *Our neighbour* and *our work* farewell."

"New every morning," which rivals Ken's "Awake my soul" and Wesley's "Christ, whose glory fills the skies" as the finest English morning hymn, belongs, as Martineau suggests, to the broad spectrum of nineteenth-century society that lived in secure homes and neighbourhoods, rural or urban, attended school and church, and trusted to attain heaven by slow degrees. Similarly, Keble's once beloved evening hymn "Sun of my soul, thou Saviour dear"[18] implies leisure to observe the sunset and the sensitivity and power of reflection to follow its sustained analogy between the sun and Christ as spiritual light. It assumes also an awareness of social position and responsibility. The observer traces God's "wondrous work" in "earth or sky, in stream or grove" (another echo of Wordsworth),[19] holds "sweet talk" with "dear friends," yet knows himself fortunate compared with the sick, the poor, and the "wandering child" who has spurned the "voice divine."

Keble's assumed persona follows the liturgical and rural calendar. At Whitsuntide, he recites "When God of old came down from heaven,"[20] at Rogation-tide "Lord, in Thy name Thy servants plead."[21] Keble constantly suffuses the natural with the spiritual and mythic. "There is a book, who runs may read"[22] refers at first to the Bible, next to the "works of God" in nature and the psyche that are its "pages." He draws analogies between the "Maker's love" and the overarching sky, between the Moon and the Church (an ancient trope of the Church reflecting Christ its Sun), the eternal music of sea and angels, the power of fire or wind and the Spirit. Above all, the myth of Eden speaks to the poet-clergyman in the paradisal Hampshire countryside. A wedding recalls the "Voice that breath'd o'er Eden" at the "primal marriage."[23] At this "pure espousal" of "man and maid" the heavenly Father, through the earthly, bestows the bride, the "son of Mary," through the priest, joins her hand with that of her earthly mate, and the Spirit seals the pair for the "heavenly Bridegroom."

The Paradise myth shapes the personal and social ethic of Keble as it did Wordsworth's recollections of his rural childhood. But it is the final Paradise that informs "Bless'd are the pure in heart," a sustained analogy between the Ascension, the Annunciation, and the prophetess Anna's passing into the presence of Christ. All of the poem that survives in the hymn-book is an application of the Beatitude to the "lowly" heart in the hymn's opening and closing verses. Between is one by another hand on the Incarnation.[24]

To trace the connotations of "pure" in the Bible from Temple furnishings or ritual incense, through the inner quality of the priest, prophet, or the righteous heart in Psalms and Proverbs, to the teaching of Jesus and St. Paul, and thence to the pure raiment of saints and gold of the Celestial City, would be to recapitulate Judaeo-Christian history and mythology. Apart from the text in the Sermon on the Mount, the nuance most relevant to Keble's poem is that of the heart purified by suffering. Another is the integrity of poet and prophet that Milton invokes in the opening of *Paradise Lost*, where the Spirit prefers "before all temples th'upright heart and pure."[25] By the Spirit's agency, Christ dwells within the pure and lowly soul. Keble has in mind, of course, not a social position but a modest, tractable disposition. Whatever range of meaning may be attached to "purity" nowadays—and Kierkegaard made out a good case for singleness of heart[26]—Victorians using this hymn thought primarily of sexual continence or love within the marriage bond, as witness its use as frontispiece to hymnals for adolescent boys, and Hardy's ironic subtitle to *Tess of the d'Urbervilles*, "A Pure Woman."[27]

From Keble's hymns, as distinct from his trenchant Assize Sermon,[28] emerges a pastoral and social idyll that the English upper and middle classes have never quite forsaken. An English Walter Mitty dream is to quit the city's noise and fumes for a village far off the highway where stands an ancient church surrounded by the thatched cottages of friendly farm labourers, a few larger houses with modern amenities, and behind its ivy-clad walls the local "hall." The few attain it, to find their place in an order long vanished from the city; the many create what they can in their suburban gardens. This ordered life of duty to God and neighbour was one face of the Learned tradition in Victorian hymnody. Its obverse, social activism and militancy, came into prominence later in the century.

Outside England, Anglican collections took their tone from the surrounding culture. One from Aberdeen that ran through eighteen editions between 1824 and 1840[29] ushers in the New Year with reflections on the feeble frames of "dying worms" with one year less to live. In Lent, they must crave mercy from an "offended" Jehovah who, even in triumphal lays for happier seasons, sits glowering at them from his "awful throne" (41) like Blake's Nobodaddy. Similarly, a selection for Trinity Church, Boston (1808)[30] was perfectly adapted for ultra-Calvinist New England. The Baptist Anne Steele has 49 of the 152 texts, and Watts, Doddridge, and Rippon many others, leaving only Cowper, Addison, Tate and Brady and the "Veni Creator Spiritus" to represent Anglicanism as known in England. Even the Protestant Episcopal hymnal issued in 1845[31] shows the same preoccupation with sin and Judgment, albeit more gently expressed. In one group among which only "There is a fountain filled with blood" offers any comfort, singers travel through life only to "reap eternal woe" unless in "Zion's gloomy hour" the Lord revive his work (140). Let none boast of duties performed, for "no man ever did" nor "ever will" fulfil the Law. Not without precedent did B.F. Skinner's ideal community forbid mutual praise in *Walden Two*.

At first the Learned tradition is difficult to document in nineteenth-century Dissenting hymnals, such was the dominance of Watts. On the social gospel of Doddridge it only remains to add that in a verse on "Israel's gentle Shepherd" visiting widows and orphans he reminds readers of the "Guardian-care" that will heal the "bleeding hearts" of all who mourn with them.[32] This strain of practical concern, found also in the more radical Montgomery, became characteristic of mid-Victorian Congregationalism. More literal than the treatment of poverty by Newton, it leads Doddridge to declare with deliberate equivocation that the "King" spreads his table for the "hungry-poor" that stray in "Sin's dark Mazes."[33]

Though he never flirted with Unitarianism, Doddridge contributed more titles than any save Watts to Martineau's *Hymns for the Christian Church and Home* (1840). The most impressive, because the least susceptible to Martineau's unscrupulous mangling of orthodox texts, were those on man and beast in England's green hills and valleys as objects of providential care.[34] If any excuse can avail for his butchery, Martineau believed (wrongly as we know from the first-century *Odes of Solomon*) that myth came as an excrescence upon primitive Christianity. He therefore felt justified in editing out the Christ-myth from some twenty-nine texts by Heber, fifty-six by Montgomery, and others by poets from Bishop Ken to Wordsworth and Keble. This very breadth, and the somewhat abstract character of the censored verses, suggest that his brand of Unitarianism, though warmer than that of Joseph Priestley or Mrs. Barbauld, has more to offer the well-read than the poor. A faith for the rational and genteel, it never in England attracted poets comparable with the Unitarian hymnists of New England.

Martineau grafts upon his rationalistic creed a romantic ideal of hymnody. "Every spontaneous utterance of a deep devotion is poetry in its essence, and has only to fall into lyrical form to be a Hymn."[35] This need not be confused with Matthew Arnold's definition of religion as "morality touched with emotion," for Martineau excludes versified morality together with dogma. The question as to whom devotion without dogma should address seems not to arise.

The editor of the imposing American Presbyterian *Church Psalmist* (1843) enunciates a classical ideal by which a hymn "should possess unity of design, and simplicity in execution." "To its one great object," "every thought and expression should be rendered subservient." While not excluding emotion, he requires like Aristotle "a beginning, middle and end."[36] No hymnal could more aptly confirm Donald Davie's distinction between the classicism of Old and the romanticism of New Dissent.

Neither definition seems to fit the Popular-by-origin tradition that had spread a generation earlier from poor white areas of the United States. Though consigned by its classical ideal to the Learned tradition, this dignified and expensive volume includes a sizeable proportion of titles by Wesley and Montgomery. Evidently the dividing line in the United States was not social position alone, but race, education, and theological attitude. The heirs of the New England Puritans reasoned about grace on Sundays and constitutional amendments during the week; the slaves and poor whites of West Virginia or Kentucky rocked and clapped their way through songs on the Exodus and Atonement in church or plantation. Both Apollonian and Dionysian Christians shared a national myth of the Promised Land, in one sense already reached by white immigrants and their descendants, in another sense to be attained by the chosen of all races in a future state. The resultant tension between white, poor white, and black has threatened American civilization.

The Learned tradition of American hymnody differed from its English counterpart in its messianic patriotism, its absence of social concern, and above all in its Calvinistic ferocity, the legacy of the Great Awakening. In the same year as Martineau's collection, *Village Hymns* (1840), a Congregational supplement to Watts that Benson judged the "brightest" American Evangelical hymnal of its time,[37] abounds with fearsome pictures of the Judgment. Echoing Jonathan Edwards, one poet bids "sinners tremble" before an "angry God" (41), while Samuel Davies, President of Princeton University, beholds them engulfed in "lakes of liquid fire" (39). The incessant self-examination that is the complement of "holy fear" appears in another text by Davies, "And what am I?—my soul awake" (237). The Abolitionist campaign being already under way, this fearsome godly book represents an obsolescent tradition.

A milder piety and a critical standpoint nearer that of Martineau govern a Presbyterian selection for the "Closet, Family and Social Circle" (1831). In contrast to "a late London collection," presumably the Wesleyan of 1830, it eschews any scheme, but by the same token caters for all of "evangelical views and pious feelings," citing an unnamed statesman for the view "Give me the making of ballads and I care not who makes the laws."[38] "Evangelical hymns" being "peculiarly suited" to convey "gospel truth" that "unlettered Christians," and especially children, retain better from "spiritual songs . . . they are accustomed to sing" than from any other formulation, the editor calls such impressions indelible if the singer's mind and heart be "excited and warmed." He thus prescribes a mixture of conditioning, instruction, and emotionalism parallel to that in English Evangelical and Methodist books, but makes no provision for celebrating even Christmas or Easter.

POPULAR BY ORIGIN, 1850-4

Hymnals of the Learned tradition presume a settled family and social life quite outside the purview of the unlettered who attended outdoor revivals in the United States and England. A "Choice Selection" for camp meetings in Vermont (1827)[39] flies in the face of the Learned tradition by referring in nearly all of its 110 items to singers as "pilgrims" or "wanderers." One called "What poor, despised company" portrays "travellers," who though "poor, distress'd," and "lacking daily bread" possess "boundless wealth" being "with hidden manna fed" (6). Beyond even Newton's assurance to his correspondent, this represents a denial or deliberate aversion of the eye from the reality of malnutrition, a feasting on collective fantasy. The hymnal's second preoccupation, with the Second Coming, takes a more subjective form than in Presbyterian hymns, in figures of a hell-bound singer weeping because not reborn (29) and a convert crying "Don't you see my Jesus coming?" (30).

That English millenarian hymnody supplied an outlet for the anger and frustration of the poor seems indicated by the strongly military cast of many Primitive Methodist hymns. A then well-known one placed at the opening of the *Small Hymn-Book* develops a metaphor of conversion as military recruitment:

Christ he sits on Zion's hill,

> He receives poor sinners still;
> Will you serve this blessed King?
> Come, enlist, and with me sing.

The refrain doubtless picked up first by children avowed "I his soldier sure shall be, / Happy in eternity."

In one of many such stories, when rowdies threatened a preacher, women stood round him singing as a spell "Wicked men I'm not to fear, / Though they persecute me here. . . . '' The verse preceding this refrain interweaves the military and millennial strains:

> Let the world their forces join,
> With the powers of hell combine;
> Greater is my King than they,
> Surely I shall win the day.[40]

In the most popular of these songs, "My soul is now united,"[41] apocalyptic images blend with the pilgrim motif, for a stranger taken in by Jesus attains rebirth by venturing his "all" upon the "atoning blood." Christ being his salvation, what has he to covet or fear? "By floods and flames surrounded" he pursues his way, Christ his "joy," "treasure," "glory," and "crown" (111). The hymn's popularity, in conjunction with the hint of psychological integration in its first line, suggests that the singers recognized their own conversion and subsequent experience in its image of the embattled pilgrim. Another of the many pilgrimage hymns represents the Christian's struggle against Apollyon.[42]

Like the Wesleyan *Collection*, the *Small Hymn-book* expresses a religion of the heart's experience in metaphors of sickness, poverty, and hunger overcome, but from a more definitely lower-class viewpoint:

> Thou chusest not the rich and great
> To spread thy truth around;
> By foolish men, of low estate,
> Thou dost the wise confound. (99)

This anti-intellectualism pervades a two-part hymn, "See how the Scriptures are fulfilling" (25, 26), in which God calls all mankind, "bond and free, rich and poor" and repays with hell-fire all guilty of "persecuting and hindering" the Saviour's work by "disputing," as well as by despising, His blood.

The hymns "popular by origin" differ from Wesley's not merely in their lamentable verse and anti-intellectual cast, but in their stronger emphasis upon the Last Things. In one addressed to "Sinners" soon to face death and plead for mercy which "may not then be found," the "travellers" cry that they have found "the rock" and "balmy dew" that "flows from Christ." Let all then "count this world below as dross," for "Who bear the cross shall wear the crown" (74). As the congregation, like Moravians, sang the chorus over and over, they doubtless fancied themselves in heaven already:

> I'm glad I ever saw the day, sing glory, glory,
> We ever met to sing and pray, sing glory, glory,
> I've glory, glory in my soul, sing glory, glory,
> Which makes me praise my Lord so bold: sing glory, glory. (50)

In compiling his *Large Hymn-book*, Bourne followed a simplified Wesleyan scheme.[43] He regressed toward the Evangelical mainstream also by taking 225 of his 536 texts from Wesley, together with many by Watts, Doddridge, Cowper, and others. He modestly pronounced 20 he had composed for this book to be "of a superior cast" and likely to "lead into the mysteries of faith." Be that as it may, the 150 contributed by himself and his collaborator Sanders strongly indicate what worshippers must have heard from their preachers.

From two lyrics by Bourne and Sanders they learned that they would pass at once to heaven or hell "When life's short journey's done" (361). Jesus, claiming then "his own," "by love united," would usher them to their inheritance of "crowns," "kingdoms," and "bright mansions" (366). Clearly preachers offered those "by the world contemn'd and slighted" (*loc. cit.*) an overcompensation for their powerless obscurity in this life.[44] A metaphor of believers as "soldiers" fighting round the Cross (398) suggests a total sublimation of aggression into a missionary or inward combat. The latter appears from a hymn that employs what comes nearest to an industrial metaphor by urging Christ to "appear in" all "waiting" hearts, "subdue and mould" them into love (115).

While one lyric on "passing through this dreary vale" refers to the body as a house "of clay" subject to "wind and rain" (280), the vast majority by Bourne and Sanders reflect the immersion of these self-taught authors in the Bible, to the exclusion of secular literature and science. One on God's "heavenly skill" in the forest and "wonder-working hand" (292) in plants and green fields, however, depicts the ordered natural world of Watts or Addison rather than the wilder scenery of Wordsworth or Coleridge.

Passing over the standard Methodist allusions to the Cross, we should notice two strains of imagery that recall the earliest charismatic Christian hymnal, the *Odes of Solomon*. A text known to have been popular, "Hark! the gospel news is sounding" calls on the sinner to observe "streams of mercy" flowing from the Cross to wash away his sin in the "fountain" of divine blood, then continues:

> Grace is flowing, like a river,
> Millions there have been supplied;
> Still it flows as fresh as ever,
> From the Saviour's wounded side. . . . (16)

Finally, it calls on all to "bathe in the full ocean" of His love.

Other hymns of Bourne and Sanders abound in water images of every kind: the believer walking "o'er life's tempestuous sea" past "rocks of pride" and "whirlpools of despair" (260); "showers" of grace blessing the earth with fruit, and "streams" overflowing the longing heart (262). Notably the rocks connote self-assertion, the sea and whirlpools passivity and helplessness, the showers and streams divine fecundity. Authors from the sodden English Midlands can hardly be thought to conjure up water mirages by wish-fulfilment. As in a presently popular example, "Peace is flowing like a river," charismatic religion appears to induce images of flow and liquefaction.

More obviously, it inspires images of liberation. In one hymn-text the collaborators internalize the Fall myth, by urging the soul to tread on sin and Satan like Christ who "bruises Satan's head." Another calls worshippers "bound in Satan's chain" to cast fear away, then run the "heavenly race" in obedience and dependence. According to the early Christian *Odes of Solomon*, the chains bound the dead, not the living.

What endeared popular hymns to mill-hands and labourers, and negro spirituals to slaves, was their blend of the Puritan or Apollonian ethos and the opposed polarity of Dionysian "enthusiasm" (God within). Like "Solomon" the Odist, Wesley conceives the state of grace as a "rest where pure enjoyment reigns," the soul's desire being "fixed on things above" (383). In this sense, Methodism, of whatever kind, created its own reality to enrich the poor. (As if to echo "Solomon," Bourne and Sanders beseech God to "stamp" on them the "Spirit's seal" [495].) C. Shaw observed this entrancement in a miner who had taught at a Primitive Methodist Sunday-school. "I have seen him lift his eyes heavenwards while singing, as if he saw a beatific vision. There was one hymn and tune which always . . . suffused his face and filled his eyes with an unspeakable serenity. . . . the one beginning . . . 'Would Jesus have the sinner die? Why hangs he then on yonder tree?' "[45]

It was this vision that inspired Primitive Methodists to translate poverty or unemployment into "floods and flames," and their adversaries into "Apollyon" retreating before the Saviour's face (80). As a minister remarked, their "popular, sacred songs . . . the most volatile and penetrating agents of religious propagandism,"[46] represented a form of conditioning. But it was the vision, so little corresponding to modern memories of soot-blackened chapels, Sunday suits, and teetotalism, that caused their souls, like that of a greater religious romantic, J.H. Newman, to dwell "apart on celestial mountains."[47] It was the vision, contrasted with daily drudgery in a pot-bank, that inspired Shaw at Sunday-school: "To me . . . it was a life within my life. In the midst of a life of hardship and temptation, this inner life shed a brightness and sweetness which always gave me an upward . . . aspiration. Sunday was verily an oasis in the desert to me."[48] The celestial vision, above all, empowered self-taught preachers to purge working-class areas of drunkenness and violence, teach labourers and children to read, and evolve a narrow but genuine culture, with a strong spirit of community.[49] Here and there this culture outlived the denomination itself (reabsorbed in 1932 into the Methodist Church) if only in the watch night service and subsequent grace hymn sung by the clan round the supper table.

To judge from the Bourne and Sanders hymns on the instant passage of the dying to paradise, congregations in the first "tin tabernacles" heard less from their preachers about an imminent Second Coming. By 1854, when their next hymnal came out, the "Ranters" had settled into a denomination, though one that never lost touch with the subliterate. In that collection, "the worst-edited and most severely mutilated ever published"[50] some twenty-eight hymns "For Domestic and Family Worship" show which way the wind is blowing. In substance, though not, alas, in style, these texts for family morning and evening worship, written mostly from the father's viewpoint and scarcely ever from the child's, bear a striking resemblance to monastic office hymns. One for Sunday morning goes:

> O bid this trifling world retire,
> And drive each carnal thought away;
> Nor let me feel one vain desire,
> One sinful thought, through all the day (531).

Parents resolve daily to talk with their children about Christ, and on their behalf to beg his guidance in the "perfect path" to "realms on high":

> May virtue crown their rising years,
> While passing through this vale of tears
> To joys that never die. (522)

Whether or not these lines were widely sung, they will represent the otherworldly ethos inherent in the collection as a whole.

Father resolves to exemplify religious obedience, show his family "their duty" and "maintain the dignity of love" (523). By analogy, the medieval abbot and prioress, called "Father" or "Reverend Mother," had a duty to guide their "children."

> A saint indeed I long to be,
> And lead my faithful family
> In the celestial road. (522)

Wesley wrote this hymn for the master of a household with servants.[51]

As for work, apart from an adaptation of Wesley's "Forth in thy name," the section says no more than:

> By thee through life supported,
> We'll pass the dangerous road,
> By heavenly hosts escorted
> Up to their bright abode;
> There cast our crowns before thee,
> Soon as our toils are o'er,
> And joyfully adore thee
> In heaven for evermore. (526)

In a rough industrial district, the poor family of teetotal believers must have lived as apart from the world as they would have in a conventual house.

Such verses show the Primitive Methodist at a mid-point between expecting the millennium and expecting in this life not wealth but a stable family life. No longer does the convert have but a single "charge to keep," for he must fit his family for his heavenly mansion, by ensuring that each child, like Red Riding Hood, lifts not an eye from the narrow way to gaze upon this world's distractions. Nor must he seek solace in "worldly" pursuits or pleasures, whether of body or mind.

POPULAR BY DESTINATION, 1800-70

Joseph Irons published *Zion's Hymns* (1816) to be used as a supplement to Watts' hymns in the Dissenting chapel at Camberwell, of which he had become pastor some years after the death of his mentor Newton. An extreme Calvinist, Irons was famous only as a preacher, yet this personal hymnal ran into three editions by 1825, and some thirty items remained in use throughout the century.[52] Of these, two openings: "I sing the gracious, fix'd degree . . . The Lord's predestinating love" (148) and "How safe are all the chosen race, / Preserv'd in Christ their Head'' (175), represent the volume's doctrinaire character. The 200 or more never widely used represent the extremes of each aspect of Evangelical spirituality: the sense of deliverance in "I was once a ruin'd debtor'' (30); world denial, in an image of the Church as oasis in "Nature's barren land'' (137); self-abasement in "Lord, I'm a sinner, vile and poor'' (245); spiritual warfare, in the promise to "soldiers of the Cross'' (239) that they will "march in holy triumph home''; above all the fountains of royal blood that flow to "thirsty souls'' (100) from "Jesus's dear breast'' (53) and wounded side. Undoubtedly Irons preached in the same vein to many of the "happy poor'' (244) who deserve "wrath and hell'' (245) yet can expect a "kingdom of eternal rest'' secure by the "precious blood'': "Ye blessed poor, come, claim your right; / The kingdom is your own'' (244). Their pastor's bloody and cruciolatrous fantasies must have induced self-abasement in the poor, or else deflected desire for change or vengeance into metaphors of Christian soldiers subjugating their foes. His hymnal also held before the overworked the prospect of eternal rest. Its compiler's name survives only because his son made our best translation of "Dies irae.''

The no less unworldly substance of Baptist hymnody is more difficult to assign to a class, for while Methodists were rising into the commercial middle class, Baptists were losing their intellectuals and becoming identified with the artisan and shopkeeper segments.[53] Paradoxically, the Arminian General Baptists resisted the use of hymns in services, while the Calvinist Particular Baptists welcomed it.[54] The major collections for "Particulars,'' by John Rippon (1787) and William Gadsby (1814),[55] the latter designed to contain "nothing Arminian,'' each included several of the texts on poverty cited from Ash and Evans, but otherwise consisted of standard Dissenting hymns, predominantly by Watts.[56] Later editions, along with Denham's *Saints' Melody* (1837), show the distinction between Arminian and Calvinist hymnody becoming outmoded: the number of Anglican hymns among the 1,174 items of the "Comprehensive Rippon'' 1844, and in John Gadsby's edition of 1853, in which he paid an eloquent tribute to Charles Wesley.[57]

Predisposed to elephantiasis by the requirement to provide for every conceivable sermon topic, these Baptist hymnals make tedious reading. Their metaphors require the singer constantly to prostrate himself before the divine majesty and give thanks for his deliverance by the blood of Christ from turmoil within and hell-fire hereafter. This life he must envisage as his pilgrimage across a desert or tempestuous sea.[58]

Since the Calvinist scheme of salvation offered less variety of topic than the liturgical calendar, brief illustrations can convey the flavour of these compilations but not their suffocating repetitiousness. A supplement

includes items by Denham on the "condescending" and "justifying" grace
of Jesus, Hart on Jesus reprieving the "convicted" sinner from the "bar"
of divine justice, and Medley on the "worthless worm" resolving to hide in
the "dear bosom" of "him who died on Calvary's tree."[59] In the main
hymnal the same poet, "washed" in the blood, joyfully anticipates passing
the "chilling flood" of death when called "home" (504), while Rowland
Hill recalls that

> Vile was my heart, deep plunged in sin;
> Dismal den of thieves within,
> Where every lust presumed to dwell—
> A hateful progeny of hell. (506)

In the final segment on heaven, Berridge envies the "happy saints who dwell
in light. . . . Safe landed on that peaceful shore, / Where pilgrims meet to
part no more" (1024).

In the "Comprehensive Rippon," Toplady images the journey of one
"launched into the deep" by Christ, his "pilot wise," whose "word" is his
"compass," steering him through "rocks and quicksands" to the "land of
endless rest" perceived by faith (304), while Wesley recalls having run to the
"desert" to hide from the "pain" of fruitless desire for "rest" from
"tempestuous things" (305, Part II). In the next hymn Kelly depicts a
journey "From Egypt" toward a "better home" in Canaan, whose
"prospect . . . cheers the pilgrim's breast" (305, Part III).

Baptist world-and-life-denial resides not in the particular hymnist, whom
the reader will already have perceived to be perhaps Anglican or
Independent, but in the accumulation of such images throughout the book.
A bird's-eye view of Baptist hymnody proper, in its social aspect, can be
gathered from some texts between its "palmy days" in the eighteenth century
and 1869, when the famous preacher Charles Spurgeon produced *Our Own
Hymn-Book*.[60]

By this time the Particulars were standing upon a rock fast disappearing
beneath a flood of undoctrinaire Evangelicalism, while popular preachers
like Spurgeon held forth to semi-literate multitudes in vast new chapels,
halls, or even theatres. This populist and anti-intellectual trend seems to
have taken over Baptist hymnody sooner in Britain than in the United States,
where the editor of the *Plymouth Collection* (1855), finds "food for true
piety" in Catholic devotional books that supplied many of his texts,[61] and in
the Gospel themes of human rights and peace that were to inspire the Baptist
President Carter.

In some lyrics anthologized by Burder, Anne Steele mingles Calvinist objectivity with personal love of the Saviour. In one, she describes the final consignment of sinners to eternal woe (117), and in another ascribes even her own ailments to sin (74) curable only by Christ her refuge (40) and "only sovereign," from whose "blissful smile" earth's "alluring joys" tempt her in vain (57). A lifelong invalid after her fiancé's sudden death on her intended wedding-day,[62] she found that from the sacred text

> . . . springs of consolation rise
> To cheer the fainting mind;
> And thirsty souls receive supplies
> And sweet refreshment find.

In this her finest hymn, "Father of mercies, in thy word / What endless glory shines," the "wretched sons of want" find in the Bible riches "exhaustless," "lasting as the mind" and beyond all that "earth can grant."[63]

The Baptist was forever travelling from the City of Destruction with a chosen few who had been reborn. As the great preacher John Fawcett says, "Blest be the tie that binds" their hearts "in Jesus' love" for "The fellowship of Christian minds / Is like to that above." The reborn who "share each other's woes" will remain "joined in heart" if physically separated and will "one day meet again," but outside that intense fellowship they will find only "toil and pain" until released by death.[64] They travel through this wilderness fortified by realizing that, in Samuel Medley's words, in "I know that my Redeemer lives" (1775), that their "constant Friend" who "once was dead" will preserve and finally raise them.[65] Their "sweet joy" in this realization depends upon the belief in the inerrancy of the Scriptures that to this day is responsible for the blinkered culture and religious argot crisply dismissed by Booth as "cant."[66]

While the Particular Baptist shopkeeper or craftsman might know only his trade and his Bible, the General Baptist joined the throng that heard Spurgeon preach a popular Evangelicalism. Severely as his preaching has been treated by Davie,[67] in his hymn collection Spurgeon espouses two admirable principles, eclecticism, and fidelity to an author's text. "Mangling" he says, "has grown into a system . . . to be most heartily deprecated."[68] Traditionally Baptist in its massiveness (1,060 items) and initial set of 150 psalm versions by Watts and others, *Our Own Hymn-Book* strikes the keynotes of mid-Victorian pietism. Notably five lyrics by Spurgeon himself furnish indications of the prevailing ethos in his, the largest ever Baptist congregation in Britain.

First comes the sense of exile. In his version of Psalm 39, he stresses man's frailty as "stranger" and "sojourner" on earth, "exiled from glory's land," but resolves to sing to "My God . . . ever near." Second comes triumphalism. In his version of Psalm 60 he hails the inevitable conquest of death and hell by the standard-bearers of "truth divine" (60), who will prevail as the Israelites over Canaan (44). Third, Spurgeon teaches a *contemptus mundi* less anti- than para-intellectual:

> Lord, make my conversation chaste,
> And all my understanding purge,
> Lest with the wicked throng I haste,
> And down to hell my pathway urge. (58)

The dogma of total depravity enunciated in the following lines, "They from the womb are all estranged, / The serpent's poison fills each vein" undercuts human reasoning and motivation.

The fourth and to our enquiry most pertinent characteristic of Baptist pietism is the kind of social concern exemplified by Spurgeon's "Jesus, poorest of the poor," in which he interweaves paraphrase of the least vindictive verses of Psalm 41: "Blessed is he that considereth the poor: the Lord will deliver him in time of trouble" and "The Lord will strengthen him upon the bed of languishing; thou wilt make his bed in sickness" (Ps. 41.1, 3) with incidents from the life of Christ. Spurgeon adds that though "crowned with loftiest majesty . . . In Thy members Thou art found / Plunged in deepest poverty." Happy these that feed "*Thy* sick and faint" and "clothe the naked *saint*," for in turn Christ will preserve their souls and revive them in sickness. We need not interpret Spurgeon's hymn as teaching his adherents to help only each other, yet it enjoins a mutual charity amounting to "ambulance work" in a fallen world rather than a struggle to bring about a more just social order.[69]

Neither Spurgeon's nor any earlier collection provides for domestic worship. The revised Gadsby collection of 1853 has no texts on home life, Denham's but two or three, among a group on the "heavenly home," and the "Comprehensive Rippon" only two.[70] Nor does Spurgeon's small section on "Revivals and Missions" (951-73) provide for national occasions. In common with its precursors his hymnal concentrates upon God, redemption, the Scriptures, and the religious life. Given a choice, Spurgeon prefers eighteenth-century texts to contemporary ones. Only Montgomery contributes anything like as many as Watts, Doddridge, Hart, Cowper, Toplady, or Stennett. Except for "Hail to the Lord's Anointed" (353), Montgomery's radical texts are passed over in favour of his otherworldly ones like "See the ransom'd millions stand / Palms of conquest in their hand" (354). One contemporary text, Bonar's call for Christ to reap the "great harvest" of this "ruin'd earth" and "restore our faded paradise" recalls a pre-industrial as well as pre-lapsarian society.[71]

To judge from Spurgeon's choice, the Baptist conception of the Christian life was, as it remains, fundamentalist and conservative. That life consists of "Holy Anxiety" (636-44) for personal salvation, "Desires after Holiness" and "Perseverance in Grace" (645-53), "Renunciation of the World" (654-7), and otherwise "Courage and Confidence," "Peaceful Trust," "Patience and Resignation," "Humility," "Zeal," and "Sacred Gratitude." The hymns collectively enjoin what Schweitzer called an *interimsethik* and Nietzsche a "slave-morality." With Steele, the believer resigns whatever earthly bliss God's will denies (696); with Cowper he resigns life, health, and comfort (698); with Charlotte Elliott he resolves while on "life's rough way" to "be still and murmur not" (699). Longing to reach his (or perhaps more often her) "glorious home" (845) the singer nightly bivouacs a day's march nearer (846), conscious like Lyte that hopes must not be built in a "region like" (848), what Bonar calls a "desert dreary" (849).[72] To particularize further would be otiose, for the mere allocation of more titles to the Last Things—including the "State of the Lost"—than to the Psalms, or even the person of Christ,[73] says much concerning the faith Spurgeon preached to his vast and predominantly lower-class congregation.

POPULAR BY ORIGIN AND DESTINATION: SOME CONTRASTS

The hymnody of Primitive Methodism originated in sublimated radical protest, that of the Baptist denominations in a world-denying conservatism. Both strains, together with the liturgical influence of the Learned tradition, can be observed in early and mid-Victorian hymnals for particular social groups.

For the household, first of all, the hundred lyrics of *Domestic Praise* (Manchester 1850) rival those for the Primitive Methodists in their world-excluding pietism:

> Lord, as a family we meet,
> Thy goodness to proclaim
> . . .
> Weary and faint, by cares opprest,
> We still are travelling on
> To that bright land of peace and rest,
> Where our forerunner's gone. (10)

Others on "Resignation" resemble Baptist hymns in the singer's passivity beneath the "chastening power" of God who gives and takes away (51). By contrast a collection of Anglican, Lutheran, and Old Dissenting texts called *The Evensong*[74] evokes an image of the well-ordered and instructed family worshipping nightly with its servants. The family that sang "Let us with a gladsome mind," "Ye servants of the Lord / Each in his office wait," "Fairest Lord Jesus," or "Now thank we all our God," but not "Abide with me" or "Jesu, Lover of my soul," neither gave up this world for lost nor pitched its tent a day's march nearer home.[75]

Selections for the *Poor of the Flock* in 1838 and for the *Working Men's Christian Association* in 1872 differ little in their ethos despite the economic growth that, as G.M. Hopkins notes in his "communist" letter to Robert Bridges (1871), had scarcely benefited the labouring class.[76] The earlier book harps not on poverty but on alienation from the "foreign land" or "desert" (321) of this world, from which the Saviour leads the singers to their "house and portion fair" (262). Despised and shunned here, with nothing to call their own, they enjoy God's love, so "perish every fond ambition" (60). The workhouse system then being set up lent credence to this bleak view of life. The "Working Men" of 1872 also find this world a "desert" (211), but now find life a "dream" (192) from which they seek rest (192) in that "happy land / Far, far away" whence music "thrills upon the heart" (211). Though richer in hymns by Wesley, Cowper, and Victorian Evangelicals, the latter still depicts the worker as dependent upon the "friend of the friendless" whose open door "Invites the helpless and the poor" (116, 117).[77] The work it presses upon them in "Christians Working" (186-93), is either religious or without meaning, for Nos. 188-91 represent "work" as soul-saving, or else as remainder as mere "toil" requisite for personal salvation. No. 187, the only text on work as ordinarily understood, conveys no sense of satisfaction or social good, for "rest" in heaven is its sole reward. The worker, an "exile, not unblest," apparently toils in solitude as his soul clings to Christ its vine (144), who bleeds copiously throughout the book.

The Radical movement exemplified in Chartism produced its own hymns, of which the best-known, "When wilt Thou save the people?" first entered a hymnal—appropriately Congregational—only in 1887.[78] Ebenezer Elliott's plea for the impoverished during the Hungry Forties has an importance beyond its simple cry for justice:

> When wilt Thou save the people?
> O God of mercy, when?
> Not kings and lords, but nations,

> Flowers of thy heart, O God, are they,
> Let them not pass, like weeds, away,
> Their heritage a sunless day.
> God save the people!

Elliott decries not religion, nor God, but a social hierarchy that has lost its meaning. Knowingly or not, he echoes Coleridge and F.D. Maurice in calling for an organic society, a whole that cares for its parts.[79] His images, however, imply that those who fail to blossom in this life can expect no heavenly Sun to bring them out hereafter. His courageous parody of the National Anthem gives utterance to a radicalism quiescent since the Restoration, but disguised in apocalyptic sects from the Muggletonians to the Primitive Methodists, who called down vengeance from Heaven rather than taking it on earth.[80] In the end, Elliott retains his Judaeo-Christian assurance that heaven and earth will maintain the right. Mountains and skies proclaim that "Man's clouded sun" shall rise, that God loves His children as His angels. He heralds the social gospel in notes learned from the Hebrew prophets. Significantly, Marxism has never found a popular poet in English.[81]

Democratic Hymns and Songs (1849) came out after Parliament had averted revolution by repealing the Corn Laws. "Hark! millions cry for justice, Lord" urges one author, "A little rest, a little corn." Echoing Shelley, the poet laureate of Victorian radicalism, another swears that "A garland on the car of pomp / Our hands shall never fling" (10). One or two voice republican, egalitarian, or internationalist sentiments; others condemn the quest for glory in battle. But the prevailing temper is moral and in a broad sense religious. "Alas for the poor," cries one poet, for "the blessings God hath seen good to bestow" in the fertile earth "Are torn from the millions to pamper the few" (1). That most Christian poet Milton said no less.[82] Another asks not for a man's "lineage" or native land, but whether he is honest (12). Another sees God's "matchless power" and providence thwarted:

> Thine hand is open wide—
> Thou has a table spread
> For all—then why is man denied
> By man, his daily bread?

The authors may cite the French Revolution as a precedent, but none would abolish the Christian faith and calendar. They decry nationalistic strife, not patriotism, for though "Britannia's sons" be "slaves," their Creator made them free.

Yet two lyrics inspired by this left-wing romanticism seem ominous portents for Christianity. Should man, asks one, confine his Maker's rule to "Gothic domes of mouldering stone?" Surely God's temple is "the face of day," his "boundless throne" earth, ocean, and the heavens. In its pantheism this breathes the spirit not of the psalmist but of Byron or Shelley. The other contrasts three preachers. The first, old, white-haired, and ascetic, preaches "every hour" with "shrill fanatic voice" that man is born to "misery," to "sweat," "suffer," and "labour" yet humbly obey his priests and kings as "God's viceregents." The second speaks softly, his aspect "sleek and slothful," his words glib, "as from a book," his air self-complacent, his message "we are happy as we are." From the eyes of the third and youngest, "Genius" flashes when he urges upon "deluded nations" that "Progress is the rule of all," that by effort "Hopeless poverty and toil" may be conquered, that none should "patiently endure" ills that can be cured. These figures fit the Oxford, Evangelical, and Broad Church moulds, but the compound of messianic romantic and positivist elements in the final verse portends the coming split between the Judaeo-Christian and the secular-liberal or socialist ethos.

In three books for sailors and soldiers, Evangelical piety takes on different meanings. The texts in the *Sailor's Hymn Book* stress dependence on Providence.[83] Those in the *Soldier's Hymn Book* (1869)[84] bear the hallmarks of the Popular tradition: the pilgrim's desert voyages to "home," "rest," and "glory," the image of soldiers as "strangers" here and heaven as their "Fatherland" (292). This book was sold in a Soldiers' Institute and Mission Hall at Aldershot, and doubtless well-used.

The *Soldiers' Book of Hymns* (1863), "compiled by an [unnamed] officer," presents the military life as one of ceaseless danger in which unaided "flesh will fail."[85] Familiar texts bear a military meaning: Heber's "The Son of God goes forth to war" and Wesley's "Soldiers of Christ," with another text calling soldiers to arms as "peace has lost its charms" (4), are headed "Christ's Army." "Take up thy Cross" and "Commit thou all thy griefs" appear under "Exhortation—Endurance." Under "Faith" appear such diverse texts as "When I survey the wondrous Cross," "Just as I am," and one highly applicable to the military life, "Father, I know that all my life / Is portion'd out for me." Under "Praise" and "Comfort" appear classics, such as "Holy, holy, holy," "O God our help in ages past," and "There is a book, who runs may read" that the compiler had doubtless learned at public school. Under "Foreign Service" the soldier whom God has posted prays to "serve" his "Queen aright" and do God's "holy will." Guardian angels ensure that he will sleep in peace until the "last dread call" awake him to "reign in glory."

Though intended for the same clientele, these two books follow two distinct traditions, and reflect different kinds of conditioning. The mission collection would have embarrassed the officer, and his would have been rejected by the missioners as too formal to "work" inwardly upon the prospective convert. The one exemplifies the Popular, the other the Learned tradition.

4

FAR APART

The religious life of this country is distinguished in its healthiest forms by a certain manly simplicity. . . .

Steal away to Jesus . . . steal away home.

he thought the idea of the spiritual world as home . . . the feeling that you are coming back to a place you have never yet reached—was peculiar to the British. . . . [1]

THE LEARNED TRADITION, 1850-75

The best English hymns of the eighteenth century were Dissenting and Methodist, the best of the nineteenth Anglican. In general the same was true of hymnals, but two Congregational collections of the 1850s marked out new directions. The "Leeds Hymn Book" (1853) shows the ministers of that city as original in treating Watts as one hymnist among many and in using translated Latin and German texts.[2] They begin their selection with 205 Psalm-based hymns by such diverse authors as Watts, Tate and Brady, Addison and Newton, Montgomery and Grant. In the central portion, hymnists range from the Baptist Steele and Anglicans Cowper and Heber to the Unitarian Sarah Adams.[3] From the book as a whole the worshipper might receive an impression of this life hardly consoling but less sanguinary than that given by earlier hymnals and more hopeful concerning our final prospect. The numberless items on death usually include the departed among the saved and virtually ignore judgment and hell-fire.[4]

The selection represents the historical and doctrinal span of English hymnody from "Jerusalem, my happy home" by a sixteenth-century Roman Catholic to "Abide with me" by an Anglican Evangelical only six years dead. Both in range and in quality, the book belongs to the Learned tradition, for the few texts declaring that after a life "portioned out" (892) we shall meet "thousands of children" (877) above can pass unnoticed among the many classics. While the best hope the book offers the poor is Montgomery's assurance, in "What are these in bright array" (661), that hereafter they will not know the hunger and disease all too familiar in Leeds or the author's home town of Sheffield, its themes extend far beyond the Fall and Atonement. Too puritan to provide for Christmas, the ministers set "Hark! the herald angels" and "Brightest and best" for Advent. For the Passion they set the finest lyrics of Watts, Kelly, and Milman.[5] Combining aesthetic sensitivity with relative freedom from morbidity and subjectiveness, their hymnal conveys a more catholic and "healthy-minded" religion than that offered Baptists or Primitive Methodists.

It formed the basis of the *New Congregational Hymn Book* (1859), intended to counteract liberalism among ministers (102).[6] While adhering to the Calvinist "scheme of salvation," this nationally distributed hymnal appears the first to urge the practice of the Christian ethic: love, kindness, and imitation of Christ. To make clear both the hitherto unexplained "scheme of salvation," and the modest shift toward the social gospel in this highly conservative hymnal, the relevant portion of the table of contents, referring to 573 texts, is reproduced at the end of this chapter.

In the scheme the first realities are God, his Word, and the Fall of Man. The conversion experience takes its place within the framework of the Christian life and ethic. The life and example of Christ, if still subordinate to the Myth, claim a larger proportion of texts than in collections for other denominations.

In the Baptist "Comprehensive Rippon" (1844) only 7.66 per cent of the hymns pertain to Christ (instead of 13.4 per cent), mostly under typological and royal titles;[7] in the *Saint's Melody* (1837), 25 per cent of the 1,026 hymns concern Christ, but 10 per cent in titles alone, 1.64 per cent his Passion (with many more on its subjective application), a mere 0.3 per cent his Incarnation, and 1.03 per cent his love and title "Friend of sinners."[8] In the enlarged Wesleyan *Collection* used from 1830 to 1875 a vast proportion relates to Christ, but only 0.26 per cent to the Nativity, 2.60 to the Miracles (0.39 objective, 2.21 per cent subjective application), 1.30 per cent to his Example, and 1.43 per cent his Resurrection and Ascension. Against these 4.29 per cent refer to the Passion and Crucifixion (0.91 per cent objective, 3.38 per cent applied), 7.02 per cent to the Atonement (3.90 per cent doctrinal, 2.99 per cent subjective), and from 3.51 per cent to 4.03 per cent to the Judgment, depending on whether those on the Second Coming only are included.[9]

As indications of a more humane and this-worldly faith, the Congregational book carries more items on Times and Seasons than on the general Resurrection and Future Life, while its hymns on the domestic life treat home as a dwelling-place rather than a corridor. Among a dozen items on the Saviour's "human life and example," "As much have I of worldly good" (348), "In all things like Thy brethren Thou" (354), "Thou Son of

God, and Son of man" (355), "Servant of all, to toil for man" (356), and especially "How shall I follow Him I serve / How copy Him I love" (358) suggest a humanitarian conception. Significantly, none have survived save the inappropriate "Lord, as to Thy dear Cross we flee" (353).

The Learned tradition, Dissenting or Anglican, eschews the "sensuous sentiment" derided by R.W. Dale, the most distinguished Congregational preacher of his age and the most active in social endeavours, in his *English Hymn Book* (1874) for his overflowing congregation at Carrs Lane, Birmingham. Can this cult of "manly" objectivity (see the epigraph to this chapter) be reconciled with Evangelical piety? The test case is the *Hymnal Companion to the Book of Common Prayer* (1870), used as late as 1892 in at least 1,400 Anglican churches, yet for different reasons also backward-looking. Its saintly editor, Edward Bickersteth, was at first refused permission to reprint several recent hymns from *Hymns Ancient and Modern*.[10] This collection, based on earlier Evangelical compilations (1832, 1858) carries many obsolescent items from the age of Watts and Wesley, such as "O thou to whose all-searching sight" and "O happy day that fix'd my choice," together with pre-Victorian hymns by Montgomery and others. Some like "Love divine, all love excelling," "O for a thousand tongues to sing" and "Bread of the world, in mercy broken" should never have been omitted from *Hymns Ancient and Modern* (1861). Bickersteth chose none that a Low Churchman would think idolatrous, but very few morbid, bloodthirsty, or egocentric enough to have embarrassed his High Church rivals.

His scheme, moreover, closely follows the Prayer Book liturgy, beginning with items for Morning and Evening Prayer, the Litany, and the thanksgivings or occasional petitions, and continuing with hymns for the major festivals and seasons and the Communion. Avoiding those obscure saints beloved of Tractarians, it departs from the Prayer Book calendar only to the extent of attaching running heads such as "Sundays in Trinity," "Holiness," or "Warfare and Pilgrimage."

In the morning both Low and High Church congregations sang "Awake my soul," "Christ whose glory" or "Forth in thy name"; in the evening "Glory to Thee, my God, this night," "Sun of my soul," "Abide with me," "At even, ere the sun was set," "Sweet Saviour, bless us ere we go," or "Saviour, again to Thy dear name we raise." The fact that *Hymns Ancient and Modern* originally carried but five Communion hymns removes all doubt as to the services at which Anglicans were expected to sing.[11] All of the above titles imply a patterned life, an ordered sequence of days and seasons simpler than yet comparable with that provided for in the Roman breviary.

Some two or three now rarely heard imply that changeless Victorian middle- or upper-class life so nostalgically evoked in films and television serials. In "Sweet Saviour" even the zealot Faber urges "gentle Jesus" to light "life's long day and death's dark night," looks back on the day's "triumphs" and failures, and pleads for "joy," "sober liberty," and "simple hearts" that long only "to be like Thee." Compare this line with Baker's on the "pleasure" and "joy" the divine word affords the "simple-hearted," or Faber's whole text with the Broad Churchman Ellerton's "Saviour again," with its recurrent evensongs and partings and its call for "peace upon our homeward way" throughout our earthly life. With the Roman Catholic, High, and Broad Church hymnists the Evangelical compiler shares a common education, class upbringing, and expectation of life. With Keble (in "Sun of my soul") and with Henry Twells, author of "At even, ere the sun" he shares also a Christ-like compassion for the less fortunate, who lack or have lost loved ones, friends, or faith. This again implies the sensitivity of the economically secure, concerned with more than mere survival.

The Low Churchman might sing mission hymns after Epiphany while his High Church cousin sang further hymns on the Magi or sing only one litany, but in Advent both would sing the hymns on the Judgment and in Lent the penitential dirges sung in Baptist or Methodist chapels throughout the year. The recurrence in all mid-Victorian hymnals of "Rock of Ages," "Just as I am" or "Weary of earth, and laden with my sin" can mislead us if we neglect the liturgical arrangement, the assumption even by Evangelicals that the Prayer Book allots a time for fear and a time for triumph, a time for guilt and a time for rejoicing. At Easter all Anglicans would sing "Jesus Christ is risen today" or "The day of Resurrection."

The common core of both *Hymns Ancient and Modern* (1868) and the *Hymnal Companion* was sung up and down the land. It consisted of: (1) translated or native hymns for the greater festivals, "All glory, laud and honour" or "Christ the Lord is risen today;"[12] (2) texts on the Last Things, "Day of wrath," "Lo, he comes" or "Abide with me;"[13] (3) psalm versions, Anglican or Dissenting, "As pants the hart" or "O God, our help . . . "[14] (4) mission hymns such as "Jesus shall reign" or "From Greenland's icy mountains;"[15] and (5) nineteenth-century texts (usually Anglican) for times, seasons, or occasions, such as "New every morning," "The Son of God goes forth to war" or "Eternal Father, strong to save." The bulk of these can without hesitation be called "objective." The proportion of hymns in common, 125 of about 368 in *Hymns Ancient and Modern* (1868) and 403 in the *Hymnal Companion* would doubtless have been greater but for difficulties over copyright.[16]

Between 1861 and 1889 (or even 1875) *Hymns Ancient and Modern* evolved from an austere Tractarian to a virtually Popular hymnal. Its genesis and history have been described too often to repeat here, but its original stuffiness, the often wooden translations that made up almost half of the 273 texts, represents an overreaction to some tart aspersions in Tractarian journals upon enthusiasm in Revival hymns. The *British Critic* had heaped scorn upon "passionate and exaggerated descriptions of moods" and "experiences" to which "the worshipper may be an entire stranger." The *Christian Remembrancer* (to which Neale contributed) had called the *Olney Hymns* "impossible" and pronounced only two by Wesley fit for a church hymnal. Even so, *Hymns Ancient and Modern* sold a third of a million copies in its first three years and four-and-a-half million by 1868. Driving out the local hymnals produced by clergy or parishioners, it reached over 10,000 parish churches by 1892,[17] thus reaching far outside the still small Anglo-Catholic wing.

Its instigator, Sir H.W. Baker, came from the same milieu as Bickersteth. At a time when Anglican clergy, whether High, Low, or Broad, came as near to being a national priesthood as at any time in history, both editors conformed to the prevailing trend of matching hymns with the liturgy and sermon. Since standards of literacy and musicianship were rising everywhere, parson and clerk no longer needed to line out psalms for illiterate villagers. Though Anglican congregations, especially rural, were by no means confined to the gentry, the professional class still supplied almost all the leadership, clerical or lay. The Evangelicals might have been at Cheltenham College instead of Wellington, but none who sang from *Hymns Ancient and Modern* or the *Hymnal Companion* called down divine judgment on their rulers or toiled alone through the wilderness. (It was the editors of "Hymns Altered and Mutilated"[18] who first changed a great hymn to "Guide *us*, O thou great *Redeemer*.") Nor, to judge from their mid-Victorian collections, did they idolize the family or nation. Being so focused on the liturgy, their hymnody was freer of intrusive secular concerns than any since.

Liturgical form channelled their missionary enthusiasm. The High Church compiler of the *People's Hymnal* (1867), best known for his translation "Come down, O love divine," supplemented ancient hymns, with their "clear doctrinal teaching" and "stern simplicity," by "more emotional and personal" lyrics from later ages, yet adhered strictly to the liturgical year.[19] Evangelical users heard the voice of Jesus, called themselves wandering sheep, washed away their sins, and strode forward to their land of rest. Anglo-Catholics invoked the day of wrath or sighed "O Paradise" in a Faber hymn spurned as "Methodistical" by an Anglican journal.[20] Both lifted a blood-red banner, unsheathed the sword of the Spirit, and urged the Saviour to sprinkle many nations. Yet though the young would live to mourn their grandchildren killed in battle, they upheld the Cross, not the flag.

Again, compared with those just arriving from across the Atlantic, the hymns prescribed for the London mission of 1874[21] were models of decorum. The self-laceration of the few lyrics that rival those of "Ranters" or Baptists by exhorting the sinner to remember his "awful guilt" while gazing on "the bleeding Head" of Christ (8) is balanced by the poetic control of "When I survey" or "Veni Creator Spiritus." Between the songs of Wesley or Cowper and those of Moody and Sankey there is a great gulf fixed. Singers of "Hark my soul, it is the Lord," "O for a heart to praise my God" or, a fortiori, "The King of Love my Shepherd is" stood yet within the prospect of salvation. They might strike fountains of blood from the Rock of Ages, or confess themselves weary of earth and laden with sin, but were not lured with offers of instant salvation. The tragic defeat of taste by "pop" religion was yet to come.

POPULAR BY ORIGIN AND DESTINATION: SPIRITUAL AND GOSPEL

Failing a clear distinction between negro spirituals and gospel hymns, genuine American folk-songs can fall under the same condemnation as mass-produced lyrics of almost depraved inanity. Both having crossed the Atlantic during the Second Revival in the 1870s, their vogue requires for its understanding an appreciation of two different historical perspectives. The period since the conversion of the Wesleys (1738) occupies 18 per cent of that since St. Augustine reintroduced Christianity to Britain in 597, but 67 per cent of American history since the landings of the Pilgrim Fathers (1620) and the first African slaves (1619). It fills 95 per cent of time since 1750, when the tobacco boom brought the number of slaves past the quarter million mark. Having passed its peak in Britain, the original Revival was well under way in America before the invention of the cotton gin (1793) and consequent demand for pickers caused their number to rise to the four-and-a-half million still enslaved at the beginning of the Civil War. The abolitionist movement stimulated British interest not only in spirituals but in many of its own songs and hymns. By the same calculation, white congregations have sung hymns for a much larger span of American than of British history, and black Americans have experienced no form of organized religion older than Methodism.[22]

In the North, their African-style dances and revels being condemned as heathen, negroes readily took to Evangelical open-air hymn-singing. In the South, they chanted psalm verses lined out by their preachers, hence the echoing refrains of spirituals or the choruses of Gershwin's *Porgy and Bess.* Their oral culture requires dramatic climax and congregational response even during the sermon. The establishment in 1815 of an independent Black Methodist church intensified this Dionysian tendency of illiterate or barely literate worshippers, such as the first Primitive Methodists. Those "heathenish" devotions that offended Lutherans of the mid-nineteenth century, those "wild" and "barbaric" songs chanted by overflowing Black Methodist congregations, were thus rooted as much in racial tradition as in the plight of slaves. "Deep River" or "Go down, Moses" readily turned into secular songs because the distinction between what may fittingly be sung on Sundays and on weekdays has never applied in Black American culture.[23] The endless repetition of choruses after improvised verses, a feature of German or Black American folk hymnody,[24] may appear incomprehensible to English church-goers conditioned to expect a clear structure of thought.

What black choirs now sing as "gospels" need not concern us, but the gospel songs that crossed over with Moody and Sankey were more deliberately formulaic than either the spirituals or the revival hymns sung by poor whites around 1800, then adopted by Primitive Methodists. A few examples from those popular in England may illustrate some differences between Christian folk-songs popular by origin and by destination. Erik Routley categorizes spirituals into: scriptural paraphrases, especially of the Exodus; songs on heaven; appeals for divine comfort; passion lyrics; and didactic or inspirational songs.[25] A rough equivalent of each can be found among the gospel songs of the Second Revival introduced by Moody and Sankey and adopted by the Salvation Army. These, as Tamke has recently shown, were sung like present-day "pop songs" by all sorts of people from schoolboys to cab drivers.[26] Their vogue coincided with home and overseas missions in the mainstream churches, especially Anglican.[27]

To this day the tune of "Deep River," sung by the Marxist Paul Robeson, commands the admiration of music lovers for its glides and audacious leaps, but the simple lyric has its own shape: a statement, "My home is over Jordan," appeals to God and to the listener; "I want to pass over" and "O don't you want to go to that Gospel feast . . . that promised land," a reiteration and a final prayer.[28] Not a word is wasted or fudged. Among the 750 *Sacred Songs and Solos* of Sankey (1874)[29] not one is fit to stand beside it.

The nearest thematic equivalent, "Shall we gather at the river,"[30] has a clear yet inorganic structure. Where the black singer appeals passionately to his Lord and his fellows in a single dramatic moment, the white soloist and chorus slowly approach the river of death (never identified as Jordan) that flows by the "throne." Successively the soloist walks and worships at its margin, having laid "every burden" down, relies on grace for his "robe and crown," and beholds in the river the Saviour's smile. Then, their pilgrimage concluded, the "happy hearts" of soloist and chorus "quiver" with the "melody of peace." In place of the spiritual's organic form, this feeble but widely used lyric offered a mechanical framework filled in with stereotyped images, redundant adjectives and inane reiteration.

Another equivalent "sacred song," "Oh, think of the home over there" more accurately conveys the scriptural images of saints and waiting Saviour, but has a merely repetitive refrain and hurdy-gurdy tune. This mid-century lyric also notably domesticates heaven, as kindred and friends await the singer.[31]

To this day, "The sweet by-and-by"[32] remains a term of contempt for the Christian hope. The fault lies not with the lyric, a clear if theologically inaccurate assertion that in a land discernible by faith the Father (not the Son) waits to "prepare us" a home, but with a tune and a refrain ("In the sweet by-and-by / We shall meet on that beautiful shore") that have the jingling sentimentality of a public house chorus at closing time.

The story-line of "Swing Low, Sweet Chariot"[33] coheres because the singer, as when appealing to God and the audience in "Deep River," looks forward "over Jordan" to the approaching angels, yet backward to the day of his conversion. Artfully, the chorus imitates both the chariot's up-and-down motion and the soul's forward direction: "I'm sometimes up and sometimes down / But still my soul feels heavenward bound."

The artistic gap between the spiritual "Nobody knows the trouble I see, Lord" and the gospel song "I left it all with Jesus / Long ago"[34] is less evident. The spiritual owes its popularity, one suspects, more to its musical leaps and intervals than to its text, a series of appeals for "Brothers," "Sisters," "Mothers," and "Preachers" to help drive "old Satan" away. Like such thanksgivings as "Nun danket" and "Praise my soul, the King of Heaven," it forms a frame whereon every singer can weave his own temptation, whether to lust, violence, or mere spite. "I left it all with Jesus" has a shapelier tune and more explicit lyric than the average gospel song. In recounting her conversion, resort to Jesus in her troubles, and attainment of peace, its author mingles the standard Evangelical formula of the Passion Applied with some prosy teaching on faith, hope and love, before her final appeal "come home." If it lacks the immediacy and shared yearning of "Nobody knows," its frequent reprints suggest that it spoke to the condition of the lonely and deprived.

The spiritual "Were you there when they crucified my Lord?"[35] has for obvious reasons entered the repertoire of hymns. Its stark succession of actions, "nailed him. . . . pierced him. . . . laid him" punctuated by the chorus "causes me to tremble, tremble, tremble" indicates less an inward realization than a formulaic retelling of the Crucifixion for the illiterate. For modern white singers it can scarcely attain the depth of meaning it must have had for slaves who had seen or suffered a flogging.

Its nearest approximation, the English lyric "Tell me the old, old story"

(1866),[36] taken up by Sankey and the Salvation Army, falls apart in that the hymnist, ill at the time of writing, longs to be told of the Passion as "a little child," yet also as to a "sinner" who has paid too dearly for "this world's empty glory." Although Jesus attributed sickness to sin, an invalid describing herself as weak and weary, yet in some worldly sense glorious, can scarcely claim that He has made her "whole." Instead of allowing the worshipper to apply a formula, as in "Nobody knows," Miss Hankey fills her canvas with incompatible images. Only its hypnotic tune and refrain "Jesus saves" can have endeared this self-centred lyric to so many.

"What a friend we have in Jesus," popularized by *Sacred Songs and Solos* and the Salvation Army, shows that kind of coherence the best gospel songs could have. It resembles the spirituals in being built upon a formula, release of overwrought feelings by prayer; in offering the singer a general matrix, "trials and temptations," weakness and desolation; and in having arisen from a situation. The author, an Irish immigrant to Canada, composed it for his mother at home, hence his wish to remain anonymous.[37] However prosy this lyric, it deserves a better tune than the mawkish jog trot that confines it to revival meetings and gospel halls.

The spiritual "Walk you in the light"[38] has never taken root in England. Its reproof of parents who fail to set an example of prayer befits a simpler, more tightly knit community. This exposes the difficulty never surmounted by gospel hymnists, that in so complex a culture as the English, simplistic teaching and threadbare lyrics appeal mainly to the young, the semi-literate, the unstable, or the deprived. Even in the melting-pot of the United States (as Mark Twain's satire underlines)[39] the eighteenth-century revivals had attracted not only a wider segment of society but poets infinitely better endowed and taught than their successors.

In an amusing instance of the appeal of gospel songs for the immature that once-popular schoolboy anti-hero William Brown disgusts his supercilious elder brother by singing "Dare to be a Daniel."[40] In his permanent rebellion against a bourgeois upbringing, William poses as a Daniel leading his "faithful few" (another phrase from the gospel hymn in common parlance). This lyric by Philip Bliss, the most balefully productive of all gospel hymnists save the indefatigable Fanny Crosby,[41] has particular interest in that its verse on the "Many giants . . . stalking through the land" who would fall if "met by Daniel's band" must have reminded English children less of an Old Testament story than of "Jack the Giant-killer." Its final verse is worth quoting for its very ineptitude:

> Hold the Gospel banner high!
> On to victory grand!
> Satan and his host defy,
> And shout for Daniel's band![42]

The popularity of Bliss's hymns in the United States seems confirmed by no less a novelist than William Faulkner, to whom "My High Tower" doubtless suggested the name and role of the reclusive confidant in *Light in August*. Like the hymnist, "In His (God's) pavilion hiding," that ex-clergyman uses his house as a refuge from life.[43]

Again a roughly equivalent spiritual, "Going to Write to Master Jesus" (140), transcends "Dare to be a Daniel" in its depth and pathos. Its two-line verses and refrain convey a petition for "valiant soldiers to fight for Christ." The finale—"You say you are a soldier, / Fighting for your Saviour / To turn back Pharoah's army"[44]—challenges the singer to such spiritual combat as gospel singers rarely face. Its shaping and matching of text and tune represents a triumph of human artistry over suffering, a power attained by those without hope in this world.

Their enslavement explains the appeal of the Exodus narrative, supremely conveyed in "Go Down, Moses."[45] Nowadays, "Let my people go" must be more familiar as refrain than as Bible verse. As sparely as a Border ballad, the spiritual recounts the journey and Red Sea crossing before drawing the only valid conclusion for slaves unable to escape: "O let us all from bondage flee, / And let us all in Christ be free."[46]

Whereas gospel songs were used to sell an Atonement-centred, simplistic faith to the young, insecure, or unstable among the faceless multitudes of British cities,[47] negro typology represented to what Arnold Toynbee calls the "internal proletariat" of slave states the genuine parallel between their situation in a supposedly free land and the captivity in Egypt or Babylon. While not forbidding personal exodus via the "underground railway" to Canada, it told the majority truly that on earth they must hope for inner freedom, and hereafter for the Promised Land. Not coincidentally, the blind Fanny Crosby's best lyric was her once popular funeral hymn "Safe in the arms of Jesus"[48] with its pathetic conclusion:

> Here let me wait with patience,
> Wait till the night is o'er;
> Wait till I see the morning
> Break on the golden shore.

To the sadness of a race in bondage, the only true parallel is in the great hymns of the First Revival that were sung by miners and mill-hands, "Guide me, O thou great Jehovah" or "Jesu, Lover of my soul." The white hymnists of the Second Revival whose lyrics so quickly entered denominational hymnals, notably for children, were dealing in a devalued currency.

HOME

From nineteenth-century hymns and translations in *Ancient and Modern* and the *Hymnal Companion* as supplemented in 1875 and 1878, it would be possible to compile a miniature hymnal embracing the whole objective teaching of the Learned tradition concerning God and man, viz.:

			AM	HC
God	the Creator:	O worship the King	167	526
	the Redeemer:			
	expected:	Hark the glad sound! the Saviour comes	53	45
	born:	Once in royal David's city	329	414
	manifest:	As with gladness men of old	79	93
	fasting:	O Lord, turn not thy face from us	93	120
	teaching:	Blest are the pure in heart	261	349
	entering			
	Jerusalem:	Ride on, ride on in majesty	99	161
	crucified:	There is a green hill far away	332	420
	resurrected:	Jesus Christ is risen again	134	183
	ascended:	See the Conqueror mounts in triumph	148	222
	worshipped:	O for a thousand tongues to sing	522	502
	the Spirit:	Our blest Redeemer, ere He breathed	207	253
	the Trinity:	Holy! holy! holy! Lord God Almighty	160	33
	His Church:	The Church's one foundation	215	285
	its services:	Morning: New every morning is the love	4	3
		Evening: At even, ere the sun was set	20	19
		Communion: O God unseen, yet ever near	320	384
	its mission:	Onward, Christian soldiers	391	322
Man:	his youth:	Children of the heavenly King	547	340
	love:	The voice that breath'd o'er Eden	350	454
	life:	Lead, kindly Light	266	18
	death:	Abide with me	27	13
	Judgment:	Day of wrath, O day of mourning	398	68
	Heaven:	For all the saints	437	354
Harvest:		Come, ye thankful people, come	382	51 [49]

Further texts could provide for Occasional Prayers, "Eternal Father, strong to save" for those at sea; "Lord behold us with thy blessing" for commencement of a school year, and so on.[50] For certain doctrines, such as Hell, none of the above list provides, and few provide for gaps in the natural calendar or the life-cycle: winter, sickness, poverty, or unemployment, the best available being "Lord, thy word abideth." A few presuppose the child's or soldier's life of simple obedience and battle against a defined foe.

Rather more share a characteristic that differentiates them from any contemporary sample of the Popular tradition and any earlier sample of the Learned. They celebrate a triumph already achieved, or victory already assured. We are, so to speak, home and dry. In hymns of the Second

Evangelical Revival home lies always beyond this life, "over there."
Moreover, many Learned texts on human life presuppose an active role for
us in securing the triumph. In gospel hymns and spirituals we remain
passive, leaving all the work to Christ. Yet these were expressly written for
the slaves, factory hands, housewives, and servants who performed the daily
(rarely "trivial") round, and common task that was to assure for working
people in late Victorian England and twentieth-century America a prosperity
and security that their forebears had never known. The implication is
obvious: the lower orders cannot by their own efforts attain happiness, their
daily work being irrelevant to their salvation. While their more fortunate
brethren can by their work and conduct at least co-operate with God, these
must let Him take charge and think for them.

This, needless to say, is an overstatement, for in "Alleluia, sing to Jesus,"
W.C. Dix cries, "His the triumph, / His the victory alone." But in the same
stanza, Dix adds "Hark! the songs of peaceful Zion / Thunder like a
mighty flood." Only a closer reading shows this to refer to the future state.
We seem, as in "The day thou gavest," to be singing of a Kingdom already
spread around the world, a harvest already in, an occupation already
completed. We sing, moreover, of a collective conquest by the Church that
some have ascribed to the Empire.

In "Fight the good fight," the outcome lies ahead, in the confirmation
from experience "That Christ is all in all." But even "Lean, and His mercy
will provide" implies not passivity but divine aid in resolving uncertainty.

A single hymn by the founding editor of *Hymns Ancient and Modern*
exemplifies the piety of the Learned tradition in its subjective aspect.
Without seeking to rival Frank Colquhoun's excellent commentary on "The
King of Love my Shepherd is,"[51] I would remark two essentials of the
tradition: the coherence of God, and the certainty of salvation. By drawing
together the Psalm 23 on God as "Shepherd," the teaching of Christ on
himself a "Good Shepherd"[52] to every stray sheep, and the "unction" of
the Holy Spirit, the hymnist draws together the Old Testament conviction
that the Israelite tribes and their individual members were in God's keeping,
and the manifestations of that care in the ministry of Jesus and the inward
working of the Spirit. The stanza most central to piety of the Learned
tradition from Watts to C.S. Lewis, of whose spiritual autobiography it
might be an abstract,[53] runs:

> Perverse and foolish oft I strayed,
> But yet in love He sought me;
> And on His shoulder gently laid,
> And home rejoicing brought me.

With a glance at the General Confession in Matins and Evensong ("We have erred and strayed from thy ways like lost sheep"), Baker brings together the psalm verse "He restoreth my soul" and the rejoicing in heaven over the lost sheep. Underlying the phrase "home rejoicing" is an assumption that both the Good Shepherd and the sheep rejoice. Within the intended context of the Eucharist, "home" refers to taking Communion. In his last hours, Baker himself muttered these lines in the expectation of heaven. To untold thousands who have sung them since, in church or school, both "home" and "rejoicing" surely denote their present state of life, neither crisis nor consummation, but simply health, cheerfulness, self-acceptance. Home is where the heart has ease. Heaven is a continuance in that state, the Cross the way thither, not solely as a sacrifice made without the beneficiary's participation, but as a burden he also must take up. The rejoicing on coming home has already begun, to continue "within Thy house for ever."

At that time the Learned tradition, in short, envisaged no radical discontinuity between this life and the life to come, no wandering here as in a desert, or a foreign land, no bondage here to be followed by liberation, no angel with a bright key releasing child sweeps to run naked in delight, for the first time free to live. It envisages instead a restrained rejoicing in the wonders of creation, in work, duty, ordered worship, in finding or returning to the path laid out, in the prospect of heaven that makes death easy. It is the ethos of those who know their good fortune as an effect not of chance but of providence, which is, etymologically, divine "foresight."

It is otherwise with the hymnody of the unfortunate, or the ill-provided. "A home in heaven, what a joyful thought" sings a Methodist of the Hungry Forties, in no satiric vein:

> As the poor man toils in his weary lot,
> His heart oppressed and with anguish driven,
> From his home on earth, to his home in heaven
> . . .
>
> as the sufferer lies
> On his bed of pain, and uplifts his eyes
> To that bright world. . . .

"My rest is in heaven, my rest is not here" sings Lyte in the same period, an Anglican whom consumption has denied the privileges of his class. Like the consumptive Brontës, he must not build his hopes "in a region like this" but look to a city not built with hands, as "the worst that can come" shortens his journey "home." The dialogue in *Wuthering Heights* between the sickly and short-lived Linton Heathcliff, whose ideal is a state of rest, and the healthy Catherine who dreams of being cast out of heaven to wake on the moor "sobbing for joy," spans the gulf between the beloved or well-provided who find home here and the unloved or ill-provided who can find it only hereafter. The strict Calvinist endeavoured to jolt the affluent out of their complacency by representing every human soul as "A limping beggar, clothed in rags," a "friendless, helpless wretch," suing "at mercy's door." The Methodist or Evangelical sought to bring home to the homeless by creating a heaven in their hearts as earnest of that to come. "I'm but a stranger here," sang one such in 1836, "Earth is a desert drear . . . Whate'er my earthly lot, / Heaven is my home."

If the latter hymnist might dangle before the deprived a "heavenly home" to overcompensate them for misfortune or injustice here, the former might idolize his class, church, or country. Such distortions and idolatries will be illustrated in the final portion of this book.

ALLOTMENT OF TEXTS IN NEW CONGREGATIONAL HYMN BOOK (FIGURES SHOW NUMBER OF TEXTS)

THE DIVINE BEING

God:
  His glory and perfections (19)
The works of God:
  Creation, providence, grace (22)
God the Son (Leeds H.B.: "The Lord Jesus Christ"):
  His glory and worship (13)
  His mediatorial character and titles (28) (Leeds H.B.:
    "Pre-existence")
  His incarnation and advent (16)
  His human life and example (12)
  His love and sympathy (10) (Leeds H.B.: "miracles")
  His passion and death (15)
  His resurrection and ascension (10)
  His intercession and reign (21)
  His second advent and judgment (9)
God the Holy Spirit:
  His office and power (21)

THE HOLY SCRIPTURES

  Inspiration, authority, and excellence (16)

MAN

His fall, mortality, probation (21)

THE GOSPEL

Statements and invitations (27)

THE CHRISTIAN LIFE

Commencement:
  Repentance and faith in Jesus (6)
  Regeneration and adoption (9)
  Personal dedication (15)
Duties:
  Holiness and love (12)
  Contentment and resignation (14)
  Trust in God, diligence (17)
  Courage, conflict (10)
Difficulties:
  Pilgrimage (4)
  Temptations and declensions (13)
Trials (7)
Privileges:
  Support and guidance (9)
  Protection and perseverance (11)
  Communion with God (11)
  Delighting in God (14)
  Aspiration and hopes (16)

DEATH AND THE GRAVE (22)

THE FUTURE LIFE

Resurrection (4)
Heaven (12)

CHRISTIAN MISSIONS

Ordination of missionaries (4)
The colonies (5)
All nations (22)

TIMES AND SEASONS

    Morning and evening (18)
    Saturday evening (13)
    The harvest (3)
    Commencement and close of the year (10)
    Youth (9)

DOMESTIC RELIGION
    Family worship (10)
    Marriage and a new home (5)

NATIONAL HYMNS (8)

5

WHAT DID THEY SING?

There's a distinction between what people, because of their social background, choose to sing, and what editors, whose background may be very different, offer them.[1]

This comment by Erik Routley, one of the greatest English-speaking hymnologists, succinctly puts a difficulty sensed by many scholars. If nine-tenths of the items in a collection remained unsung, to make any valid generalizations on its social influence we need to pin down the remaining one-tenth. Of several possible methods the first, a hunt through newspapers, essays, magazines, and novels for allusions to hymns sung would take too long and in any case reveal only what the highly literate sang. The second, a search of ecclesiastical and educational archives, has proved marginally useful in the case of late Victorian schools, but again would be prodigal of time. The third, a study of sermons, service-sheets, religious journals, and church magazines would not only require long-term residence near a centre such as London or Edinburgh,[2] but given the proportion of material lost or destroyed could only yield fortuitous inferences, again as to the preferences of clergy.

While occasionally drawing on material of all three kinds, I have sought to attain something better than guesswork by two further means: a computer search of some 140 first-line indexes for the number of times each hymn was reprinted between the mid-eighteenth and early twentieth centuries; and an analysis of some Victorian surveys and supposedly representative selections, checked against two recent lists of hymn-texts in common use during this century.[3]

So wide-ranging a computer search has obvious shortcomings. It gives undue weight to hymnals that interest the investigator, in this case those for the young, favours older as against more recent texts, and only reveals the choices of editors who, in the heyday of cheap printing, rarely thought to undertake market research. I have therefore drawn inferences primarily from the Victorian items among the 150 texts most frequently reprinted, on the ground that to have established themselves so quickly they must have attracted many compilers. In addition, I compared the hundred items most often used in adult denominational hymnals of the Learned tradition with the hundred used most in those of the Popular tradition, repeating this comparison for Sunday and secular (ie, "public" versus "Board") school hymnals.[4]

The surveys and representative selections were: an Anglican set of 100 hymns for domestic and school use (1861); a magazine poll of the "100 best in English" (1888); a collection of *Victorian Hymns* (1887) counteracting the tendency of cumulative hymnals to favour older texts; and a survey of Anglican hymnals (1885) for the 325 most common items. A further check was a list of 100 hymns for schoolchildren made in 1956.[5] Any texts found in all clearly had some enduring appeal. A subsequent check against the extensive lists of Routley (1979) and David Perry (1980) has eliminated many lyrics that died before the First World War.[6]

COMPUTER SEARCH AND CLASSIFICATION

Of the 140 hymnals searched, the overwhelming majority were published in Britain between 1750 and 1914. A few American ones were included in order to ascertain any differences of taste, and some British school ones published between the two world wars.[7] This main survey includes all major denominational collections save the *Methodist Hymn Book* (1875), unavailable at the time, and by oversight the *English Hymnal* (1906). The 1868 edition of *Hymns Ancient and Modern* was preferred to the 1875 edition as being more distinctive of Anglican taste.

Since the following classification of themes provides for school as well as adult collections, not all of its categories will be used in this chapter:

    1 praise and providence of God the Creator or Father
    2 "myth" of Christ in hymns on Advent, Christmas, Easter, etc.
    3 Holy Spirit
    4 subjective devotion, usually couched in first-person singular
    5 missionary
    6 military image of spiritual life
    7 pilgrimage, self-dedication, and life-work
    8 death and Heaven
    9 Heaven alone
    10 the act of worship, or the Church
    11 morning, evening, or other time of day

12 nature or the seasons
13 the Christian ethic
14 the Bible
15 the nation or homeland

Though these are mostly self-evident, an example of No. 8 would be "Let saints on earth in concert sing" and of No. 9 "Light's abode, celestial Salem."

The hymns printed over sixty times all date from before 1830. When compared with those printed less often, they illustrate a shift during the Victorian age in the proportion of hymns of certain classes. Of the sixteen hymns, five belong to class 1, Praise and Providence, and range from "All people that on earth do dwell" (1561) through "God moves in a mysterious way" (1779) to "Holy! holy! holy! Lord God Almighty" (1827). The only ones on the mythos or sacred story of Christ are "Hark! the herald angels sing" (1739) and "When I survey the wondrous Cross" (1707). The latter was placed in class 2 rather than class 4 (devotional) because it portrays the figure of the Crucified, whereas "Jesu(s), Lover of my soul" (1740) and "Rock of Ages! cleft for me" (1775) stress the singer's dependence on Him. Of the two in class 5 (mission hymns), "Jesus shall reign where'er the sun" (1719) remains in use but "From Greenland's icy mountains" (1827) has not outlived the British Empire. Of the remaining four "Come, let us join our cheerful songs" (1707) alone represents class 9 (Heaven) and "Awake my soul, and with the sun" (1695) and "New every morning is the love" (1827) class 11 (times and seasons). Bishop Ken's nocturnal hymn "Glory to Thee, my God, this night" (or "All praise . . . ") was placed not in 11 but in 4, its substance being the individual's dependence on God. Numbers of reprints are given in the Appendix after the concluding chapter.

With the notable exceptions of "Jesu, Lover" and "Rock of Ages," these embody an objective or, in William James' phrase, "healthy-minded" religion concerned with praising God and affirming his care for man. The same may be said of the 22 printed between 48 and 59 times, but the only (almost) Victorian text in class 1 is "Praise, my soul, the King of heaven" (1834), "Now thank we all our God" being a mid-Victorian translation of a seventeenth-century German text. The five in class 2 range from "Rejoice, the Lord is King" (1746) to "As with gladness men of old" (1861). Like several introduced in *Hymns Ancient and Modern*, the latter very soon came into wide use. So did that battle hymn of Victorian schoolchildren "Onward, Christian soldiers" (1864). A pilgrimage hymn (class 7) "Lead us, heavenly Father, lead us" (1821) also came into its own during that age of earnestness. In each case, a stirring tune vastly increased the popularity of the text.[8]

Reprinted between forty and forty-seven times were such quintessentially

Victorian hymns as "Eternal Father, strong to save," "The King of love my Shepherd is," "Jerusalem the golden," "There is a green hill far away," and "Lead, kindly Light." Dates here can mislead, for though Newman wrote the last in 1833, it only became a popular hymn when given a singable tune for *Hymns Ancient and Modern* (1861). Though both text and tune are eighteenth-century, "O come, all ye faithful" entered Protestant hymn-books via an early Victorian translation, on a wave of carols and nativity hymns. Although this group includes three famous hymns in class 1, and several in class 2, "I heard the voice of Jesus say," "Jesus calls us o'er the tumult / Of this life's wild, restless sea" and "Just as I am, without one plea" signify a trend toward subjective devotional lyrics. "God bless our native land" (1836) and "For the beauty of the earth" (1864) spread rapidly as part of increasing tendencies to identify love of God with love of country and of nature.

Not much can be inferred from the older hymns in this bracket, beyond the resistance of nonconformist editors to liturgical hymnody of medieval origin ("Come, Holy Ghost, our souls inspire," "Come, thou Holy Spirit, come") and of Anglican editors to the emotionalism of "There is a Fountain filled with blood."

The hymns printed forty or more times (listed in the Appendix) point to a declining emphasis upon the fatherhood and providence of God. The infrequency of military, patriotic, or naturalistic hymns might indicate either the weighting of anthologies toward older texts or the preference of editors. The analysis of those listed thirty or more times, however, and the grand totals of the two groups, more definitely indicate shifts of focus.

Classification can present difficulties, particularly with regard to class 12 (Nature). "For the beauty of the earth" exemplifies a tendency to see God in nature that began with Keble's "There is a book, who runs may read" (1827), which treats the natural order as an emblem of the divine, as God's book. In its original context of the *Christian Year*, a cycle strongly influenced by Wordsworth's *Ecclesiastical Sonnets*, the ancient analogy is perfectly clear. "For the beauty . . . ," however, adapts so well to a non-sacramental context that its original designation as a eucharistic hymn has been known to surprise the expert.[9]

With such caveats, it is safe to make the following inferences. Texts concerning the military image of the Christian life, self-dedication thereto, and the natural world belong primarily to the nineteenth century. Neither "military" nor patriotic hymns, however, took compilers for adults by storm as they did those for schoolchildren. The focus of hymns on the Christ myth shifts from the Passion to the Nativity. Victorian hymnody otherwise shows an existential concern with the moment of commitment to the Christian life ("Just as I am"), with that life itself, and with the hour of death. It also shows a post-Romantic interest in the natural world.

The very inclusiveness of this survey conceals class differences shown up by a search for the 100 titles most reprinted in thirty-six hymnals of the Learned (Anglican, Congregational, Presbyterian) and eight of the Popular (Baptist, Primitive Methodist, etc.) traditions.[10]

Ten lyrics printed in at least three-quarters of each group of hymnals, and therefore ranked in the top quartile of each set of a hundred lyrics, were evidently universal favourites. In class 1 comes "God moves in a mysterious way"; in class 2 Wesley's classics on Christ born and risen "Hark! the herald angels sing," "Christ the Lord is risen today" and "Rejoice, the Lord is King"; in class 4 "Rock of Ages" (the most ubiquitous of all), and "How sweet the name of Jesus sounds"; in class 5 "From Greenland's icy mountains" and "Thou whose almighty Word"; in class 6 Wesley's "Soldiers of Christ" and, surprisingly as sole item on heaven, Watts' "There is a land of pure delight."

Three also in the first quartile of the "Learned" list but the last of the "Popular" were "Lord, dismiss us with Thy blessing," "Come, Holy Ghost . . . " and "Let us with a gladsome mind." Conversely, "Guide me, O Thou great Jehovah" and "Lead us, heavenly Father, lead us" appear in the last quartile of the Learned list and the first of the Popular, being favourites of those not free to choose their own way of life. To a lesser degree, Wesley's "Lo! he comes, with clouds descending" was a favourite among educated classes and his "Jesu, Lover of my soul" among uneducated worshippers. Likewise, "Abide with me" and Ken's nocturnal hymn "Glory to Thee, my God" were preferred by the educated, "All hail the power of Jesu's name" and, surprisingly, the harvest hymn "Come, ye thankful people come," by the uneducated.

The most definite indications of differences in taste, however, are those texts not among the hundred most often printed by the one group of denominations but in the top quartile of the hundred most printed by the other. Eleven predominantly objective hymns are thus indicative of the Learned tradition: "All people that on earth do dwell," "Holy! holy! holy!," "Praise, my soul . . . " and "Now thank we all our God" in class 1; "As with gladness . . . ," "Hail to the Lord's anointed" and "When I survey the wondrous Cross" in class 2; and otherwise "Jesus shall reign . . . ," "Awake, my soul . . . " and "Sun of my soul . . . ," the last two redolent of the ordered life of public school or middle- and upper-class household. The eleven in the top quartile of the Popular hundred but not in the Learned list are a mixed bag. Cowper's "O for a closer walk with God" and Anne Steele's Bible hymn "Father of mercies, in Thy word" deservedly survived from the eighteenth century, as perhaps did Doddridge's "Jesus, I love Thy charming name." Most significantly working-class are "Another six days' work is done" and "Dear refuge of my weary soul," one of six subjective devotional hymns connoting pietist world-and-life denial.

The contrast between class attitudes appears more clearly in the following analysis of hymns according to types, from which categories 13 to 15 have been omitted as insignificant. The figures refer to numbers of texts.

Class	1st Quartile		4th Quartile		In list (of 100)		Subject
	L	P	L	P	L	P	
1	6	4	1	2	13	10	God: praise, providence
2,3	7	4	8	6	27	17	myth: Christ & Spirit
4	2	9	8	4	17	26	subjective devotional
5	3	2	0	1	3	6	mission
6	2	1	0	0	3	3	military
7	1	2	2	1	6	6	pilgrimage, dedication, work
8	0	1	1	2	6	6	death & Heaven
9	2	1	1	1	6	5	Heaven
10	0	1	1	1	4	7	church & worship
11	3	0	0	1	6	2	time of day
12	0	0	2	1	2	2	nature

Clearly hymnals of the Learned tradition emphasized praise and thanksgiving, the coming of Christ and the Spirit, and the daily round of services, elements to the fore in the worship of the ancient and medieval Church. Those of the Popular tradition emphasized subjective devotion, involving emotional dependence, the act of worship itself, and missionary activity. Surprisingly, the traditions did not differ as regards their emphasis on the death and the future state, a fact again casting doubt on the Marxist critique of religion.

While it yields firmer conclusions, this more specific survey has three defects: the preponderance of eighteenth-century texts, the considerable proportion sung at one time of year, and the reflection of clerical tastes.

VICTORIAN SURVEYS

Victorian Hymns (1887), being limited to 176 native and 48 translated texts produced during the Queen's reign, meets our first difficulty; a compilation of non-liturgical hymns by an Anglican layman for "Schoolroom Services, Cottage Meetings, Family Worship and Private Devotion" (1861) our second; and between them "One Hundred Hymns" selected in 1888 by readers of *Sunday at Home* and a selection in 1885 of 325 by an Anglican clergyman our third, that of differentiating between lay and clerical tastes.

Victorian Hymns, a mish-mash of lyrics inspired by the Evangelical and Oxford movements, can best be labelled "Catholic-Evangelical." A list of titles at the end of its alphabetical sequence will convey one of its two strains:

> Thou to whom the sick and dying
> Thou who didst on Calvary bleed
> Throned upon the awful tree
> Thy way, not mine, O Lord
> Voice of Jesus—Calling, Calling
> We ask for peace, O Lord
> We come to Thee, sweet Saviour
> Weary of earth, and laden with my sin
> When my feet have wandered
> When this passing world is done
> When wounded sore, the stricken soul
> When shall we learn to die

The other and healthier strain is evident in "As with gladness," "Crown Him with many crowns," "Praise to the Holiest in the height," and some sentimental but reputable children's hymns, such as "Once in royal David's city" and "Jesus, meek and gentle."

In textual accuracy and indexing, *Victorian Hymns* typifies the Learned tradition, but it represents the extreme of the Popular in its use of egocentric devotional lyrics that harp on the singer's burdens and weariness, or on the blood streaming from the Crucified. In so scholarly an edition the pervasive womb-longing and death wish might signify that convergence of the traditions to be demonstrated later, or simply a preference of the compilers, or the Queen, for neurotic verse. Some poems of Tennyson, Arnold, Clough and Morris[11] exude a world-weary pessimism ironically justifying the editor's claim to have produced a "specimen and summary" of the "mode of devout expression" characteristic of "the last fifty years."

In common with many compilations for the young, the Anglican layman's choice was apparently governed by generation lag, the tendency to prescribe as for the days of one's youth. Barely half of his hymns selected in 1861 survived until 1900. "Happy the man whose hopes rely," "Let the minds of all our youth," or "O God, my inmost soul convert" might have been sung by Samuel Butler's Ernest Pontifex at Evangelical gatherings in the 1830s.[12] The choices for the poor, "When languour or disease invades" or "Another six days' work is done," had survived mainly in mid-century Baptist collections.[13] The latter, composed in 1732, bids the tired worker pass his day off in "holy duties" and "holy pleasures": "How sweet a Sabbath thus to spend, / In hope of one that ne'er shall end!"[14]

A better-known text, "Thine earthly Sabbaths, Lord, we love" imparts a more definitely escapist quality to the "nobler rest above," promising "No more fatigue, no more distress."[15] Its author, Doddridge, envisages relief, however, from the hereditary ailments of fallen man, toil, sin, and death. Thus, the Anglican layman assigns to the poor hymns that represent work as the penance of fallen man, rather than the means of improving their lot. Otherwise, his selection represents the best of eighteenth- and early nineteenth-century Anglican and Dissenting hymnody, with nothing more sanguinary or morbid than "Rock of Ages" and "Jesu, Lover of my soul."

Those two classics of the Revival were at the top of the hundred chosen by readers of the Evangelical magazine *Sunday at Home* as the "best in the English language." The reporter of that survey, evidently a hymnologist familiar with original titles—"Our God, our help . . . " and "Hark! how all the welkin rings"—must have found the priorities of readers discouraging. Their "top ten" were:

1 "Rock of Ages"
2 "Abide with me"
3 "Jesu, Lover of my soul"
4 "Just as I am"
5 "How sweet the name of Jesus sounds"
6 "My God, my Father, while I stray"
7 "Nearer, my God, to Thee"
8 "Sun of my soul"
9 "I heard the voice of Jesus say"
10 "Art thou weary, art thou languid?"

To spend a moment on those unfamiliar to us, No. 6, by Charlotte Elliott, the invalid better known for "Just as I am," describes afflictions or deprivations encountered while "Far from home, on life's rough way," each followed by the refrain "Thy will be done." The author hopes to sing that refrain "on a happier shore."[15] In No. 9, by the Scottish Free Churchman Horatio Bonar, the "voice" invites one "weary and worn and sad" to "Come and rest," promising "living water" as refreshment.[17] In No. 10, John Mason Neale inspires the languid to follow the example of the suffering Christ attested by "Saints, apostles, prophets, martyrs."[18]

The readers prefer those ten hymns to "God moves in a mysterious way" (No. 11), "When I survey the wondrous Cross" (14), "Lead, kindly Light" (15), and "O God, our help in ages past" (19). The appearance of so many death-oriented and subjectively devotional lyrics among their first twenty preferences[19] compels us to believe these religious attitudes profoundly meaningful even in the most tranquil and secure age the English middle classes have ever known. Many objective texts come far down the list: "O for a thousand tongues" is No. 89. That "Hail to the Lord's Anointed" is No. 49, "Hark the glad sound" No. 67 and "As with gladness men of old" No. 88, can be set down to their seasonal use. "Great God, what do I see and hear?" as No. 51 might be an effect of the generation lag. But that "I could not do without thee" (No. 85), "I lay my sins on Jesus" (No. 43), "Weary of earth, and laden with my sin" (No. 59), "Safe in the arms of Jesus" (No. 65), or "Tell me the old, old story" (No. 98) could ever have been thought among the "best in the English language" points to a corruption of taste comparable to the excesses of church restoration. The readers show sounder judgment in choosing "Guide me, O Thou great Jehovah" as No. 24 or "Hark my soul, it is the Lord" as No. 29. Of their hundred, 9 date from the seventeenth century or earlier, 33 from the eighteenth, 16 from the early nineteenth, and 42 from the Victorian era. The hundred fall into the following classes:

1 (praise of God)	11	7 (pilgrimage)	10
2 (Christ)	20	8 (death)	9
3 (spirit)	1	9 (Heaven)	6
4 (devotional)	25	10 (worship)	5
5 (mission)	1	11 (time)	6
6 (military)	3	12 (nature)	1

There were none in classes 13 to 15.

Save for the higher totals in classes 7 and 9, these proportions correspond with those of the hundred most-printed hymns in the two traditions. That for class 4 agrees with the figure for the Popular and that for class 11 with that for the Learned tradition. Presumably most readers of *Sunday at Home* were women regularly engaging in private prayer and public worship.[20]

In 1885 a clergyman ranked 325 hymns from Anglican hymnals in order of frequency, ranking them in three groups. In the following comparison, the abbreviation SH refers to the magazine title, AH to the Anglican hymnal survey, and the adjectives to the ranking groups of approximately 33 in SH and 108 in AH: *First* in SH and AH, 24 hymns; *Middle* in each, 6; *Last* in each, 3; *First* in SH, *Last* in AH, 1 ("At even when the sun was set"). None of SH choices are unlisted in AH. *First* in AH, *unlisted* in SH, 47 (ex 105); *First* in AH, *Last* in SH, 14. Among the 33 common to both surveys, only "Art thou weary, art thou languid," "Brief life is here our portion," "Jesu, the very thought of thee," "My God, my Father while I stray," and "Sun of my soul" in the first two ranks of each would be unfamiliar to present-day congregations. All three in the third of each, "Come, thou Fount of every blessing," "I was a wandering sheep," and "O Lord, how happy we should be" have passed into oblivion. Their keynotes of languor, resignation, and *Weltschmerz* cannot be missed. The superior taste of the clergy who compiled the Anglican hymnals can be judged from some of their most frequent choices not selected by the magazine readers:

1 (praise):	"Now thank we all our God"; "When all Thy mercies, O my God"; "Praise my soul, the King of heaven"; "Praise the Lord, ye heavens adore Him"
2 (Christ):	"All glory, laud and honour"; "Ride on, ride on in majesty"; "Rejoice, the Lord is King"
4 (devotional):	"Love Divine, all love excelling"
5 (mission):	"Thou whose Almighty Word"
7 (pilgrimage, work):	"Forth in Thy name, O Lord, I go"
9 (Heaven):	"How bright those glorious spirits shine"; "There is a land of pure delight"
11 (daily):	"Christ, whose glory fills the skies"

Allowing for generation lag, for feminine preferences, for the possibility of liturgical or seasonal hymns being overlooked, and for the obsolescence of some by Watts, it is reasonable to infer that some of the finest hymns and translations by Wesley and others had never taken root among the magazine readers; and that equally long-established objective hymns of praise and thanksgiving meant less to them than to Anglican clergymen, schoolmasters, hymnologists, and in all probability the laity in churches of the Learned tradition, who doubtless had the most reason to offer thanks and praise.

6

CONVERGENCE

The sameness of late Victorian hymnals can be demonstrated by tracking favourite hymns through five published between 1884 and 1900 for Congregational, Primitive Methodist, Anglican, Scottish Presbyterian, and Baptist worship.[1] If three texts that came into prominence after 1870, "O sacred Head surrounded," "The day Thou gavest, Lord, is ended," and "Dear Lord and Father of mankind" be added for convenience to the 247 resulting from our consideration of late Victorian surveys, 96 of the 250, or 38.4 per cent, occur in all five, 71 or 28.4 per cent in four, 63 or 25.2 per cent in two or three, and 20 or 8 per cent in one only. The first two figures combined show an astonishing 66.8 per cent printed in at least four of the five books. An overlap of 72.6 per cent would result from basing the percentages on 230, on the assumption that the 20 printed but once reflect some personal or denominational taste, such as the predilection of the *Hymns Ancient and Modern* editors for translations from Latin. There is even an overlap of better than 60 per cent between the Primitive Methodist and Anglican collections. To draw the most cautious inferences, three-fifths of the favourite hymns among the five congregations, ranging from Anglo-Catholics and Presbyterians to definitely working-class Methodists, were identical.

A text in four of the five and also in two important twentieth-century collections, the *Methodist Hymn Book* (1933) and *Hymns Ancient and Modern Revised* (compiled 1938-9, published 1950), obviously was still spreading, but such a text included in neither twentieth-century compilation was probably on the way out, as was a text included in one late Victorian collection only. The Primitive Methodist and Anglican compilers showed the most strongly marked tastes in their exclusions; the Baptist the greatest and the Congregational and Presbyterian the least capacity to select hymns destined to survive. Of 23 omitted by the Primitive Methodists only, 15 turned up in both twentieth-century books and 8 in one of them. Of 23 omitted only in *Hymns Ancient and Modern* (1889), 11 turned up in both and 11 in one. The Baptists alone chose four that turned up in one or both, and the Congregationalists five found in neither.

The Primitive Methodist and to a lesser extent the Baptist compilers omitted liturgical hymns, native or translated, accruing from the Oxford Movement, but included some obsolescent devotional ones.[2] The Congregationalists left out some eucharistic and Confirmation hymns, while retaining obsolescent ones by Watts.[3] The Baptists introduced new or newly sung texts such as a poem by the seventeenth-century Anglican divine Samuel Crossman "My song is love unknown." The Scottish Presbyterians, while omitting Christmas hymns and, predictably, substituting their Paraphrases for those based on psalms, showed in their section for children an astonishing fondness for Gospel hymns like "Safe in the arms of Jesus."[4] Although the *Hymns Ancient and Modern* editors naturally chose Anglican hymns, their omissions of Heber's "Brightest and best of the sons of the morning" and Milton's "Let us with a gladsome mind" cannot be explained on this or their other principle of omitting the feebler devotional and nature lyrics.

As the Primitive Methodist editors suggest, the Popular and Learned traditions were converging for two reasons: rising educational standards and a growing ecumenical sentiment. The editors give the "progress made in hymnology" owing to "the spread of education" and hence the "altered tastes" of "vast numbers who worship with us" as their reasons for superseding the wretched hymnal of 1854 and for abjuring its mangling of texts and cutting of them to an "arbitrary" length. They not only tried to restore original texts, but went beyond Watts and Wesley to "numerous . . . authors and translators," on the principle that "no church" has monopolized the "gift of sacred song."[5] A likely cause of this catholic and literary trend in a once anti-intellectual sect was the opening in 1864 of a seminary for training full-time clergy. Though replaced by the Salvation Army as the church of the homeless, the Primitive Methodist Connexion continued to recruit largely from the unskilled.

Its hymnal compilers even reprinted Catholic hymns such as "Crown Him with many crowns" (M. Bridges) and "Praise to the Holiest in the height" (J.H. Newman), the latter published only in 1866. Even more indicative of the rapid and widespread use of both the best and the worst lyrics were the listing for the Primitive Methodists of "We plough the fields and scatter" ("Wir pflügen"), first printed in an English hymnal in 1868, and for the scholarly Presbyterian Kirk of "Tell me the old, old story," first published in 1866.[6]

To judge from items rarely heard now but printed in at least four of the collections, if a time-machine took us on a whirlwind tour of late Victorian church services, the piety of our ancestors would surprise us by its combinations of activism, or the Victorian work ethic, in "Christian, seek not yet repose" or "Fight the good fight," with passivity in "Thy way, not mine, O Lord" and "Father, I know that all my life / Is portioned out for me"; and of Evangelical with Roman Catholic pietism in "Lord, as to Thy dear Cross we flee" and "O Paradise, O Paradise." Even if unable to hear the Advent hymns "O quickly come, dread Judge of all" or "Great God, what do I see and hear?" we should find our elders obsessed with nightfall and the end of life. They even augmented their heritage of evening hymns ("Saviour, breathe an evening blessing," "How sweet the hour of closing day," "Now the day is over," etc.) by transferring "Abide with me" from its proper place among "For ever with the Lord," "A few more years shall roll," "When this passing world is done," and other funeral hymns.[7]

For all their energy, our ancestors show a surprising preoccupation with their weariness and need of rest. This shows in the hymnody of High Churchmen from whom more bracing lyrics might have been expected: W.C. Dix ("Come unto me, ye weary"), J.M. Neale ("Art thou weary, art thou languid") and most of all S.J. Stone (known by "The Church's one foundation") in "Weary of earth, and laden with my sin," which epitomizes not merely a countercurrent to ruling-class activism, but a convergence of the two traditions.[8] Longing to enter Heaven, where "no evil thing may find a home," Stone's "vile" speaker hears a voice bid him "Come," and sees divine "hands stretch'd out" to draw him. Yet while he would "tread the heavenly way," he is impeded by his sense of sin. The hands are those of Jesus whose "Blood . . . can for all atone":

> 'Twas He Who found me on the deathly wild,
> And made me heir of Heav'n, the Father's child,
> And day by day, whereby my soul may live,
> Gives me His grace of pardon, and will give.

In these lines Stone sums up the whole Popular, indeed Christian, tradition of man's exile from Paradise in terms of the lost child-heir figure of Victorian novels like *Oliver Twist*. But whereas Baptists or early Evangelicals locate their singers within the desert during the journey home, Stone, like Baker, places his nearer the entrance to heaven than to the "deathly" wilderness. Like Keble, he foresees daily progress in the spiritual life.

The pervasive undercurrents of world weariness and gathering darkness convey the sense of a running down of those titanic energies whereby the Union Jack and the Cross had reached every inhabited continent. In Arnold Toynbee's view, empires attain their greatest extent as decline sets in.[9] Such lyrics composed at the height of commercial and missionary expansion evince, like the fantasies of Lewis Carroll, a subversion of high Victorian confidence and activism.[10]

Christianity has often functioned as a counter-culture, opposing to the chaos of dark ages the ordered life of the cloister, to the impersonal ruthlessness of the factory system God's infinite concern with the individual soul, to the masculine and acquisitive energies of Victorian industrialism the feminine and world-denying strain latent in Evangelical and Tractarian hymnody alike. Some of the most vigorous hymns composed or adopted by mid- or late Victorians reached their peak of popularity in this century. None of our five collections includes either form of "He who would true valour see," only one "Father, hear the prayer we offer," and only three "Fight the good fight." The Baptists alone reprint "Immortal Love, for ever full" and "Immortal, invisible, God only wise."[11] Even more surprisingly, not one of them carries "City of God, how broad and far."

The subsequent fortunes of three hymns beloved by Victorians shed light on this convergence of traditions. An old Evangelical stand-by, "Sweet the moments, rich in blessing," has of late appeared only in Anglican and Salvation Army hymnals. Bishop How's social gospel hymn "Soldiers of the Cross, arise," dropped out of the Methodist and Salvation Army books to which it appeared most suited. "For the beauty of the earth," excluded only from *Hymns Ancient and Modern* (1889), has in this century entered all hymnals save that of the Salvation Army, neither nature nor the Eucharist being objects of ultra-evangelical devotion.[12]

Carols that appear quintessentially Victorian—"Away in a manger" or "O little town of Bethlehem"—appear in not more than two books, while the unimpeachable "While shepherds watch'd" is missing from those of the Congregational and Presbyterian churches.[13] "It came upon the midnight clear" was denied the vast numbers that used *Hymns Ancient and Modern*. The circumstances and social import of the Nativity appeal to us, but the hope-giving doctrine of the Incarnation appealed to our forefathers. To emphasize the slow spread of the now ubiquitous "social gospel" from Watts and Doddridge, "Thy kingdom come, O God," Hensley Henson's demand for the promised era of justice and peace, appeared only in the Anglican and Presbyterian books.

In their songs the churches, though beginning to decline relative to the increasing population, were forming a community of feeling that presaged the informal but substantial unity they know today. In this way, the shaping Spirit operated through these poems and tunes, mediocre or sentimental as they often were. In no small measure, this growing body of common hymns contributed to the renowned British social consensus, as to the tribal unity of public school alumni.[14]

The expanded core of favourite hymns on God, on man here and hereafter, and on the Christian life, both individual and social, reveals convergence, but not identity. The Primitive Methodist hymnal, if far less doom-laden than that of 1825, continues to insist on man's "Fallen condition," to invite sinners to repent, and, under "Content and Resignation" to reflect a harsher time by reminding its users of the "poverty and pain," "privations, sorrows . . . scorn . . . life of toil," and "mean abode" endured by Christ. Prayers that with "humble mind" workers may see God's will "in all things" and turn to Jesus, "the weary wanderer's rest," justify to a degree the Marxist indictment of religion,[15] yet some better-known texts common to all these churches concern griefs that beset even the prosperous.[16] The collection, moreover, devotes as many lyrics as any save the Congregational to missionary and national endeavours. "For all the saints," "Onward, Christian soldiers," and "Forward be our watchword" reveal not a jingoist but a distinctly military impulse.[17] What this hymnal fails to do is give religious meaning to work. Its New Testament metaphors of vineyard, harvest, straight race, and good fight bear no relation to work in a mine, mill, or tool-room.[18] No Primitive Methodist hymns suggest that work could be hard to get, underpaid, or injurious to health.

Nevertheless, the sense of alienation from a doomed world has disappeared. One of the unprecedented number of Anglican hymns celebrates "holy household love" in the "happy homes of England" as a manifestation of the divine love evident also in fields and forests that likewise sing God's praise.[19] Home is no longer a heavenly outpost in an unheavenly world, no longer an oasis in the wilderness.

On work, or "Christian Service," the Baptists offer the usual biblical metaphors of seeds sown in the morn and fishermen's nets let down, together with injunctions applicable to work on the land rather than in factories or mines.[20] An example used from 1868 until the First World War tells singers to "Work, for the night is coming," and depicts the life-cycle by analogy with the (Canadian) farmworker's day:

> Work, through the morning hours,
> Work, while the dew is sparkling,
> Work, 'mid springing flowers;
> Work, while the day grows brighter,
> Under the glowing sun;
>
> . . .

> Work through the sunny noon;
> Fill the bright hours with labour,
> Rest comes sure and soon.
>
> . . .
>
> Under the sunset skies,
> While their bright tints are glowing,
> Work, for daylight flies.
> Work till the last beam fadeth,
> Fadeth to shine no more.[21]

To have watched rows of women sit in a Birmingham factory before machines were installed in 1854, when Mrs. A.L. Coghill wrote this lyric, is to realize its irrelevance to the drudgery of unnumbered thousands where the sun never glowed, and dew never glistened. Otherwise, as in " 'Forward!' be our watchword,'' life takes the forms of a journey through the desert behind the pillar of cloud, of endeavours (as in "Awake, my soul, stretch every nerve") to run the "heavenly race," or of combat by "Christian soldiers" in a mission field.

Hymns on the Judgment by the Countess of Huntingdon and Wesley, or by Tuttiet and Mrs. Alexander, show the Baptists to have laid a more definite stress than other denominations on the inner life and on eschatology.[22] That by directing attention to existential anxieties, evangelical Christianity distracts it from the struggle for daily bread is the charge made by the Marxist against religion, or indeed by the extrovert against any form of introversion.

The patriotic hymns common to the Baptist and Congregational books will be explored later, but one popular at this time was "Praise to our God, whose bounteous hand." In this, the Broad Church hymnist John Ellerton also begged God's forgiveness for the neglect of the poor and "untaught" by those whose "greed of gain" or "slothful ease" deserved punishment.[23] As will be shown in Chapter 14, the social and patriotic concerns of Broad Church hymnists went hand-in-hand, so that upon the outbreak of war emotions were readily transferred from the one to the other.

But for its Unitarian texts by Martineau ("A voice upon the midnight air" and Sears "It came upon the midnight clear"), the *Congregational Hymn Book* could be *Hymns Ancient and Modern* as regards its liturgical hymns such as "Ride on, ride on in majesty" or "All glory, laud and honour." From so catholic a selection almost any attitude could be demonstrated, from the triumphalism of "Hail the day that sees Him rise" or "The Day of Resurrection" to the escapism of "Come ye sinners, poor and wretched" or the pietist devotion of "Jesu, Lover of my soul."[24] If from this book the young D.H. Lawrence derived a "vague, hymn-singing piety," the fault lay with the minister who chose the hymns,[25] but the future novelist might have gathered both from the adult and Sunday-school collections, a somewhat vapid impression of God's dealings with children. At a child's funeral, he could have sung of blessed dead reposing their weary heads on the divine breast, or even sung the appalling "Safely, safely gathered in."[26] It all depended on the minister's choice. The adult hymnal confirms the judgment by Davie that the Congregational denomination had "reneged on its inheritance" only by sharing in a common heritage from Latin, German, and Wesleyan hymnody.[27]

That said, the American Congregational (and Presbyterian) hymnal of 1897, co-edited by the great hymnologist Louis F. Benson, must be accounted more consistently satisfying in both poetry and doctrine. Even the eccentricity of listing "We plough the fields and scatter" among a dozen items for children calls attention to their robust tone and freedom from the English cult of children's littleness.[28] Though, in his history too kind about the literary taste of his English counterparts,[29] Benson rejected many sentimental or moralizing texts that overemphasized subjective and inner events.

As compared with the Congregational hymnal of 1884, *Hymns Ancient and Modern* (1889) again shows a greater consistency of tone and choice. Some 160 hymns added since 1875 included some neglected masterpieces by Wesley ("Love Divine, all loves excelling," "O for a thousand tongues"), Newton ("Glorious things of thee are spoken") and Cowper ("for a closer walk with God") and some Victorian hymns now part of the common stock ("Fight the good fight," "Lord enthroned in heavenly splendour," "O perfect Love"),[30] but by introducing "There is a fountain filled with blood," Anne Steele's resigned "Father, whate'er of earthly bliss" or even Mrs. Alexander's "All things bright and beautiful," with its notorious verse on the "rich man in his castle," the compilers showed themselves in the worst sense behind the times.[31] Conversely, by admitting "Stand up, stand up for Jesus" and, above all, "Safely, safely gathered in"[32] they converted the famous tractarian compilation into a people's hymn-book.

For all its liturgical texts and high literary standard, the first-ever Scottish *Church Hymnary* went much further in that direction. Intended for all Presbyterians, whether Highland crofters, Glasgow shipyard workers, or Edinburgh civil servants, it carried many of the military hymns of the Primitive Methodist and Baptist collections, an even more glutinous selection of children's hymns than the Congregational,[33] and a section on "Faith and Penitence" for the Calvinist Evangelical obsessed with sin and woe, who, weary of earth and wandering from God, would wash away his "crimson stain" by laying his sins on Jesus, Rock of Ages.[34]

In common with the Supplement to *Hymns Ancient and Modern*, it carried among its few and decidedly "Learned" texts on Work the now rare

> Sons of Labour, dear to Jesus,
> To your homes and work again;
> Go with brave hearts back to duty,
> Face the peril, bear the pain.

Later, the hymn reminds the worker that his Saviour was born in a stable and "Had not where to lay his head," exhorting him to be chaste and kind as "Husband, father, son and brother," to bear the Cross in this life and to offer his work as "worship" in the hope of a "golden morrow . . . Home with Jesus, home at last!"[35] As these details show, the hymn failed to take root among the working class owing to its air of clerical exhortation from the elevated pulpit.

The incalculable harm done to the Anglican church in particular by Mrs. Alexander's verse:

> The rich man in his castle,
> The poor man at his gate,
> God made them, high or lowly,
> And ordered their estate.[36]

resulted not from the misunderstood intention of that devout friend of the poor but from the use of this verse among late Victorians who had the vote, could read, and for the most part no longer resided in the countryside under feudal conditions. By failing to observe their usual practice of excising incongruous lines, the editors of *Hymns Ancient and Modern*, if not Mrs. Alexander herself, perpetuated as an idol a class image no longer valid. If God had made the country, man had subdivided it and ordered its estate.

In 1891 the Unitarians designated their *Essex Hall Hymn Book* to enable "all persons familiar with the . . . varied experiences of the religious life, whatever their profession or creed" to express "their real sentiment."[37] They used a vast number of eighteenth-century hymns on the Creator with surprisingly little retouching. Cowper's "Jesus, where'er thy people meet" became "O Lord . . . " but "Sometimes a light surprises" and "God moves in a mysterious way" survived unscathed, as did Addison's "The Lord my pasture shall prepare" and even such later favourites as "Lead, kindly Light" and "In the Cross of Christ I glory."[38] The compilers added to these a great many composed in New England by Unitarians or kindred spirits: Sears, O.W. Holmes, Stuart Longfellow, Whittier, and Hosmer.[39] Though the compilers moralized miraculous events such as the Nativity, their real originality was the introduction of American nature hymns depicting untamed forest rather than the tidy English landscape.[40] This represented both the American form of Romanticism and the reversal of the driving out of Nature by the Christian mythos a millennium earlier.

They went further in their revised collection of 1902, trimming 15 lyrics by Watts to 7 by elimination of those with a supernatural or missionary theme ("There is a land of pure delight" or "Jesus shall reign . . . "), and representing the New England poets by 20 texts instead of 12 by Hosmer, 25 instead of 21 by Longfellow, and 14 instead of 9 by Whittier.[41] No doubt to improve the poetic quality, such orthodox poets as Heber were better represented too, but the general direction was toward the naturalistic and away from the mythic. The editors now placed hymns on Worship, Aspiration, Praise and Praise in Nature before those on God's Presence, Love and Inspiration and the human duty to respond. Behind these they placed those on Christ, the Church and the Future Life, and those on Christmas, Easter, Baptism and Communion just before those on church and school routine. In the neo-orthodox collection of 1891, compiled in reaction against Martineau's extreme liberalism,[42] the mythic and sacramental sections had come much earlier.

Orthodoxy in the poet by no means warrants orthodoxy in the verse, for Herbert and Newton are represented by "Let all the world in every corner sing" and "Kindly spring again is here" to the exclusion of Christ-centred lyrics, while even Wesley's "Rejoice, the Lord is King" appears without the lines on the Saviour's reign.[43] Consequently the hymns dwell on God as Father and Spirit or inner light, to the neglect of the miraculous. "Our blest Redeemer, ere he breathed" becomes "Our blessed Master" (239), while by more radical butchery Herbert's lovely and unsectarian poem "Virtue" (391) acquires a new but by no means simpler conclusion. For

> Only a sweet and virtuous soul,
> Like season'd timber, never gives,
> But though the whole world turn to coal;
> Then chiefly lives.

the editors offer this wretched substitute:

> Only a sweet and holy soul
> Hath tints that never fly:
> While flowers decay, and seasons roll,
> It lives, and cannot die.

At the beginning of this century a Unitarian would inevitably view the third line in terms of evolution rather than the Last Judgment, and it takes a sensitive ear to pick up the hint of the final Resurrection in the rhythm of "Then, chiefly lives." The substituted lines imply the naturalistic absurdity of indefinite survival through the recurring seasons. To eliminate all mythic elements from so profoundly Christian a poem was to drain out its life-blood.

In a hymn by Hosmer, the pilgrim dwells always in God's presence, his "one thought" a sufficient creed for the poet, "secret strength" to the martyr and "light," "staff and rod" to the pilgrim. What does this but give the journey through the wilderness a meaning drawn from the singer's own culture and circumstances?

One sequence of titles gives this naturalistic flavour: "Earth with her ten thousand flowers"; "Easter flowers, Easter carols"; "Eternal Life, whose love divine"; "Eternal Ruler of the ceaseless round"; "Eternal source of light divine"; "Evening and morning"; "Everlasting! Changing never"; "Ever more as years roll round."[44] Forty-five titles begin with "Father" or "God," but only two with "Jesus" and none with "Christ."[45]

In this context, Hosmer's splendid evocation of divine social justice "Thy kingdom come, on bended knee," or J.W. Chadwick's no less impressive "Eternal Ruler of the ceaseless round"[46] become expressions of a humanism little less secular than that of the South Place Ethical Society's *Hymns of Modern Thought*,[47] in which the demythologizing amounts to a virtual editing-out of specifically Christian language. Another text by Chadwick represents at its best the social and natural order envisaged by Unitarians in common with Broad Church Anglicans, and by the Congregational and Presbyterian denominations that otherwise constituted the Learned tradition.

> Eternal Ruler of the ceaseless round
> Of circling planets singing on their way,
> Guide of the nations from the night profound
> Into the glory of the perfect day;
> Rule in our hearts, that we may ever be
> Guided, and strengthened, and upheld by Thee.
>
> We are of Thee, the children of Thy love,
> The brothers of Thy well-beloved Son;
> Descend, O Holy Spirit, like a dove,
> Into our hearts, that we may be as one. . . . [48]

If this realized eschatology, this aspiration toward human oneness should prove an illusion, it is one to be respected.

It is difficult to tell where demythologized Christianity shades into the surrogate religions of secular humanism and positivism. Such lyrics as "How happy is he born and taught," "O brother man, fold to thy heart thy brother," "Ring out, wild bells," "Say not the struggle nought availeth," "These things shall be!," and "To mercy, pity, peace and love" appeared not only in school hymnals around the turn of the century[49] but, with some editing, in *Hymns of Modern Thought*.[50] Why the humanist editors felt obliged to delete the opening line of Wordsworth's "Ode to Duty" ("Stern daughter of the voice of God") becomes clear from their statement that in their hymnal: "Spiritual aspiration . . . is . . . towards the highest ideal of human goodness, and even the name of 'God' as typifying this conception has been avoided. The gradual fading of the old ideas of heaven and hell has left untouched every worthy motive for striving towards goodness of heart and life; and no allusion to these ideas will be found. . . . "[51]

Here they record that progression from demythologized Christianity to atheism in which Newman had viewed Unitarianism as a half-way house.[52] They tried to make the transition painless by exploiting the negative connotation of "dogma" in asserting that "all religions (of the Western world at least)" were becoming "more practical and less dogmatic," so that hymns should convey "the spiritual aspirations of men in regard to daily life, character and conduct."[53] They were not dishonest in this, for at that very time Sir James Frazer was completing his *Golden Bough* on the assumption that "myth" and "truth" were mutually exclusive. When Jung and T.S. Eliot were unknown, and the best verse of Yeats still to appear, few would have agreed that to edit myth out of religious poems was to empty them of substance. To the positivist or rationalist, myth represented the disposable element of dogma, in the sense of untrue propositions.

As Chadwick's "Eternal Ruler" suggests, Unitarian hymnody in America had more of poetic substance and less of moral platitude than that in England just because its authors, having remained nearer to the orthodox position on Christ, retained more of its "mythic" element.[54] In the lines quoted above, the myths of Creation, the Parousia and the Coming of the Spirit remain as vestiges, alongside the Newtonian myth of the cosmos. The "natural piety" of Wordsworth encouraged American Unitarian hymnists to transplant Judaeo-Christian myths into the seeming infinitude of the American outdoors. "On the lone mountain's silent head" says one, "There are thy temples, God of all." The poet's eye travels upward in worship to the heavens where "planets trace their ceaseless march," thence down in prayer to the tombs, "thine altars." Then he reflects that

> All space is holy, for all space
> Is filled by thee; but human thought
> Burns clearer in some chosen place,
> Where thy own words of love are taught.[55]

St. Augustine, who found God in the heavens, earth, and (subterranean) hell, would have endorsed the opening, but the verse as a whole implies that the imagination needs a focal point, if not an incarnate deity or church (for to Unitarians the teaching, not the teacher, was divine), then some venerated natural scene, Wordsworthian "spot of time" or Joycean "epiphany." It was for students, on either side of the Atlantic, to endow the school or college chapel with a special holiness or transcendence by fusing their consciousness of spiritual growth in worship with an imaginative awareness of earlier generations. By such acts of imagination, citizens of what was once known as Christendom can make an idol of the ancient cathedral or parish church, or Americans make an idol of "America the beautiful" or Russians of "Mother Russia." How easily the sense of God immanent in Nature could evolve into one of transcendence identified with the natural or man-made object itself. To demythologize was not merely to discard superfluous "dogma," but to drain away that focus of vision or personal attachment that, far more than moral abstractions, can inspire action and self-sacrifice. The tragic consequences of creating a spiritual vacuum, to be filled by idols, will be considered later in this book.

7

NURSELING AND INFANT SCHOLAR

PRINCIPLES AND NURSERY CLASSICS[1]

By the mid-twentieth century, manipulation of public opinion and taste through propaganda and advertising had imparted a sinister overtone to the whole notion of conditioning or even training in good manners and behaviour, as we see from Aldous Huxley's *Brave New World*, George Orwell's *Nineteen Eighty-Four*, or Vance Packard's *The Image-Makers*. More recently, even the most conservative have learned from the Marxists to sniff out class conditioning, whether in the "rich man in his castle" verse or the now ridiculed manual of etiquette. In such a climate, distinctions need to be drawn between education, moral training and class conditioning in verse intended for young children.

The pejorative associations of "dogma" conceal the vital difference between Isaac Watts or Charles Wesley and the staunchest believer or most open-minded enquirer of today. Convinced beyond doubt that the central Christian doctrines concerning the Creation, Fall, Redemption, and future state of man were true, the hymnist had no choice but to impress them upon children who might at any moment be snatched from their play by "death's resistless hand" to face their Maker. When the most permissive of us would never let an infant learn by trial and error how to cross a road, can we condemn a Watts or Wesley for seeking to implant truths essential for the child's salvation? In our day the most convinced parent must know that before attaining maturity the child will encounter indifference, agnosticism, unbelief, or some other faith held with equal sincerity.

Admitting the right of Watts or Wesley to implant Christian doctrine and morality, how did they propose to implant them? In practice, Watts could not teach children of his host and congregation that God had predestined them to heaven or to hell. He could and did teach them the substance of the ten Commandments, Summary of the Law, and Golden Rule: to fear God, observe the Sabbath, honour and obey their parents, refrain from lying, stealing, or covetousness, and in general do as they would be done by. His *Divine and Moral Songs* offer a sterner image of God and a stronger emphasis on the Commandments than would be acceptable today, but are far more humane than the "good, godly books" of Janeway or Bunyan that were his models.[2] What earned them ridicule in the mid-nineteenth century was their author's celebrated principle of *kenosis*, enunciated in their full title "*attempted in easy Language for Children.*" Undoubtedly the "other plan" proposed in John Wesley's posthumous edition of his brother's hymns for children, of expressing in "plain and easy language" such "strong and manly sense" as to induce spiritual maturity in children, is more calculated to win respect from the critical adult. As Routley insists, a "fairly heavy emphasis" on *kenosis* caused Victorian hymns to harp on the "littleness" and feebleness of children, and invite the adolescent to "grow out of" religion.[3] Of looking down upon children from adult height Watts was never guilty. Lewis Carroll parodied "How doth the little busy bee" in *Alice in Wonderland* because he rejected the moralizing tendency of children's literature during his own childhood, in what has been dubbed "The Age of Admonition."[4] By Carroll's time, flora and fauna had acquired their own interest for botanists, biologists, and the public in general.[5] Watts' reflections on dogs, who "delight to bark and bite / For God hath made them so" represented an advance on the theological inferences likely to be drawn in say, the *New England Primer.*[6] His success in "speaking to children as children" is attested by the sales and prolonged currency of his *Divine Songs.* Whether and to what degree they inculcate the values, manners, and viewpoint of the mercantile aristocrats for whose children he designed them, and so represent a form of class conditioning, depends on the attitude of the child-speaker.

In the eighteenth century they circulated to varying degrees among children of all classes, but by the early nineteenth had become nursery classics. At that time, they were joined by *Hymns for Infant Minds* produced by Ann and Jane Taylor, daughters of the Independent minister.[7] These two books give a clear indication of what children of the literate classes learned at that time from their nursery poets.

WATTS: *DIVINE AND MORAL SONGS*

Since human beings tend to divide and segregate, that each one entered this world by the same route, at first lacked all sense of modesty, devoted much time to sleep, feeding, and excretion and cuddled up alike with human, animal, or doll is a truism in need of constant reiteration. If nineteenth-century aristocrats and bourgeois draped and repressed their shameless offspring more earnestly than lower-class parents; if they shielded them from the violence and corrupt communications that poorer children very soon experienced; if to escape the chaos of the nursery they employed wet-nurses and nannies, their offspring had in common with children of the working class helplessness, frustrated wishes, tantrums, and the fantasies of those unable to distinguish their inner from the outer world. Above all, the young obeyed orders or else were "spoilt." As Butler's *The Way of All Flesh* reminds us, Evangelical parents took care not to spoil their children. Ever since the Puritan Commonwealth and settlement in America, poets had assured the young that having shed His blood to reclaim them God did not intend to spoil or keep them in idleness. Watts' *Divine Songs* were among the milder messages from their permanent parent.

What underlies these Songs is a pessimism about the human condition derived from the Calvinist dogmas of Original Sin and Election and man's uncertain tenure. "How sad our state by nature is," begins a once-famous hymn for adults. Until Christ freed our "captive souls," asserts another, "Plung'd in a gulph of dark despair / We wretched sinners lay." Given the shortness of life and prospect of hell, "Time, what an empty vapour 'tis." Given the prospect of heaven, "Why do we mourn departing friends" summoned by Jesus to His arms?[8] His inescapable pessimism made Watts' pre-eminence as a children's poet the more astonishing. Between 1715 and 1900 his *Divine Songs* sold over seven million copies, ran through six hundred editions[9] and, a century after being published, was called by Watts' editor George Burder "the delight of infant minds from that day to the present."[10] Its influence upon great Victorians weaned upon it has yet to be explored. A book that had captivated eighteenth-century children became a bore as Victorian parents and teachers forced children to recite passages, an infallible mark of obsolescence. It remains important for the suggestions it implanted about life and conduct. Like many great children's books, it was written for particular children, those of the Watts' hosts the Abneys, but after trying the book out on each child under fifteen in his congregation, Watts knew that he had found the right register for children.

The first and paramount reality of his *Divine Songs* is God. This distinguishes them from the child-centred poems and stories of later origin. By sinking to a simpler level of discourse than that of his own childhood Watts underwent, as Johnson says, "the hardest lesson that humility can teach."[11] Obliged to impress upon his child readers that they could face divine judgment without ever having grown up, Watts conveyed this more gently than earlier puritans who had scared children into virtue. His originality, like that of Lewis Carroll, lies in his charm of manner and identification with the child reader.

Only when advances in medicine and hygiene had immeasurably improved the survival rate of chidren could parents and teachers confidently prepare them for this life. Their forebears had to rear them with an eye to eternity. An incident cited by Burder typifies the difference:

> A poor wretched girl, religiously educated but now abandoned to misery and want, was struck with horror at hearing this infant repeat, so soon as she could speak, some of the profane language she [the mother] had taught her by example. She instantly resolved that the first sixpence she could procure should purchase Watts' *Divine Songs*, of which she had some recollection, for her infant daughter. She did, and upon opening the book, her eye caught the following striking stanza:
>
> > Just as a tree cut down, that fell
> > To North or Southward, there it lies,
> > So soon man departs to heaven or hell,
> > Fix'd in the state wherein he dies.
>
> She read on—the event was her conversion, and she died an honourable professor of religion.[12]

In the *Songs*, God combines the remote rationality of the Supreme Being who had wound up the universe then let it run by impersonal law, with the capriciousness of the tribal deity who struck children dead for jeering at the bald Elisha. Both figure in "I sing th'almighty power of God" (No. 2), printed in children's hymnals to the beginning of this century.[13] On the one hand His power "made the mountains rise . . . spread the flowing seas abroad," "built the lofty skies," and ordained the courses of sun, moon, and skies. On the other hand, in Heaven He "shines with beams of love" but in Hell flames with wrath, while His all-seeing eye watches over every child that still breathes His air.[14] Watts wrote within Isaac Newton's lifetime yet within living memory of Milton's publication of *Paradise Lost*. This and other lyrics in the *Divine Songs* convey to perfection these contradictory attributes of the abstract yet patriarchal deity so brilliantly mocked in Blake's epithet "Nobodaddy."

In the *Divine Songs*, Christ has three aspects. As victim whose blood paid the ransom of children enslaved to sin (7), he recalls Christ the Lover. As sun of Heaven that rose at his Father's bidding to reign in glory (3, 27), he recalls Christ the Victor. As model for obedient children (14, 16), he inspired many early Victorian children's hymnists, notably Mrs. Cecil Frances Alexander, who must surely have read the *Songs* in childhood.

God inspires both terror and trust. The child-speaker fears lest by sudden death he come unforgiven to judgment. At nightfall, however, he feels more secure for God's presence:

> With cheerful heart I close mine eyes,
> Since thou wilt not remove;
> And in the morning let me rise
> Rejoicing in thy love. (26)

Trust in the omnipresent divinity is religion's very essence.

The fear of sudden death so memorably expressed in *Hamlet* and in Cranmer's Litany depended upon a medieval belief which, tricked out in Watts' silvicultural image, shocked the mother in Burder's anecdote. Our culture maintains an unacknowledged continuity of belief via folk-tales and poems heard in our earliest years, that return to consciousness in times of crisis.

In other ways, too, Watts' poems for children combine his current view of the world as a harmony in which every prospect pleases but only man (and, curiously enough, dog) is vile, with the medieval conception of earth as the child's exemplar and bestiary. The stars instruct and the earth feeds him. The "busy bee" that "improves the shining hour" (20) exemplifies patient industry, not sin as in the source-poem by Bunyan.[15] Birds that "in their nests agree" (17) set examples of family concord, the rising and setting sun a daily example of duty. The fading flower shows the brevity of life, the fallen rose-petal a good soul's sweet savour to its Lord (*Moral Songs* 3). Lambs and doves set examples of cleanliness and innocent play, ducks and dogs examples of dirt and brawling (*MS* 2, *DS* 16). Like Locke, but unlike Wesley, Watts approved of play.

Everywhere, the child-speaker makes the right resolve from examples and situations objectively presented, in Watts' characteristic pattern of divine action prompting human response.

However wise or logical his conclusions, the child-speaker must strike the modern reader as a prig. At first, his very terror compels sympathy, as he cowers beneath the "all-piercing eye" that "strikes through the night" to observe his "most secret actions." These and every "wicked" word God sets down in his "dreadful book."

> And must the crimes that I have done
> Be read and publish'd there?
> Be all expos'd before the sun,
> While men and angels hear? (9)

Who does not know the child's fear of exposure before the school? The child-speaker, lying ashamed at God's feet, begs God remember the blood that washed out "our stains" and prays he may ever fear "T'indulge a sinful thought" since God observes and records "every fault." With what terror the young must have read of the "all-seeing God" after yielding to auto-erotic or other temptation.

What makes the child-speaker a prig is his intrusive sense of nationality and class. Under seemingly innocuous titles—"Praise for Birth and Education in a Christian Land" (5) or "Praise for the Gospel" (6)—he plumes himself upon his birth and upbringing. In "Great God, to thee my voice I raise" (5), a common Sunday-school hymn, he ascribes to God's "sov'reign grace" his birth "on British ground / Where streams of heavenly mercy flow." He pities those that dwell "Where ignorance and darkness reign," those that "know no heaven" and "fear no hell." Warned by "preachers of the word . . . t'escape eternal fire," he resolves not to waste his "blessings." Ascribing his birth "of Christian race" to divine grace, "not to chance," he fears that both Gentile and Jew might denounce him at the Judgment for failing to respond (6). Writing just after the Act of Union but before British expansion overseas, Watts set a fashion for identifying patriotic with religious commitment that reached its peak shortly before the First World War.

A *Divine Song* much reprinted for Sunday schools enshrines a parallel class-consciousness. "Praise for mercies temporal and spiritual" (4) begins:

> Whene'er I take my walks abroad,
> How many poor I see;
> What shall I render to my God
> For all his gifts to me?

Upon his elect, God has bestowed food while "others starve / Or beg," warm clothing while other children go "half naked," a home while "some poor wretches scarce can tell / Where they may lay their head." The analogy with Christ seems not to strike the favoured child, who returns thanks for having learned to fear God's name and do his will rather than "swear and curse and lie and steal." The model child in Watts' source, Janeway's *Token for Children*, would "be oftentimes admiring God's Mercy for such Goodness to her rather than to others; that she saw some begging, others blind, some crooked, and that she wanted nothing that was good for her."[16] The poem, which evidently rang true to the Abney children, distinguishes Watts' attitude from that of Fielding or Dickens, implicit in the secular pilgrimage from beggary to inherited wealth that forms their plots, and still more from that of British lower-class parents who sought a secular salvation for their promising children in the heyday of selective education.

Living before Britain became an imperial and industrial giant, Watts had no reason to foresee upward migration. As a Calvinist, he inevitably saw the distinction between rich and poor as ordained by God. A kindly man, he lost no opportunity of persuading rich adults to aid poor children. His child-speaker pities but has no power to help the poor, and so turns to self-congratulation upon an upbringing both prosperous and religious. For the street urchin there was starvation here and hell-fire hereafter. In this and a later Song the poet tried laudably to inculcate compassion and a sense of social obligation:

> Should I e'er be rich or great,
> Others shall partake my goodness;
> I'll supply the poor with meat,
> Ne'er showing scorn or rudeness. (*MS* 6)

Within the framework of the book, the child proves by no means so obnoxious as in songs printed out of context. His agonies of conscience earn our pity as he wonders whether he can escape the doom of sinners (11), or why, lost in sport, he forgets his prayers and the realities of heaven and hell (17). What brings out his streak of self-righteousness is the presence of profane children, especially of the lower class. Observing how "wicked children" dare abuse God's "dreadful, glorious name," he ponders their final state of "everlasting fire and pain" wherein no drop shall "quench their burning tongues," and decides to give up "profane companions." (19)

Contrasting this puritan image of the child as inherently sinful with the paradisal image in writings by Vaughan or Boehme, Harry Escott thinks it the more useful to educators. Such adult realism imputed to a child annoys us in "Against Evil Company" (21) just because the little pharisee is so damnably right.

> Why should I join with those in play
> In whom I've no delight
> Who curse and swear, but never pray;
> Who call ill names and fight?
>
> I hate to hear a wanton song,
> Their words offend my ears;
> I should not dare defile my tongue
> With language such as theirs.

As in Janeway, whose exemplary boy, "fearful of wicked company" trembled at their "wicked words,"[17] the speaker fears being sent "where none but sinners are." Like any maximum security jail, hell must be the more intolerable for its selective entry.

The child whose passions may lead him there but who can sometimes teach employers a lesson seems preferable to the paragon who resolves that if "poor and mean" he (or perhaps she) will "engage the rich to love me" while remaining "modest, neat and clean," and submitting "when they reprove me" (*MS* 6).

Watts, who like Gerard Manley Hopkins combined remarkable powers of reasoning with small stature and a nervous disposition, favours the submissive lamb or dove to the aggressive dog or bear, dislikes dirt, noise, and violence, worships a patriarchal despot, and in general strikes feminine rather than masculine attitudes. Although the substance of his poems has been traced to earlier Puritans, their style and flavour suggests an identity between his child-speaker and his recollected self. In the little denouncer of pride in clothes, we seem to encounter the dissenting minister's child. After unfavourably contrasting the gayest human attire to that of tulips and butterflies, this child resolves to find "adornings of the mind" and those "robes of richest dress" knowledge, virtue, truth and grace. Yet this judgment must remain tentative, for the preference for inner to outer adornment goes back to Sidney and Shakespeare.[18]

That in their time the *Divine and Moral Songs* had an immense influence upon generations of children Burder leaves no room for doubt: "by two societies alone (the Society for Promoting Religious Knowledge among the Poor, and the Religious Tract Society), more than 100,000 have been circulated . . . not less than thirty editions are kept in print in England only, and . . . the annual circulation in this country considerably exceeds 50,000, besides the multitudes printed in Wales, Scotland and America."[19] To his evidence must be added that of individual poems reprinted in day and Sunday-school hymnals until our own century.

In a chapbook version about 1845, an illustration to "Whene'er I take my walks abroad" (4) shows a beggar touching his forelock as a richly dressed girl absently drops a coin in his cap. In Mrs. Gaskin's illustrated edition of 1896, a merely well-dressed girl gazes compassionately at two poor children begging.[20] This points to a sentimental identification with the poor very noticeable in such late Victorian public school hymnals as that used by Winston Churchill at Harrow.[21]

These illustrations and Carroll's parodies of "How doth the little busy bee" and " 'Tis the voice of the sluggard" imply that the book had become the birthright of middle- and upper-class children. Mrs. Gaskin's edition probably marks the end of its vogue. With every poem illustrated and beautifully printed under titles in red capitals, the book has the look of a collector's item. Its boy and girl in nightgowns kneeling with folded hands anticipate that consecration of post-Victorian nostalgia, A.A. Milne's Christopher Robin. The picture for "Against Pride in Clothes" shows a richly-dressed girl preening herself before a plainly-dressed one who seems none too willing to accept inequality as providential.

Long after the book had outlived its usefulness among poor children it instilled in the better-off a cosmology and social psychology no longer taken seriously by adults. If the wondrous complexity of Charles Dodgson's psyche forbids any inference from his ridicule, the historian Esmé Wingfield-Stratford attests its influence. Through the medium of his hymns, "the good Doctor Watts made the divine name more terrible to successive generations of children than that of 'Boney' was ever destined to become." In an old edition of "this dreadful book" Wingfield-Stratford found alongside " 'Tis dangerous to provoke a God" (13, vv. 5-6) a woodcut of a four-year-old girl's tombstone implying that she suffered eternal punishment.[22] While Wingfield-Stratford's vehemence makes him an unsafe witness, it shows how a late Victorian liberal would loath the teaching about Hell in eight of the thirty-six poems. Its effect upon a sensitive child all too likely to find these texts in a Sunday-school book may have been far more lasting than that of the "gangster movies" to which A.P. Davis compares such "brimstone poetry,"[23] not least because Watts pictures Hell more concretely than Heaven:

> *Heaven and Hell*
> There is beyond the sky
> A heav'n of Joy and love;
> And holy children, when they die,
> Go to that world above.
>
> There is a dreadful hell.
> And everlasting pains;
> There sinners must with devils dwell
> In darkness, fire and chains. (11)

Even his tender and justly praised "Cradle-Song" (*MS* 8) alludes to the Redeemer's mission to "Save my dear from burning flame, / Bitter groans and endless crying."

Burder cites a clergyman on the "sweet delight and joy" with which children read the *Divine Songs* especially when dying.[24] While poems like "Heaven and Hell" probably affected most the child who read them silently or out of context, such flat contradiction between an editor in 1810 and a historian in 1930 suggests that earlier and later children read them in quite different ways. Eighteenth-century children accepted heaven, hell, and the divine authority for the class system as universally received truths. Late Victorian children found these asserted only in the *Divine Songs*, the Prayer Book, or Epistles. That each minor dishonesty built up habits liable to bring one to hell via the gallows was a truism in the eighteenth century, the age of associationist psychology.

Undoubtedly the *Moral Songs* exercised a wholesome influence by inculcating the puritan virtues of honesty, diligence, and cleanliness. The all-seeing eye that beholds each theft need terrify only the thief. The 1845 illustration (*MS* 4) showing a public hanging, and one to "The Sluggard" (*MS* 1) showing a ragged youth yawning before his tumbledown cottage, register the point these poems made for pre-Victorian children. It was Watts' poem on the bee that made "Satan finds mischief for idle hands to do" a universal folk-epigram. Obviously children continued to derive pleasure both from the poems on bees, lambs, doves, dogs, and above all boys and girls, and in Watts' characteristic pattern of observation followed by inference.

Out of context, individual poems amusing enough to the critical adult must have terrified the sensitive child. In 1838, pupils of a "Model Infants School" in London were catechized in *Questions with Answers Taken from Dr. Watts' Hymns for Children*. To "Does God see you, and know all you say?" Dr. Watts replies, "There's not a sin that we commit / Nor wicked word we say" unrecorded in God's "dreadful book." To "What should be our prayer, on account of our sins?" he responds on the children's behalf "Lord, at thy feet asham'd I lie," then assures them that they must die, and that the good ones will enter a "heaven of joy and love," the "wicked sinners" a "dreadful hell" of "darkness, fire and chains." Every one that lies must have his portion in the lake of "brimstone and fire," every thief risk the gallows for "taking other people's things."[25] Such penalties were sober reflections of Puritan teaching and the Bloody Code. By the mid-nineteenth century, the *Divine and Moral Songs* read aloud by nursemaids or teachers of infants were passing down outmoded customs and beliefs to children. As it became a rarity for prosperous families to lose a child, fewer and fewer parents could willingly have confirmed the portents of hell-fire and possibly no mother have read her infant the offending verse of the "Cradle Song." All that could have made sense to them was the teaching about the Christian virtues and the natural order.

Nevertheless, throughout the Victorian era "Almighty God, thy piercing eye" (9) assured Nonconformist Sunday-school children that no misdeed went unrecorded, "How doth the little busy bee" (20), continued to teach diligence and "I sing th'Almighty power of God" (2) to acclaim the wonders of the divine Creation. The patriotic song "Lord, I ascribe it to thy grace"

(6) taught a self-complacent patriotism until mid-century and even turned up in a Quaker collection of 1903. "Whene'er I take my walks abroad / How many poor I see" (4) encouraged social compassion right into our century. The threats of "Heaven and Hell" ("There is beyond the sky") (11), however, resounded only until about 1860, at least in major children's collections.[26] That group of titles being a fair cross-section of Watts' *Songs*, it can be seen that God the author of nature comfortably outlasted God the holy terror, as eschatology gave place to reverence for the natural world.

ANN AND JANE TAYLOR: HYMNS FOR INFANT MINDS

The fables and cautionary tales of Ann Taylor and her more gifted sister Jane have a naïve charm and freshness traceable to Jane's practice of addressing them to an imaginary child-listener. Of her contributions to *Hymns for Infant Minds* (1809), however, she wrote that she had failed because she so often had to tell the imaginary child, "Now you may go, my dear. I shall finish the hymn myself."[27] Even so, by 1877 the book had gone into its fifty-second edition. Some half-dozen or more lyrics recur in children's collections, three throughout the century.

Alternately inspired and discouraged by the "very excellence" of Watts' *Songs*, and sharing his Independent heritage, the Taylors conveyed puritan doctrine and ethics even more humanely. Having in childhood been on Christian-name terms with villagers in Ongar, they were distinguished by literary and artistic interests rather than social pretensions. As children of a Dissenting minister, they had early experience of the poverty to which their hymns counsel resignation. Their lyrics bespeak a sympathy with the poor and with animals that they had learned as children in their lovely but forgotten corner of Suffolk.

While saying nothing that would have offended Watts, the Taylors convey "evangelical truths in the language of children"[28] in a very different tone. God, no longer "Jehovah" but "Father," manifests himself sometimes as an All-seeing Eye with "piercing view" (74), or a Presence the child cannot flee (30), but never as the capricious Thunderer. His "rod" is not lightning and tempest but sickness (60), his holy will not to torment the ungodly but to summon mother or infant to Himself. God indeed favours England, the "Land of the Bible" (37), but his "love" protects "in every land" the beggar or negro slave, while amid "forest shades" and "silent plains / Where feet have never trod" he reigns "in majestic power." Whether or not they knew the poetry of the Romantic movement, the sisters were touched by its spirit.

One hymn mingles love of the Redeemer with induced guilt, for "See! the blood is falling fast," from his "tender limbs . . . torn."

> Down to this sad world he flew,
> For such little ones as you!
> You were wretched, weak and vile,
> You deserved his holy frown;
> But he saw you with a smile,
> And to save you hastened down. (34)

Many more, however, focus attention upon the "secret, gentle voice" warning against sin, that if ignored, will eventually die away (52). Conscience condemns the smallest deceit, insists that God cares not "what I say / Unless I feel it too," hears no prayer that "comes not from my heart" (11).

The Taylors were hymnists more of what might be called "Christian behaviourism" than of evangelical conversion. They instruct the child how to form her Nonconformist conscience by putting out "the smallest spark of Pride" (15), suppressing "thoughts impure, or false, or vain," which having nursed, she is "already defiled" (19). Most insistently, they inculcate habitual obedience to parents, whose "kindness" the child cannot otherwise repay (36). The hymn headed "For a Child that is sorry for a Fault" even begins: "Lord, I have dared to disobey / My friends on earth and Thee in turn," the "friends" presumably being parents and teachers. Anger and rebellious spirit they perceive always as effects of pride. Christ was above all things "pure and spotless . . . meek and lowly" (66). They clearly instil his teaching, not only about the sin nurtured within the heart, but about concern for the poor and the Golden Rule: "Do we mind our neighbour's pleasure / Just as if it were our own?" (78).

Their vision of Christ was again a feminine one intended for girls, whom they unwittingly trained for submissive Victorian womanhood. In "For a very little Child" (22), the speaker resolves to "cheerfully obey," by leaving her "pretty play" to "learn my hymns to say" so that she can read and spell. Play is least to be thought of on the Sabbath, when at school "poor children" learn to "read and pray" (55) instead. On Sunday evening the child must confess if guilty of "idleness and play" (45).

The Taylor sisters can to a considerable extent be credited with the formation of the Nonconformist conscience, but also with the Victorian cult of "littleness." If less obsessed with size than later hymnists, they compose hymns on "very little" children; (22, 24) invite a "little one" (33) to look within for childish sins (self-will, anger, deceit); envisage "little hands" (34) lifted in prayer, presumably from a "little heart" (21); on good authority wish "little children" suffered to approach Jesus (35), and include one text for a "Little Family." Their emphasis on children's smallness can be traced to their help in rearing younger brothers and sisters.

To their credit, the Taylor sisters show a keener insight than Watts into the plight of the poor, for their "Child of Affluence" wonders how, if "destitute, friendless and poor," she could "such suffering endure" (89), yet neglects the text "Blessed are they who consider the poor." Their "Child of poverty" prays for "daily bread," remembers how God sustains the ravens and lilies, and aspires for better gifts than gold, "grace" and a "humble, pious mind." While not preaching revolution, neither do the sisters make light of suffering or proffer pie-in-the-sky.

More creditably still, they spare childish sensibilities when writing about hell. In a dialogue between a child and its mother "About Dying" they eschew all images, describing the lot of the "wicked" that "chose to be so vile" as to be abandoned by God "to the way they took" (28). On the Day of Judgment, the wicked child (apparently male) who "fled from every serious word" of "his pious parent" on God, will stand, "poor guilty wretch" with "shame and terror and despair" to hear his "everlasting doom" (51). They focus on the child's feelings rather than the thundering heavens, withered earth or dreadful book.

Otherwise the sisters neither threaten nor do they use the allurements of heaven to devalue life on earth. Usually they mention heaven only in the final line, without image or elaboration. They devote far more attention to family relations and personal integrity within this life. Apart from their admitted didacticism, they can at worst be charged with over-seriousness:

> 'Tis easy to squander our years
> In idleness, folly and strife;
> But oh! no repentance or tears
> Can bring back one moment of life. (56)

Summer and winter they treat, conventionally, as paradigms of youth and age, when "stripped of our blossoms and fruit" we remain with nothing left but root, "For spring will not cover our branches again." If in youth we "prepare for the end of the year" old age will "come pleasantly on" and "bring us to glory again." They show less poetic talent than Watts at his best, but more appreciation of nature and the simple pleasures of this life: seedtime and harvest, when each plant creeps from its "prison" at God's behest (64), family love and friendship. Even their patriotism is rooted in love of the English countryside "so green and so fair," of hedges blooming and the cuckoo calling in springtime, not in the typological parallel between England and Israel.

Of hymns by the Taylors, those most extensively printed in Victorian collections were "Great God, and wilt thou condescend" (6), "Now that my journey's just begun" (7) and "There is a path that leads to God" (41). The first and commonest of these asks whether God will "condescend"

> To be my Father and my Friend,
> I a poor child, and thou so high,
> The Lord of earth, and air, and sky?

These lines blend the remote deity of Calvinist theology with the more accessible one of the eighteenth-century revivals. To this awesome yet benign figure the singer resolves to be a "meek, obedient child" and ultimately a "better child above." Within this context, "poor" refers unmistakably to the child's imperfection and helplessness, evident in "Canst thou bear / To hear my poor, imperfect prayer?" or "listen to the praise . . . such a little one can raise?"

"Now that my journey's just begun," however, varied in significance according to the worshipper's environment, the more so as its length necessitated cutting. The sisters had in mind a return from "sinful paths" to "wisdom's pleasant way" and a trust in God to befriend and fortify the Christian whether rich or poor, whether orphaned or old and solitary. In the first collection for Manchester elementary schoolchildren,[29] the verses on trusting God who "feeds the ravens" to "fill his poor with bread" and on resignation to His will, "whatever grief or ill" it may ordain, read as if designed by mill owners to appease the starving masses. Out of context, childlike trust in Providence could appear very like the submissiveness enjoined upon industrial workers in the Manchester that Marx and Engels took as their paradigm. Less common texts, "How kind, in all his works and ways" (19), "When little Samuel awoke" (85), and "As Mary sat at Jesus' feet" (86) enjoin an untroubled faith and "meek, attentive mind" that modern parents, as well as modern employers, might envy.

In a Bunyan-inspired text, "There is a path that leads to God, / All others lead astray," the "Little Pilgrim" of the title resolves to follow the way that "Christians love" through this "world of sin," ignoring the "Broad way" down which so many turn. With the Lord as guide, the pilgrim keeps in view the gate of heaven till she "shall enter there." Compared to that of Bunyan, Jane Taylor's was, however, a minor and derivative talent.[30]

While no one could accuse the Taylors of snobbery, small indications— the bourgeois or upper-class word "Mamma" for "Mother," and allusions to regular Sunday worship—imply a readership drawn from the "respectable" classes. A few of their *Original Poems*[31] enable us to define their public more precisely. In "A True Story," a mother cures her little girl of envying the nobility inhabiting a West End mansion by pointing to the disparity between themselves and the bare-footed girl begging in the street. The model children of "The Industrious Boy" and "The Shepherd Boy" read books in a cottage and play the pipe on a hillside, the latter's joy in life being the envy of the local magnate. The sisters know country life and can identify with those of modest means who pursue a craft, or scholarly or artistic interests, or who study to support themselves. They know nothing of industrial work or life in manufacturing towns. Small wonder if, in the alien context of Manchester or Birmingham Board school hymnals, their hymns appear unreal.

Few if any collections were designed for small children of the mainly Anglican aristocracy and professional classes. In 1841 Charlotte M. Yonge published *A Child's Christian Year* to "raise and purify the standard by which the poor judge of religious poetry."[32] She endorses John Wesley's principle that the young will "find deeper meanings" in the hymns "as they grow older and consult their own consciences more." Ironically, the book's format ensures its use primarily by children of the educated, for only they or their parents could find an unnumbered hymn set to a scriptural text for a Sunday or feast in the Prayer Book. The exclusion of Dissenting and Methodist material, finally, deprives the book of many texts that would enliven its chilly rectitude. Addison and even the brilliant but short-lived poets Heber and Joseph Anstice[33] lack the inspiration of Watts and Wesley. Though happily devoid of threat or blood-lust, the *Child's Christian Year* remains of interest mainly to historians of the Oxford Movement.

INFANT-SCHOOL HYMNALS

The difficulty of providing for poor children can be illustrated from a selection based on experience at a model school in London. Desirous that "the pleasure children generally find in verse should be early consecrated to the Lord" the compilers intend some poems merely to afford "amusement and cheerful relaxation to the very young," and hope that early instruction "will ere long be more extensively introduced into the manufacturing districts." Once the Factory Act forbidding work for children below nine is enforced, they expect parents to keep their children longer at school, reaping "the benefit of their more orderly and obedient behaviour at home."[34]

The very inception of this pioneer infants' school justifies the term "nursery classics" for both the *Divine Songs* and *Hymns for Infant Minds*. Parents who could not afford a governess had to teach their children as best they could, send them to a dame school, or in manufacturing areas hope to find a Sunday- or evening school at which writing and non-biblical literature were taught.

Despite their enlightened intentions of cultivating "kindly affections" and a "taste for the beauties of nature," the compilers began their selection with supposedly easy texts likely to have defeated the brightest infant: "Come, let us search God's holy word" or "Jesus, that condescending King." They included, moreover, threatening poems by Watts and others: "Against Lying," "Heaven and Hell," and "Delay is Dangerous."[35] The second verse of "Lord, teach a little child to pray": "A sinful creature I was born / And from my birth have strayed" shows exactly that Calvinistic reprehension guyed by Dickens in the dismal Christmas dinner episode of *Great Expectations*. Under *Happiness in Heaven* occurs "Here we suffer grief and pain," which Hardy's Tess Durbeyfield sang to her orphaned brothers and sisters half a century later.[36]

The book was nevertheless ahead of its time in both its humane, child-like Christ-figure and its adaptations of folk-songs ("O dear! what can the matter be") and play-jingles. The tutorial voice rarely falls silent, reminding children even in the playground that they are safer there than in the street, but the poems on play and on kindness to animals imply a healthier attitude than do earlier threats of hell-fire or later sentimental effusions.

Jane Leeson's *Hymns and Scenes from Childhood* (1842) taught that sickly subservience to parents so unforgettably satirized by Samuel Butler. That her lesser poems survived so long in hymnals suggests that they exerted some influence, whether or not they represented any existing pattern of family life. "I cannot bear Papa to frown . . . Nor would I grieve my dear Mamma / So gentle and so mild," says one. Another thanks Jesus for clothes and food, then for "tender and so kind Mamma / And my watchful, good Papa." The child-speaker loves to talk of "heavenly things" at Mother's side or on Father's knee. On hearing of Jesus' birth and dying love, or Jerusalem's "white-robed multitude," she hides her glowing cheek and tearful eye.[37] No wonder Ernest Pontifex chose to have his children reared by a bargee.

Two much superior poems by Miss Leeson, a member of Edward Irving's Catholic Apostolic Church, deservedly remain in use: "Loving Shepherd of thy sheep" and "Saviour, teach me day by day / Love's sweet lesson to obey."[38] The latter, presenting Christ as model of child-like trust and obedience, has a refrain "Loving him who first loved me" that indicates how seriously Victorians took the analogy between filial and religious duty. "Loving Shepherd" illustrates the rule that the more the text is based upon the Scriptures, and the less upon current social attitudes, the longer it will endure. The child, as "lamb," pleads to be kept safe by the "Shepherd," commemorates the sacrifice on Calvary—"hands outstretched to bless" that "bear the cruel nails' impress"—, and resolves like His "blessed ones above" to follow in His footsteps "Till before my Father's throne / I shall know as I am known." Such essentially Christian verse for children will remain relevant as long as the faith itself.

A selection of hymns intended for memorization (1856) illustrates more central tendencies in middle-class upbringing, by alluding to God's All-seeing Eye and omnipresence in Nature, noticed earlier, and by endorsing resignation, restraint, and the social hierarchy. Like daisies in the meadows, normal children should be "modest, meek and quiet . . . contented with their lot," in contrast with the "beauteous" children of the great, who "serve God in their estate." In Newman's "Prune thou thy words," children must learn self-control, for

> . . . he who lets his feelings run
> In soft luxurious flow.
> Shrinks when hard service must be done
> And faints at every woe.[39]

Here children of the upper and middle classes learn to behave like strong, silent Englishmen.

Inhibition, the basis of Victorian child-rearing, as of creative neurosis in poets such as Arnold, Clough, and Hopkins, appears in book after book for younger children of the educated. A child-speaker in *Twenty-Six Hymns for Nursery School* urges himself: "When I cannot have my way, / I must no ill-will display" (6) and prays God to keep him from every "sin" and "wicked thought within" (14). A child of "tender years," helpless and "deprav'd and filled with fears" (19), "conceived in sin" with a heart "wicked and unclean," consoles himself with the knowledge that Christ "for little children died." These poems printed in large type for pinning on nursery walls labour the paradox of childhood being unclean yet consecrated.[40]

Between the early and mid-Victorian periods the balance tilted from the depravity of childhood to its consecration, from threat and prohibition to sentimentality, from God the Hanging Judge to God the Friend of Children or Jesus our Elder Brother, and so begins a shift of emphasis from a transcendent deity to one immanent in nature and society. The one kind of immanence underlies the ecological, the other the Marxist movement.

An early example of softening occurs in sixteen *Hymns for Very Little Ones* (1866), put out by the Society for the Propagation of Christian Knowledge[41] and which children "liked to hear . . . again and again, and thus unconsciously learned . . ." The first gives the All-seeing Eye a quite new sense, for the child-speaker's realization that God "hears all I say" and "knows my thoughts" implies no divine condemnation of secret vices but a "Great Eye of Love" looking down from the throne to reassure him. God differs only in degree from the parent figures in the next poem who provide love, food, and clothing. "Jesus loves me better / Than I can ever tell," the keynotes of infinitude now being love rather than power.

The baneful sentimentality of other poems resides in their forced emotion: "O don't you love the pretty flowers?" begins one, asking the same question with reference to God's birds and "golden sun." Heaven, a place "far more bright," comes as a bonus rather than a consolation prize. What governs these poems is neither terror nor discontent but inane happiness and social sentimentalism. The benign shadow of Mrs. Alexander lies over the book, for the hymn on the flowers recalls "All things bright and beautiful," while "The Holy Child" alludes directly to an even more famous hymn of hers in depicting the sun as shining upon a "green hill side" where a "little child" plays beside his "mother dear." Jesus' obedience to Mary turns into an insidious plea to children to given up their "own way," for they still must not be spoilt. The era of permissiveness has yet to begin.

Palgrave's more honest plea for the child to be made "gentle, kind and true" after the example of Christ "who once on mother's knee / Wast a little one like me," remained in print as late as 1932, in *Prayers and Hymns for Little Children*.[42] This collection, revealing the influence of hymnologists such as Percy Dearmer and G.S. Briggs, still includes Jane Leeson's "Saviour, teach me," but also lyrics by Wesley, St. Theodulph, St. Francis, Christina Rossetti, and a charming carol by Watts. The sentimental Jesus, the guardian angles, daisies, buttercups, and raindrops still predominate, but the insidious parental conditioning has gone the way of all religious perversions.

8

THE SUBMERGED CHILD

Children's voices should be dear
(Call once more) to a mother's ear;
Children's voices, wild with pain—
Surely she will come again!
. . .
From the church came a murmur of folk at their prayers,
But we stood without in the cold blowing airs.[1]

If nowhere else, Christianity for the lower classes prevailed in charity-
schools, orphanages, ragged-schools, and evening institutes. Charity-
schools, in the words of M.G. Jones, "came into being chiefly, though by no
means exclusively . . . to *condition* the children for their primary duty in
life as hewers of wood and drawers of water."[2] The Jesuits founded the first
in 1687, followed within a year by Anglicans and Dissenters. Within fifty
years England alone had some fourteen hundred, run mainly by Low
Church or Dissenting ministers. Charity-school children marched annually
on Ascension Day to St. Paul's Cathedral for a fund-raising anniversary
service that included a sermon by an important divine. The occasion was
somewhat ambivalently described by Blake:

'Twas on a Holy Thursday, their innocent faces clean,
The children walking two and two, in red and blue and green,
Grey-headed beadles walk'd before, with wands as white as snow,
Till into the high dome of Paul's they like Thames' waters flow.

O what a multitude they seem'd, these flowers of London town!
Seated in companies they sit with radiance all their own.
The hum of multitudes was there, but multitudes of lambs,
Thousands of little boys and girls raising their innocent hands.
Now like a mighty wind they raise to heaven the voice of song,
Or like harmonious thunderings the seats of heaven among.
Beneath them sit the aged men, wise guardians of the poor;
Then cherish pity, lest you drive an angel from your door.[3]

Similar functions took place in provincial centres. Their common themes were the rich man's obligation to lay up treasures in heaven by contributing, and the social value of turning waifs into law-abiding citizens. As was customary, Isaac Watts reassured the gentry by advising trustees to refrain from educating the children beyond their station, in his address of 1728, published in 1741 as "Towards the Encouragement of Charity-Schools."[4] Responding to an attack on free education as likely to unfit children for their unpleasant but essential tasks,[5] Watts conceded that Providence, having in all ages "wisely ordained" that there should be "some rich and some poor," had "allotted the poor the meaner service and the rich the superior and more honourable business in life." The poor, therefore, "should not be generally educated in such a manner as may raise them above the services of a lower station." This he qualifies by inquiring whether masters objecting to minimal education wish to "keep the poor in profound ignorance that they might turn their servants into perfect slaves."[6]

While agreeing with the Bishop of London that charity-schools should turn out "good Christians and good servants" rather than teach music or "fine writing,"[7] Watts adds a more enlightened argument on schools in manufacturing towns. Boys without the connections to enter the over-crowded field of service, could become apprentices, for "mechanics and manufacturers . . . increase the commodities, and thereby the riches of a nation."[8] His case for technical education, alas, went unheeded.

Watts also defended charity-schools on conventional religious, moral, and social grounds. Children of poor and ignorant parents should not be "abandoned to the wilderness of their own natures," and "run loose and savage in the street." Care must be taken to "inform their minds," curb "their sinful passions," teach them to speak and act "like reasonable creatures," and "support themselves by honest labour,"[9] as "useful citizens of Church and State." From the age of eight or nine, within three full-time years or the equivalent, the children should be taught the Bible, patriotism, obedience, and a useful trade.

At that time the Birmingham Blue-coat Schools for Boys and for Girls held their fund-raising services on different Sundays at St. Philip's, now the Anglican Cathedral, and St. Martin's, now the Parish Church. Often the preacher would be the Bishop of Lichfield or a college principal from Oxford. By the early nineteenth century, the schools had to make do with a local vicar, a college chaplain, or even a curate, a measure of the function's decreasing importance. The hymn to accompany the sermon would emphasize at first the needs of poor children, the social and religious obligations of the wealthy, and the heavenly reward of charity. According to the first hymn-sheet (1724), God decrees that "the poor are eased" and protects "orphans," "strangers," and "widows." Those whom God has favoured in this life will receive a "temp'ral and eternal crown" for their "Favours to the Poor."

During this first period, the children sing praises to their benefactors in less unctuous tones than in a later and harsher age. In 1726 God has found them "grov'lling in the Dust / Yet not beneath His care," in the form of "useful learning," the knowledge of by whom their "precious souls were bought."[10] "Again the kind, revolving year" (1734), soon a standard hymn for charity services, asks with what "Incense" the children shall pay "grateful, humble homage" to God, for their rescue from "Want, and Vice, and Shame." It praises human benefactors in a lower key:

> Each Hand and Heart that lent us Aid,
> Thou didst inspire and guide;
> Nor shall their Love be unrepaid,
> Who for the Poor provide.[11]

The fawning submissiveness taught the young Uriah Heep is not yet in evidence.

By 1747, the emphasis shifted from God's material to his moral benefactions. Orphans for whom "Heaven contrives" aid resolve to "magnify the Deity / Whence flows "their Happiness" in being taught at school "to know His will" and "walk the perfect way."[12]

After a forty-year gap,[13] the series resumes in a more strident and dramatic tone, befitting an age both of sensibility and of economic desperation. The smiles of Charity

> unbend the wrinkl'd brow of care
> And bid the helpless Orphan's cry
> Soothe the wild rage of madness and despair.[14]

By 1811, tear-jerking and *Weltschmerz* reaches a climax, as "suppliant" orphans bend before God's altar:

> Cast on a world where scenes of woe
> And crimes . . . prevail
> [They know] No other Sire than Thee.[15]

We are in the world of Blake's *Songs of Experience*.

Even in 1811, however, the Birmingham leaflets exude a relatively cheerful Anglican piety. A far darker picture emerges from the hymnals published to raise funds for other charity-schools and for orphanages. The tear-jerking hymns for annual appeals point to the economic consequences of the war, to

booms and slumps, and uncontrolled migration to new manufacturing
towns. One for a girls' orphanage in London (1801)[16] laments the "dread
decree" by "stern death" that left the girls "helpless and forlorn" till
"benignant mercy" redeemed them from their "wretched state" (7). A
charity-school hymn in Dublin (1812)[17] strikes an even darker note:

> Great God, when famine threaten'd late
> To scourge our guilty land,
> O did we learn from that dark fate
> To dread Thy mighty hand? (22)

In the first poetic allusion to secular training at Birmingham, in 1812,

> . . . smiling Bounty waits
> To teach our hands the best employ
> And give us useful lore.[18]

The preface to a hymn-book for a girls' orphanage at Bristol specifies the
institution's object as "to instill . . . principles of Religion and Morality,
and to inure them [the girls] to habits of industry and cheerful obedience, by
instructing and employing them in every kind of household work which may
qualify them for acceptable servants in any reputable place . . . "[19] How the
heart aches for the poor little drudges whose very reading must be limited to
"such as may be useful to them in any future situation." This product of the
Evangelical Revival has Wesley's "Supplication for Seriousness" (34),
inviting a girl orphan to consider herself "a worm of earth," living "on a
narrow neck of land," and to resolve "with serious industry and fear" to
assure herself of heaven at the general resurrection. Another by Cowper (73)
implores her to fix "wond'ring eyes" on the Saviour's "bleeding glories."
The Bristol orphan is invited by Addison to imagine how on the Last Day
she will appear to her Maker (40), and by Doddridge is shown the "fiery
deluge" (70).[20]

In the London girl orphan, this Advent hymn must have inspired terror by
its very incomprehensibility:

> The Judge ascends His awful throne;
> He makes each secret sin be known.
>   . . .
> O then! What int'rest shall I make,
> To save my last important stake,
> When the most just have cause to quake. (21)

A note records that in 1684 its author, the Earl of Roscommon, repeated on his deathbed "with an energy that expressed the most fervent devotion" the last lines: "My God, my Father and my Friend, / Do not forsake me in the end." Evidently the noble earl believed his own propaganda.[21]

Many of the hymns commendably endorse love, courtesy, or cheerful industry, and in no way reveal principals or trustees as the skinflints and hypocrites of *Jane Eyre*. An episcopal introductory sermon praises music for promoting a "pious disposition," and "advancing that most heavenly passion of love" that "reigns always in pious breasts," as the "sweet mark of true devotion." Harmony, the Bishop declares, offers a "very earnest and foretaste of Heaven," while on earth "All selfishness and narrowness of mind, all rancour and peevishness, vanish from the heart that loves it." His Lordship clearly valued music more highly than did his forerunner in Watts' day.

In the Dublin charity-school hymnal, the compiler praises his "dear children" for having memorized the "excellent hymns of Dr. Watts and Dr. Doddridge." The aim behind all instruction being to make children "wise unto salvation," and poetry being easily remembered, he trusts that the ensuing hymn will "improve" their hearts and strengthen their "good principles." The children should learn these "Religious poems" not as a school task but because in sickness, sorrow, or insomnia they will "afford peace and comfort which the world can neither give nor take away." Can this man be insincere?

His hymnal, nevertheless, represents a social conditioning for the lower orders. In one poem children pray to become "mild as he [Christ] was mild" (5). Two further poems on the subjugation of pride (6, 7), and a great number on resignation to "whate'er kind Providence hath sent" (24) enjoin the "sweet" humility (58), obedience, and industry required of prospective servants or shop assistants:

> Thy gracious hand, to diff'rent ranks
> Hath diff'rent lots assign'd;
> 'Tis ours to tread the lower path,
> And bear a humble mind. (60)

It is easier to condemn this than to determine what those responsible for the nurture of orphans and foundlings could have done to change the social and economic order. The bishop and the principal evidently hope that pupils will develop an inner strength and life to sustain them in the absence of status or possessions.

Appeals reached a second climax of desperation during the Hungry

Forties. While magistrates were reading the Riot Act to famished multitudes in nearby Black Country towns, charity-school hymnists in Birmingham indulged in melodramatic images inspired, perhaps, by *Oliver Twist*. Let God regard the "dreary . . . road . . . aching heart" and "falling tear" of widow or orphan, sings one chorus, after the girl soloist has begged Him hear the dying mother who "with disease and want oppress'd" commends her infant to His care. The boy soloist points to the "clay-cold brow . . . woe-worn cheek and haggard eye" of the father, who wishes but to "see his child preserv'd and die." The final chorus predicts that by rescuing such children from folly, vice, and untimely death, patrons will "avert a guilty nation's doom."[22]

Tear-jerking may have foundered upon the law of diminishing returns, for by 1847 the children's theme had shifted to a resolve not to waste "holy Sabbaths" in "sinful play."[23] Alternatively, in the fifties, improving economic conditions caused the charity-school to become marginal and in any case better endowed. The task of educating the deprived fell upon the ragged-schools and evening institutes staffed by volunteers, mostly young ladies of Evangelical convictions. Generally speaking, hymnals for these institutions enjoined work and profitable use of time, while those for orphanages inculcated moral attitudes requisite for communal living followed by domestic service.

One side of Evangelical conditioning for the lower orders appears in the hymn-book for a "Ragged-School" in Manchester,[24] the other in that for an evening school near Leeds.[25] The Manchester book calls for love to entwine all hearts that teachers may enjoy "large success / In winning souls." Its hymns, described as "old favourites," invite children to accept the Saviour's offer of grace purchased by His blood, so as to avoid "eternal fire" (202). The bulk of the 253 hymns concern the life to come. The Oulton book features the *Divine Song* by Watts on the "piercing eye" of Jehovah, who writes every sin and "wicked word" in his "dreadful book" (6). Work is a trial to be borne that one "as poor as I . . . whose blood for me was shed . . . will bless me with his smile" (11). If the working day be long, can it compare with the "long, long time" with God "in eternity" (25). Though in a "foreign land," the singers are "not far from home" (96), for Christ has sought them "In the wilderness" of this world (39). Weary their life to come, full of "sorrows . . . toils . . . dangers . . . strife" (69) and they "in it but strangers" (69), but let "poor sinners" sail with Jesus in the "Gospel ship" through life's rough sea" (41), rather than set their hopes in "a region like this" (72). Though Lyte's sentiment seems a fair comment on working-class areas of Victorian Leeds or Manchester, such books conditioned poor children to view work as the necessary evil it undoubtedly was, and to set their hearts on things above. In this way they transmitted both an obsolescent Evangelical and the perennial Christian ethos.[26]

A further keynote of virtually all hymnals for lower-class children was the naïve and rigid moral teaching echoed half a century afterwards by Shaw's Peter Shirley. A text telling Manchester children to "heed the voice of conscience" lest it "hardened grow" might even be acceptable in our cynical age, but young people brought up to believe that "to speak the truth is . . . always best" and that it "must ne'er be denied / Whate'er the consequence"[27] may have found it difficult to prosper in the Victorian market-place.

An altogether more cheerful collection produced about 1860 for Dove Row Ragged School, London,[28] exemplifies a complementary feature of lower-class religion, the consecration of domestic love, together with a patriotic sentiment more common in collections for the higher classes. After wondering whether to love England more because all nations own her "wide command" or because "her children" know "home comforts and the fireside glow," one author decides to love her as the "Bible-land" that spreads the message "Jesus died for sinners" (58).

In another way, this book signals a period of transition, for it anticipates the later neglect of hell and sentimental pictures of heaven as "beautiful Zion" with "pearly-white gates" and "streets of shining gold" (11). In similar vein, it includes the well-known hymn on the Bible as a "sweet story of old."[29]

Sentimentalism represents both a decline yet also a relief from the obsession with the Atoning Blood that stamps the hymnals from Bristol and Manchester. Though absent from the Birmingham Blue-coat hymns and attacked as early as 1810 in a collection for charity- and Sunday-school children at Walworth (London),[30] cruciolatry pervades even the dignified and eclectic hymn and anthem book for the Foundling Hospital (1874).

While including many of the finest Anglican hymns and translations, this collection for the most famous of all orphanages[31] rubs in the bleeding Victim's demands upon the young inmate who during Lent, might sing "O Lord, turn not thy face from me / And call me not to strict account," lest "my guilty conscience" own "How vile I shall appear" (40). Some sixty years earlier the Walworth compiler had courageously disclaimed "sentiments and feelings to which . . . children in general are strangers" lest he constrain them to "utter the language of hypocrisy" and form habits of "insincere worship."

Our final collection for a charitable institution, coincidentally from Birmingham, illustrates the general trend of Victorian hymnals toward increasing editorial sophistication and scholarship. It was produced in 1883 for the Orphanage founded by Sir Josiah Mason, founder of the science college that became the University. Advised by the hymnologist Julian, the editors compiled an accurate index, included canticles, anthems, and psalms, and spared the feelings of inmates by omitting hymns about parents.[32] Immeasurably superior to the crudely printed and tasteless collections of the early nineteenth century, which so unmercifully (or unwittingly) rubbed in the inmate's dependence, this selection mainly avoids blood-lust, threats, or sentimentalism, and provides for the girls, who stayed until older than the boys. Undoubtedly it has some Victorian vices, such as the ubiquitous cult of littleness in "Lord, look upon a little child" (175) or "We are but little children weak" (84). Children of today would benefit from being taught to resist the "many voices" urging "a pleasant, easy way" (196) on creatures "made for better things," or to prefer "worthy, pure and noble ends" (256) to material acquisition. Yet the plethoric generalities and prevailing tenor of submissiveness. ("In sickness and in health / To every lot resigned, / Grant . . . before all worldly wealth / A meek and thankful mind") (266) epitomize the conditioning of nineteenth-century orphans for subordinate roles in life. Many hymns instil this ethic for lower paid workers, who "must not seek for ease nor rest," nor lay down their burdens if "such work / Thy neighbour prizeth not" (279). Unction reaches a handwashing climax in:

> My God has given me work to do
> I have . . . to strive with evil thoughts . . .
> To try to learn what I am taught
> And humbly obey. (268)[33]

Two hymns on work that enjoyed wide circulation must have changed their meaning according to the circumstances of their singers. In writing "Though lowly here our lot may be / High work we have to do" (1857) for his congregation in Manchester, the Unitarian William Gaskell, husband of the novelist whose *Mary Barton* drew attention to slum conditions in that city, cannot be accused of cheating the poor into submission. The "work" consists of following Christ, "Whose lot was lowly too," leaning in "days of darkness" upon the "almighty arm" of God and remaining "firm" to duty and "true" to conscience: "In God's clear sight high work we do, / If we but do our best." By thus brightening "the lowliest lot" with "rays of glory," the child may "turn a crown of thorns / Into a crown of light" (28). This hymn appeared in day- and Sunday-school collections until the mid-twentieth century. Clearly its envisaged work and troubles meant one thing to the orphans of Birmingham in 1874 and quite another to the pupils of a highly competitive London grammar school in 1923.[34]

Godfrey Thring's "Work is sweet, for God has blest / Honest work with quiet rest" (276) has a more complex ambiguity. The "rest" refers to sleep and to the heavenly rest from the "work of life." That work, though a "battle," is by definition neither "for gold" nor "bought and sold." In that case, it can refer either to the clerical or professional callings for which Thring's brother Edward prepared boys at Uppingham, or to the more menial tasks that awaited Birmingham orphans.[35] It excludes only the business of the commercial middle class. As much as doctrinal substance, it is poetic quality and breadth of application that distinguishes the genuinely Christian hymn for children from those written to instil class-conditioning.

One of the many hymns on heaven complementary to those on work raises an interesting question about paradisal hymnody for deprived children. Following the divine promise of ascent to the "upper room," it continues: "Dark is the passage through the grave, / But Jesus went before," having lived on earth as "a little child" (313).[36] Did it unwittingly represent death as a repetition of the birth trauma, while overcompensating orphans for their lowly social position?

9

THE AVERAGE CHILD

Day by day we magnify Thee
"Te Deum"

Before the first Education Act (1870), most children sent anywhere attended a "National" or Anglican school, the minority a "British," or Nonconformist, or (from the 1850s) Roman Catholic school. After 1870, Church of England schools remained the rule in country districts, but most urban children attended municipal "Board Schools." In 1902 a further Education Act established municipal secondary schools, together with scholarships to the older grammar schools. Since scholarship winners were expected to remain until at least sixteen, hymnals for grammar schools will be considered alongside those for the public schools. The vast majority of children continued to receive a basic education first until thirteen, then fourteen, at "Council Schools" run by boroughs or counties.

Very little evidence survives of the hymns sung in elementary schools before and sometimes after school. Few hymn-books remain from the eighteen-thirties and fifties, though rather more from the seventies and the beginning of the new century, compared to the multitude from between the world wars. Between 1870 and 1940, children in both church and secular schools can be presumed to have sung at least one hymn per school service.[1] In county archives for Surrey and two East Midland counties, inspectors record near the end of the century that pupils in Anglican schools learned hymns along with passages of scripture, a practice then universal in German Protestant schools.[2] That so few Board School hymn-books are preserved suggests that children often learned from blackboards or wall charts hymns familiar to their teachers. Alternatively a church or "chapel" school could have used its denominational Sunday-school book.

The few Victorian collections, therefore, tell us more about the thrust of worship and instruction in their time than about what the nation's children sang each morning. Edwardian hymnals, on the other hand, being designed for use by the children in the industrial areas of Birmingham and the West Riding of Yorkshire, and in one case throughout England, more reliably indicate what hymns most English children knew. After surveying public school hymnals, I shall in Chapter 12 draw some conclusions about religion in Edwardian schools from the few hymns that were and the many more that were not common to Council School books and the *Public School Hymn Book* of 1904.

CHURCH SCHOOLS

In 1831, the managers of the National School for Pannal and Low Harrogate brought out a hymn-book to be presented to school-leavers with the Bible and *Book of Common Prayer*, intending this "little library of spiritual knowledge, devotion and recreation" to "fortify" boys and girls against "the allurements of sin" and solace them in "toils and privations in this vale of tears."[3] Even this most aristocratic of churches addressed village children a few miles from the fashionable watering-place in puritan accents, while endorsing the class system of this "ungodly world." Though divine "wisdom fixed" their "lowly birth" (9), the children share in the divine goodness and so hope for "heaven on earth." Saints who in this world respond to "eternal love" find that their "heaven on earth's begun" (6). This verse from a hymn sung when the Archbishop of York preached here in 1829 epitomizes the distinctly Calvinistic attitude of the Establishment to the rural poor:

> Born in life's humblest, neediest state,
> Subject to toil and fear,
> Our ills unable to abate,
> We ask a blessing here.[4]

Though not deluged with fountains of blood, these children "kindly brought" to school to "sing Jehovah's praise" (1) learned their duty of submission to His order in church and state and to economic vicissitudes.

As if to remind us that they lived within a few miles of the Reverend Patrick Brontë and his gifted daughters, a text in the Supplement strikes a familiar chord of puritan and lower-class alienation: "This is not our rest. . . . We've no abiding city here."

Near the end of the book, the hopeful school-leaver could, but one hopes did not, read that

> The day is fixed . . .
> When heaven and earth shall flee away
> . . .
> The body, cursed and blighted
> To ceaseless torment rise.

In that midnight, "secret faults" and "midday crimes" must appear (160). Also in 1831, a tiny hymn-book issued by the National Society proclaims the mission of Christ as to "warn of sinners' doom" and turn them from "woes to come" (27).[5] No doubt the children found somewhat unreal Watts' warning against wearing fine raiment but took more seriously another hymnist's threat of hell-fire for lying,

> Children, never tell a lie:
> Don't you know that when you die,
> God for every lie you tell
> May remove your soul to hell? (10)

or Sabbath-breaking,

> On the holy Sabbath day
> Christian children must not play;
> . . .
> They who do this day profane,
> Soon may dwell in fire and pain. (14)

A version of the Golden Rule at least indicates a deeper level of ethical teaching than this naïve rigidity, but can hardly have been chanted with glee,

> To do to others as I would
> That they should do to me
> Will make me honest, kind and good,
> As children ought to be. (19)

Even twenty years later, in the year when the Great Exhibition ushered in the prosperous and hopeful mid-Victorian era, the National School child opened his penny hymn-book[6] to read at once:

> That day of wrath, that dreadful day
> When shrivelling like a parched scroll,
> The flaming heavens together roll. (1)

Since the Church's year begins with Advent, he soon read and doubtless sang "Great God! what do I see and hear! / The end of things created," followed by Wesley's scarcely more reassuring "Lo! He comes in clouds descending." Five years later, his younger brothers or sisters were invited to sing, or perhaps to recite, as "Timely Preparation for Judgment," Addison's fearsome lines

> When rising from the bed of death
> O'er whelmed with guilt and fear,
> I see my Maker face to face
> O how shall I appear.

Even if they never turned to the section "Hope of Full Immortality" to learn that "The hour of my departure's come," they could hardly have read Addison's next verse, on their prospect of being "amidst a ghastly band / Dragged to the mercy seat" without at least a nervous giggle.[7]

More dismal even than the threats, moralizing or prosy verse was the languorous escapism of such hymns on heaven as this well-known text:

> Thine earthly sabbaths, Lord, we love,
> But there's a nobler rest above;
> O that we might that rest attain
> From sin, from sorrow and from pain,
>
> . . .
>
> No sighs, no rude alarms of raging foes;
> None cares to break the long repose.
> Fain would we leave this weary road
> To sleep in death, and rest in God.[8]

The tendency of hymnists to turn heaven into lotus-land was not more reprehensible than this devaluing of a life scarcely begun. Against threats and pi-jaw children can grow thick skins, but against life denial they have no defence.

Between 1856 and the 1870s the whole spirit and ethos of the National School changed under Tractarian influence. Moreover, the section of its *Graded Hymn-book*[9] intended for children under eight evinces a way of life more secure than their parents, or perhaps any working people, had ever known. One hymnist offers thanks for "happy homes," "cosy fire and candle bright" and "those who love us there" (Supplement, 3). Another rejoices that

> When the corn is planted
> In its deep, dark bed,
> Mothers know their children
> Will have daily bread. (7)

If reminded overmuch of their littleness and helplessness,[10] the children sang no jeremiads on blood, sin, and judgment.

Though the sexual implication of a petition to rise "pure, fresh and sinless" next morning (26) would pass them by, even children under eight might subliminally gather from "God has given us a book full of stories"—supremely of the Nativity (14)—that the scriptural narratives were folk-tales. Certainly another text represents missionaries as telling "stories we love" to "little brown babies."[11]

Between the ages of Wordsworth and Hardy, the archetypally complacent account of nature and society is "All things bright and beautiful" (31), but a number of nature lyrics in this collection exemplify the sentiment "God's in His heaven, all's right with the world." A parallel in the social sphere, "God bless all the workers," describes Jesus as "Brother to all workers" in mine or mill on the evidence of His having worked alongside Joseph (30).

Among many standard liturgical[12] hymns set for older children, one text blends the now well-established domestic images with the new strain of military and chivalric metaphors. Beginning

> The saints of God, their conflict past
> And life's long battle won at last,
> No more need shield and sword. (53)

it continues by picturing heaven as a "dear home" and concludes with the anticipation of "sweet rest" in that "bright Paradise." Evidently, like Newman in the conclusion of "Lead, kindly Light," the hymnist views Heaven as a return to childhood. In this book, nevertheless, God appears as altogether kindlier and fairer than in the earlier collections.

Ironically, the old-fashioned Evangelical currents flow most strongly in a selection issued in 1883 by the Sisters of Notre Dame, that became a model hymnal for Roman Catholic schools.[13] The threatening Jehovah, not otherwise in evidence, can be inferred from a line in St. Francis Xavier's "My God, I love Thee not because," asserting that those who do not must "burn eternally" where the milder versions used today say, "must die" or "are lost" (1). A manipulative sentimentalism, a wringing of the childish heart by images of suffering, must have served to increase guilt.

> O Heart, for sinners riven,

> By sheer excess of love,
> The spear thro' thee was driven—
> 'Twas sin of mine that drove. (27)

Even children who did not sing those particular lines probably had to recite or sing an "Act of Contrition" in the chorus of which they renounced sins leading to "endless misery" and resolved "Never [to] sin again." To fix this resolve in each penitent heart the final verse held up a picture:

> See our Saviour, bleeding, dying,
> On the cross of Calvary,
> To that cross my sins have nailed Him.
> Yet he bleeds and dies for me. (8)

A hymn to the Holy Spirit smuggled in the guilt-fixing assumption that devotion and amendment were never enough:

> O, we have grieved Thee, gracious Spirit!
> Wayward, wanton, cold are we;
> And still our sins, new every morning,
> Never yet have wearied Thee. (5)

The echo of Keble's morning hymn points for us the contrast between unhealthy and healthy religion.

A further Evangelical current is an erotic escapism focused on the Wounds and the Sacred Heart. These lines from "To Jesus' Heart all Burning" could have come from the pen of any Moravian:

> Within the cleft I'll cower
> Of Jesus' wounded side;
> In sunshine or in shower,
> Securely there I'll hide. (27)

The child not made to sing those lines certainly had to recite the prayer "Anima Christi," with its petition "Within thy wounds hide me" (25). In "O Jesus, Open Wide Thy Heart," the singer pleads:

> . . . seal the entrance o'er,
> That from that home my wayward soul
> May never wander more. (31)

Here in a less morbid way the Sacred Heart is urged to enclose and shield the child. Both cults imply womb-regression.

Yet the major Evangelical trope, the Gospel re-enacted in the heart, made no real inroads into Catholic objectivity. If a pre-Communion hymn pleads, "my Jesus come! / Make this poor, sad heart Thy home" (9), the collection as a whole treats the spiritual conflict as outward rather than inward. A hymn to the Sacred Heart describes earthly life as "warfare" against "foes without, foes within" (32), but another pleads to the conversion of England from the rule of "misguided men" (29), presumably the Anglican establishment. Conceivably the strong resemblance between this Roman Catholic and many Evangelical collections for children can be attributed to their having been intended for children from the same class and environment. In the same spirit, a text in a collection for Irish children in 1900 describes "home" as the heart of Christ, "the exile's rest."[14]

BOARD SCHOOLS, 1870-80

Both Evangelical and nature religion can be discerned in the first compilations for the new elementary schools. The former is uppermost in those for children in Huddersfield (1873), Manchester (1878), as in *Hymns for Day-Schools* (1874);[15] the latter in one for children in London (1873). Time has spared but few of the cheaply produced collections for lower-class children, compared with the many handsome and elaborately indexed public school hymnals to be found in libraries. The whole field of hymnody provides no more illuminating contrast than between the hymnals for the boys of Harrow School (1855, 1881) and those for their contemporaries in National Schools (1856) and the Board schools of Manchester (1878).

The London compiler of the *Book of Sacred Song* eschewed hymns beyond the child's understanding as making for "formal and unreal" worship.[16] Pressed to its limits, this principle excludes not merely Evangelical but Christian theology, for the book has but one hymn of penitence and one on the Passion, with none on the Resurrection, Holy Spirit, or Judgment, nor even a Christmas carol. What remains is a virtually unitarian collection of hymns on nature, didactic poems and a few sadly mangled lyrics by Herbert, Milton, and other poets. Of the 203 items, Jane Taylor has seventeen,[17] Watts seven (including "O God our help" though not "When I survey" or "Jesus shall reign"), but there are none by Wesley. This book sets before children not a bleeding but a bloodless Christ. "I want to be like Jesus," says an effusion often found in children's collections,

> So lowly and so meek;
> For no one marked an angry word
> That ever heard him speak. (78)

Another by Anne Steele ("Whene'er the angry passions rise") invites children to lift their eyes to Jesus so "benevolent and kind," and imitate his "humility and holy zeal" in doing his Father's will (80).

If asked "What is wrong with this?" I would reply that the selected lyrics illustrate only one side of Christ's personality. From the whole treasury of Passion hymns, editors too anxious to spare children blood or deep feeling have chosen only "'Tis finished!' so the Saviour cried, / And meekly bowed His head and died" (78).

Revealingly, the compiler cites Dean Stanley on "our common Christianity" as "the religion of children"[18] in a book that portrays heaven as the "home and fatherland" (130) of children where their "great Forerunner's gone," a "beautiful land of rest" (132), where "we dwell together / As children dwell at home" (135). "Shall we meet beyond the river?" asks a variant of the well-known gospel hymn, with "many a loved one . . . torn from our embrace" (134)? The collection thus presents the children of London with an idyll, unsupported by Christian theology, of perpetual childhood and domesticity.

The anonymous and otherwise unknown lyric "I have a dear and happy home" (140) contrasts the happy family home with the "better home above," thereby remaining on this side of idolatry. The author of "Never forget the dear ones / Around the social hearth" (171) oversteps that line in a later stanza, by following the refrain-line "Never forget . . . " with "Be heart and treasure there," a misapplication of the Gospel saying "For where your treasure is, there will your heart be also," which in Matthew 6.21 and Luke 12.34 follows the verse on laying up treasure in heaven. This idolatrous hymn also paints a domestic idyll of "sunny smiles of gladness" unlikely to have corresponded with the experience of working or lower middle class children in London, as does the next one "There is beauty all around, / Where there's love at home" (172), found also in the Huddersfield collection (157). In this, the poet depicts home as a "cottage" near a sweetly singing "brooklet" before concluding that love transforms earth into a "garden sweet" with roses blooming. In this nostalgic daydream, domestic love restores the imagined paradise of pre-industrial England. The cottage bears little resemblance to any dwelling that board school children in East London, Manchester, or any West Riding mill town were likely to have known.[19]

Even more remote from the daily experience of most children was the imagery of some lyrics offering a mish-mash of home, heaven and native land, as in:

> Many happy homes are found,
> Homes of peace, on British ground,

> And our Fatherland we love
> Free, and blessed by God above;
> But more happy homes by far
> Are beyond the brightest star. (137)

How sincerely could waifs and louts in the East End have sung of an England "holy . . . happy" and "gloriously free" or prayed for "joy in all her palaces, cottages and halls" (200)?[20]

Equally foreign to the experience of most metropolitan children must have been the sentiments of "I love this world so beautiful," which after recording the poet's love of flowers, trees, brooks, breezes, birds, showers and stars concludes:

> I love to hear of heaven my home,
> Where all is bright and fair;
> I love to think the time will come
> When I may enter there. (230)

With those pathetic early photographs of slum school children in mind, we cannot dismiss such daydreams as unreal, yet by almost excluding Christian theology the compilers ensured that the hymns would represent a retreat from diurnal, as well as spiritual, reality.

Among three dozen texts on "Daily Life" (142-77), only the undistinguished call to repentance "If Jesus Christ was sent / To save us from our sin" (159), enunciates a central doctrine. Symptomatic of the inverse relation between divinity and doctrine are these lines from a mangled version of Herbert's "The Elixir":

> Teach me, my God and King,
> *Thy will* in all to see; (for "In all things *thee* to see")
> . . .
> If done beneath Thy laws,
> E'n servile labours shine;
> Hallowed is toil, if this the cause,
> The meanest work, divine.

The latter verse is based on two by Herbert on the "tincture" of divinity that makes the meanest object "bright and clean" and "drudgery divine," so that the servant "Who sweeps a room as for thy laws, / Makes that and th'action fine." By substituting a judgmental abstraction for Herbert's concrete figure of divine immanence, the adaptation turns a sacramental act into one of mere obedience.

Otherwise, these lyrics, like the "Moral Poems" of the Manchester book, consist of injunctions on love of God and neighbour, restraint, truthfulness, and diligence. Some of these a boy from a tough area may well have judged unwise (e.g., 161: "be the matter what it may / Always speak the truth") or unreal (e.g., 169: "Be kind to your father" who "loved you so dearly"). As a "volunteer in the army of the Lord" he probably failed to gather what combating "Envy, anger, hatred . . . self and pride" involved (160). But such lyrics as "Courage, brother, do not stumble" (147) and the following text on work and commitment (found also in Unitarian hymnals), convey, if less concretely, the activism characteristic of public school hymnody:[21]

> Live for something; be not idle;
> Look about thee for employ;
> Sit not down to useless dreaming,—
> Labour is the sweetest joy.
> Folded hands are ever weary;
> Selfish hearts are never gay;
> Life for thee hath many duties:
> Active be, then, while you may.

Poets capable of Herbert's concreteness, alas, rarely write school hymns.

The inclusion of hymns by Ken, Watts, Doddridge, Wesley, Cowper, and Montgomery gives the Huddersfield book a dated but genuinely Christian flavour and a literary quality setting it above the rest.[22] Again, however, Victorian lyrics so distort Christian teaching on the Last Things as to invite the Marxist indictment of religion as an opiate. The "joyful thought" of a "home in heaven" consoles poor men toiling in their "weary lot" who, like the tramps of Samuel Beckett, "wait in hope on the promise given" (2). While one offers long life here and heaven hereafter as the child's reward for filial devotion, a great many more, as in the other books, promise heaven as compensation or escape rather than a state to be attained or a kingdom within.

A brief selection will show how heavily the Huddersfield and Manchester books sell the next world as compensation for a life of deprivation and humble passivity, never of achievement or moral choice. Some first lines in the Huddersfield book run:

1 Above the waves of earthly strife . . . My home is (5)
2 Here we suffer grief and pain (62)
3 I'm but a stranger here / Heaven is my home (77)
4 My rest is in heaven / My rest is not here (105)
5 There is a beautiful world . . . where tears . . . never fall (149)

6 There is a better world, they say (150)
7 There is a happy land / Far, far away (152)
8 Though here we're often weary / There is sweet rest above (164)[23]

While the hymnals no longer threaten children with hell-fire, they present death as a reunion of family and friends, and heaven as an assembly of children round the throne. Both these and *Hymns for Day-Schools* harp on heaven as "land of perfect rest" (74), but in the latter the disguised death wish of "O for the robes of whiteness!" (112) and escapism of "There is a happy land" (143) supply their own unintended comment on the lot of the poor in Victorian England.

As a rural child, the little brother of Hardy's Tess Durbeyfield learned to sing "Here we suffer grief and pain" at a National school, but had he lived in Huddersfield could have sung its hypnotic tune "Rejoicing" at Board school. "Here," he sang before the family wagon ran into the mail coach, "we meet to part again; / In heaven we part no more."[24] After each of the six verses, he would chant repeatedly "Joyful . . . When we meet to part no more," expecting to meet in heaven "all who love the Lord": "little children," teachers, pastors, parents, and best of all the Saviour "Exalted on his throne." In the end, this favourite of Victorian children has more of Christian jubilation than of sentimental manipulation, for

> There we all shall sing for joy,
> And eternity employ
> In praising Christ the Lord.
> O, that will be joyful!
> Joyful, joyful, joyful!
> . . .
> When we meet to part no more.

Through the inane verse comes the hope that inspired better poets: Bernard, Abelard, Watts, and Wesley. Perhaps this, after all, rather than class conditioning, reached the souls of Victorian children.

In the Manchester book class conditioning obtrudes. "My God, my Father, while I stray / Far from home, on life's rough way" (76) has a refrain, "Thy will be done" quoted on the highest authority.[25] The mischief lies in its application to the life of a healthy child, rather than the invalid hymnist:

> Though dark my path and sad my lot,
> Let me be still and murmur not.
> . . .

Though Thou hast called me to resign
What I most prized, it ne'er was mine.

. . .

Should grief or sickness waste away
My life in premature decay . . .

By equating all these forms of adversity, the refrain precludes any effort at self-help. The equally well-known hymn of the Taylors, "Now that my journey's just begun" (8), offers the child of poor parents a scriptural assurance that God who "fills the ravens when they cry" therefore "fills his poor with bread," but again imputes to him whatever his ensuing ills, the resolve to be "submissive to Thy will."[26] Nowhere does it state that God helps those who help themselves.

Hymns and Moral Songs did the wealthy city of Manchester little credit, being not only the most cheaply printed and poorly chosen collection, but that which most distorts the Christian ethos into one of spineless resignation. Its 32 *Moral Songs* by Watts and others urge the same habits of diligence and productive use of time, patriotism, kindness, and truthfulness as in the London collection, but its 136 hymns, arranged in alphabetical sequence, pour into the child as pernicious a brew of submissiveness and wish-fulfilment as undernourished children can ever have drunk. The three dozen hymns known today, including "Abide with me" (1), "Jerusalem the golden" (67), "Guide me, O thou great Jehovah" (46), "O God our help . . . " (83), "Once in royal David's city" (87), "Take up thy cross . . . " (100), "All people that on earth do dwell" (2), "Praise the Lord, ye heavens adore Him" (92), and "Blessed are the pure in heart" (15) were, one hopes, sung the most frequently. Some eighteen figured in the repertoire for nineteenth-century children, including "There is a path that leads to God, / All others lead astray" (110), "Do no sinful action" (24) and "By cool Siloam's shady rill" (17). One of these, by Mrs. Alexander, represents a major theme ceaselessly reiterated:

Every morning the red sun
Rises warm and bright,
But the evening cometh on,
And dark, cold night.
There's a bright land far away
Where 'tis never-ending day. (25)

Stir together this theme and those of resignation in "My God and Father" and many other texts, God's sanctioning of the class system in that of the "rich man in his castle" verse (6), his unsleeping Eye, the "home in heaven" and, above all, that of the "meek, obedient child" (45), and the opiate is ready to drink. It consists of a pervading ethos wherein even that admirable poem, Wesley's "Gentle Jesus, meek and mild" (35) or the following application of the dominical injunction to become as a little child, are calculated to dull curiosity and resilience:

> O! not unless our childish hearts
> In simple Truthfulness obey;
> Unless our souls be guileless found,
> And meek and gentle, day by day,
> O Saviour, make us good and mild,
> And fill our hearts with simple joy,
> And bless us with thy gentle hand
> As Thou didst bless that Jewish boy. (3)[27]

How can the adolescent so conditioned distinguish what Providence denies from what employers might wrongfully deny? Meek, obedient children could grow into submissive, diligent mill-hands made content by their visions of a bright land far away to toil in the half-light and foul air of Victorian Manchester.

10

THE TIME-CONDITIONING OF
SUNDAY SCHOLARS

A highly-developed culture of self-help, self-improvement and respectability, which nurtured many of the political and trade union leaders of the working class, emerged from the late eighteenth-century and nineteenth-century Sunday-school world. The school joined together the world of respectability and roughness, political activism and resigned quietism.[1]

That children from order-giving classes sang into their systems an expectation of responsible service, those from order-receiving classes one of subservience here and triumph hereafter, does not explain the common change of tone in collections for Sunday-schools of all denominations. Founded to enable the poorest to read the Bible, and never attended by those born to rank and fortune, these institutions do not easily fit into a study of class conditioning, since their character depended more on district than denomination. Anglican Sunday-scholars in the East End had more in common with neighbouring Primitive Methodist children than with Anglicans in a fashionable area. Even more did Sunday-school hymnals vary according to their generation. A contrast to be drawn in the next chapter between compilations for pre-Victorian and late Victorian public schools would apply at least equally to those for Sunday-schools.

For children to have absorbed the spirit, beliefs, and idolatries of their times only requires explaining because the verses purported to convey eternal truth. The improving economy and expectation of life which explain the more cheerful tone of the later church day-school and Harrow School hymnals does not fully explain the contrast between these brought out for young Methodists and Independents by Joseph Benson and Rowland Hill (1808, 1819) and those issued by five major denominations between 1879 and 1886.[2] Thomas Hardy and Flora Thompson leave us in no doubt that agricultural workers, at least, had known better times than the eighteen-seventies and eighties.[3] Hymns for children, moreover, were at their grimmest when Shelley (if no longer Wordsworth) was composing his most inspiring verse for adults, while the sunniest late-Victorian children's hymnals were contemporary with Tennyson's "Locksley Hall Sixty Years After" or the early novels of Gissing. It is for social historians to assess the spirit of an age. A hymnologist can merely offer his findings in evidence, but the sea change that came over Sunday-school hymnals demands explanation.

EARLY NINETEENTH CENTURY

Early collections had the flavour of all children's literature in the "Age of Admonition" that succeeded the publication of John Newbery's "Pocket Books" and Christopher Smart's *Hymns for the Amusement of Children.* Editors and authors like Mrs. Barbauld, Mrs. Sherwood and Mrs. Trimmer were in tacit agreement with parents on what middle- and upper-class children should read and recite.[4] Yet neither their cautionary tales nor Mrs. Barbauld's *Hymns in Prose for Children* nor her well-known "Give to God immortal praise" have the peculiarly threatening tone of Sunday-school hymns. The influence of the "graveyard school" of eighteenth-century poets upon the Anglican collection of 1834 for "Young Persons" of the "higher classes" is attributable to generation lag. Despite a good selection of texts by Watts, Wesley, Cowper, Newton, and Heber, its many hymns on death must have given pupils a sober, not to say dismal view of their future prospects. One headed by the psalm verse on man's days being as grass infers from the rustle of autumn leaves an "awful truth" to be learned by "Youth, on length of days presuming." On the opposite page, one headed by Job's lament that his days are few and full of trouble ranges over "millions" whose "life was but a spark," who ignorantly trod "paths of ruin" or else knew but scorned God, before it exhorts the young to live and so die unto the Lord.[5]

In the collections of Benson and of Hill death has a personal sting and Jehovah a frowning face. In the former, young Methodists confess themselves "vile, conceiv'd in sin," "children of wrath by nature," and conscious of God's all-seeing Eye within the very curtains of their beds. Addison's "When rising from the bed of death," Wesley's "And am I born to die" with "And am I only born to die" and, supremely, the only Wesleyan hymn on hell, have a grimness exceeded only by accounts of the Nazi death camps that the latter seems to predict:

> Shall I—amidst a ghastly band
> Dragg'd to the mercy seat!
> Far on the left with horror stand,
> My fearful doom to meet?

> While they enjoy his heavenly love,
> Must I in torments dwell?
> And how (while they sing hymns above)
> And blow the flames of hell?

The Wesleys' fiercest critic, Rowland Hill, opened an Independent Sunday-school at his Surrey Chapel for poor children "exposed to all the wretched consequences of ignorance and sin." In the 1819 edition of his hymnal, the Wattsian praises of God have a dignified objectivity but the penitential hymns, couched in the first-person singular, invite the child to apply personally the shock-and-relief formula of Evangelical preaching. A "confession to be said when sorry for a fault newly committed" begins:

> O what a wretched heart have I,
> How full of sin and blame;
> How justly I deserve to lie
> In one eternal flame.

Another, "I dread the vengeance of thy rod," asserts that divine justice "bids me sink to endless flames." Its subsequent plea "Jesus, to thee alone I fly . . . trusting on thy sacred blood" seems unlikely to have brought the intended relief.

An ex-Anglican, Hill took High Church objectivity to the point of substituting "we" for "I" throughout "When I survey the wondrous Cross." Metrical psalms such as

> Behold the lofty sky
> Declares its maker God;
> And all his starry works on high
> Proclaim his power abroad.

confer a dignity lacking in headings like "Advice to youth to prepare for death." In such lyrics as Watts' "There is a God that reigns above," with its "dreadful hell" of darkness, fire and chains, the Jehovah who confronts the child resembles the "austere and wrathful" deity of the Murdstones, who requires such endless humility and obeisance from the charity boy Uriah Heep. In 1819 Dickens was of about the same age as were David Copperfield and Pip when menaced by their surrogate parents.

In the collections of both Hill and Benson the child sings, or more probably recites, "After receiving Correction":

> Lord, I confess I am chastis'd
> Deservedly for sin;
> And all my evil actions flow
> From a vile heart within.

Hill insisted in his editorial upon the "total depravity of *our* nature," the Murdstones upon that of the *child* David, while the Christmas dinner guests in *Great Expectations* call the *young* as a whole "naturally wicious." The lyric continues,

> And shall I let proud anger rise
> Because I am reprov'd;
> No, rather let me grateful be
> That I am so belov'd.

Its next lines imply more than mere reproof:

> For not to please themselves at all
> My parents cause me smart. (Hill No. 109, Benson p. 261)[6]

In discussing current children's literature, Wordsworth was calling for "a race of real children, not too wise, too learned or too good."[7]

In *David Copperfield* Dickens superimposes a child-hating father-figure upon a loving but fading mother-figure. The juxtaposition of the above lines with these from the preceding hymn,

> Dearest Lord, upon each child
> Send a heavenly shower of grace;
> Make us lowly, meek and mild,
> Fill us with sweet joy and peace.

leaves a similar impression. In Samuel Butler's paranoid retrospect of his Evangelical upbringing, Christina employs feminine gentleness to subvert her son's resistance to the threatening father.[8]

A similar doubleness in the Canadian reprint of a Sunday School Union collection takes the form of a Blakean or rather Barbauldian frontal design of a child being taught under a tree near grazing cattle, that is belied by the threatening Jehovah of the hymns.[9] The child, recognizably the little pharisee of Watts' *Divine Songs*, congratulates himself on being British not heathen (6, 68, 152), warmly clad, not shivering like the "many poor" around (79), at Sunday-school not playing like the "sons of darkness" (99) and warned by "kind teachers" to escape "eternal fire." The threatening father-God dominates the group of lyrics on the future state. "There is a pit beneath the grave" (200) where the "everlasting flame" of God's "holy wrath" is "kindled by his almighty breath." "There is a land of pure delight" (201) and "beyond the sky / A heaven of joy and love" (though also a "dreadful hell") (202), but the gloom returns in "What a dreadful place is hell / Where bad children ever dwell" (203).

All aspects of the child's depravity appear in a single text: "O Lord, forgive a sinful child / Whose heart is all unclean" (84). After reflecting on his defilement by the "vile work" of sin, the child fears being doomed by the divine wrath to "feed the worm that never dies / In endless flames to dwell" unless God change his "stubborn heart" and make him "pure within." While a girl might also have a "wild" and "untractable" [sic] heart, impurity was presumed of boys. As the conclusion makes clear, sin comprises lust, pride and anger, holiness their repression: "O Lord! to me thy chaste, thy mild, / Thy holy mind impart." A verse of "Lord, we are vile, conceiv'd in sin" unhappily marries Calvinist total depravity with Evangelical inwardness: "No outward forms can make us clean; / The leprosy lies deep within." (83) An early Victorian compiler printed this text by Watts as "Lord, I am vile . . . ''[10]

Objective mythology and inwardness meet in a *Divine Song* of Watts, "Almighty God, thy piercing eye" (11). To God's view "lie open" at night "our most secret actions"; in His "dreadful book" every "sin" and "wicked word" are recorded against the "judgment-day." "And must the crimes that I have done / Be read and publish'd there" exclaims the child, who inwardly prostrates himself "at thy feet asham'd." The Redeemer's blood having blotted them from the Book, the child begs that he may "for ever fear / T'indulge a sinful thought." In another text, the "eye" surveys alike "public walks," "private ways, / The secrets of my breast," yet in this "wondrous knowledge" the child feels security, for he lies in God's "circling arms" shielded from evil by the "bulwark" of grace. The hymns of the Evangelical Revival completed the internalization of judgment. The God of Watts' *Divine Songs* knows "our inmost mind" and sees through the "disguise" worn by "painted hypocrites," but remains external to the child. Only when the images of all-seeing eye and bleeding Saviour had been fused by Newton and internalized by Wesley could fear of the Lord turn into the self-searching repression of the young John Ruskin, Augustus Hare, or Arthur Hugh Clough.

Benson's collection has much to say on family and school life. Of his "Family Hymns," one after another praises Christ for bringing domestic concord. One reveals the upward mobility of Methodism at this time:

> To thee may each united house,
> Morning and night present its vows;
> Our servants there, and rising race
> Be taught thy precepts and thy grace. (p. 243)

Another presents the ideal boy at work, not play, and the ideal girl at her housework like any Agnes Wickfield. Finally, as in Hill's book, the future Victorian child "weak and helpless," humbly seeks to be "thine own, / Meek, dutiful and mild" (p. 237). Mrs. Proudie or Mr. Slope could have asked no more. Butler's Christina might have wept with the mother who "with streaming eyes" beheld her unconverted son "entirely dead" to God (p. 226).[11]

As is shown by an earlier collection by Benson, *Hymns for Children and Young Persons*,[12] the Methodist Connexion, like all revolutionary institutions from the early Church to the Soviet Communist party, was undergoing a repressive reaction from initial euphoria. Benson's use in 1816 of John Wesley's principle, the expression in "plain . . . easy language" of "strong and manly sense," has a twist earlier remarked of the reproving adults in novels by Dickens. In his preface Benson aspires to "lift" children "up to *us*," implying that adults were redeemed from depravity. Thus parents of the early Victorians made an idol of their own maturity. Benson urges children to request explanations of hymns about religious "experiences" to which they are "strangers." Like an ancient Byzantine or a future Salvation Army leader, he intends his lyrics to work by usurpation, for children should "memorize" the "praises of God" to sing "at work" so as to induce "cheerfulness" and avert the "temptation to sing vain and foolish songs." Early Primitive Methodists were at that time setting hymns to popular tunes with a view to having working-class children introduce them into their homes.[13]

The ecstasies of Wesleyan gatherings long past, Benson enjoins the *gravitas* proper to worship. Let children "be sincere," remember "that the Lord searcheth the heart," be serious in addressing "the Majesty of Heaven whom angels worship and at whose name devils tremble," for to sing His praise below is to fit themselves for that "better world" where their mouths will be "eternally filled with the high praises of Jehovah."

I have quoted so extensively to show how this second- or third-generation Methodist instils an ethos essentially similar to that of upper-class Evangelicals such as the Wilberforces, John Ruskin's parents, or the fictional aristocrats who forbid acting in *Mansfield Park* or impose sobriety in *Vanity Fair*. Behind that ethos lay a theology more Calvinist than truly Wesleyan. Though Benson's hymnal is Methodist in its focus on family life and the believer, its early section headings have that flavour of reprobation proper to Hill's Calvinist scheme of salvation, evident also in the Anglican

Sunday-school book issued at Hull in 1823.[14] Where the latter begins with God (1-14), Christ (15-57), the Holy Spirit (58-9) and Scriptures (60-70) and continues with the "Fall of Man" and "Depravity of our Nature" (71-7), the Methodist begins with "Scriptural Doctrines re God, the Scriptures, Creation, Fall, Redemption" (1-23) and continues with "Sins of Youth: Sabbath-breaking, Disobedience to Parents, Pride, Cruelty, etc." (24-38).

The gloom that enveloped the Sunday-school hymnal from the Hill's first edition in 1790 to that of the Leeds Sunday School Union in 1834 was the combined effect of the repressive Jehovah, the short life-span, and the puritan work ethic adapted to the factory system. In the Sunday-school hymnal reprinted at Montreal, well-nigh every hymn mentions death. One verse may serve as comic epitome:

> Religion should our thoughts engage
> Amidst our youthful bloom;
> 'Twill fit us for declining age,
> And for the awful tomb.[15]

Just as Revival hymns extended the life of seventeenth-century tropes for the Christian life, so their editors directed the devotion of children to the paternal deity of the Reformed churches. While G.R. Taylor hardly distinguishes between Methodist and Evangelical in his account of womanhood repressed in consequence of the Revival,[16] Wesleyan devotion to the suffering Christ becomes overlaid in such compilations as that of Benson.

Christ the Victor predominates in one of the rare missionary hymns of Hill's collection, the once famous "O'er the gloomy hills of darkness," by the Welsh Calvinistic Methodist who wrote "Guide me O thou great Jehovah." Let Christ's "wide dominion. . . . still increase" exclaims Williams, via his translator:

> Let the Indian, let the Negro,
> Let the rude Barbarian see
> That divine and glorious Conquest
> Once obtain'd on Calvary.
> Let the gospel
> Loud resound from pole to pole.

As late Roman poets transformed the victim into a king reigning from the Cross, so during British imperial expansion missionary hymnographers stamped Him with the warrior's image. The ethical contraries of submission at home and conquest abroad were central to the culture of pre-Victorian England.

If Sunday-schools regularly taught child and even adult workers to read and write, would they have taught them habits of submission? Hannah More, founder of Evangelical schools, and the Methodist Jabez Bunting forbade the teaching of writing as likely to make poor children discontented with their station. By the accession of Victoria, only Congregational, Unitarian, and some Baptist and Primitive Methodist Sunday-scholars could officially be taught writing. In 1825 the editor of a *Baptist Sabbath School Hymn Book* laments that some "are more anxious to teach the art of reading and writing than the way to heaven." "Mere knowledge," he adds, "will never convert the soul."[17]

The demanding vocabulary of a hymn to be sung before the Litany at St. John's (Anglican) Sunday-school, Newcastle implies that the children came from the literate if not exactly critical middle class:

> Bright source of intellectual rays,
> O Father of Spirits! God of grace!
> O dart, with energy unknown,
> Celestial beamings from thy throne.

"The sacred Book," continues the hymnist, will teach children the way to "happiness and God." After the Litany, children besought Christ, "God of Truth," to crown their teachers' "kind instructions" by blessing His "rising race."[18] Unlike the young Baptists urged in their ferocious hymnal to shun the way of destruction, these Anglican children could expect some enjoyment in this life.

Even upon the most privileged, the *zeitgeist* of the early nineteenth century imposed a measure of sobriety and restraint. Young Quakers in hymns to be recited "for the Instruction of Young Persons" (1818) had their full portion of blood, guilt, fear of death and sententious admonition. Thirty of their 253 lyrics came from the *Divine Songs* of Watts, and almost as many from each of the Calvinists Cowper, Newton and Kelly. In the editor's view, children should be "early stored with that knowledge best calculated to promote their . . . advancement in a religious life."[19] Though less threatening than most, their anthology resembled a well-built meeting-house, handsome but mournful.

The young Quakers of 1903 lived in a quite different world, for according to the compiler of the seventeenth edition "true Christians," that is those dwelling not upon "theological controversy" but the "grand essentials of Christian truth" experienced a "wonderful and beautiful harmony." The poems, no longer exclusively sacred, were to suit the children's "present circumstances and age" and "varying conditions" in the future: "joy or sorrow . . . health or sickness" and life's "closing scenes." Though poetically even better than the earlier volume, this selection of 138 recitation-pieces—among them Milton's "On His Twenty-Third Birthday," Tennyson's "Strong Son of God" and Wordsworth's "Ode to Duty"—no longer conveys theological "knowledge" requisite for "a religious life."[20]

Also common to nearly all denominations was the increasing prevalence of Watts' principle of *kenosis* or "sinking" of style to the child's level, over Wesley's principle of "manly sense" intended to raise comprehension to the adult level. Disastrous as his method proved in the hands of lesser poets, Watts contributed lyrics in no way puerile, while, ironically, Wesley's best hymn for children has incurred unmerited notoriety on this ground.

Both poets were to impress upon Victorian children images and concepts valid for an earlier time. Watts perpetuated the Augustan cosmology. In "I sing the almighty power of God, / That made the mountains rise," the divine wisdom "ordained" the motions of sun, moon, and seas which "obey," "filled the earth with food" and "form'd" all creatures. As his metaphor "*built* the *lofty* skies" reminds us, Watts wrote during the rise of Freemasonry, with its image of God as "Great Architect." Architectural imagery is subordinate to monarchical allusions to clouds and tempests rising "by order" from God's "throne," plants making known His "glories," creatures "subject to his care" inhabiting "his earth." Despite a passing reference to hell in a disused verse, the divine "hand" and "eye" protect rather than oppress the child-speaker.[21] The imagery of cosmic and providential order, further evident in Addison's "The spacious firmament on high," Pope's "Essay on Man," Thomson's "Seasons" and supremely the text and music of Haydn's *Creation*, was to survive in children's hymnody for generations after the researches of Lyell and Darwin had thrown it into question.

In Wesley's unfairly condemned "Gentle Jesus, meek and mild"[22] the monarchical image is subordinate to those of the Lamb and divine child, that were further developed in Blake's "Little lamb, who made thee." Beyond even Wesley's basic texts, "Suffer little children to come unto me" and the Lord's Prayer, the paternalism of petitions such as "Give me thy obedient heart" and "Let me, above all, fulfil / God my heavenly Father's will" governs and distinguishes the thought of this poem from Blake's otherwise similar moral idea in "The Clod and the Pebble":

> Thou didst live to God alone;
> Thou didst never seek thine own;
> Thou thyself didst never please:
> God was all thy happiness.

Having combined with other Revival hymns to form the Victorian Sunday-school ethos of paternal dominance, this highly scriptural lyric became a byword in the reaction against these Sunday-school hymns, mostly by women, that enjoined passive resignation. Yet its conclusion shows a more virile as well as more Christian spirit than that of most children's lyrics during the age of religious terrorism or the succeeding era of sentimental naturalism:

> I shall then show forth thy praise,
> Serve thee all my happy days;
> Then the world shall always see
> Christ, the holy Child, in me.

MID-NINETEENTH CENTURY

To judge from the paucity of Sunday-school hymnals surviving from the eighteen-sixties and seventies, the rag-and-bone men must have been especially active in carting away their barrowloads of dog-eared volumes. This hiatus throws into prominence the contrast between hymnals for children in the iron time after the Napoleonic War and for those of the more prosperous 1880s. To epitomize that change, as this life became more secure, so nature, the life-cycle, and social institutions—school, family, and country—acquired a sacredness formerly reserved for the Christian mythos. Conversely the treatment of the Creation, Redemption, and Last Things evolved in a secular direction, by the distancing of the Nativity and Passion, the representation of Jesus (more than "Christ") as Friend, Brother, and role model for this life, the disappearance of hell and domestication of heaven.

Although like a fellow Tractarian, Charlotte M. Yonge, the future Mrs. Alexander directed attention to the whole mythos and ethic, not just the Passion, three of her best known *Hymns for Little Children* (1848) heralded a change. "All things bright and beautiful" portrays nature as a present rather than a long-lost paradise. "There is a green hill" conveys the idea, rather than the sanguinary image, of redemptive sacrifice in a "far away" setting like that of Keats' "Grecian Urn," before exhorting children to love and imitate the Saviour in this life. "Once in Royal David's city" treats of a model family life, with the Christ-child as "pattern" of obedience and dependence. Add to these "Do no sinful action, / Speak no angry word," a text on resisting the devil, and you have an ideal of family life that remained intact until after the First World War. It involved a gentler form of repression than had the earlier Evangelical stereotype, for "little children" were to follow Christ in being "kind and gentle . . . pure and true." This element overlays that of spiritual combat mainly because reduction and internalization of the devil to a "wicked spirit" and "the bad within you" left the feminine anima of Christ as the only real figure. In this sense, to depersonalize the Devil was to emasculate God.

Mrs. Alexander's verse on "The rich man in his castle, / The poor man at his gate," in common use until about 1900, deserves condemnation not for its literal sense (perhaps recalling the happy relationship of her father with his gate-keeper) but for making an idol of the obsolescent hierarchy supposedly "ordered" by God.[23] The alteration of her "We are but little children poor, / And born in very low estate" to " . . . weak, / Not born in any high estate" sheds a sidelight on the class system, for originally children of the poor and now children in general, having little scope for deeds of heroic martyrdom, must wage inward combat against pride and anger. But as in all her hymns the class system is tangential, for the keynote is restraining "thoughts of pride and anger," "bitter words," "tears of passion" or the "angry blow."[24] Can we condemn her for teaching a principle so essential for attaining maturity? The defect lies in the description of an effort at self-control as a "little cross" that "little children" must bear daily in imitation of Christ and the martyrs. Aside from the author's two-eyed viewpoint, at once above and within the "little" child, suppression of infantile anger and egoism (as distinct from self-control in adolescence) is thought by most child psychologists to do more harm than good.

As a metrist well versed in the Scriptures, Mrs. Alexander must be accounted the most successful Victorian hymnographer for children; as a high-born lady unavoidably patronizing the poor whom she served with such devotion, she played her part in the naturalizing and domesticating of the Christian ethic and mythos that continued through the second half of the century.

LATE VICTORIAN CONSENSUS

Nowhere is consensus more apparent than in the collections issued between 1879 and 1886 by the Methodist, Anglican, Congregational, Baptist, and London Sunday School Union authorities. A group of hymns found in all five and also among the hundred most often reprinted for Sunday and day-schools exemplifies *kenosis*, consecration of nature and the life-cycle (especially childhood) and of home, school, or country, sentimental distancing of the Christian mythos, especially the Nativity and Passion, identification with Jesus as ethical model, domestication of heaven and disappearance of hell. The lyrics concerned were:

"Around the throne of God in heaven / Thousands of children stand"
"Brightly gleams our banner"

"Gentle Jesus, meek and mild"
"I think when I read that sweet story of old"
"I love to hear the story"
"Just as I am . . . " (either of two versions)
"There is a green hill far away"
"There's a Friend for little children."

All but the Anglican book included also "I want to be like Jesus" and "Tell me the old, old story."

Full reading of these inevitably modifies one's first impression that heaven had become the peculiar abode of children and the Gospel events acquired the "once upon a time" dimension of fairy-tale.

To dwell no further upon the classics of Wesley and Mrs. Alexander, the opening lines of "Around the throne" speak for themselves, while "I think when I read" (1841) begins in a retelling of "Suffer little children to come unto me" and ends in the child-speaker's yearning for the "thousands" ignorant of the "heavenly home" to join the "little children of every clime" who shall finally "crowd to" the Saviour's arms. Its middle stanza, resolving to seek Christ in prayer and so meet Him in that "beautiful place he has gone to prepare / For all that are washed and forgiven," depicts heaven as a continuation of the Victorian home, entered immediately at death, and populated by "many dear children . . . gathering there, / 'For of such is the kingdom of heaven'."[25] Note also the two-eyed stance, the child observing "dear little" children.

The underlined expressions in the opening lines of "I love to hear the story," which concerns the Saviour's personal love for the child, though theologically sound, combine with later phrases to convey an impression of infantilism:

> I love to hear the *story*
> Which *angel voices tell*,
> How *once* the King of Glory
> *Came down* on earth to dwell.

The Saviour who was "once a child like me," having "come down to save me," showed His "little ones" how to be "pure and holy," and "kindly promised" that the child-singer might "go" to "sing among His angels."[26]

The still extant "There's a Friend for little children" properly describes Christ as one "whose love," unlike earthly friendships, "will never die," but represents heaven as "rest" and "home" for the "little children" who will each wear a "crown" and "robe" while singing a song that even angels cannot address to Christ, their King but not their Saviour. The refrain line "Above the bright blue sky," the only line children were bound to remember, conveyed an outmoded image of the cosmos that must have invested heaven with a sense of unreality. By coincidence, this hymn appeared in the same year as *The Origin of Species*.

"O little Child of Bethlehem" crossed the Atlantic too late to be included in these hymnals, but such established favourites as "Once in Royal David's city" and "Good King Wenceslas" exemplify the distancing and poeticizing of the Gospel event already evident in "There is a green hill."

"Brightly gleams our banner" and "I want to be like Jesus" invite the child to identify with Christ. In the first, the Evangelical trope of Christian "soldiers" marching homeward through the desert, gives place to the Victorian trope of "children" following in the "narrow way" of Christ, "Pattern of our childhood." The second, discussed in the previous chapter, presents a Saviour never known to speak in anger, who died "meekly."

The two versions of "Just as I am" most clearly point to the contrast between early and late Victorian time-conditioning. The original version " . . . without one plea / Save that Thy blood was shed for me" represents an invalid's adaptation to her lot in Evangelical tropes that extend to all forms of doubt or conflict. The believer's sickness and poverty are relieved by her poignant vision of the Saviour's love to be proved "Here for a season, then above . . . "[27] The revised version, "Just as I am . . . Thine own to be," dated 1887 by the authorities yet printed in the Congregational collection of 1881, has become a standard expression of "healthy-minded religion" for the "young, strong and free" who in the "glad morning" of life vow devotion with "no reserve and no delay."[28] If by no means heterodox, since she offers the final hope of casting a "victor's crown" before Christ, Mrs. Farningham regards the faith as "dearer than," not alternative to the "dreams of fame and gold, / Success and joy" that embolden her singer.

We cannot fairly accuse the earlier poet of escapism in anticipating fulfilment hereafter and the later of secularization in envisaging it here. Rather we should ask what aspirations and objects other well-used hymns held before late Victorian or Edwardian children.

Table 1 records recurrences from 1868 to 1923 in up to seven Sunday-school books of the Learned (Anglican, Congregational, Presbyterian) tradition, seven of the Popular (Methodist of all types, Baptist) tradition, and seven Board (elementary) day-school books. Wesleyan schools, to which non-churchgoing parents sent their children in preference to Anglican schools, are considered Popular.[29]

TABLE 1

		L	*P*	*B*
A	I love to hear the story	7	7	4
	Little drops of water	5	6	3
	There is a green hill far away	7	6	3
	There's a Friend for little children	5	5	3
B	Brightly gleams our banner	7	7	0
	Gentle Jesus, meek and mild	5	6	0
	I think when I read that sweet story . . .	5	5	0
	I want to be like Jesus	6	7	0
	Just as I am (usually "without one plea")	5	5	0
	Tell me the old, old story	6	7	0
C	Soldiers of Christ, arise	5	0	0
D	I sing the almighty power of God	0	6	Under 3
	There is a path that leads to God	0	5	Under 3
E	Forward be our watchword	0	6	Under 3
	God bless our native land	0	6	7

All children seem likely to have known those in group A, "Little drops of water" in either its English or the American version. Most if not all Sunday-school children knew those in group B, which have a more explicitly devotional flavour. "Soldiers of Christ" appeared in most Sunday-school books of the Learned tradition and in at least ten for public (boarding) schools.[30] Those by Watts and the Taylor sisters (in D) rarely appeared in Board school or in Learned tradition books. Three more, "Come, sing with holy gladness," "Lord, teach a little child to pray," and "It is a thing most wonderful" (that Christ became a child) appeared in all but one of the five denominational Sunday-school books of 1879-86 but rarely in those for day-schools.[31]

The first three lyrics, universally known, distance the Passion and present heaven as home for children. "Tell me the old, old story" (1886), expressing a convalescent's regressively simple emotion, employs the request for a story as a metaphor of conversion. Its neurotic elements of fixation, unfocused guilt and dependence overlay its biblical elements. If understandable in one struggling back to health, they should have ruled out its use for healthy children:

> Tell me the old, old story
> Of unseen things above,

Of Jesus and his glory,
Of Jesus and his love.
Tell me the story simply,
As to a little child,
For I am weak and weary,
And helpless and defiled.

Tell me the story simply,
That I may take it in:
That wonderful redemption,
God's remedy for sin.

* * *

Tell me the same old story,
When you have cause to fear
That this world's empty glory
Is costing me too dear . . . [32]

Dean Alford's "Forward be our watchword" represents the opposite pole of Evangelicalism in its trope of the spiritual life as a march through the wilderness behind the "fiery pillar" of Christ. It disdains regression, forbidding the Christian to cast "a thought behind" as he passes from infancy to manhood and beyond. Clearly intended as a processional, it blends apocalyptic images of city and river with the Judaic and ecclesiastical images of God's "high temple" and finally with the Victorian trope of progression through darkness to light, as in Newman's "Lead, kindly Light." This conventional but unexceptionable marching hymn remained a Sunday-school favourite into this century.[33]

In the American version of "Little drops of water," just as an accumulation of droplets and grains make up ocean and earth, so small acts of love can make earth into Eden, while small misdeeds lead to great evil. In the English text, the case is proved from a miscellany of examples: the sparrow building her nest, letters making up books and erosion wearing away cliffs.[34] Each amounts to a sound idea ill transmitted.

"Come, praise your Lord and Saviour" (1872) and "Come, sing with holy gladness" (1868) are the only English examples of gender-conditioning I know. In the former, Bishop How (of "For all the saints") has the boys singing praise of Jesus for sojourning here "A pure and spotless boy" and pattern of obedience and virtue, while the girls praise the "lowly Maiden's Son" in whom "gentlest graces / Are gathered," while praying for that "best adornment . . . Christian maid can wear," his "meek and quiet spirit. . . ." In the latter, used as late as 1905 by elementary-school children, the High Churchman J.J. Daniell exhorts boys to be "strong in" and toil for Jesus, girls to "live for" the "maiden's Son" and perfect the "grace begun" by being "patient, pure and gentle."[35]

The preference of "Learned" hymnals for "Soldiers of Christ, arise" and "Popular" ones for "God bless our native land" calls for comment. Though also paraphrasing St. Paul's elaborate metaphor of taking up arms against the powers of evil, Wesley differs from the Gallican poet of the contemporary "Pugnate, Christi milites"[36] in directing his metaphors toward the soul's standing "entire at last." The monastic poet beautifully depicts the attainment of eternal life and joy by those who have spurned earth's transitory pleasures so as to attain eternal light. Wesley's existential images suited the devotional context of the Sunday or public school service, while the literal petitions of both American and British versions of "God bless our native land" (1832, 1836) suited the extravert setting of the elementary school. The American version, originally a translation from German, ends in the alarming petition "God save the State," the English one in a wish for "peace and love" in every land.[37] Considering its earlier petitions that "Britain's power depend / On war no more," "just and righteous laws" guide this "land of liberty" and nations "form one family," we must acquit the English lyric of the idolatrous patriotism that was to mar so many hymns near the end of the century.

During Victoria's reign there set in a poetic decline which is evident in the practice of writing down for children, or else of adopting their supposed viewpoint, in the tacit assignment of Gospel events to a remote or even legendary context, and in some romantic nature images the feebleness of which may be contrasted with the increasing stridency of military and patriotic images.

In devotional hymnody, the wind finally shifted from northeast to southwest around 1870, when a committee of teachers compiled *Songs of Praise for Sunday-school Children*.[38] While including some highly scriptural texts—"How glorious is the heavenly King," "To thy father and thy mother" or "Young children once to Jesus came," they chose for the very young such unpromising titles as "Beautiful Zion! built above," "I want to be an angel," "Little child, do you love Jesus," and "Yes, there are little ones in heaven."

Our five denominational hymnals (1879-86) exemplify all these trends. In compiling the Anglican *Children's Hymn Book* Mrs. Brock Carey, advised by the hymnists Ellerton and How, tried to combine "excellence" with "a healthy religious tone" by choosing texts within the "experience" and . . . "comprehension" of children yet which they could "love and value all their lives."[39] This trade-off between the Watts and Wesley principles and the Broad Church ideal suffers from a child-centred view of education reflected in the lack of a section on death and judgment, presumably in consequence of an improved economy and life expectancy. The results of passing over hymns on the conversion experience in favour of some with no scriptural basis were a sentimentalized Christ-figure and a saccharine tone regrettable in what must with all its faults be adjudged one of the leading late Victorian children's collections. A few comparisons must suffice for illustration.

In the original twelve stanzas of Keble's "There is a book, who runs may read" (1827), interwoven allusions from both Testaments portray the cosmos as God's handiwork. The encompassing sky typifies His love, the moon his Church, the sun Christ, the stars His saints, the dew grace, fire and wind the Holy Spirit. Only sinful man fails to reveal his divine origin. Let God grant "a heart to find out" and "read" Him "every where." The stanzas selected for this hymnal develop this central Judaeo-Christian analogy with an exactness and economy undeserving of the sneer "Wordsworth-and-water" flung at the *Christian Year*:

> The works of God above, below,
> Within us and around,
> Are pages in that book, to show
> How God Himself is found.
>
> The glorious sky embracing all
> Is like the Maker's love,
> Wherewith encompass'd, great and small
> In peace and order move.

Despite its lively tune, how feeble by comparison is How's "Summer suns are glowing" (1871), still sung in some churches and schools. Most specific when most credal, in "Light of Light! shine o'er us / On our pilgrim way," this drifts into sheer inanity in "Happy light is flowing, / Bountiful and free." The only nature image with a clear meaning is the Tennysonian metaphor of clouds obscuring "our sky" till God lift the veil. In a single stanza "God's free mercy" that "streameth" and His "banner" that "gleameth / Everywhere unfurled" are jumbled up with solar and celestial images for love in the concluding lines:

> Broad and deep and glorious
> As the heaven above,
> Shines in might victorious
> His eternal love.

Neither this nor the following verses on responsive love and God as light for this our pilgrimage can unravel this tangle of military and nature images.[40]

Only in its title does G.R. Prynne's "Jesus, meek and gentle" (1856), intended for adults, resemble Wesley's more famous lyric. While Wesley develops a complex image of the child seeking and receiving comfort from its parent and Saviour, Prynne exhorts a "Pitying, loving" Christ to hear the "children's cry," pardon their offences, loose their "captive-chains" and break every "idol" their "soul [sic] detains," then to draw them through "terrestrial darkness" to "eternal day."[41] Outside the mission field, children, in particular, may have wondered what idols or chains the poet had in mind.

A decline of taste or skill attributable to the *zeitgeist* must be distinguished from an author's limitations and from the inherent difficulties of writing for children. As if to exemplify the first, opposite "When I survey the wondrous Cross" (113) the compiler prints J.M. Neale's "A time to watch, a time to pray," a passion hymn which descends to the bathos of "The saddest, yet the sweetest hour" men or angels knew. As an example of the second, on a double-page spread of Ascension hymns, Wesley's "Hail the day that sees Him rise" (130) cruelly exposes the conventional imagery of Frances Havergal in "Golden harps are sounding" (129) ("Pearly gates" are opened) and her propensity for reverting from concreteness in recounting the event to emptiness in describing the risen Christ "Praying for his children . . . Calling them to glory."[42] Two lyrics published by women poets in 1841 reveal individual differences in skill. The short-lived Mary Duncan's night prayer "Jesus, tender Shepherd, hear me," makes the child-speaker call himself *"little* lamb" but concisely recounts the day's blessings ("clothed . . . warmed and fed") and offers succinct petitions for forgiveness, friends, and salvation:

> Let my sins be all forgiven,
> Bless the friends I love so well;
> Take me, when I die, to heaven,
> Happy there with thee to dwell.

In Jemima Luke's otherwise substantial "I think, when I read that sweet story of old" (discussed earlier), a plethora of adjectives ruins the conclusion.

> I long for the joy of that *glorious* time,
> The *sweetest*, the *brightest*, and *best*,
> When the *dear little* children of every clime[43]
> Shall crowd to his arms and be blest.

With the adjectives excised, the ending would read like one by Duncan or even Keble:

> I long for the joy of that time,
> When the children of every clime
> Shall crowd to his arms and be blest.

Another double-page spread highlights a major difficulty in writing for the very young. Baker's metrical psalm "The King of love my Shepherd is" (183) employs the archaism "Perverse and foolish oft I strayed" and hints at experiences verifiable only by the mature. The naïveté of Havergal's "God will take care of you" (184) makes it as transparent to the infant as it must be unacceptable to the critical teenager:

> Jesus is near to keep you from ills,
> Waking or resting, at work or at play,
> Jesus is with you and watches you still.

As Wesley might have predicted, Baker's hymn has become a classic for all but the very young, while Havergal's has sunk into oblivion.[44]

By comparison with its predecessor of 1816, the *Methodist Sunday School Hymn Book* of 1879 has a scheme simplified and, apart from the nativity hymns, almost demythologized. Of his 327 items the eighteenth-century editor allotted 23 to "Scriptural Doctrines on God . . . Creation, Fall, Redemption"; 15 to the "Sins of Youth"—Sabbath-breaking, Disobedience to Parents, Pride, Cruelty—; 65 to prayer for "Divine Knowledge, Guidance and Protection . . . Repentance, Pardon and Holiness"; 27 to praise of "Sincere Christianity, Creation, Providence, Redemption" and the "Universal Church"; 30 to "Historical" accounts of scriptural characters and events, especially the "Birth, Life, Death, Resurrection and Ascension" of Christ; 36 to "Time and Eternity," that is, New Year, morning, evening and Sunday followed by Death, Resurrection, Judgment, Hell and Heaven; 29 to the "Family" worship detailed as parents or "Masters" and children praying for each other and prayers for "Boys at Work," "Girls," dying parents and orphans; and 66 to "School Hymns" on such topics as "Catechism, Being Commended" or "Corrected" and the "Death of a Schoolfellow." Save for its emphasis on the family, his format differs little from the Calvinist scheme of salvation in Hill's book and in the early Anglican collection at Hull. By contrast, that of 1879 has 583 titles but a format pared down to "God" (205 titles), including the Trinity and Father (74), Christ (119 in all), and the Holy Spirit (13); the Scriptures (22); the

Christian Life (198) including "Early Piety, Prayer, Repentance, Faith, Confidence and Joy (rather than Hope and Charity), Conduct and Service"; then "Times and Seasons" purely in this life (48), with a separate section of 40 on the "Life to Come" that eschews all mention of the Second Coming, Last Judgment, Hell, and the powers of evil. In effect, salvation is contrasted not with damnation but with this life. "Here we suffer grief and pain" (No. 431), meeting but to part again, but "in heaven we part no more." Here wheat and tares grow together (443); hereafter wheat will endure and who knows what will happen to the tares?[45]

Late Victorian children, however well instructed, no longer sang the Christian eschatology into their bones. Instead they sang, less insistently, of a general progression to family life with the universal Father, after an instantaneous passage eased in some way by the death of "gentle Jesus," Friend or Brother. The young Methodist was taught submission to parents and teachers not by threats but by having his littleness constantly rubbed in. An emphasis on his small stature beside his parent or teacher replaced that on his social inferiority to a landlord or employer.

The little Methodist might sing "I am Jesus's little friend" (324) or "I love to tell the story / Of Jesus" which "satisfies my longings" like nothing else (405) but no longer went "Forth in thy name" to work. In the mission field however, he might lift high the Gospel banner (394), or spend and be spent (595). At home he had a charge to keep, his soul (397), that being the "only wisdom" to require "serious industry and fear" (250). His range of classic Wesleyan hymns did not include "Lo! he comes, with clouds descending" or any that told him what he had to fear.

In the *Congregational Sunday School Hymn Book* of 1881, the substitution of new and feeble for old and strong English texts is countered somewhat by a goodly number of translations from Latin. These and a generally eclectic choice preserve the poetic superiority expected of Congregational and other "Learned" collections. Though far more suitable for children than Hill's fearsome volume, it represents the conditioning of a later day. Twenty-two of its first hundred authors are women. By *kenosis* beyond all reason, some of Watts' finest lyrics, including "When I survey the wondrous Cross" and "Come, let us join our cheerful songs" are passed over in favour of, for example, "How doth the little busy bee" (167).

Above all, the patriotism that Watts had kept in measure the then popular hymnist T.H. Gill did not. At times a merely cultural nationalist, like an Elgar or Kodaly, Gill thanks God for his "English land," its "good laws" and "great" history while acknowledging the pre-eminence of the "heavenly fatherland" and "country of Emmanuel" (499). In "Lift thy song among the nations, / England of the Lord beloved" (498), however, he resorts to religious and patriotic rant on the defeat of the Armada "vainly . . .

assembled / 'Gainst the isle of his delight'' or on Cromwell's defence of the
"Good Old Cause.'' Children doubtless sang with gusto this amalgam of
patriotic, missionary and liberal fervour:

> Sing how He, the Lord, hath brought thee
> Onward still from height to height,
> How the Heavenly Lustre sought thee
> Ere it made the world more bright.
> Let the freedom long-descended
> Gloriously uplift thy voice.
>
> . . .
>
> Sing how He His England crowned
> When He loosed the yoke of Rome;
> Sing how He His truth enthroned
> In this consecrated home;
> How He trusts thee with the treasure
> Of His word to send it forth:
> Mightily fulfil His pleasure;
> Send His word o'er all the earth!
>
> Sing how gleamed His sword victorious
> In the hand of heroes thine![46]

The point of quoting this so fully is to show with what blend of patriotic and
religious fervour the generation that fought in Flanders had been imbued.
Such now forgotten lyrics were to abound in school hymnals between 1880
and 1914.

A more gifted poet, the Anglican John Ellerton, addressing the tribal
deity in the "Praise to our God, whose bounteous hand / Prepared of old
our glorious land'' (300), employs rhetoric on the "garden fenced with silver
sea'' or "A people prosperous, bold and free'' that echoes Shakespeare and
could have inspired Churchill. At all events,

> Praise to our God; His power alone
> Can keep unmoved our ancient throne,
> Sustained by counsels wise and just,
> And guarded by a people's trust

is the kind of assertion still heard at public school speech days and
Conservative party rallies from speakers who no longer call their "guilty
nation'' to seek God who has spared it. Like such renowned Congregational
preachers as R.W. Dale, Victorian sacred poets blended the patriotic with

the social and religious spirit of mission in, for example, "Christ for the world we sing" (497), on bringing "the world to Christ" while ministering to "The poor, and them that mourn."

This male activism, sometimes impatient as in Bonar's plea against unemployment (171) ("Make use of me . . . Let me not be forgot; / A broken vessel . . . whom thou needest not"), alternates with a treacly feminine didacticism. Fanny Crosby (Mrs. Van Alstyne) begins a series of contingencies with one that appears to reflect self-observation:

> Suppose a little cowslip
> Should hang its golden cup,
> And say, "I'm such a tiny flower,
> I'd better not grow up." (172)

Her "little child" is to employ its "little strength" in "deeds of kindness." Mrs. Alexander's "We are but little children weak" (174) teaches a more coherent and sensible ethic of restraint, but the archness of her lyric and the silliness of Mrs. Van Alstyne's typify these female excesses that made the Sunday-school the butt of male wit, and half-way house to male apostasy.[47] To demonstrate here the male excess of militant patriotism would be to anticipate a later chapter.

RETROSPECT: TIME-CONDITIONING IN THE KIRK, 1815-1914

Rather than contrast the threats of hell-fire in the Baptist *Sabbath-school Hymn Book* of 1825 with the prospect of "Heavenly Happiness" in a section in *Psalms and Hymns for School and Home* (1883), or draw similar contrasts between early and late Sunday School Union books,[48] I shall recapitulate the time-conditioning that took place between the Napoleonic and First World wars from a series of Scottish and English Presbyterian hymnals.

A New Selection . . . for the Use of Schools (1824)[49] paints so dismal a picture of this life as to render otiose all threats concerning that to come. The children who like "crowded forest trees" (8) stand marked for cutting down may bloom for "a few short years" until the "awful hour," but when "sickness wastes the frame" must fly to "One hanging on a tree" (6). The religious melancholy that, to judge from novels by Scott and Hogg, haunted the young in Edinburgh continues unabated in *The Sabbath School Minstrel* (1835). It is if anything exacerbated by poems on total depravity and the "Pit beneath the grave" (44) that awaits the unchosen. Further to cite Watts and others on human nakedness before Jehovah were to compound melancholy with tedium. A paraphrase of St. Paul that is reminiscent of

"Tam o' Shanter" must serve as Last Post of old-style eschatology:

> When the last trumpet's awful voice
> This rending earth shall shake,
> When op'ning graves shall yield their charge,
> And dust to life awake;
>
> Those bodies that corrupted fell
> Shall uncorrupted rise,
> And mortal forms shall spring to life
> Immortal in the skies.[50]

Thus far, the scheme of salvation and use of Scots Paraphrases preserved the dignity proper both to Old Dissent and to the Established Kirk. In a *Presbyterian Hymnal with Sunday School Supplement* (1876) printed in Edinburgh but used also in England,[51] the structure remains but the dignified reserve begins to crumble. Though Presbyterian logic still mainly informs the hymnal, in its section "For the Young" and Sunday School Supplement (328-52) the rot has set in. If the drivel provided elsewhere for children is still absent, "Around the throne of God in heaven" (331), "I love to hear the story" (335), "I'm a little pilgrim" (347), and "Little travellers Zionwards" herald a similar decline. The gulf between verse for adults and for children widens in the proposed Supplement printed in 1882 for the committee producing a Scottish Hymnal.

> Away from sorrow, doubt and pain,
> Away from worldly loss or gain,
> . . . temptations, tears and care
> Beyond the bright and pearly gates
> Where Jesus, loving Saviour, waits (369)
>
> I love to think of the heavenly land
> Where white-robed angels are,
> Where many a friend is gathered, safe
> From fear, and toil, and care. (384)[52]

The hymns proposed for adults still belong decidedly to the Learned tradition, those for children to the Popular tradition of escapism and hot-gospelling, the less bearable for the pervasive "littleness." That some members could propose them for children speaks volumes about the decay of taste. Many of these, with some more worthy, appeared in the Scottish Kirk's *Children's Hymnal* (1885).[53]

The Free Church of Scotland produced a *Home and School Hymnal*[54] remarkable for its many egocentric items and its funeral hymns, the latter headed "Homegoing." A double-page spread setting Wesley's "Come, let us join our friends above" beside a lyric ending

> A few short years of evil past
> We reach the happy shore
> Where death-divided friends at last
> Shall meet to part no more (253)

registers the loss of substance and stature in eschatological hymnody during the late nineteenth century.

A bracing nationalism accompanies an effeminate Christianity in two hymnals produced in 1910 and 1912. In the *Scottish National Hymnal for the Young* (1910), "Sound the Battle Cry" (106) and "There's a Royal Banner" (107), depict the Christian life and mission as a medieval war, with standards raised and armour, shield and banner gleaming as singers battle "for the right" against the "raging" foe. In the former hymn that victorious singers hope to "wear the crown before Thy face" implies lifelong inner combat, but the preceding images suggest a black-and-white morality readily transferable to the impending war. The same can be said of the latter, in which the "royal banner" for "soldiers of the King" to flaunt before the foe works against the final identification with the Cross that soon "the world shall sway." While clearing the hymnist of idolatry, the image reminds us that the Union Jack consists of superimposed crosses. The juxtaposition of the National Anthem (135), "O God, our help in ages past" (136) and "Scotland for Christ"[55] implies a convergence of nation with deity to be noticed in the ensuing chapter on Edwardian hymnals.

This *Scottish National Hymnal*, first issued in 1889 when the Glasgow Foundry Boys and Boys' Brigade amalgamated with the national Sabbath School Union, shows rather a lack of discrimination than of good hymns. Thus "Tell me the old, old story" appears opposite "Jesu, Lover of my soul" (43, 45). Only hymns on nature and heaven show unvarying mawkishness. One runs:

> The world looks very beautiful
> And full of joy to me;
> The sun shines out in glory
> On everything I see. (131)

In the next, a "little pilgrim" undertakes in a variable refrain to "follow Jesus all the way" in happiness, suffering, trouble and death. His admirable sentiments are undercut by their glib expression:

> The trials cannot vex me,
> The pain I need not fear,
> For, when I'm close by Jesus,
> Grief cannot come too near.

In the Flanders mud this, like the "happy land" of heaven "far, far away" (148) wherein is neither death nor night (150), must have seemed equally unreal. In one Sunday-school hymnal after another, such feeble verse planted its Judas kiss on the once-mighty Presbyterian faith.

Regression and escape characterize the hymns for "Little Children" and those on the "Heavenly Home" in *School Praise* (1912)[56] issued by the Presbyterian Church of England. Amid the usual thousands of children surrounding their enthroned Friend in the happy land so far away, two lyrics reveal what the prospect of heaven had become. The singer of "There is a city bright" (231) prays to be Christ's "living child" till ensconced in "snow-white dress" above. As if to proclaim the Brothers Grimm his inspiration, another hymnist offers to "work for Jesus" with "little ears . . . feet . . . eyes" and other organs of a dwarf (283) in a song small children would have done better to mime than to sing.[57]

While not fairly representing a selection distinguished by many fine hymns, these show how, in verses for the young and impressionable, the envisioned journey to the heavenly city that had so long enabled the faithful to live well and die at peace had declined into the quest motif of a romance or fairy-tale. The very concept of life as pilgrimage that inspired Dante and Bunyan had been relegated to verse for children. In how many souls were the terrible realities of war to extinguish this feeble lamp of faith, kindled with inferior fuel.

11

PRIVILEGED YOUTH

But public schools had their own corpus of . . . songs that echo down the 19th century and deep into the 20th. . . . the splendid hymns of the Church of England, collected together in Hymns Ancient and Modern. *Hymns bound the public schools together. . . .* [1]

Victorian public school hymn-books exist in such profusion and variety that any study can only be kept in bounds on a principle of graph-drawing once whispered by a school-fellow in Midland dialect: "Mek a curve on it." More precisely, three "curves" extending from about 1825 to 1900 illustrate the range of purpose, ethos, and content in the hymnody of the boarding-schools, predominantly Anglican, for sons of the gentry. Their hymnals varied so widely because each school took its tone from the personality of its head, a scholar or public figure comparable in prestige to a modern university vice-chancellor, but less subject to criticism and constraint. Not only Thomas Arnold of Rugby, but Edward Thring of Uppingham, Charles Vaughan and Henry Montagu Butler of Harrow, and supremely Dorothea Beale of Cheltenham Ladies' College, were subject only to the Lord, the school governors and the unperceived compulsion of generation lag.[2] The headmaster-compiler could usually spare no expense in producing his elaborately indexed hymnal.

THE CHANGING PURPOSE OF HYMN-SINGING

The earliest service-books, for Rugby in 1824 and Leeds Grammar School in 1826, were primarily intended as psalters and anthem-books. Rugby's had only four hymns, for morning, evening, Easter, and Whitsun. By 1843 it had 56, against 18 psalms and no anthems, by 1897 some 360 in elaborate liturgical sequence and by 1906 an editorial review of Rugby hymnals, the title "Hymns and Tunes . . . " and indexes of composers, tunes and metres as if to signal a musician's collection, with performance an end in itself.[3]

The headmaster of Leeds Grammar School expounds an associationist theory similar to that we have seen expounded by a Primitive Methodist contemporary of his: "The impressions made upon the mind in early life are so strong that they mix with our feelings, mould our opinions, become maxims of belief, and principles of action; even at an advanced age they return as something natural and congenial, and are seldom removed but by extreme violence." He calls it "an act of prudence" at the "dawn of understanding" to "tincture it" with the "doctrines" and precepts of spiritual religion, that "truths which in their origin are supernatural, may have an habitual and instinctive power, and be early incorporated into the moral nature." He finds no medium more suitable than "hymns or short pieces of religious poetry," wherein the "impression of truth is deepened by the force of imagination, with memory sided by the charm of the verse." To be lasting in effect, hymns should be "scriptural" in substance and "simple" in expression, yet "contain nothing offensive to the mature judgment."[4]

True to the law of generation lag, the headmaster employed an associationist principle derived from Locke and Hartley and accepted by the early Wordsworth. His endeavour, more acceptable in the generally Christian culture of his day than in our pluralist society, precludes both the *kenosis* of Watts and the sentimentalism of late Victorian child-centred hymnody. His collection, *Hymns and Paraphrases of Scripture*, conveys a Calvinistic moral theology that eschews any Wesleyan hymns, an effect, no doubt, of his own upbringing. In printing Ken's midnight petition for God to take "sole possession" as protective against nightmares and "thoughts impure," the headmaster clearly has in mind private reading for moral purposes. His printing of "There is a fountain filled with blood" under "Praise for Redemption," and "When darkness long has veil'd my mind" under "God Unchangeable" likewise implies private reading of poems that expound Calvinist doctrines. Other than by printing "O for a closer walk with God" under the simple and un-mystical heading "Walking with God," the headmaster makes no concessions to youth. Even now, when boys mature earlier, Cowper's metaphor of the soul as "nightingale" pouring forth "solitary lays," in "Far from the world, O Lord, I flee" would be adjudged outside a boy's emotional range. No doubt some lines under "Affliction Sanctified," "Thou madst me feel the chast'ning rod, / And straight I turn'd unto my God," had a more literal meaning.[5]

Consistent with his emphasis upon revealed truth, the headmaster prefers dogmatic to emotional expressions of Calvinism, excluding "Rock of Ages" and lyrics by Anne Steele in favour of some assertions extremely rare in school hymnals:

> What thousands never knew the road!
> What thousands hate it when 'tis known!
> None but the chosen tribes of God
> Will seek or choose it for their own.[6]

Some sentiments on Redemption appear straight out of Burns's "Holy Willie's Prayer" or Hogg's *Private Memoirs and Confessions of a Justified Sinner*:

> As man, he [Christ] pities my complaint,
> His pow'r and truth are all divine;
> He will not fail, he cannot faint,
> Salvation's sure, and must be mine.[7]

Such an assurance is further evidence of a schoolmaster's tendency to endorse ideas that were conventional in his own youth. Generation lag accounts also for the listing of "O God of Bethel," "The race that long in darkness pin'd" and "Hark, the glad sound!" not as hymns but as scriptural paraphrases. In general, the selection conveys an old-fashioned Calvinist emphasis on the omnipotence of God and helplessness of man, upon the impending judgment and the salvation of the chosen few cleansed in the blood of the Lamb. As a further mark of old-world belief, images that later generations would take literally have a theological sense, so that "Ye sons of earth, prepare the plough" is a meditation upon the Parable of the Sower.[8]

To the generation-lag characteristic of public figures whose ideas were formed in an earlier day can be traced a set of "Hymns for the Days of Creation," printed nearly fifty years later for the boys of Uppingham and Sherborne, two schools set in landscapes that make literal belief in the Garden of Eden seem the most natural thing in the world. Their headmasters took the lead in forming the Headmaster's Conference to defend their classical curriculum and social exclusiveness against proposed modernization and entry by competition.[9] Generation lag mainly accounts for a sermon that Thring wrote in 1887, but died before he could preach. Opening with an unequivocally fundamentalist assertion that man had chosen "knowledge-power" in preference to the love of God, so that his body, intellect and moral instincts that had "worked together in perfect order and . . . peace, were by the Fall set in rebellion and made enemies to one another," it expounds a Wordsworthian or Rousseauist antithesis between "city-vices" of corrupting knowledge and the "manly" virtues of "bravery, endurance, patience, temperance, purity, hardihood" and obedience to divine law to be ingrained by the muscular Christian discipline of the school. "God's plan" is fulfilled in that of "a School like this" where the alternation of games and studies affords "opportunities for manliness and self-denial" and the communal life "calls for gentleness and forbearance." Finally, Thring admonishes boys in "this sheltered home, this Garden of the Lord" to beware of sexual temptation and "pride of knowledge separate from God," so as to apply their gifts "in His kingdom of love."[10]

Though theologically pre-Darwinian, Thring's sermon is socially of its time in assigning to the school the function of a secluded garden (*hortus conclusus*) or enclave of heaven in a fallen world which St. Benedict had assigned to the monastery, and Watts to the Dissenting church, and that of character-building which Primitive Methodist hymnody, in particular, had assigned to the home.[11] Its emphasis upon "manliness" rather than scholarship is also of its time.[12]

Three years later, at Cheltenham College, the editor claims that a school hymnal should "link itself in the minds" of boys with "religious associations in the past, and memories of hours spent in the service of God in boyhood."[13] Compared with the Leeds headmaster's statement of threescore years earlier, this emphasizes the emotional associations of school worship rather than "truths" of supernatural origin to be "incorporated into the moral nature." As at Rugby hymn-singing apparently becomes an end in itself, so at Cheltenham, as at Uppingham, school replaced church and home as the formative influence. The Romantic cult of childhood developed into a Victorian cult of (boarding) schooldays that was to linger on in boys' stories until the Second World War, superimposing an anti-intellectual ideal of athleticism upon readers who mostly attended elementary or grammar schools.[14]

Between the fall of Napoleon and that of Kaiser Wilhelm II, the spiritual songs of the future rulers of the nation mainly responsible for their eclipse evolved from being wholly God-centred to being in some degree focused upon secular objects: school, social class, and country. Whereas the hymnal of Leeds Grammar School in 1826 was designed to reinforce the values of "godliness and good learning," most of those for public schools of the late nineteenth and early twentieth centuries instilled into the officer and gentleman class an ideal epitomized in a hymn for Manchester Grammar School in 1913 as "high manliness."

Service-books for the usually Anglican chapels of boarding schools, however, inevitably followed the liturgical calendar. Better than his subordinates, the ex-public schoolboy who rejected Christianity knew what he was rejecting. How far this applied to alumni of day-schools or those such as Bedales, at which hymns followed the rhythm of the school year, is more doubtful. The hymns sung in the vast majority of public schools conveyed "strong and manly sense," though to pupils older than those who used the inferior selections available at council schools.

CHANGING IMAGE AND ETHIC

Any public school hymnal issued before the mid-sixties differed radically from its successor in its Evangelical emphasis upon sin, death, and judgment. The year after Dr. Arnold's death, the boys he imbued with his liberal-Protestant ideals were among the first to sing Keble's socially compassionate hymn "Sun of my soul," yet also read or sang

> Dust or ashes though we be,
> Full of guilt and misery;
> Make us Thine, O son of God,
> Wash us in Thy precious blood.[15]

Seven years later, "Dies irae" and "Rock of Ages" were introduced by compilers presumably educated about the time of the Leeds hymnal.

At Harrow in 1855 C.J. Vaughan brought out a selection that comes as a breath of fresh air after the penny hymnals of National School children. Yet of the 242 hymns 38 (other than those on the Passion or Judgment) allude, often with grim concreteness, to death.[16] To confront youths less mature than their descendants with the dying man's "feeble pulse," "gasping breath," and "glazed eye" (143) or the "dark river" ahead argues a preoccupation with death, even among the aristocracy, only to be explained by the general susceptibility to disease before the coming of modern hygiene and medicine. Such verses as "What if death my sleep invade? / Shall I be of death afraid?" "When in the solemn hour of death, / I wait Thy just decree" (74), and the inevitable "Rock of Ages," suggest a comparable preoccupation with guilt, to be inflicted upon the growing boy. The book's collective viewpoint, Bunyanesque metaphors, and encouragement of boys to stride manfully toward the "bright city" rather than wallow in self-abasement are refreshing.[17] The death-wish of "Fain would we leave this weary road" (19), "Soon shall thy faithful people change / Their wilderness for heaven" (180) and (sung at Evensong) "Abide with me" (20), however, shows up the balance and moderation of John Percival's collection for Clifton College in 1863.

With Evangelicalism receding before the Oxford Movement, this young headmaster, who has been unfairly ridiculed in a recent book, but who was to show singular courage in opposing the British declaration of war in 1914, brought out a hymnal that also emphasized sin and the Last Things, but mingled newer and translated texts with those of Watts and Montgomery.[18]

Whether through generation lag or school tradition, an updated reprint of

Hymns for . . . Cheltenham College (1864), marks the extreme limit of Evangelical "unhealthy religion."[19] Centred like Bickersteth's *Hymnal Companion* (1870) upon the Passion rather than the Incarnation, it subjected boys to a forty-day Lenten barrage that included "Turn not Thy face away from me" (67), "Have mercy, Lord, on me" (68), "Oft in sorrow, oft in woe" (74), "When our heads are bowed with woe" (82), "Lord, as to Thy dear cross we flee" (81), "Lord, when we bend before Thy throne" (72), "O for a closer walk with God" (71), and of course "Rock of Ages" (80) and "Jesu, Lover of my soul" (79). In youth, a thick skin can be a blessing.

Of some dozen translations from Latin, three treat of death and judgment, and three of the exile's longing for heaven, while one of the "Vexilla regis" chronologically distances the "wonder . . . Which saints of old rejoiced to sing," yet brings the present worshippers into that most impersonal and objective of passion poems:

> Lord, in Thy Cross may we discern
> Our only hope, our way to heaven;
> To Thee in deep repentance turn,
> With longing eyes, to be forgiven.[20]

By the final quarter of the century, service-books in the now far more numerous "public" boarding-schools spanned the whole range of churchmanship. One for Wellington College, in 1880, resembled a breviary in providing hymns for twice-daily offices throughout the ecclesiastical year:[21] "When I survey the wondrous Cross" for "Eve of Good Friday," "Abide with me" for Tuesday Evening in Winter, and for the corresponding time in summer the Ambrosian hymn "Ere darkling wanes the day" with its plea for "stainless sleep." As in other late Victorian school hymnals, there are Latin texts for liturgical hymns ("Dies irae," "Veni Creator Spiritus") and for psalm titles. The selection includes Communion hymns by John Wesley and Conder,[22] but no sanguinary passion lyrics or sentimental nature poems.

The hymnody of the "Oxford malignants" seeped into the very tent of their long-dead foe, Thomas Arnold, for in 1876 the Rugby hymnal provided thirteen pages for Saints' Days, eighteen (pages) for the Christmas feasts, and twenty-one for Easter and Whitsun, though still thirty-one for Lent. By 1897, no distinctively "Noetic" flavour remained, for the 360 hymns, elaborately indexed and arranged according to the feasts and ferial Sundays of the Prayer Book, included some in the original Latin, and "Praise to the Holiest" by Newman the foremost "malignant," who had once enquired whether Dr. Arnold was a Christian.[23] At the opposite extreme stand one or two sentimental Victorian lyrics like "Jesu meek and gentle."

The collection best representing a central Anglican tradition, that for Clifton in 1885, balances some of the finest High Church lyrics—"As with gladness," "Earth has many a noble city," or "The King of Love . . . " —with translated German texts, "Sleepers, awake" or "Now thank we all our God," and previously omitted classics by Wesley ("Rejoice, the Lord is King") and Watts ("There is a land of pure delight"). Most typical of this "strong and manly" central Anglican tradition are the old psalm version "Through all the changing scenes of life" and the modern "Eternal father, strong to save."[24]

Inspiration was the raison d'être of hymnals set in the "muscular Christian" and Broad Church moulds. Though readily confused, these terms refer respectively to a stern yet bracing ethos of competitive struggle and an insistence upon the duty of social service. The one sent explorers to the South Pole, the other volunteers to East End settlements. Traceable, like Evangelicalism, to the Puritan legacy, these are not mutually exclusive. The "muscular Christian" hymnal for Uppingham and Sherborne (1874) eschews alike sentimental nativity and bloodthirsty passion lyrics for hymns of praise and pilgrimage.[25] Among these, a verse of "Through the day thy love has spared us" clearly bears a different meaning for the disciples of Thring than it had for those of Kelly during the Napoleonic wars:

> Pilgrims here on earth and strangers
> Dwelling in the midst of foes;
> Us and ours preserve from dangers,
> In Thine arms may we repose,
> And when life's sad day is past,
> Rest with Thee in heaven at last. (17)

To a mid-Victorian upper-class adolescent this could only refer to external struggles in distant lands or internal struggles against sexual and other temptations. Complementary to this puritan ethos of struggle was the gentlemanly ethos of "Work is sweet for God has blest / Honest work with quiet rest," by Thring's brother Godfrey, which exhorts boys to strive for what is "great and good" rather than "bought and sold" (154).[26] Where but in Rutland or Dorset could it seem so right to condition the young to fight manfully while despising the spirit of Victorian commerce?

The competitive ethos found its strongest voice in the redoubtable Miss Beale, who in 1889 issued for Cheltenham Ladies' College a supplement to *Church Hymns*. As such, her *School Hymns* need have neither liturgical pattern nor comprehensiveness. Miss Beale groups her extraordinary lyrics under yet stranger titles, that oscillate between randomness and intrusive logic. Thus Nos. 2-14 are headed: Joy; God's Workmen; Daisies; The Way, the Truth, the Life; The Glory of God; One Church, One Faith, One Lord; Praise; I have the Keys of Hell and Death; This is the House of God; Harvest; Choral Hymn; Morning Hymn; while Nos. 23-7 appear under God's Infinity, Eternity, Sovereignty, Spirituality, and Blessedness.[27]

Miss Beale brands her compilation with her realized eschatology and undiscriminating idealism. One soon ceases to count the reiterations of "Onward and upward." Confirmation candidates enlist as "God's soldiers" (1), workers as "God's workers" who with might and main "labour for the right" (3). Ladies-to-be must lead a life of constant challenge:

> Onward! the goal thou seekest
> Is worth the quest of a life;
> High is the prize above thee
> In the light of the golden sky. (37)

The sexual sublimation of "Dear Lord, in Thee I seek my rest . . . In deepest thankfulness / For Thy great love of me" and of "Shall this life of mine be wasted, its joy pass by untasted / And this soul remain unfilled" (49), is matched by sublimated ambition in "Never hasting, never resting. . . . Onward, upward ever press" (76), one of many hymns on work.

In one eschatological text, a bizarre image pleads for guidance from the "Judge" and "Eternal Fire of Wrath," identified with the fire of the Spirit that must "our baser dross consume" (9). This military image of the spiritual life might have frightened even St. Paul:

> Unfurl the Christian Standard, with firm and fearless hands
> For no pale flag of compromise with error's legion bands,
> And no faint-hearted flag of truce with Mischief and with Wrong
> Should lead the soldiers of the Cross, the faithful and the
> strong. (35)

Broad Church optimism, the tendency to seek the kingdom of God in social action, were within a few years to turn into a strident nationalism all too evident in some Unitarian lyrics that greeted the outbreak of the First World War.[28]

Miss Beale's book, needless to say, admits no such perversions, though it does include virtually Unitarian praises of an abstract deity in "Holy and Infinite! Viewless, Eternal" (23), of whose "essence pure" (26) we can form no image. Its predominant heresy is a pelagian view of Heaven as reward for good works and ceaseless effort; its defect, for which one is almost grateful, a lack of clear sense and of poetic rhythm that must have rendered most hymns unsingable. Both characteristics emerge from

> Now the sowing and the weeping,
> Working hard and waiting long;
> Afterward the golden reaping!
> . . .
> Now the plunge, the briny burden;
> . . .
> Afterward, the pearly guerdon. (36)

It is the rare hymn that eschews this triumphalist, this ultimately egocentric gospel of work, "our highest mission" on which "all blessing centres" (112), this assurance of, rather than resignation to, a "life portioned out" (81). A revealing text in the Appendix of 1908 foists a male identity upon the girls, "youthful soldiers of the Lord" seemingly destined never to beat their swords into knitting needles. Miss Beale envisaged a post-Victorian woman neither dependent upon the male nor circumscribed by home and church, but making her own way in the world.[29] For all their strident rhetoric, the lyrics of her pioneer venture in feminist hymnody hold out more hope than the verses on life resigned or deferred that were thrust before Sunday or elementary school children, or even middle-class girls and women.

Predictably, the other Broad Church specimen came from Bedales, a *Psalm and Hymn-book* (1901),[30] in which the forty-three psalms and thirty-eight hymns imply that, *pace* Blake, there *is* a natural religion. This selection has no carols, no passion-hymns, nor any on sin or death. It represents a "healthy-minded" conditioning to activism, belief in progress, and worship of a Creator confined neither by dogma, tribe nor class. A mere cluster of early psalm-heads will make the point about God: Nos. 1, "O Lord our Governor" (Ps. 8); 2, "Preserve me, O God" (Ps. 16); 4, "Lord who shall dwell" [in thy tabernacle] (Ps. 15); 5, "The Lord is my Shepherd" (Ps. 23); 6, "The earth is the Lord's" (Ps. 24); 7, "The heavens declare (the glory of God)" (Ps. 19); 8, "God is our hope" (46); 9, "Rejoice in the Lord" [alway] (Ps. 33).

The hymns, arranged in general progression through the school year, develop two related themes. The first is a collective pilgrimage in, for example, "Soldiers of Christ, arise" (3), "Onward, brothers" (4), and "Through the night of doubt and sorrow" (5); the second, collective trust in a broadly religious tradition, evident in "O God, our help in ages past" (6) and "All people that on earth do dwell" (7). Here we have what Coleridge, inspirer of the Broad Church leader F.D. Maurice, called the fundamental polarity within English society, that between permanence and change.[31]

Some lyrics, "Strong Son of God" (21) or "Through all the changing scenes of life" (32), represent a hopeful pressing forward; others, such as "City of God, how broad and far" (23), "Now thank we all our God" (25), or "Ein feste Burg" (28), a restful assurance of divine favour.

A group of American hymns bears witness to the prevailing liberal ethic: "Life of ages, richly poured / Love of God . . . flowing in the Prophet's word / And people's liberty" (8) or the Abolitionist song "Once to every man and nation" (9). Others, mostly American, affirm a unitarian theology: "O God, in whom we live and move / Thy love is law, Thy law is love" (10), the law fulfilling both "Man's hope, and God's all-perfect will."[32] A few, like "Praise the Lord! ye heavens adore him" (33) affirm the transcendent Creator.

While the Bedales collection would refresh any reader wearied by enervating, sentimental, or patriotic hymnody for lower-class children, the faith that idealistic teenagers acquired in that most hopeful of modern communities can scarcely have been Christianity. Too many of their hymns ignored those realities of evil, suffering, and death into which the boys, at least, were destined to undergo so terrible an initiation in 1914.

More than any other, the service-book used in the chapel of Harrow School by Winston Churchill brings together diverse strains in contemporary school religion, indeed in contemporary life.[33] Such was the influx of new hymns that H.M. Butler, while deleting a quarter of the previous 242, raised the total to 453. Those omitted mostly concerned death, affliction and the vanity of this life: "O'er the gloomy hills of darkness" or "The world is grown old, and her pleasures are past." Some no less evangelical replacements had more literary merit: "Hark, my soul, it is the Lord" or "Love Divine, all love excelling." A few like "There is a fountain filled with blood" should doubtless have stayed out.

The collection as a whole exhibits High Church and Broad Church lying uneasily in one bed, with Low Church's covered body just visible between. The liturgical arrangement, the evocations by Bernard and others of the heavenly Jerusalem (121-8), the "Dies irae," "Veni Creator Spiritus" and the lovely "Veni, sancte Spiritus," all in Latin as well as in English, proclaim a powerful Anglo-Catholic influence. A number of items, nevertheless, brand this collection as late Victorian. Appeals to sanctify "each brave and holy vow" (309); petitions for social justice to invalids, widows and orphans (31); resolutions that "farm and merchandise . . . freely given . . . be freely shared" (53); above all, Carlylean praises of work, a "soul be up and doing" strain, show how Broad Church piety had spread from Dr. Arnold. Life no longer begins at the death-bed, for Christ has become a brother, guide and comrade. School disperses singing: "Be our pattern ne'er forgot; / Friend of boyhood, leave us not." (391)[34] Like the "childhood's pattern" phrase in "Royal David's city" (one of twenty carols, compared with scarcely any in 1855), this betokens moral will rather than awe, worship or fearful dependence.

Even secular work has religious meaning, for the singers are not prospective miners or foundrymen but future civil servants, officers, politicians, or judges, whom God must teach to live, for " 'Tis easier far to die" (420). Yet many happily ephemeral verses, whether sung or thumbed over in sermon-time, show this late Victorian social conscience tinged with sentimentality.[35] Though hymns formed but part of their indoctrination, these young patricians seem too earnest, their world too kindly. An after-dinner speaker at Hurstpierpoint carries more conviction about public school life: "I was sent to Mr. Baring-Gould. He gave me 32 cuts, then went back to writing 'Onward, Christian soldiers'." His story cannot be true, for the dates will not fit, yet it sheds a truer light upon Victorian male psychology.[36]

As the God once regnant in dreadful majesty walks beside the growing boy, the future English establishment enjoys its sense of mission, its belief in the consecration of its class and country. No hymn better embodies this than a curious variant of "Let us with a gladsome mind," by Dean Arthur Penrhyn Stanley, Dr. Arnold's ex-pupil and biographer. Its eight stanzas give thanks: that "Long our Island throne has stood"; for this "Home and refuge of the free"; for monarchs from Alfred to Victoria; for statesmen like Chatham; for Shakespeare and Milton; for soldiers, sailors, scientists, and engineers. The final stanza epitomizes most of what late Victorian England stood for:

> Give us homes serene and pure,
> Settled freedom, laws secure;
> Truthful lips and minds sincere,
> Faith and love that cast out fear:
> Grant that Light and life divine
> Long on England's shores may shine;
> Grant that people, Church and Throne
> May in all good deeds be one. (446)[37]

No wonder that the greatest Old Harrovian, who doubtless sang these lines, felt himself walking with destiny as he entered the Palace in 1940, and ordered "Fight the good fight" and "John Brown's body" sung at his funeral.

One oddity in the Harrow book, a frontal reprint of "Blest are the pure in heart" outlined in red, serves to illustrate a taboo more explicit in a preparatory school hymnal of 1894. This time the frontispiece also includes a mysterious Greek text on homosexuality, while various hymns obliquely reprove that vice and masturbation.[38] A translation of the Ambrosian hymn "Lux surgit aurea" urges boys to "cast aside the works of darkness" that have "led" their "souls astray," warning them that "All day long an Eye is o'er" them, which "every secret knows" (24). Next, one by Neale enquires whether their "toils and woes" and "the foe's attacks" increase, urging them to gaze with "unshrouded" eyes upon the Cross (25). In the context of these and further lyrics in this vein, another Ambrosian petition, for "faith deep rooted in the soul" to subdue their flesh and control their minds, must in a sexual sense have implied to precocious boys that "guile" and "discord" should give way to "inner joy and peace" (3).

This survey has somewhat overrepresented some extremes to highlight an evolution of public school religion through the century from a dignified yet sombre view of this life *sub specie aeternitatis* into an ethic ranging from the Anglo-Catholic routine of future Army officers at Wellington to the strenuous work ethic of future missionaries or suffragettes at Uppingham or Cheltenham, or the kindlier ideals of future rulers at Harrow. If anything united this "tribe" of privileged young people, it was a body of stock hymns that returned collective thanks for their freedom to choose a worthy calling in life.

In literary taste, the hymnal for Marlborough College (1878)[39] excels all its rivals. Less optimistic than that of Harrow, it shows even less preoccupation with blood, death, and self-laceration. Its preponderance of translations from German, rather than Latin, reflects an Evangelical tendency, but its Wesleyan and Victorian items were chosen with discrimination.[40] Its acknowledged source, *Hymns Ancient and Modern*, doubtless prompted a use of plural pronouns even in penitential hymns.

How does this best primer of Victorian public school religion differ from any modern equivalent? First, it attaches religious import to the close of day, at which time the modern schoolboy would not expect to sing "Sun of my soul" or "Through the day Thy love has spared us," still less "Abide with me." Second, it treats life more solemnly, for in Advent it offers not only still familiar texts but two versions of the "Dies irae," and Bonar's melancholy reflection that after "A few more years" have rolled, "we shall be with those that rest . . . within the tomb."[41] From a heart "athirst to know" Christ within, the Marlburian could sing "Just as I am," "My faith looks up to thee" or even "Lord, as to Thy dear cross we flee," with its plea for "our selfishness" to be supplanted by divinely induced kindness. In Passion Week, he could sing "Rock of Ages" or a translation of "Stabat mater" but never "There is a fountain filled with blood." At no time would he sing of pearly gates or golden harps.

This impression of *gravitas* without morbidity comes over most strongly from the confirmation hymns "Thine for ever," "Soldiers of Christ arise," or How's now forgotten "Lord, thy children guide and keep," a text that in working-class vein pictures life as a "weary wilderness" but in public school vein condemns "slothful ease" in "flowery glades." The work ethic of "Christian, seek not yet repose" and "Strive aright when God doth call thee" (211-12) is set out in two hymns set for Ember Days which epitomize the Victorian upper-class sense of responsibility. "O Thou who makest souls to shine" (146), dangles no pie-in-the-sky to ensure continuing submission:

> Give those who teach pure hearts and wise,
> Faith, hope, and love, all warmed by prayer;
> Themselves first training for the skies,
> They best will raise their people there.
>
> Give those who learn the willing ear,
> The spirit meek, the guileless mind;
> Such gifts will make the lowliest here
> Far better than a kingdom find. (146)[42]

Likewise Montgomery's "Lord, now Thy Spirit from on High" (147), sets before the clerisy a better principle than exploitation: "To bear Thy people in their heart (*sic*), / And love the souls whom Thou dost love."

CHANGING SUBSTANCE

Neither hymn can be counted among the "simple, stirring songs" that, according to Gathorne-Hardy, bound together the ruling class educated at public schools. The filament had other strands: a modicum of classical literature, superseded increasingly by an obsession with sport, and after that by a military ethos of officers and gentlemen.[43] Undeniably, from about 1860 the morning and evening hymns sung in the solemn setting of the school chapel (Charterhouse being the main exception)[44] had an importance second only to that of the Lord's Prayer. But did boys at different schools, or father and son at the same school, sing the same hymns? A computer search of selected hymnals for two periods, 1870-85 and 1890-1905, enables us to answer these questions with some certainty.

In the earlier period, those of Uppingham and Sherborne (1874), Harrow (1881), and Rugby (1885) exclude only the extremes of churchmanship. To compensate for omissions from the shortest list, titles omitted from the Uppingham book were checked against those for Clifton and Marlborough, and the 79[45] found in at least four are presumed to have been widely accepted in public schools. Among 35 found in any three,[46] "Just as I am" and

"Guide me, O thou great Jehovah" might be given out by any chaplain not avowedly anti-Evangelical.

In the later period, indexes for Cheltenham College (1890), Harrow (1895) and the *Public School Hymn Book* (1904) offer a wider range of churchmanship and a greater certainty that the 135 hymns found in all three[47] were widely used. The 51 found in at least three earlier but not all later lists fall into the following groups: (1) superseded translations and psalm-versions, or obsolescent texts by Watts or Wesley, the exceptions being "Stabat mater" and "Deck thyself, my soul, with gladness";[48] (2) redundant, "bloody," or sentimental texts, "As the hart the brooks desireth" or "The roseate hues of early dawn," but also, unaccountably, "Just as I am," "Lord, thy word abideth," and "Ye servants of God"; (3) omissions from the Cheltenham book of some standard Christmas and Easter hymns (perhaps on account of school holidays) but also, unaccountably, of "Praise the Lord! ye heavens adore him"; (4) omissions from the Harrow revision of "O worship the King" and two Nonconformist eucharistic hymns with Anglican equivalents.[49] Oddly enough, of eleven preserved in but a single book, "Father, I know that all my life / Is portioned out for me" lived on only at Harrow.

Of eleven found in all three later books but none of the earlier, several have a military flavour: "Conquering Kings their titles take"; "Fight the good fight"; "O Son of God, our Captain of salvation" and "Onward, Christian soldiers," while "Father let me dedicate" and "Through the night of doubt and sorrow"[50] have notes of pilgrimage and service.

As an alternative to the tedium of lists, let us imagine hearing a series of broadcasts in, say, 1885, entitled "From the School Chapels," including hymns found in at least four of our earlier indexes. Being designed to illustrate school worship, the services take place on weekdays or Sundays throughout the year.

The voices, which surprise us by being largely treble, greet the new day with the hymn that has given its name to the BBC morning service, with "Awake, my soul" or else Wesley's canticle to the sun within the heart.[51] As an alternative, the chaplain may have set a versified psalm of praise, "O worship the King," "Praise the Lord, ye heavens adore Him," or even one familiar only to our grandfathers, "Before Jehovah's awful throne." A day of thanksgiving may call for "Praise my soul, the King of Heaven." More often a keynote of pilgrimage or self-dedication calls for "Lead us, heavenly Father, lead us," "O God of Bethel," "Just as I am," or a hymn so unfamiliar that we strain to catch the words:

> Thy way, not mine, O Lord,
> However dark it be:

> Lead me by thine own hand,
> Choose out the path for me.

Why must these late Victorian young gentlemen, among the most privileged ever to walk the earth, sing of a path, smooth or rough, that leads "Right onward to thy rest," of daring not to choose their lot? Surely these lines are not for them:

> Choose thou for me my friends,
> My sickness or my health:
> Choose thou my cares for me,
> My poverty or wealth.[52]

Bonar had a wider spectrum of society in mind, yet his words mean much to the new boy exposed to the predictable bully or occasional epidemic, and very much at the mercy of the system.

In the evening, especially in winter, the songs have a mournful tinge. Their words, however, exude a sense of trust in Providence, in "Through all the changing scenes of life," or "All praise to thee, my God, this night" with its prayer to be forgiven the "ill that I this day have done" and filled with "heavenly" rather than "impure" thoughts when lying awake in the dark. The melody by Tallis touches the heart with nostalgia for days when all counselling came from the clergy and young men hoped by chaste living to "rise glorious at the awful day."[53] The alternative, "Sun of my soul," brings to mind the candles and frock-coated doctor by the sickbed of the affluent, while the poor, in humbler dwellings, depended on charity or providence. "Abide with me" at Evening Prayer may even raise a smile at Victorian sentimentality.

What we hear on Sundays depends on the scripture-reading, sermon, and liturgical season. At any time we might hear "As pants the hart," "God moves in a mysterious way," "Love Divine," or "Blest are the pure in heart." In Advent, "Lo! he comes" or "Hark the glad sound" will be familiar, but the sombre chorale of "Great God, what do I see or hear,"[54] and still more the plainchant of "Dies irae," in Latin or English, may appal us notwithstanding that in our day the young can "see the end of things appear" while recognizing no likeness between the threat of nuclear war and the predictions of the biblical Apocalypse. Near Christmas the boys will sing "Hark! the herald angels" or "While Shepherds watched" rather than those sentimental carols on King Wenceslas or the Child of Bethlehem usually associated with late-Victorians, and for the commencement of the Lent (not "Spring") Term familiar Epiphany hymns by Montgomery, Heber, or Dix. As Lent drags on through the fag-end of winter, "Jesu, Lover," "Rock of Ages," "Saviour, when in dust to thee," or "Father of heaven, whose love profound'' may remind us how necessary penitence and resignation must have seemed to the boy supposedly sheltered from the world, but actually exposed to the wrath of headmaster, prefect, or bully and the blandishments of the dormitory seducer. How otherwise can these dark-suited boys vent emotions that would embarrass us: "Before thy throne, we sinners bend" or "Wash me, Saviour, or I die"? At Passion-time, we are sure to hear "When I survey" or "Go to dark Gethsemane" but listen in vain for "There is a green hill" or even "Ride on, ride on in majesty" and "Vexilla regis."

At Easter-tide our favourite hymns resound in lusty chorus, but in Ascension-tide not "Crown him with many crowns" nor at Whitsun "Breathe on me, breath of God." Indeed, though their tunes be familiar, "Veni Creator Spiritus" and "Veni, sancte Spiritus" may well be sung in Latin, so we can only join them in singing "Our blest Redeemer, ere He breathed."

At Trinity, the boys are not limited to "Holy! holy! holy!," for their chaplain might prescribe the "holy chant and psalm" of "Three in One, and One in Three," including either the morning petition for "Light Divine" and the "balm" of charity or the "vesper" prayer for "sin forgiven." If it be audible, does the initial metaphor of the next line "*Fold us in the peace of heaven*" refer to God as Shepherd or as mother?[55] The boys, perhaps, envisage heaven as sheepfold and unconsciously long for it as the maternal embrace. For a number of "green Sundays" in Trinity they will be on vacation, but on missionary occasions they sing Anglican classics, "Thou whose almighty word" and at All Saints "The Son of God goes forth to war" instead of the expected ones "Jesus shall reign" and "For all the saints." If privileged to hear an ancestor confirmed, after the episcopal sermon we may well hear "Thine for ever" (but not "O Jesus, I have promised"), then at the First Communion, "O God unseen, but ever near." At the end, the schoolfriends and the proud parents of the newly-confirmed will raise the chapel roof with "Soldiers of Christ, arise" or "Lead us, heavenly Father, lead us."

To hear "Onward, Christian soldiers" we should need to listen to the following series of "From the School Chapel," covering services of the next generation in, say, 1901.

In that year, "O God, our help in ages past," "Jerusalem the golden," "Nearer, my God, to thee" or, of course, "Abide with me" might record the school's grief at the passing of the Queen. Now, however an occasion for national relief or jubilation prompts the chaplain to set "Nun danket" rather than the once-common "Ein feste Burg." (Of necessity, English schoolboys have always sung German hymns in English.)

During our second series of broadcasts, most of the former hymns will be heard again. Additions to the repertoire will be old favourites unaccountably neglected earlier: "Ride on . . . in majesty" or "We sing the praise of him who died." Conceivably, generation lag might have kept from the earlier repertoire "It came upon the midnight clear," "Through the night of doubt and sorrow," and "The King of love my Shepherd is," which now replaces "The Lord my pasture shall prepare." Why the earlier boys had to sing "Christian, seek not yet repose" instead of the older text that has replaced it, "Forth in thy name, O Lord, I go" is not the mystery it first seemed. As the Evangelical tide receded, to "Watch and pray," gird on heavenly armour "night and day" against evil powers, and listen to the inner voice no longer attracted the chaplains and headmasters compiling hymnals, who preferred the healthier spirit of Wesley's hymn on work. In fact, activism was now in fashion, with "Fight the good fight" a great favourite, together with "There is a book who runs may read," or in harvest-time the rousing "We plough the fields and scatter," even though it was father's tenants who ploughed. In keeping with this more bracing tone is a hymn on the healing miracles, "Thine arm, O Lord, in days of old," which encourages boys to improve the lot of those less fortunate. Its tune, "St. Matthew" (fortuitously recalling the contemporary guild of Christian Socialists) is sung in rousing unison during the petitions of the final verse, which are surely more appropriate for the order-giving class than those of the earlier hymns on resignation:

> Restore and quicken, soothe and bless
> With thine almighty breath;
> To hands that work, and eyes that see,
> Give wisdom's heavenly lore . . . [56]

At the same time, some curiously subjective lyrics by Bonar have crept into the repertoire. Admittedly, boys sing not "I lay my sins on Jesus" or "I was a wandering sheep," but examples more suited to their estate: "Here, O my Lord, I see thee face to face," or "I heard the voice of Jesus say" at the Communion service. In the latter case, they may occasionally feel "Weary, and worn, and sad" but attend more to the final resolve to "walk" in Christ, that "light of life," "Star," and "Sun" till "travelling days are done."[57] No doubt any broadcast that includes "A few more years shall roll" takes place soon after the death of a beloved master or boy.

To conclude, in the final quarter of the nineteenth century the new paganism by which the nation acquired a sacredness formerly imputed to the Church had not overtaken the public schools, much as the "military" hymns of that era might have lent themselves to it. The generation that furnished the harassed administrators and senior officers who directed operations during the First World War sang a range of hymns representing a faith at once more profound and less distorted by jingoism or sentimentality than was to be found in the hymnody of their contemporaries at Sunday or elementary school.

12

CLASS IN THE DOOMED GENERATION

What of the faith and fire within us
Men who march away?[1]

In the prosperous and secure England of Edward VII, the man who cried aloud in the streets that its schoolboys stood as little chance of surviving into their middle age as any since the Black Death would have been ignored as a lunatic. The spokesmen of that "lost" generation, who composed bitter sonnets or autobiographies during or after the deluge, a Wilfred Owen or Robert Graves, belonged to a tiny minority that had attended "public" boarding-schools and perhaps Oxford or Cambridge before being commissioned for hostilities only as "trusty and well-beloved" junior officers. Few privates had the skill, influence or, strangely enough, incentive, to publish their recollections. At all events none became household words like Rupert Brooke and Donald Hankey before disillusionment set in, or Owen, Siegfried Sassoon, and Graves thereafter.[2]

We can lift the curtain a little on how the convictions of privates may have differed from those of their officers by considering the religious lyrics sung at council schools in general, and specifically in a great industrial city. To judge solely from the *Council School* (1905), *Birmingham School* (1901, 1904), and *Public School* (1903) hymn books, the differences amounted to one religion for the semi-literate and another for the well-educated. The gap was the narrower for the fact that those children of tradespeople, artisans, or clerks who attended Sunday-school sang devotional hymns that were also printed in public school collections. Even they did not sing them day by day, while the barely literate children of the casually employed probably sang only those printed in the council school book, or, in poorer districts, copied out on wallboards.

Our three chosen collections—hereafter called P for Public School, C for Council School and B for Birmingham—had but 16 items in common. C and B shared 39, P and B 11, P and C 28, while P had no fewer than 293 (out of 348) all to itself. That P catered for older pupils, unlikely to leave day-schools before sixteen, or boarding-schools before eighteen, matters less than may appear, the question being what impression of Christian faith and devotion school-leavers seem likely to have formed.

Of the sixteen common hymns, six were for Christmas or other seasons and at least three for morning services. Of the remaining eight, "O worship the King" and "O[ur] God, our help in ages past" also belong to the slender national inheritance. The Christmas and Epiphany lyrics known to all included neither the most sentimental, "Away in a manger" and "O little Child of Bethlehem," nor "Good King Wenceslas" nor, surprisingly, "O come, all ye faithful." Not a single passion lyric or Easter hymn appeared in all three, and only the sentimental "Our blest Redeemer, ere He breathed" for Whitsuntide.

All but three of the sixteen listed at the end of this chapter remain in common use and for the most part represent "healthy-minded" and objective religion. A few, however, may have meant different things to pupils from different social backgrounds.

For all who knew its biblical source, "Fight the good fight with all thy might" carried the invigorating message "Lay hold on life"; for those who did not, mainly future private soldiers, it probably had a more literal meaning.[3] Again, Wesley's great hymn on work might mean one thing to the singer from a professional-class home and another to one whose father came home in dirty overalls after bearing his "easy yoke" in a furnace or machine-shop.

Before embarking on a detailed contrast between public and elementary school hymnody in the early twentieth century, we should notice the rather different set of titles common to P and either B or C, also printed at the end of the chapter. P and B share one Easter hymn, one for Confirmation, and a number used in evening or other devotions: "Abide with me," "Lead, kindly Light," and "Jesu, Lover of my soul" or "When all thy mercies." P shares with C some further devotional hymns, "Love divine, all loves excelling" or "Sun of my soul," for example, but also the most invigorating of Palm Sunday, thanksgiving, and praise hymns, "All glory, laud, and honour," "Nun danket," and "Praise the Lord, ye heavens adore Him," as well as the most healthy-minded of all on heaven, "Come, let us join our cheerful songs."

It is reasonable to infer that except for a few characteristically solemn nineteenth-century lyrics on the existential journey through doubt, darkness, and the grave, this core of hymns would have conveyed joy in life and thankfulness, but that the only liturgical season commonly celebrated was Christmas.

Another way of inferring the trend of school hymnody is by comparing obsolescent with brand-new lyrics. Cennick's "Children of the heavenly King" (1742), now little used outside the churches, presents life as a journey to heaven "In the way our fathers trod." In this context, two lines near the end, "Lord, obediently we go, / Gladly leaving all below" imply apostolic submission to the divine will, not obedience to superiors in factory or front line. Again, "Fair waved the golden corn" (1851), no nature poem but an account of how the Israelites gave their first fruits to the Lord, likewise encouraged self-dedication. "Go, when the morning shineth" (1831) instils the habit not of work but of prayer.[4]

By contrast, "From homes of quiet peace" (1901), composed for the Boer War and too late for B, enlists the Almighty on the side of the British troops as their "strength and stay" in peril, with them when they "fight" and when they "fall," though with the reservation

> Let Thine Almighty Arm
> Be their defence and shield,
> And whosesoever cause is Thine
> To them the victory yield.

The author, the Anglican clergyman R.P. Draper, composed the much more nationalistic "What can I do for England / That does so much for me?" but redeemed himself by fashioning from the Franciscan "Canticle to the Sun" one of the few established classics of this century, "All creatures of our God and King."

Though his battle hymn is more illustrative of the Anglican penchant for having things both ways than of jingoism, Draper, a former barrister and once Master of the Temple, unwittingly participated in the secularization of hymnody by sanctifying the tendency to regard the national interest in a religious light, to accord the earthly realm a veneration once reserved for the heavenly. To what extent compulsory Scripture teaching counteracted this tendency depended on the school. In the early 1930s a head-teacher educated near the end of last century made children salute the flag each afternoon on leaving my first elementary school, and in 1935, at my next, we sang "What can I do for England" when celebrating a royal jubilee.

That lyric, which Draper composed for the *Council School* book of 1905, is simply a secular song instilling love of "ancient cities," "villages," "cottages," oneness with the "merry children / Who with me work and play," and pride in the nation's history, its "great and glorious name" which the singer must not stain. Idolatry becomes evident in the religious language and motifs appropriated to patriotic devotion, the resolve to be "One of England's 'faithful children'," the sense of being "Safeguarded" and "Watched over day by day" by her "armies," rather than by guardian angels.[5]

Two texts common to P and C illustrate secularization and class signification. In Wesley's "A charge to keep I have" (1762), based on Matthew Henry's scripture commentary, the singer gives first priority to saving and fitting "for the sky" his "never-dying soul." To this he regards serving "the present age" in his "calling" as subsidiary. The second verse, on preparation for Judgment by self-examination and dependence on God, originally ended "if I my trust betray, / I shall for ever die," altered in the Council School book (106) to "and let me ne'er my trust betray, / But press to realms on high." Even without the threat of hell (in Wesleyan phrase the "death that never dies"), the eighteenth-century master clearly regards work as ancillary to the quest for salvation.[6]

The Unitarian minister William Gaskell, husband of the novelist, composed his "Though lowly here our lot may be" for poor children in mid-Victorian Manchester. Their "high work" consists of following "Him / Whose lot was lowly too." Admirably avoiding celestial day-dreams, Gaskell has his singers bear their "days of darkness" strengthened by "a Father's love" with hopes "fixed . . . above" yet resolved to live here the Christian life "enriched with gentle thoughts" and "loving deeds." That life is a "stream" that "nobler grows" when "nearer to the sea" of death. In God's "clear sight" they do their "high work" if faithful to duty and conscience "However tried and pressed," thus making the "lowliest lot / With rays of glory bright" and turning their "crown of thorns" into a "crown of light."[7] I give so much detail of this lyric, which evidently owes something to Wordsworth's "Ode to Duty," to show how the Unitarian tilts the balance from myth and soteriology toward the Christian social ethic. In what sense, it may be asked, could the privileged pupils at boarding or independent day-schools have found this hymn applicable to their circumstances? In the former, they served their seniors as fags, and in both were encouraged to think of work as duty or service rather than a means of acquisition.

Upon elementary school pupils destined to become infantrymen or sailors, as upon their Victorian forebears, the hymn enjoined a kind of stoicism or quietism, an identification of their lot with the Way of the Cross. More moralist than poet, Gaskell stood at the mid-point between Wesley's internalizing of the Christian mythos and George Eliot's rejection of God and Immortality in favour of Duty, in the famous story of her walk in the Cambridge college garden.[8] Gaskell's sentiments must have seemed very real to the soldier who remembered them in the trenches, or to the soldier's wife struggling to rear their children.

Some texts must always have required too much of singers due to leave school at thirteen. In Wesley's "O for a heart to praise my God" the difficult lines on the heart not resting till of its "Eden repossest" was omitted, but the qualifiers "resigned, submissive, meek . . . humble, lowly, contrite . . . believing, true and clean" epitomized religion for the lower orders. The child, however, can rarely have sung from a heart that "Always feels Thy Blood / So freely spilt for me," and in which "only Christ is heard to speak."[9]

Any final judgment of the difference between the beliefs and attitudes hymns transmitted to the officer and to the private must depend on the texts common to B and C but not to P, and the much larger number found in P alone. The former are listed at the end of this chapter; of the latter only an impression can be given.

Some lyrics found in B and C—"Let us with a gladsome mind," "There is a green hill," "Once in Royal David's city," or "Lord, Thy word abideth"—the Public School editors did wrong to omit. As the list will show, the remainder found in B and C alone represent the worst elements in Victorian hymnody for children: the cult of littleness, didacticism, escapist visions of heaven, imitation romantic nature poetry, and a patriotism more secular than messianic.

Elementary school children, though not public school adolescents, must have sung one or two at least of "A little kingdom I possess," "O what can little hands do?," "There's a Friend for little children," "We are but little children weak," and "Jesus, from thy throne on high," in the last of which "little lambs" with "little hearts," "little ears," and "little lips," leading "little lives," offer their praise. The many who ceased to worship between leaving school and attending their first church parade must have remained theologically fixated, having tacitly assigned to childhood the "sweet story of old," and rejected it in adolescence like other fairy-tales. Even the sound ethic of self-restraint in "We are but little children . . . " came tainted with adult and class patronage of the lower-class bearer of "little crosses." Public School editors could put away childish worship as compilers for younger pupils could not.

The latter failed in discrimination. They rightly included "New every morning," which they could sing as adults, and children sing as children. They wrongly included "Kind words can never die," the sentimentalism of which they projected upon the children they invited to think of such words lying deep in the heart as "childhood's simple rhyme / Said o'er a thousand times." To neither adults nor children would it occur to compare the recurrence of "sweet thoughts" with the blooming of flowers after dew (st. 2). Both could believe that though the body lie in the tomb the peacefully departed soul will live with Christ (st. 3) without seeing how this follows from the earlier comparisons.[10] Again, "We plough the fields and scatter" expresses what grown-ups have often thought and felt, "All things bright and beautiful" what adults assuming a child-like naïveté have felt. "Summer suns are glowing," sung with the élan of its tune, was omitted by the more critical editors of the Public School collection, doubtless on account of some inane lines.

Even the finest hymns based on the argument from design—"We plough the fields . . . " or "The spacious firmament on high"—pose an insoluble problem for the post-Darwinian compiler. "There's not a tint that paints the rose," found in both elementary school hymnals, as in many others for children, may lack the dignity of Addison's "The Spacious firmament" but on the author's assumption makes perfectly good sense, from its opening statement that God "placed" the hues and patterns to its final ascription of light from distant stars to "heavenly skill" and providence.[11] Any modern Christian must in some degree concur while knowing that genetics and physics have relegated both the celestial flower-painter and the geocentric cosmos to the nursery. "All things bright and beautiful," with the aid of a sprightly tune, has survived because Mrs. Alexander remained content to list flora, fauna, and features of landscape and climate in general terms, as objects of her refrain-clause "The Lord God made them all," and finally shift into the viewpoint of the children who play, gather rushes, and acknowledge the gifts of senses and consciousness wherewith to enjoy "all things" and praise their Creator. The "rich man in his castle" verse having died with Queen Victoria, only the verb "made" and the "Lord God" epithet from Genesis remain to tie her text to the old Judaeo-Christian world-picture. It doubtless embarrasses the adolescent more than the adult.

The Public School editors provided texts that early adolescents about to put away childish things could sing without embarrassment. While their students were singing "God moves in a mysterious way," their compeers at senior elementary schools were being fobbed off with infantile texts like "God will take care of you," with its eye of Jesus watching each "little one" work or play. Those alumni of public schools who rejected Christianity did so on other grounds than as something to be grown out of, like short pants or picture-books. For generations the clergyman's most intractable problem in working-class areas of industrial cities such as Birmingham has been the inability of working men to envisage Christianity as a religion for grown-ups. His colleague in Hampshire or Sussex, where a larger proportion of parishioners were educated at public or grammar schools, has had an easier task.

The 293 texts in P alone convey the substance of a religion for grown-ups: "When I survey the wondrous Cross" (84) or "How sweet the name of Jesus" (92) commitment to the Redeemer; "As pants the hart" (214), "Blest are the pure in heart" (218) or "O for a thousand tongues" (291) hunger and thirst after God and His righteousness. Those who had used this hymnal carried into adult life lines that embodied fundamental Christian teaching and experience, on the Passion, of religious longing, on growth through adversity, of sacramental worship, and on the Last Things. All too probably the worker from a non-worshipping home carried only favourite carols and memories of hymns embodying the largely non-scriptural religion he had left behind with childhood. His condition was foreign to the North American worker or even the British Catholic.

As regards patriotic hymnody, the distinction is more complex. B and C carried the National Anthem and "God bless our native land" (set, ironically, to the tune "Moscow"). This was by no means jingoistic, pleading first for British rights to depend "on war no more," and subsequently for the sovereign to be inspired with "wisdom from above," and for "just and righteous laws" to govern peoples who formed "one family." If the initial wish for Britain to extend her power in peaceful ways has a trace of double-think, the universalism of the remaining petitions qualifies British pride in the "home of the brave and free." The author of the English version, a journalist named William Hickson who campaigned for popular education, would surely have been repelled by Edwardian jingoism.[12] Two world wars and the threat of a nuclear holocaust having made nonsense of idolatrous nationalism, how much sounder appear this early Victorian layman's sentiments than those of the Edwardian priest Draper, let alone those of Kipling's notorious lines for the Diamond Jubilee. In Hickson's time neither public nor council school pupil was invited to praise God as "Lord of our far-flung battle-line" granting "dominion over palm and pine."

The public schoolboy, nevertheless, could like his German contemporary sing "Ein feste Burg" as a "National" hymn (188). Under the same heading, he could sing How's "To thee, our God, we fly" (189), with its refrain "O Lord, stretch forth Thy mighty hand, / And guard and bless our fatherland" and its prayer for "powers ordained by thee." How's petitions in general refer more to the Church and to sin than to the civil power or crime, the "Majesty" insulted by sin being God. The whole prayer was appropriated to the patriotic use. It was one thing for the compilers of P to annex for their country Luther's phrase for the Guardian of the young Protestant community, "mighty fortress." It was quite another to appropriate the American Civil War hymn "O Lord of Hosts, Almighty King" (184), with O.W. Holmes's plea for the "holy faith that warmed our sires" and his claim that God's hand had "made our nation free" so that "to die for her is serving Thee." Against the morally indefensible cause of slavery, Holmes and his fellow Abolitionists could invoke the Almighty with a clear conscience. Transplanted to English soil, lines like "God of all nations,

Sovereign Lord, / In Thy dread name we draw the sword" seem to turn any conflict into a holy war.[13]

The schools served by P being predominantly Anglican—hence its office and sacramental hymns and its Latin texts such as "Adeste fideles" and "Veni Creator Spiritus"—confirmation candidates understood the chivalric imagery in "When thy soldiers take their swords" (152) as referring to the struggle against temptation.[14] Out of the sacramental context, the "strife" and "battle cry" take on a patriotic sense. Even the splendid missionary hymns of Watts, Heber, or Marriott could acquire patriotic overtones once the nation that supplied the missionaries became a world-wide empire. One less well-known, Montgomery's "Hark the song of jubilee" (165) acquired such an overtone in "He shall reign from pole to pole, / With illimitable sway" after the widely expected apocalypse had failed to come in the author's own age. A.C. Benson's "O Lord of Hosts, who didst upraise / Strong captains to defend the right" (185), though a prayer for peace, appears as a "National" hymn and so unavoidably identifies the sacred with the national cause.[15]

It is this "chosen people" complex that differentiates national and mission hymns in P from comparable items in B and C. It was associated with the whole ethos of responsible service that pervaded late Victorian and early twentieth-century hymnals for public school use. Hymns that the working-class adolescent need not jettison with the infantile lyrics on Christ and heaven had stirring tunes and military or patriotic images: "Fight the good fight" or "Lead us, heavenly Father, lead us" (the pilgrim metaphor). Unlike the lower-class hymnody of an earlier day, these and "Now thank we all our God" are characterized by world and life affirmation.

From texts found in P alone, a propagandist with a good pair of blinkers could prove that "Rock of Ages" (82) or "Weary of earth and laden with my sin" (72) made public schoolboys introspective Evangelicals; that "Adeste fideles" or "Dies irae" predisposed them to Catholicism; that "Lord of the brave" (149, discussed in the next chapter) or "Praise to our God, whose bounteous hand" (188) made them warlike nationalists. The actual effect depended on which hymns were most frequently sung in a given school, and in what context of scripture readings, prayers, and exhortations. We may safely conclude that the wider range available gave the public school principal more freedom to conduct the kind of worship he or she believed in; that the superior selection permitted a choice of hymns giving a truer impression of what adult Christians believed and felt; and that in consequence the pupils need not carry into life a distorted view of Christian teaching concerning Christ and the life hereafter. No doubt individual schools could and did teach a religion tailored to suit a ruling class. From this hymnal they could not have taught one especially suitable for lower-class adolescents. But they could and often did teach a core of Christian doctrine and ethics without regard to chronological age or social class, one representing the elements common to the major English Protestant denominations at the end of the nineteenth century.

APPENDIX: PUBLIC SCHOOL, BIRMINGHAM SCHOOL BOARD, AND COUNCIL
SCHOOL HYMN BOOKS

	Time/Season	P	B	C
A *Common to all three*				
As with gladness men of old	Epiphany	052	009	040
Awake, my soul, and with the sun	Morning	002	010	002
Brightest and best of the sons of the Morning	Epiphany	053	011	143
Children of the Heavenly King		222	013	050
Fair waved the golden corn		240	108	095
Fight the good fight with all thy might		247	021	113
Forth in Thy name, O Lord, I go		005	022	005
Go, when the morning shineth	Morning	254	025	007
Hark! the herald angels sing	Nativity	046	034	137
It came upon the midnight clear	Nativity	048	042	138
New every morning is the love	Morning	008	058	003
O God, our help in ages past		294	061	100
O worship the King, all glorious above		306	068	099
Our blest Redeemer, ere He breathed	Pentecost	107	070	118
We plough the fields and scatter	Harvest	175	085	133
While shepherds watched their flocks by night	Nativity	050	090	141
Total	16			
B *In Public School and Birmingham H.B.* (11)				
Abide with me: fast falls the eventide	Death, Evening	013	003	
All people that on earth do dwell		211	005	
Jesus lives! thy terrors now	Easter	092	046	
Jesu, lover of my soul		063	047	
Lead, kindly Light, amid the encircling gloom	Evening?	272	050	
O God, of Bethel, by whose hand		292	060	
O Jesus, I have promised	Confirmation	154	062	
Prayer is the soul's sincere desire		315	071	
The King of love my Shepherd is		327	074	

Through all the changing scenes of life		336	082
When all Thy mercies, O my God		343	088
Total	11		

C *In Public School and Council School H.B.* (28)

A charge to keep I have		200	106
All glory, laud & honour	Palm Sunday	077	039
Come, gracious Spirit, heavenly Dove	Pentecost	101	083
Come, let us join our cheerful songs		227	111
Eternal Father, strong to save		190	145
Father, let me dedicate	New Year	191	126
From homes of quiet peace	Wartime	182	147
Lead us, heavenly Father, lead us		273	040
Lord, we thank Thee for the pleasure		279	053
Love divine, all loves excelling		281	084
Now thank we all our God	A Thanksgiving	287	110
O for a heart to praise my God		290	087
O happy band of pilgrims		296	097
O little town of Bethlehem		049	136
O Lord of heaven and earth and sea	A Thanksgiving	163	131
Praise the Lord, ye heavens adore Him		313	064
Round the Lord in glory seated		114	051
Songs of praise the angels sang	Nativity	321	074
Stand up, and bless the Lord		323	093
Sun of my soul, Thou Saviour dear	Evening	027	017
The day is past and over	Evening	029	015
The Son of God goes forth to war	Martyrs	117	042
The spacious firmament on high		329	076
Thine for ever! God of love	Confirmation	151	036
Though lowly here our lot may be		334	078
Through the day Thy love hath spared us	Evening	031	016
To Thee our God we fly		189	102
We thank Thee, Lord, for this fair earth		342	092
Total	28		

D *In Birmingham and Council School H.B.* (39)

A little Kingdom I possess		002	109
All things bright and beautiful		007	071
Come sing with holy gladness		014	089
Courage, brother! do not stumble		015	058
Day by day we magnify Thee	Morning	016	009
Every morning, the red sun		017	069

Father, lead me day by day		020	115
Gentle Jesus, meek & mild		023	024
Gently think and gently speak		024	067
God bless our native land		026	149
God make my life a little light		028	080
God save our gracious King		030	150
God will take care of you all through the day	Morning?	031	090
Hushed was the evening hymn		036	038
I think when I read that sweet story of old		040	072
In our work and in our play		041	116
Jesus bids us shine		044	029
Jesus, from Thy throne on high		045	075
Jesus, meek and gentle		048	081
Kind words can never die		049	061
Let us with a gladsome mind		051	124
Little drops of water		054	063
Lord, I would own Thy tender care		055	041
Lord, Thy word abideth		056	028
Loving Shepherd of Thy sheep		057	046
Oh, what can little hands do		067	120
Once in royal David's city	Nativity	069	135
Summer suns are glowing	Summer	073	130
The morning bright with rosy light	Morning	075	014
The wise may bring their learning		076	107
There is a green hill far away	Passion	078	070
There is beauty all around		079	068
There's a Friend for little children		080	079
There's not a tint that paints the rose		081	085
We are but little children weak		084	101
When his salvation bringing		088	119
Winter reigneth o'er the land	Winter	092	134
Work, for the night is coming		094	123
Yes, God is good; in earth and sky	Morning	096	011
Total	39		

13

WILD TONGUES UNLOOSED:
PATRIOTIC HYMNS FOR EDWARDIAN SCHOOLS

If, drunk with sight of power, we loose
Wild tongues that have not thee in awe,
Such boastings as the Gentiles use,
Or lesser breeds without the Law—
Lord God of Hosts, be with us yet,
Lest we forget—lest we forget!

These lines in Kipling's "Recessional" are usually thought to epitomize the idolatrous nationalism that they in fact reprove. They are, however, idolatrous in a more traditional sense. Their identification of Britain with Israel and the Mosaic with the English Common Law goes back, as I have shown, to Watts and beyond him to Milton and the Puritan Commonwealth.[1] The "wild tongues" were loosed in three Edwardian service-books for fee-paying schools in London and one for young Methodists.

By coincidence the year 1907, when Mill Hill School issued its Supplement to the Congregational Hymn Book and St. Olave's and St. Saviour's Grammar School its hymnal,[2] saw the formation of the Territorial Army in face of the perceived menace from Germany. Fear and hatred of the "lesser breed" that Kipling had in mind contributed to the hysteria so evident in a hymnal issued in 1910 for Emanuel and its sister schools. Sunday-school children had been putting on armour, flaunting banner or Cross, and blowing the martial trumpet for a generation or two, but can never have found spiritual warfare so indistinguishable from literal as in the *Methodist School Hymnal* of 1911.

Mill Hill's beautifully produced set of eighty-eight devotional poems and hymns meets the literary standard to be expected of this famous Congregational school. Its poems by Herbert, Gascoigne, and Wither set the fashion for using seventeenth-century Anglican verse in school hymnals.[3] If its seventeen Latin texts encourage a suspicion that public schoolboys sang in Latin what they might not believe in English, the collection also includes some of the best Victorian hymns: "For all the saints," "Fight the good fight,'' and "The day Thou gavest, Lord, is ended.'' It shows something of the sentimental idealism of the Harrow collection (1881), in "O merciful and holy'' or even "O Love, that wilt not let me go.''

The one disturbing feature in an otherwise unexceptionable book is a distinct strain of battle imagery that is most explicit in lyrics composed especially for public schoolboys. In "When Thy soldiers take their swords'' (61), first sung for Confirmation at Cheltenham College, a stanza on temptation begins "When the world's sharp strife is nigh, / When they hear the battle cry.'' The singers who "rush into the fight'' fear the "conqueror's pride'' of the self-satisfied and finally plead for aid to the "wounded.''[4]

The military image of the spiritual life is worked out most explicitly in a text composed in 1893 and published in a small personal collection for public schoolboys by J.H. Skrine, no soldier but a classicist who taught for some years at Uppingham.[5] "Lord of the brave'' appeared in the *Public School Hymn Book*, then in those for Mill Hill, St. Olave's, and Emanuel, then in a small Anglican collection soon after the outbreak of war in 1914. Its relevant verses therefore repay scrutiny.

> Lord of the brave, Who call'st Thine own
> In love's fair name to fearless war,
> Behold us where God's musters are,
> His viewless banners o'er us blown.
>
> Lo! we that dare the all-holy fight,
> Our soldier oath we pledge today,
> Our soldier hands 'neath Thine we lay,
> Dread Captain of the Hosts of light.
>
> To-day we dare. To-morrow who
> Can guard the soldier faith unshamed?
> For valour faints as valour flamed.
> We dare: 'tis Thou must make us do.
>
> This soul of youth that springs to prove
> Heaven's knighthood on heaven's olden foe,
> O God in Man, 'tis Thine to know,
> 'Tis Thine, O Man in God, to love. (63)

The other verses entreat the loving help of Christ "when war is higher'' and recapitulate the opening.

By war in "love's'' name under "viewless'' banners, Skrine clearly signified conflicts internal and social. His metaphor of the "soldier oath'' originates in Victorian works by Tennyson and others that were based on

Malory's *Morte d'Arthur*. That of the "soldier hands 'neath Thine" and the whole act of self-dedication seem inspired by the Anglican rites for Ordination and Confirmation. Even in a Nonconformist school the context of scripture-readings and instruction can have left the singers in no doubt of the intended meaning. What the metaphors meant to singers elsewhere would depend upon the interpretive context. The plural "banners" (the Cross requiring a singular), the special role assigned to youth, and the sense, in the third stanza, of self-preparation for a supreme ordeal, lent themselves all too readily to the combination of youthful idealism with militarism that led young men to enlist in droves in 1914, and of which traces remained in the youth movements of Nazi Germany and Soviet Russia, and even in the admirable Boy Scout movement, coincidentally launched in 1907.[6]

The editor claimed that the texts had been used "nearly twenty years" at Mill Hill. His selection was an excellent example of the Congregational tradition epitomized by a former student at Mill Hill, H.M. Gunn:[7]

> As faithful as our fathers were,
> May we their children be;
> And in our hearts their spirit live,
> That gained our liberty. (60)

Elsewhere, however, Gunn records God as having "led our sons . . . / To realms beyond the sounding sea."

Again the St. Olave's hymnal, with its Jesuit motto, Roman numerals, and biblical or devotional texts alongside each of its 361 hymns, supplies a full theological context for a selection mingling classic hymns with secular poems. Wordsworth's "Ode to Duty" indicates the book's commitment to an ethos of service. To juxtapose praise of all who "leave the world behind" for the "rough path of duty" amid "suffering, meek and patient poor" (51) with a prayer by George Macdonald for a "quiet . . . submissive, meek" heart, was to cross the bourgeois and aristocratic ethos of service with the lower-class ethos of submission. In general, however, the "onward-and-upward" activism of Miss Beale's collection for Cheltenham prevails, so that Ann Brontë's poem "Believe not those who say / The upward path is smooth" appears alongside "Guide me, O thou great Jehovah," "Forward be our watchword" and "Go labour on" under a heading *Via Ardua*.[8]

This Broad Church idealism proved all too compatible with militaristic patriotism. Under the heading *Faithful unto Death*, a translation from the German poet Klopstock, on the labour whereby the Christian "warrior wins his crown" would be innocuous were it not followed by these lines of Newbolt:

> England! where the sacred flame
> Burns before the inmost shrine,
> Where the lips that love thy name
> Consecrate their hopes, and thine.
>
> . . .
>
> Watch beside thine arms tonight;
> Pray that God defend the right.

This poem, doubtless an inspiration to many for whom a sacred flame burns on Remembrance Day, was alluded to by Neville Chamberlain, when announcing the declaration of war in 1939. Chamberlain, never a jingoist and in his mid-thirties by 1907, quite properly referred to the impending war against Nazi Germany as a defence of "the right."[9] The use of this idolatrous poem in a Christian hymn-book for the young was altogether more deplorable. Next to it the compilers placed that earlier expression of the social gospel, "When wilt Thou save the people?"

The clearest evidence of the Edwardian interpretive context appears in *Hymns for School Use* (1910), compiled for the six Dacre Foundation schools by H. Buchanan Ryley, Head of Emanuel School, Wandsworth.[10] Military and patriotic motifs elsewhere placed in contexts of religious idealism became this book's raison d'être owing to Ryley's placements, headings, and astonishing preface. Acknowledging the St. Olave's hymnal as source of his 101 hymns, he omits any others "incomprehensible to youth" or expressing "emotions" that "young life has no business to feel." He finds even the choicest hymnals lacking in expressions of "high hope, and valiant trust, and the fire of youth." On this basis, he continues: "Exceptions may be taken to the patriotic hymns . . . inserted of set purpose . . . for if a man love not his own land, which he has seen, he gives little warrant for belief in his love for the heavenly land, which he has not seen." Conversely, patriotic would imply Christian commitment.

Arranging his hymns according to the school year, Ryley places first a hymn of Skrine for "Beginning of term" that mingles chivalric and modern military images. "Rank on rank again we stand. . . . once more to war addressed" with God as aid against temptation:

> Forward then our battle go,
> Comrades sworn one troth to render;
>
> . . .
>
> Strong for war, for helping tender:
> Strong for war, whom Christ hath led. (1)

Under the heading *A Living Sacrifice*, a recently altered version of "Just as I am, thine own to be," hailing Christ as "Friend of the young" (no longer "of sinners"), expresses a commitment that in this context takes on new meaning:

> In the glad morning of my day,
> My life to give, my vows to pay,
> With no reserve and no delay,
> With all my heart, I come. (6)

The side motto "Never glad confident morning again" recalls an epigraph over the gilded list of the fallen at my old school: "These, in the glorious morning of my days, / For England's sake gave all but England's praise." Opposite "Just as I am," the text "O God of Truth, whose living word" (7) includes a resolve to join the "blest array" of those who fight in "raiment clean and white" for "Truth and God," having resolved that to "wage war on earth" one must "first be pure within."[11] In Nazi Germany "purity" referred to race, but here it and the apocalyptic motifs dramatize life as a moral conflict with a nameless foe.

Under the general heading *Work and Battle* and an epigraph "Suffer hardship with me as a good soldier of Christ Jesus," "Lord of the brave" (16) already bears a meaning Skrine can hardly have intended. Junior officers such as Donald Hankey,[12] brought up in religious homes and educated at public schools, were to claim Christ as their inspiration and, in the words of Ryley's next epigraph "fight, because the Lord was with them." "God with us" is the root-meaning of the school's name. The ensuing hymn, "Through earth's wide round let the tidings sound" (17) has the singable refrain

> March on, march on, O ye soldiers true,
> In the cross of Christ confiding,
> For the field is set, and the hosts are met,
> And the Lord his own is guiding.

Its second stanza runs "We march to fight with the powers of might / That have held the world in sorrow," and its third

> We fight with wrong; and our weapon strong
> Is the love which hate shall banish;
> And the chains shall fall from each ransomed thrall,
> As the thrones of tyrants vanish.

Here the religious and military conflict become one, the Lord's cause the nation's. In the faith that the "God of Right" was "ever near," that the "sunrise . . . of the day of God" would "declare the Victor's glory," the young men marched away—on either side.

His messianic patriotism and cult of youth inspired Ryley to print alongside Kingsley's Christian-socialist lyric "Who will say that the world is dying" the motto "The seeds of godlike power are with us still":

> Still the race of hero-spirits
> Pass the lamp from hand to hand;
> Age from age the words inherits,
> Wife and child, and fatherland;
> Still the youthful hunter gathers
> Fiery joy from wold to wood;
> He will dare as dared his fathers
> Give him cause as good. (31)

To do Ryley justice, he must have dreaded the very war for which his earlier choices seem to call. Among seven hymns *For England* (77-83), the early Victorian "God the all-terrible" (79) has a refrain "Give to us peace in our time, O Lord" that could also have inspired Chamberlain, when announcing the ill-fated treaty of Munich. By coincidence, the penultimate lines of each verse express anticipation and dread: "Doom us not now in the moment of danger," "Bid not thy wrath in its terrors awaken," "Falsehood and wrong shall not tarry beside thee," and even "Through the thick darkness thy kingdom is hastening."

The following hymn, however, under the epigraph "Blessed is the nation whose God is the Lord," contrasts that nation with one oppressed by "tyrants." In this setting, boys must surely have applied to their own nation the following lines:

> The race that strove to rule thine earth
> With equal laws unbought;
> Who bore for Truth the pangs of birth,
> And broke the bonds of Thought. (80)

"Praise to our God, whose bounteous hand" (81) appears under an epigraph "That good land which the Lord thy God giveth thee for an inheritance" and the typological side motto "I have given Egypt as thy ransom . . . " The inevitable "Recessional" (82) has an epigraph "Some trust in chariots and some in horses; but we will remember the name of the

Lord our God" and a lengthy side motto admonishing a well-fed people living in "goodly houses" and with abundant "herds . . . flocks . . . silver and gold" not to forget God, nor say in their hearts that their own "power" and "might" have gotten them their wealth. With the headline "For England" printed in capitals above, the youngest boy must have realized the intended parallel between the English and the Chosen People.

Since the book contains many hymns expressing a masculine but scriptural devotion,[13] should we make so much of a handful of lyrics manipulated by a hysterical headmaster? Ryley attached labels to texts, but chose only those already used at other schools. A group of twenty-four headed "Temptation and Conflict" in the *Methodist School Hymnal* (1911) included fourteen "military" hymns that denote a profound reorientation of religious emotion since the age of the Wesleys, or even that of Luther.

Most of the metaphors represent spiritual conflict as a crusade or tournament. The four-times repeated refrain of "Hark to the sound of voices," by "Colin Sterne" (H.E. Nichol),[14] runs:

> Marching beneath the banner,
> Fighting beneath the Cross,
> Trusting in Him who saves us,
> Ne'er shall we suffer loss.
> Singing the songs of homeland,
> Loudly the chorus sings
> We march to the fight in our armour bright
> At the call of the King of Kings. (376)

Similar images in more famous hymns by Wesley and Heber—"Soldiers of Christ arise" (368) and "The Son of God goes forth to war" with "blood-red banners" (369)—or the "heavenly armour" of Kirke White's "Oft in danger, oft in woe," more directly emanate from St. Paul's sustained image of putting on the "whole armour of God" (Ephesians 6. 11-17). Whether a clerical hymnist immersed in the Scriptures draws on St. Paul, on the *Christus Miles* trope of Latin hymnody[15] or on Victorian pseudo-medieval literature is not easily determined. Baring-Gould, in "Onward Christian soldiers" used what looks like a medieval standard for his "cross of Jesus / Going on before." The Abolitionist G. Duffield perhaps drew on all three sources for the armour, trumpets and banners of his "Stand up, stand up for Jesus" (374). This favourite of Evangelicals more specifically raises the issue of religious orientation. The campaigns against slavery and against Nazism were genuine cases of battles against "principalities . . . powers . . . rulers of the darkness of this world" and "spiritual wickedness in high places," that could induce pacifists to change their minds. How can the adult, let alone the child, distinguish such rare instances of a just war from mere struggles for power, territory, or wealth? Furthermore, how can the singer determine when battle images apply to internal and when to external conflict, the passage in St. Paul being applicable to both?

Throughout history Christian leaders and authors have alternated between three kinds of warfare against the powers of evil: resistance to temptation within, reformation of abuses in the church or secular society, and conflict with other religions, whether by mission or crusade. In hymnody the emblems of internal and external warfare are interchangeable, their significance depending upon their immediate context. The crusaders directed hymns against the Muslims,[16] the first Lutherans against their princely and ecclesiastical opponents. The Puritans marched against the royal armies, singing psalms. The early Methodists employed hymns as weapons against the foe within, the Abolitionists against the social evil practised in slave-holding states. Duffield's text allows for ambiguity, instructing the singer who meets evil within or without to "Charge for the God of battles," and so has survived the conflict for which it was designed.

Alternatively the compiler determines the interpretation of hymns by his grouping and labelling. The patriotic headmaster-compiler directed his hymns outward, identifying the national with the divine cause and eschewing introspection; the Methodist compilers directed them against both temptations and social evils. They could not, however, control the future meaning of their hymns to alumni caught up in a conflict yet more tragic than the Civil War. "Who is on the Lord's side?" (1877), though it directs a stream of chivalric images toward the spiritual conflict, must have rung equally true to Victorian imperial soldiers "In an alien land" and to members of the British Expeditionary Force. Out of context, even Wesley's lines "Stand to your arms, the foe is nigh . . . The day of battle is at hand, / Go forth to glorious war" (386) could have adorned a recruiting poster, as could Sterne's refrain "God on high is watching o'er you: / Be a hero in the fight" (388), F.A. Jackson's "Fight for the right, boys" (389) or W.F. Sherwin's "Sound the battle cry! / See! the foe is nigh" (390).[17] When asked whether the First World War had been worth fighting, a Methodist veteran brought up on this hymnal cited the finest of all Victorian "military" hymns, "Fight the good fight" (384), having redirected its Pauline text from spiritual to national strife.

The generation that fought the First World War had become conditioned to feeling for their country the reverence their forebears had felt for God, not denying Him but enlisting Him on its side. While this goes back to the "God of battles" in the Old Testament, or the Puritan belief in Britain as the Second Israel, the drift of adults away from the churches converted it into a worship of two gods. They had come to view the Union Jack, a pattern of superimposed crosses, as equivalent to the Cross, a sign of ultimate value for which lives were well lost. Originally a feature of Dissenting, then of public school religion, this patriotic conditioning had by the accession of George v spread to all classes.

To say that as Armageddon drew near the English, in common with other Europeans, transferred their allegiance to God's supplanter, the nation-state, would grossly overstate the case. Certainly the majority of those educated at public and grammar schools used the *Public School Hymn Book* or some school hymnal quite free from propagandist manipulation.

That of Edinburgh Academy (1904),[18] for example, adhered to Presbyterian tradition by deriving half of its sixty-four hymns from the psalms and supplying biblical source-texts for all. Its remaining hymns amount to a select anthology of the strongest and most durable in the common repertoire: for Christmas "Hark the herald angels" but no sentimental carols; for Easter "Jesus Christ is risen today"; from the Wesleyan hymn-book "Soldiers of Christ," "Rejoice! the Lord is King," and "Wrestling Jacob," but no fugitives sheltering in Christ's bosom; from the *Olney Hymns* "God moves in a mysterious way" but no fountains filled with blood; otherwise "O worship the King" or "Praise the Lord! ye heavens adore him" but no text that would embarrass the adolescent taught to discern poetry from mush. From the neurosis or idolatry discernible in some collections for children, this robust and unsentimental collection, abounding in praise and awe of the Creator, comes as a relief.

The last service-books before the war were that of E.M. Palser used in grammar schools in Suffolk and that for Manchester Grammar School, both issued in 1913.[19] The former is best considered in the context of the new critical awareness that informed the post-war compilations. The latter is a late offshoot of the Victorian era. Only its Roman numerals visually distinguish this clothbound manual, with its small print, alphabetical sequence, and listing of translators as authors, from that designed for humbler children of Manchester in 1878. The selection belies the drab format. Supernatural religion, though to the fore in "As pants the hart" or "Let saints on earth in concert sing," takes neither a liturgical nor a sentimental form, the main themes being the divine praises, as at Edinburgh, the service ethic or the honorable ambition of Milton's "Fame is the spur." Texts in the last vein vary from the puritanical to the secular idealistic, one describing "feeble steps" on the "rough and steep" pathway through this world's "weary wilderness" (20); another the struggle for inner purity by conquest of sin like any medieval, Wesleyan or Tractarian hymn (30); a third the "toil of brain or heart" as "man's appointed lot" (42). The last seems more hellenic than Christian:[20]

> Toil is no thorny crown of pain
> Bound round man's brow for sin;
> True souls from it all strength may gain,
> High manliness may win.

In other verses, "our Brother," Christ, who "made all life divine," shares our "lot and strife." Compared to the replacement of godliness by "manliness" and the exaltion of the noble and gifted above the poor and despised, the inconsistencies of orthodox faith seem but minor difficulties. Nevertheless, this stanza belongs to a Victorian mainstream, being exemplified in the prose and verse of Arnold and to a lesser degree in the poems of Tennyson and Browning. David Newsome has most fully documented this transition from "godliness" to "manliness" as the end of public school education.[21]

Although some of the forty-seven texts employ military images, none alludes in any way to patriotism or even to England. One or two, such as Butler's "O merciful and holy" recall the Harrow hymnal of 1881 that imbued secular work with religious meaning, and some likewise sentimentalize Christ. The genesis of "military" and patriotic hymnody in the needs of home and foreign missionaries, and the reaction against it that set in during the First World War, are the subjects of the next chapter.

14

SOLDIERS OF CHRIST AND THE SOVEREIGN

We were perpetually in a state of slight euphoric fever.
There was something mystical in the atmosphere.[1]

In his autobiography the playwright Carl Zuckmayer describes his upbringing in the Roman Catholic faith, attending Mass in childhood as unself-consciously as if going "to a bakery," the ritual that awakened his "inner life," the "happiness of unconditional belief" that in adolescence gave place to "struggles, doubts, spiritual crises" but never indifference or apostasy, until he attained "serene knowledge" of its truth. The *Te Deum* or chorales sung after Mass filled him with an "elation . . . comparable to no other joy," at the "tangible presence" of God's "creative power."[2] How deceptively similar was his elation as he hastened back from holiday to enlist in 1914. Forgotten were his pacifism, his verses pleading "Lord, avert it . . . Do not thrust me into the grave" and predicting that mothers would weep, brides wail, and survivors forever carry "shards" within their hearts. His schoolmates smiled at each other, all doubts swept aside, shouting "freedom" as they rushed into uniform, the prospect of death meaningless beside the "intoxication," the "craving for immolation in blood" common to youth in Germany, France, England and, in time, the United States. In civilians patriotic hysteria inspired acts of mindless violence, comparable to the looting of German shops in England, but in recruits every communiqué intensified the conviction of having enlisted in a "just cause," to defend their native soil.

As Zuckmayer reflects, every country believed it was waging war in self-defence. Germans thought the British government, Britons thought "the Hun," had plotted the whole conflict, leaving "us" no option but to fight, even before press reports of atrocities incited xenophobia and thus opened a gap between believing civilians and disillusioned troops.[3]

Zuckmayer is describing transference of religious emotion to the nation-state observed in pre-war English hymnals for the young: the sense of transcendence, the sinfulness of doubt or enquiry, the generous self-giving, the external enemy that had replaced the Devil. This new faith, I have argued, did not replace but lived upon the body of the old, appropriating its signs and symbols. National churches and even the multinational Catholic church endorsed patriotic devotion and military service, the latter treating conflict between Catholic states as a civil war, and blessing combatants on either side.

The German hymn having reached its peak in the seventeenth century, the transference was accomplished by usurpation of existing texts. "Ein feste Burg" lent itself to reinterpretation, the recently united Germany beset like the new Protestant church of Luther's day. English hymnody, having grown as the German declined and having received transfusions from North America, showed a more complex mixture of motifs and attitudes. Its ambivalence toward missionary and imperial expansion applied also to the making of war. In the first two, the motives of service and conquest were as inextricably mixed as were patriotic fervour and the sense of duty in the third. To understand how the older hymns were read as consecrating the war effort, how the war swept aside doubts that the peace was to multiply a hundredfold, we must look at some mission hymns and martial images.

MISSIONS

In India, the arrogance of the first missionaries astounded even the Brahmans, never noted for humility. Launched into unknown territory with every likelihood of dying young by disease if not by martyrdom, they found Hindu suttee and infanticide even more abominable than European rapacity.[4] The instant condemnation of any signs and symbols that recalled the idolatries of Rome, like the later suppression of Amerindian tribal feasts, originated in a culture shock the more intense for the lack of present-day anthropological understanding. The first mission hymnists, who lamented "slaughter'd heaps" as "trophies of sin" and called on the Almighty to "cast" away Hindu "idols,"[5] had no means of understanding the economic and cultural bases of death rituals. More durable texts transmitted the lack of discrimination evident in "O'er the gloomy hills of darkness" (1772), which lumps together "Indian," "Negro," and "rude barbarian."[6] Even the learned Reginald Heber, later Bishop of Calcutta, who when he composed "From Greenland's icy mountains" had never been abroad, offended natives of Ceylon, where "every prospect pleases / And only man is vile" and "the savage in his blindness / Bows down to wood and stone." Yet in "icy mountains" and "coral strand," he hit off exactly the arctic and tropical environments and in the "many an ancient river" the age-long suffering and ignorance. Perhaps the first intimations of his future vocation inspired "They call us to deliver / Their land from error's chain" and "Can we to men benighted / The lamp of life deny?," lines that few who have been delivered from fear and superstition would condemn. The tune "Aurelia" conveys a sadness as appropriate for peoples without the Christian hope as it was for the troops who set it to "We are Fred Karno's army."[7] The same tone pervades some lines by Mrs. Alexander on the "cruel places" of earth from which "Slaves in bondage" look "heavenward" but not to God.[8]

The common impression that the Cross and the Flag went together is not borne out by the great missionary hymns "Jesus shall reign where'er the sun," "Hail to the Lord's anointed," "Hark! the song of jubilee," and "Thou whose almighty Word." Far more typical is a universalism that Watts and Montgomery caught from the Psalms. The themes of liberation and love in "Jesus shall reign" need no demonstration. Even the long-omitted stanza

> There Persia glorious to behold,
> There India stands in Easter Gold;
> And barbarous nations at his word
> Submit and bow and own their Lord

distinguishes those fabled realms from the unnamed "barbarous" peoples, and follows one requiring a like tribute from European princes and nations.[9] Neither Montgomery nor Marriott casts aspersions upon non-Europeans, or their faiths. The intolerance of Wesley's "For Mahometans" had been a matter of doctrine, Islam being "the Unitarian fiend."[10] Marriott's call for light "in earth's darkest place" refers in context to all without the "lamp of grace," the "sick in mind" and "inly blind" of the previous stanza. Montgomery alludes in a neutral tone to "Arabia's desert ranger" and the "Ethiopian stranger," and reserves submission for kings yielding up their gold in fear and love of the Messiah who succours the "poor and needy."

An earlier mission hymn, "Behold! the mountain of the Lord" (1767) paraphrased the prophecy of Micah that nations would cease from war to join in worship.[11] Victorian authors handled this theme of the Great Gathering in various ways. Tennyson foresaw a universal parliament, C.E. Oakley, in "Hills of the north, rejoice," a proclamation of the Second Advent to each region in turn. Two late Victorians took diametrically opposed positions, G.T. Coster, in "From north and south and east and west" (1884) foreseeing "heathen darkness roll away" from arctic and oriental lands in turn, George Matheson, in "Gather us in, Thou Love that fillest all" (1890) discerning in "rival faiths" and "diverse forms" a "common soul." Each believed worshippers to seek "one spirit-land" and one God, the goal of aspirations from the Buddhist longing for Nirvana to the Christian expectation of the millennium.[12]

The appearance shortly afterwards of a number of patriotic mission hymns by "Colin Sterne" showed that the day of ecumenicism had yet to dawn. In "We've a story to tell to the nations" (1896) Nichol waxed as triumphal as "Solomon," the earliest mission hymnist, for the "story" will "conquer evil" and shatter spear and sword, yet even in this naïve song for children, he talks not of submission or idol-smashing but of a "kingdom of love and light."[13] Though Kipling tarnished his name for ever by writing of "lesser breeds without the law," his theme was the need to restrain pride and lust for power. Admittedly he reformulates and Nichol implies the old trope of England as the Second Israel, but to judge from surviving hymn texts the chauvinism of missionaries has been much exaggerated. What has been taken as such often amounts only to a pardonable complacency. In the centenary year of the Church Missionary Society (1899), a hymnist may "scan the years" with satisfaction, for has not the Lord done marvellous things that "many a tribe and tongue" unite in praise?[14]

John Ellerton's "The Day thou gavest, Lord, is ended" (1870), designated "for Missionary Meetings," has drawn fire from Susan Tamke, who notes its choice by the Queen for the Diamond Jubilee service: "In this hymn, the expanding Christian British Empire becomes synonymous with the Kingdom of God." While Ellerton concedes that "earthly empires are ephemeral," "there is no mistaking" his "pride in British missionary accomplishment." Earlier, however, she notes that "the great expansion of foreign missionary work occurred only in the last third of the century," beginning "in approximately 1870" and coinciding with the Moody and Sankey revival and "the popular revival of imperialism."[15] Apart from the logic of detecting pride in the expansion that only began in the year of the hymn's publication, she surely overemphasizes the image of the unsetting sun in the fourth verse:

> The sun that bids us rest is waking
> Our brethren 'neath the western sky,
> And hour by hour fresh lips are making
> Thy wondrous doings heard on high.

to the neglect of the main theme, convincingly defined by J.R. Watson as "the way in which the praise of God is never ending, because the earth is moving, so that as one part . . . sleeps, another is waking and praising

God."[16] From the thanksgiving for the "Church unsleeping, / While earth rolls onward into light" to the final contrast with "earth's proud empires" that "pass away" while "Thy kingdom stands, and grows for ever, / Till all thy creatures own thy sway," the hymn epitomizes the Christian view of history. Watson rightly judges the fourth verse structurally the weakest but in context it contrasts the unending praise of the Church with the life-cycle of its members.

Like other vesper hymns "The day thou gavest" has become less familiar with the decline of Evensong, but remains in demand for ecumenical services. In the last half-century ecumenicism, now almost synonymous with mission, has reaped a harvest of late Victorian hymns. Between the publication of "Hills of the North" (1870) and of the apparently similar "In Christ there is no East or West" (1908), there began an important shift of consciousness. Ironically, "Hills of the North" became popular only after the First World War, when already anachronistic. Its third verse calls on "Lands of the east" to "awake" for "Soon shall your sons be free," the "everlasting day" having dawned on their "far hills." If seeming to apply to Russia, the verse actually concerns the Far East. More clearly, the next verse, on the "Shores of the utmost west" that "Unvisited, unblessed" await the good tidings, alludes to natives in the Americas. In each case, the hymnist assumes the pre-anthropological posture toward the Confucian, Hindu, or Buddhist, or the Great Spirit worshipper, that Tamke describes as "condescending paternalism."[17] No doubt some Anglican missionaries had that attitude, commonly associated with a public school and Oxbridge education, but the large proportion of mission hymns by hymnists of other denominations diminishes the force of this criticism. Although the Christian claim for Christ implies in His adherents a unique insight, that most assured of all churches, the Roman Catholic, has for centuries equipped Jesuits in particular with a commendable understanding of Far Eastern cultures. The real shortcoming of Protestant missionaries was surely ignorance. Once this was dispelled by the geographers and anthropologists who followed the explorers, humility and discernment could take its place. How far they did would depend on the missionary's personality and education.

Within ten years of the CMS centenary, another London missionary congregation found itself singing lines that despite their male orientation are even now ahead of human consciousness in general:

> In Christ there is no East or West,
>   In Him no South or North;
> But one great fellowship of love
>   Throughout the whole wide earth.

In Him shall true hearts everywhere
Their high communion find,
His service is the golden cord
Close binding all mankind.

Join hands then, brothers of the faith,
Whate'er your race may be.
Who serves my Father as a son
Is surely kin to me.[18]

Here Oxenham sketches two concentric rings, the one enfolding brethren "of the faith," the other "true hearts everywhere." No longer need the one group condemn the other, however intent upon its conversion. By an unhappy trait of human nature, missionary "enthusiasm" abounds in the converted, who feel delivered from darkness into light. Moreover, as Tamke reflects, belief in the damnation of the unconverted spurred Evangelicals to missionary endeavour as more liberal beliefs would not have done.[19] Those who first preached in darkest Africa or furthest India were caught in a tragic bind, for without intense conviction no young man could undertake service so risky and ill-requited, and with it few could maintain the detachment needed to amass information and draw distinctions. The missionary doctors and teachers of this century may have conferred more tangible benefits on native peoples, but without the earlier evangelists and missionary societies they could never have begun.

Economic and imperial expansion supplied opportunities and to a degree incentives for mission work. Only upon hearing highly coloured reports of misery and customs of paganism among the multitudes of India and China did churches establish missions. Anthropology and economic geography being as yet unborn, no one knew why shamans treated disease with blood or urine, or why South Sea islanders ate each other. Without doubt, fund-raising services were too emotionally charged to permit discrimination between primitive and highly developed cultures. Evangelical missionaries to the North Pacific coasts should certainly have paused to observe the native cultures before combining with rapacious traders to smash them. While indigenous churches flourish long after the Union Jack has been hauled down in former African colonies, Christianity has made little headway in the literate and more mature civilizations of East Asia.

For all the absurdities that abound in missionary hymn collections—negro impersonations, thanksgivings by natives apparently recruited into the Victorian bourgeoisie—for all the blood-stained banners and images of conquest, as in the unpleasant Irish Evangelical hymn "Jesus, immortal

King, arise" (1810) where the "victorious Conqueror" asserts his sway till "distant lands obey," the keynote of the great hymns for overseas missions known to every Protestant churchgoer is not quasi-military conquest but universal love and liberation.

Compared with these or with Abolitionist lyrics, late Victorian mission hymns lack a clearly defined objective. In "These things shall be" (1880), by the Oxford historian John Addington Symonds, the central image of a "loftier race" with the "flame of freedom in their souls" who by practising nobler arts than blood-letting will turn earth into paradise, springs more from Shelley and William Morris than from the New Testament.[20] It is difficult for the proselytizing spirit to co-exist with tolerance, inclusiveness, idealism, or disinterested inquiry. As an early Victorian lyric insists, the "youthful blooming throng" of missionaries little knew what tortures or temptations awaited them as they traversed "ocean's foamy ways / To plant the cross abroad."[21] Scholarship requires a security then confined to the upper and professional classes. While such Broad Church hymnists as Ellerton lauded the spread of Christian institutions, the Evangelicals who largely supplied the manpower strove to make dramatic conversions.

MILITARY IMAGES

Foreign missionary societies, then, did not inaugurate either the transference of religious emotion to the nation and Empire or the images of military conquest. It was on the home front that Charles Wesley ordered the soldiers of Christ into action. By hindsight, the heroes and heroines who spent themselves to spread the Gospel abroad can be charged with ignorance, hasty judgment, failure of discrimination, and an overly simple view of life, but not with idolatry. Single-mindedness they shared with home evangelists, soldiers, sailors, schoolchildren, indeed all whose situation requires them to struggle toward a well-defined goal. The black-and-white ethos of Frances Havergal's "Who is on the Lord's side?" (1877) now restricts it to the revival meeting or a confirmation by an Evangelical bishop. The Church Missionary Society properly included in its centenary collection her "Take my life and let it be / Consecrated, Lord, to thee" (1874) for had she not given that very Society her jewels? In this, her only hymn still widely used, she offers her time, her will and her artistic musical and intellectual gifts "Ever, only, all for thee" (a line she dashed off after making ten converts) with an all-embracing dedication quite beyond the majority who must earn a living and raise children.[22]

Recently John Batts found among CMS and Salvation Army hymns an astonishing 25 and 34 per cent couched in military terms, with images of violence in a further 17 per cent used by the fervently pacifist Salvation Army.[23]

The classic text for the transference from secular to spiritual warfare is St. Paul's:

> Put on the whole armour of God, that ye may be able to stand against the wiles of the devil. For we wrestle not against flesh and blood, but against principalities, against powers, against the rulers of the darkness of this world, against spiritual wickedness in high places. Wherefore take unto you the whole armour of God, that ye may be able to withstand in the evil day . . . having your loins girt about with truth, and having on the breastplate of righteousness. And your feet shod with the preparation of the gospel of peace. Above all, taking the shield of faith, wherewith ye shall be able to quench all the fiery darts of the wicked. And take the helmet of salvation, and the sword of the Spirit, which is the word of God . . . (Eph. 6. 10-17)

To understand the reverse transference, by which soldiers on each side could attribute religious meaning to secular warfare, we need to know the identity of the Christian soldiers exhorted by hymnists from Wesley to Baring-Gould, the nature of the spiritual war, and the way it turned into a literal war against other Christians. Some half-dozen well-known texts composed between 1736 and 1897—"Pugnate, Christi milites," "Soldiers of Christ, arise," "Soldiers of the Cross, arise," "Onward, Christian soldiers," "Fight the good fight," and the "Recessional" tell us more than volumes of forgotten hymns stuffed with chivalric weaponry.

The Gallican poet of "Pugnate, Christi milites" (1736) promises his fellow monks that God will reward them for renouncing home and world with a heavenly home. As late as the 1880s the English Jesuit Gerard Manley Hopkins draws admiring analogies between "dexterous and starlight" orders, celestial and military.

The Protestant parallels to the religious orders were the Moravian and Methodist societies. What is now "Soldiers of Christ, arise," the closest paraphrase of the Pauline text, originally ran to some sixteen eight-line stanzas, of which John Wesley printed twelve as three adjacent hymns under "Believers Fighting" in his *Collection*.[24] By this time the poem was forty years old. Originally Charles Wesley, a High Churchman, addressed as "soldiers" the new converts and the members of the former Holy Club at Oxford. With a verse from Romans in mind, he assures the singer, through the "strength of Jesus" of being "more than conqueror," and inseparable from His love in the "fellowship" of believers and their families. In this context, the "armour" represents God's grace supplied "Through his eternal Son," the "shield" faith, the "Captain" Christ. Within the three hymns printed in 1780 no offensive weapons appear save "arms of heavenly light" and the "fiery darts" of Satan. Classicist as he is, Wesley subsumes all under the term "Panoply," that is the whole gear of God's *hoplites*, or foot-soldiers.

The spiritual war, then, was defensive, the foe the mythological "Legions of wily fiends" and "sons of night," the armament (in another Pauline phrase) "the mind / That was in Christ." The troops were to "Leave no unguarded place, / No weakness of the soul," yet fortified with every "virtue" and "grace" they fought not singly but "Indissolubly join'd" to Christ and to each other. The soldiers may hope, "conflicts pass'd," to "stand entire at last" collectively, rather than singly like modern existentialists.

In the *Collection* four stanzas beginning "Soldiers of Christ" concern the armament, the next four from "But, above all, lay hold / On faith's victorious shield" the assurance given by prayer and belief in the Atonement, the last four from "In fellowship, alone, / To God with faith draw near," the duty of worship, repentance, praise and prayer "for Sion's peace." In a striking figure, the poet bids them "Extend the arms of mighty prayer, / Ingrasping all mankind." Even after victory, union with God will be attained only by the Spirit's call for Christ to "descend from high / And take the conquerors home." The demonic foes are never identified with human institutions and the battle takes place within the mythic context of fallen angels, Redemption, and Parousia.

This three-part hymn was read by "People called Methodists" before a whole sequence on the believer arming for spiritual conflict and attaining the Christian character. In hymn after hymn the believer relives a scriptural episode demonstrating the divine assistance.[25] To later Methodists only the First Part has come down just as John Wesley printed it, that is in mythological terms. To members of other churches, and especially school congregations, a mid-Victorian cento mainly of the First Part conveys a more limited set of battle orders. In both versions, printed in an appendix to this chapter, the "fight" has become a more secularized and less well-defined "battle of life" signifying to the adolescent the struggle with temptation and the formation of character. In the cento the Second Advent and departure for Heaven have vanished with the satanic personages, for "powers of darkness" can mean anything from sexual desire to the school bully or corrupt adult. Sung to either Monk's "St. Ethelwald" or Naylor's "From strength to strength," the hymn's march-like resonance can inspire to the adolescent or fervent evangelical. Poetry lovers might find "From strength to strength" distracting. To them that phrase, a late insertion, could imply in Wesley's sense that God equips the soul for the fray, in

Wordsworth's that Nature feeds and forms it with lofty thoughts and a power of quiet joy, so equipping it to find its happiness in this world.[26]

By 1854, when W.W. How composed "Soldiers of the Cross, arise," both soldiers and battleground had evolved. The soldiers "are all that bear the Good News to those that know it not." "Gird you with your armour bright" suffices for defence, for the whole stress is upon raising the "banner" over the "faithless, fallen world" surrounding the Christian church. In his detail How depicts the "darkest England" of contemporary novelists: the "homes of want and woe" that are "Strangers" to the "living word," the dens of crime where "shadows deepest lie," and "soldiers" must display the "saving sign" of the cross, the "weary" and "worn," "outcast" and "forlorn" to be told of "realms where sorrows cease." The battle against sin and unbelief will be fought by clergy and laity alike within British society. Only in the last verse does How allude to missions overseas:

> Be the banner still unfurled,
> Still unsheathed the Spirit's sword,
> Till the kingdoms of the world
> Are the Kingdom of the Lord.[27]

Of triumphal jingoism this verse has no trace. The poet, like the early Christian mission hymnist "Solomon" the Odist, indeed like Paul of Tarsus, envisages a saving faith and knowledge spreading over the globe so as to make nonsense of frontiers and racial distinctions.

In the most famous (or notorious) of Victorian military hymns, "Onward Christian soldiers," composed for a Whitsun Sunday-school procession,[28] the "cross of Jesus" becomes equivalent to a Roman standard before which in the second verse "Satan's legions flee." By then, it has become personified into "Christ the royal Master" leading "into battle" young soldiers whose shout makes "Hell's foundations quiver" like the walls of Jericho. In what way this procession puts fallen angels to flight never becomes clear, for the poet turns from recounting the Christian mythos to exhorting his "Brothers" to sing louder. In the remaining verses he draws out the resemblance and contrast between the Church and "a mighty army," its unity and triumphal singing, its capacity both to outlast and prove more "constant" than earthly kingdoms. The hymn ends with an apparent allusion to the singing by medieval children of the great Palm Sunday processional "All glory, laud and honour": [29]

> Glory, laud and honour
> Unto Christ the King;
> This through countless ages
> Men and Angels sing.

Baring-Gould modifies the *Christus Victor* trope by enlisting the boy singers, at least, as participants in the conquest. In Victorian activist hymnody, the believer plays his part in attaining the common goal. Though the very explicitness of Baring-Gould's analogy restricts the "battle" to an ecclesiastical procession, the believer's continuing battle can more readily be transposed into a crusade against a rival faith or empire, identified with the powers of evil, than can the once-for-all victory of the crucified Christ celebrated by Prudentius or Fortunatus. Its martial imagery and simplistic theology (was the Anglican Church of 1864 "one . . . in doctrine"?) endeared "Onward Christian soldiers" to child and adult alike, once Haydn's strangely mechanical melody had been replaced by Sullivan's rousing march "St. Gertrude."

In the commonly used cento from "Soldiers of Christ, arise" first published in *Hymns Ancient and Modern* (1868), the existential conflict of believers who must wrestle, fight, and pray, so as to tread down the powers of darkness within and "stand entire at last," engages more mature warriors than those who first marched with Baring-Gould. It can fairly be compared with the famous Victorian military hymn, "Fight the good fight" (1863), a paraphrase that changed the meaning of some New Testament verses by quoting them out of context. "Fight the good fight of faith, lay hold on eternal life, whereunto thou art also called" (1 Tim. 6.12) follows a warning against the love of money. Monsell does not define his "good fight," and in "Lay hold on life, and it shall be / Thy joy and crown eternally" misses St. Paul's contrast between worldly and spiritual goods. Again the advice "Wherefore seeing we also are encompassed about with so great a cloud of witnesses, let us lay aside every weight, and the sin which doth so easily beset us, and let us run with patience the race that is set before us" (Hebrews 12. 1) is transformed into an endorsement of activism more optimistic as regards this life than anything in the Epistle, identifying Christ not merely with the "path" but with the "prize." To cast care aside and lean on Him as Guide is the gesture of blind faith Evangelical preachers have always advised, but since 1834, when Montgomery composed the hymn of the same title that was Monsell's model, the Christian ethos has shifted from a world-denying self-defence by souls intent upon salvation to world-affirming activism.[30] "He changeth not, and thou are dear" and "Only believe," in the last verse, seem to hint at the mid-Victorian struggle for faith that reached its height after the publication of the *Origin of Species* (1859).

"Through the night of doubt and sorrow," composed in Danish in 1859 and translated by Baring-Gould for the High Church *People's Hymnal* (1867), represents the Christian life in the older Protestant image of the pilgrimage to the "Promised Land," brothers clasping hands as they defy doubt and surrounding darkness. The translator replaces "Jesu Christ" by "the one almighty Father" and generalizes the detail of Golgotha to "onward with the cross our aid," with the effect of intensifying the focus on the apparently all-male "band" that sings one song, braves one peril and expects one "great awaking." The imagery dates from the Reformation, the brotherhood from the pre-capitalist world, the "night" of doubt and sorrow from the dilemma of nineteenth-century intellectuals, who must either like Newman or Liddon defy biblical and scientific criticism, or like Maurice or Arnold try to construct a new framework of belief, or else, like so many, abandon their faith.

Somewhat lower in the scale of rationality, hot-gospellers from General Booth to Jerry Falwell have hammered into the young, the unstable, or the ill educated a simplified message in defiance of logic or fact. The quest for personal salvation has been considered earlier in regard to the Moody and Sankey "Gospel hymns." That for mutual assurance during the last third of the century took the forms of transplanted Abolitionist marching hymns like "John Brown's body" and of the "military" hymns that cluttered up Sunday-school and revival hymnals, the best being filtered into denominational collections. Batts has observed these common features: (1) Christ as captain, the Christians as soldiers; (2) military accoutrements—armour, shield, and sword—conventions, I would add, of pseudo-medieval romances by Scott, Tennyson, and Morris; (3) an ethos of simple truth, unswerving faith and resolve, reflecting conviction of a righteous cause; (4) an aggressive, activist Christianity, requiring a lifelong "march" toward a heaven pictured in biblical images of Canaan or the New Jerusalem, a land of rest and peace, where the soldiers exchange their swords for crowns.

The best examples of the military analogy, such as "For all the Saints," may last as long as the English hymn itself, but others, such as "Onward, Christian soldiers," have declined into bywords for an outmoded convention. The soldier-knight image of Christ (*Christus Miles*) being hallowed by a thousand years of poetic usage,[31] and the Christian's weaponry by St. Paul himself, what was new and distinctive about this Victorian military hymnody? First, collective salvation, whether by social amelioration or safe passage through this world, demanded unity, brotherhood, and total commitment to Christ as leader. Personal doubt was equated with sin or surrounding paganism. At times, especially in High Church hymnody, the "army" and the march seemed ends in themselves, and mystic union attainable by the very act of joining up, submerging personal doubts and cares. The images and unquestioning faith were drawn from a past seen in simpler and brighter colours than the present. The bind of the educated Christian, was that hymns all could sing with abandon could not encompass the complexity of industrial life, or the reforms needed to make Victorian England a more loving and mutually responsible community. The hot-gospeller could raise the roof with his marching songs, or lyrics on salvation in the Blood of Jesus, but to cease drinking, stop one's ears against ideas, and trust in Providence would no longer work the miracles they had in Wesley's time. The education needed to run schools, to design sewage systems or hospitals, or to market products, would sooner or later expose one to the doubts of Darwin, Huxley, and the biblical critics.

Above all, what conditioned soldiers of Christ to become soldiers of the sovereign, and prepared the youth of Britain, Germany, or in our time the United States to sacrifice themselves in war, was the activism and belief in progress evident in the swinging tunes and insistent themes of oneness and impending triumph common to "Onward, Christian soldier," "Forward be our watchword," and many other hymns. But in British culture another cause was at work.

TRANSFERENCE AND SECULARIZATION

In my previous book I have described the transference of the Second Israel archetype from Covenanters and Independents to the union of British peoples formed in 1707 and cemented by the struggle to preserve the Protestant Hanoverian dynasty. This can be epitomized in the history of "Our God, our help in ages past," also recounted in the preceding volume. Published five years after Queen Anne's death had preserved Dissenters against proposed new disabilities, the hymn gave Dissenting "saints" whom "Our God" had hitherto sheltered from persecution of "hope for years to come." Five stanzas now omitted contrast His eternal changelessness with the frailty of the civilization that barely tolerated Dissent. Their subsequent omission and John Wesley's change of "Our" to "O" God (1737) did away with the idea of death as a divine sentence upon all save the elect, and removed all reference to a tension between Dissenters and society at large that eased once the Hanoverian dynasty had survived the rebellions of 1715 and 1745. After the emended text was set by founding editors of *Hymns Ancient and Modern* (1861) to the sturdy tune "St. Anne,"[32] with its thoroughly English hint of melancholy, it became a tribal lay. As such, it first appeared under the heading "National Hymns" about the turn of the century, and became a standard hymn for the Remembrance Day services throughout the Commonwealth (originally signifying the Puritan regime) that were designed to ensure that fallen soldiers should *not* fly "forgotten as a dream."[33] Although the implication that the throne, Parliament, and national Church would outlast war and change was precisely the opposite of what he had said in the omitted stanzas, Watts the patriot would certainly have approved the new interpretation, for by his very act of naturalizing and Christianizing the Psalms he endorsed that transference of divine favour from Israel to Britain already visible in George Wither's hymns and Milton's *Areopagitica*. "Israel" and "Judah" were replaced by England and Scotland.[34]

Several hymns by his fellow Independent Philip Doddridge entreated God to love and chasten the British Isles as He had Israel. "Great God of Hosts, attend our Pray'r," urged God to "make the British Isles" his care when "angry Nations" would "tread our Glory down" and "defile" the Hanoverian crown, and described Britain as "Emanuel's land." In another, God's faithful "Remnant" pleaded "Our Nation shield, our Country spare."[35] After the rebellions, another hymn offered thanks for the defeat of the conspiracy between the Stuart Pretender and French king in images partly naturalistic and partly scriptural (Britons now seated under vines and fig trees) that blend in the line "Drove back the tide, that delug'd half our land."[36]

During the American war Newton pictured the Angel of the Apocalypse pouring "vials of fierce wrath" upon the "guilty land" of Britain as brother strove against brother,[37] while Benjamin Beddome realistically described "loud cannon" and blood polluting the earth, and urged the renunciation of "useless sword" and "glittering spear." Beddome's hymn was entitled "On Britain, long a favour'd isle" (1778).[38]

During the Victorian era Britain the chosen nation became the source rather than the object of judgment, and perhaps for that reason patriotic hymns declined in quality. The combination of religious with secular patriotism in T.H. Gill's "Lift thy song among the nations," has already been demonstrated.[39] Only near the end of that era did jingoism predominate. "Now pray we for our country" (1840) appealed for England to remain not only a "holy" but a "happy" abode of peace and freedom.[40] Wreford's well-known hymn for Queen Victoria's accession, "Lord, while for all mankind we pray" appeals for secular forms of happiness: peace, freedom, and prosperity. Even "sepulchres" has secular meaning in these lines on the attachment of Britons to their land:

> Our fathers' sepulchres are here,
> And here our kindred dwell,
> Our children too; how should we love
> Another land so well?[41]

While the Congregational lyric "Our fathers were high-minded men" (1844) can be read as celebrating either Protestant or national heroes, the mid-Victorians Arthur Penrhyn Stanley, in "Let us with a gladsome mind" (1873), and Ellerton in "Praise to our God, whose bounteous hand" (1871) (both discussed earlier) gave thanks for the secular blessings of throne, land, famous men and, above all, national security. Even H.M. Gunn in "To realms beyond the sounding sea" (1859), though describing the colonies as promised lands by which God has led English settlers, beats no jingoistic drum.

The "wild tongues" were loosed in 1887, in a booklet for the Golden Jubilee. Bishop Bickersteth of Exeter, compiler of the Evangelical *Hymnal Companion*, permitted use of his doggerel verses "God of our fatherland," designed for singing to the tune of the National Anthem. Bickersteth prayed that the "guardian sea" remain under God's smile, the "Gospel's light" its "buckler and sword" by day and night. While the Bishop of Southwell contented himself with an account of the Queen's reign, S.J. Stone, whose "The Church's one foundation" had already verged upon ecclesiolatry, burst into a torrent of idolatrous rhetoric in "God of supreme dominion," culminating in the allusion "her realm lies . . . 'Neath an unsetting sun." Baring-Gould's paean rivalled in extravagance, though not in art, the poetic compliments paid to Queen Elizabeth three centuries earlier, descending from the "thousand stars . . . burning" in Heaven and planets turning in their orbits, to Britain in its God-ordained pre-eminence, its Queen "commanding . . . As a bright peculiar star." Like other late Victorian hymnists, he cast over the national history a religious and mythological aura, urging God to "extend the stately story" of "our nation great, serene, / Faithful, loyal, well-compacted" as in ages past. A then eminent theologian named Mason distilled the essence of the peculiarly Anglican church-and-throne worship by calling on "daughter Churches" from "East to West" to praise God who "raises monarchs" and "gives his people rest." Lauding the "happy Queen" in whose time peace has flourished in "rich abundance," he saw no anomaly in rejoicing that "with her flag, the Gospel / Speeds to every clime," so that "India's sons of freedom / Give thanks for England's Queen." Ellerton adds that "Dusky Indian," "strong Australian," "Western forest" and "Southern sea" cry "God save the Queen."[42]

But for their evidence of national self-deception, these lyrics that never reached the hymn-books could be left in decent obscurity. They and the preceding hymns show how the Second Israel archetype, that originated with the Anglican George Wither and grew with the Puritan Commonwealth and Dissenting communities, culminated in an identification by the Anglican Establishment, especially its Broad Church wing, of the nation's prosperity with the divine favour. A similar activism and sense of enjoying divine protection can be observed even now in the United States, but with two differences. First, the American patriotic hymnist tends to glorify the land of liberty in the abstract, the British to praise the sovereign and famous men. Second, instead of praising physical features or institutions such as the

English coast, fields, castles, cottages, or ancient churches, the American praises his vast land's very emptiness, its limitless forests and plains, and inexhaustible resources. Until late in the nineteenth century these endeared it to Unitarians in particular. The American could sing "O beautiful our country" or "America the beautiful" without having mentally to exclude a great chunk of heartland given over to industry. Even New Jersey has its stretches of woodland. Victorian hymns never exalted the manufacturers, inventions, transportation, and industrial cities that were the chief cause of England's wealth and influence, these being resistant to Christian sentiment and symbolism.[43] Hymns on the American nation and landscape tended toward abstractness. "God bless our native land" could conclude in "God save the State"[44] without self-contradiction because for American patriotic hymnody the poet conveyed the idea of a Promised Land of freedom rather than the geography or social system, the ideals of liberty and patriotism rather than the rights and fealties. Had the Old Testament related the occupation of Canaan from the viewpoint of the dispossessed Canaanites, Americans might have bought less readily the myth that God had prepared for them a continent to which native Indians had no right.

Space permits but few illustrations. The myth of the exodus from European oppression to the God-given homeland informs the opening stanza of "My country, 'tis of thee" (1832) (also to the tune of "God save the King"):

> Sweet land of liberty
> Of thee I sing;
> Land where my fathers died,
> Land of the pilgrim's pride,
> From every mountain side
> Let freedom ring.[45]

The illimitable landscape is implied also in "O beautiful our country" (1884), but Hosmer dwells less on "wealth of commerce" and "harvests waving" than on freedom, classlessness, and racial mixture. Let it be America's pride to "lift up / The manhood of the poor"; let her represent "Freedom's open door" to the oppressed; let her exult that the "blood of noble races / Commingled flows."[46]

A single issue compelled American hymnists to face the contradiction between ideal and reality. "Once to every man and nation" (1845) has in British ears a priggish ring of the mission hall. For Abolitionists, Lowell described precisely this issue confronting Americans, who must support "the good or evil side." But even he devotes this hymn mainly to the abstraction, the cause he styles "God's new Messiah."[47] Likewise singers on both sides of the Atlantic have mythologized John Brown into an abstraction typifying man's struggle for liberty and justice, whose soul marches in his successors rather than toward heaven. Transplanted to Britain, the black-and-white ethos and tub-thumping tune of "Stand up, stand up for Jesus" (1858), based on an Abolitionist's last words, again have a whiff of the mission hall, even though the text has far more theological substance than the average military hymn.[48]

In modern times, no English crisis has so focused the imagination as the American Civil War. The First World War inspired a wealth of secular and sacred poetry because of the losses, not the cause. During the Second World War, despite the clear moral issue, poets of quality no longer wrote hymns.

As Donald Davie has recently shown, Kipling probably drew on the Calvinist trope of the consecrated people under divine judgment for his "Recessional," the only poem of note composed for either of the royal jubilees.[49] I shall discuss it later in conjunction with admonitory hymns composed after the Great War but would here remark its realistic images of war ("reeking tube and iron shard"), its sombre tone inspired by the German menace, and its dawning historical perspective in the apprehension lest the Empire pass into oblivion like Nineveh. Reprehensible as were both Kipling's excess of patriotism in "lesser breeds" and his insincerity in assuming a faith he did not hold, he saw beyond the seemingly endless triumphs of British arms.

Kipling's lyric stands between two kinds, the patriotic and the socially judgmental. The former, as I stated earlier, infiltrated day and even Sunday-school hymnals after the Boer War, and can be found in those for adults. It is doubtful whether the average church or chapel-goer often sang patriotic hymns in services until after 1918, by which time the slaughter had made elegies of them. The place for "Land of hope and glory" was the music hall, the rally or even the drawing room. Until the Great War the God who had made Britain mighty took his place not on the cross but on the saluting base. Only the young were made to sing patriotic hymns, but their parents caught the jingoist infection during the Diamond Jubilee and Boer War. After the coronation of Edward VII, "Land of hope and glory" rapidly acquired the status of a sacred song.

The lyric of social concern entered the adult Nonconformist hymnal as early as the Chartist "When wilt Thou save the people?" Sometimes it was more socialist than Christian, as when Edward Carpenter's "England, arise! the long, long night is over," appeared under a heading "Patriotism" in the humanist *Hymns of Modern Thought* (1900). Alternatively, it was Anglo-Catholic. Scott Holland's "Judge Eternal, throned in splendour" and G.K. Chesterton's "O God of earth and altar" call for a cleansing of empire and nation by application of the Christian ethic.[50] Carpenter's lyric, summoning the English to awake from their "evil dream of toil and sorrow" for "the day is here" has the keynote of secular apocalypse, as if the author had come under Marxist influence from William Morris and the workers' rallies of 1889.[51]

The next patriotic hymn comparable to those of Kipling and Chesterton did not appear until 1918. The excellence of the verse prompted by the American Civil War and First World War indicates that struggle and grief stimulate the poet more than jubilation.

WARTIME HYMNODY

Conversely, as Archbishop Randal Davidson remarked in 1914, "Most of us have discovered" that in time of "overwhelming stress . . . poetry can do for us what prose words cannot do." Davidson was commending the forty lyrics of *In Hoc Signo: Hymns of War and Peace*, one of four small collections issued soon after the outbreak of war.[52] To judge from the Latin title, the compilers intended the book mainly for officers. At all events, this selection does not bear out the popular impression that Anglican clergy turned their pulpits into recruiting stands. Among the initial "Hymns of Battle" "God the all-terrible! King who ordainest" was, as we have seen, a plea for peace. A new one, "Lord, while afar our brothers fight" (printed in all four books), though leaning toward the Allied cause in trusting that "right shall triumph over wrong" pleads for the mortally wounded and their loved ones and acknowledges neglect of God as in some sense a cause of the war. Indeed the best poems, on the "Coming of the Kingdom," Milton's "The Lord will come and not be slow" or Montgomery's "Hark! the song of jubilee" appear scarcely relevant to the war. Even the seven "National Hymns" include the far from jingoistic "When wilt Thou save the people?" and "Judge Eternal, throned in splendour," while Gill's "Lift thy song among the nations," as we have seen, initially commemorated the English Reformation. An idealistic young officer might find inspiration in the American hymns on "God as Peacemaker": "Eternal Ruler of the ceaseless round" and "O brother man, fold to thy heart thy brother."[53] Among those on "God's Victory," "Thy kingdom come, on bended knee" and "These things shall be" were similarly idealistic, while "Praise to our God, whose bounteous hand" lauds not English power but the English environment. Only to the section on "Spiritual Conflict" can exception be taken. In this context, "Lord of the brave, who call'st Thine own to fearless war" and "Who would true valour see, / Let him come hither" obviously sound the call to arms.

All told, *In Hoc Signo* was far less reprehensible than the sermons of the then Bishop of London and other dignitaries,[54] and infinitely better balanced than the Unitarian booklet of twenty-six *Hymns in Time of National Crisis,* among which only "O God our help" and "Once to every man and nation" impart any tinge of sobriety. An early Victorian text dug out for the occasion typifies the heady optimism of that disastrous time:

> In a noble cause contending,
> God speed the right!
> . . .
> Truth shall win, whate'er delay it,
> There's no power on earth shall stay it.[55]

Even the Roman Catholic Faber's "Oh, it is hard to work for God" came in useful, for "Upon this battlefield of earth . . . right the day must win" receive a literal application by which "to doubt" the national cause was "disloyalty," to "falter would be sin." From the Unitarian convert Stopford Brooke, once chaplain to Queen Victoria, came the metaphorically intended "Arm, soldiers of the Lord" (1891), now literally applied to urge troops to right "wrong" with "shield and breastplate, helm and sword."[56] The coincidence of this booklet's title with that of one issued in 1804 for the "Alarming Crisis" of the Napoleonic War underlines our tendency to think of major wars in apocalyptic terms.

The Church of Scotland's booklet of twelve *Hymns Suitable for Use in Time of War* begins in a more humane spirit. Its first author admits to the collective waste of divine gifts before pleading for "our brethren" fighting in the "cause of truth." Then S.C. Lowry, author of "Lord, while afar brothers fight," laments like Newton long before, "Behold, Lord, how the nations rage / In fierce and deadly strife . . . their wrath assuage, / And stem this waste of life." In war he sees only a "raging tide of sin," and universal "wail of agony" from wounded men and "homes bereaved." Let God forgive all combatants, who "know not what they do." To publish this pacifist poem must have taken much courage.

Subsequent lyrics forsake all moderation. Another clergyman, W.J. Mathams, calls on the "God of Battles" to hear the Nation's heartfelt prayer for its "brave defenders" by girding them for the conflict when "The trumpet call resounding / Speeds them forward." If a realist in replacing the clash of swords and shields by the "awful cannon's roar," he shares the prevailing apocalyptic view of this "war to end war" by beseeching Christ to act as Captain and Guide till "the world's last war is o'er."

Another clergyman, J. MacBeth, urges the "glorious Guardian of our land" to inspire courage in "duty's dread baptismal fire":

> When hosts on earth presume in might

> To scorn the sacred law of right;
> Let counter hosts in justice rise
> And right the wrong through sacrifice.

He pleads, however, that none on field or ocean "destroy where love can save" and that Christ may unfurl the "flag of peace" upon a "blood-stained, weary world."

The same church's substantial selection of *Psalms, Paraphrases, Hymns and Passages of Scripture Suitable for Use in Time of War* represents an effort to construct a small-scale hymnal relevant to the war out of standard congregational and mission hymnals. None can be found on the life of Christ, and only one each on the Resurrection or the Scriptures, but four each on "Holiness and Aspiration" and "Discipleship and Service" and half-a-dozen each on "Temptation and Conflict" and "Trust and Resignation." These larger sections and mission hymns entitled "Faithful warriors," "March, march onward soldiers true," "Pass the word along the line," and "Breast the wave, Christian, when it is strongest" highlight the soldier's dilemma. In Flanders, the soldier needed the courage of the early martyr to do a duty the martyr would have refused. But the Christian hymn, like the faith itself, fortified him for moral and spiritual combat. "Am I a soldier of the Cross" and "The royal banners forward go" had treated of a quite different combat. Shrapnel and bullet struck at random, regardless of faith or character. Alone of the combatant powers, Britain had a moral imperative in her obligation to defend Belgium, but the weapons employed and the interminable casualty lists soon made nonsense of knightly honour.

In 1914 the influence of the churches remained such that a joint declaration by the Pope, the Orthodox patriarchs, the Archbishop of Canterbury, and other leaders, forbidding any Christian to wage war, might have caused the fighting to peter out as it did on the first Christmas Day, but the churches were too fragmented and alienated. In the late twentieth century, when the mainstream churches could conceivably issue such a declaration, they have lost their hold over the masses. They had lost it by 1939, when in any case Hitler and Nazism represented a far graver threat to civilization than the Kaiser's military machine. Even in 1914, the national church that acted alone to deter its members from fighting would have lost a great many of them. As it was, the Church of Scotland prescribed "Fight the good fight," "Soldiers of Christ, arise," "Onward Christian soldiers" for the living and, under the title "Heavenly Glory," "Safe home, safe home in port" for the slain. Many who survived to recall the recruiting sermons, of Anglican clergy in particular, drifted away from religion in disillusionment.

By 1914, to judge from Zuckmayer's recollection printed as epigraph to this chapter, the secularization that began once Luther nailed his theses to the church door was complete. Transcendence had been reassigned to the nation-state. The flood of Lutheran hymnody had long since dried up, yet the Evangelical Church, being responsible for the religious education of most German Protestants, required pupils to recite the great hymns with passages of Scripture.[57] "Ein feste Burg" lent itself even more readily to patriotic interpretation than "O God, our help in ages past." Battle imagery in this and other Lutheran texts could be reapplied to Bismarck's purpose of forging old princedoms into a modern imperial power. But the real triumph of post-Reformation nationalism lay in the directives to Roman Catholic and Orthodox laymen to fight their fellow believers in other countries, a requirement never yet imposed upon the essentially English-speaking members of the Anglican Communion.

In England only pupils at church schools had to recite hymn texts,[58] yet the daily services at both public and council schools, and the tradition of Sunday-school attendance, ensured widespread use of the best-known hymns for both adults and children. The great hymns of Watts, Wesley, Heber, and Montgomery appeared when the nation was waging wars against France, so that almost from the beginning singers could apply in a patriotic sense both the Chosen People archetype and the Pauline military metaphors. Dissenting hymnists even identified Rome, and by implication Catholic France and Spain, as the enemy. By the time Germany became the national enemy, the greatest hymns were common knowledge. Essentially, therefore, congregations reapplied "O God, our help," "Soldiers of Christ," "Fight the good fight" and the like.

PATRIOTIC IMAGES

In wartime, both patriotism and disillusionment found expression in secular poems by Rupert Brooke, Siegfried Sassoon, and Wilfrid Owen. Even Studdert-Kennedy reached his audience more through his poems than his hymns.[59] The time-lag between the hymn's composition and congregational singing unfitted it for the task of registering responses to the crisis. To their eternal credit, young British poets and novelists—Owen, Graves, or Vera Brittain—perceived the war for the unrelieved disaster it was, yet only one hymnist found in it the "terrible beauty" that Yeats discovered in the Irish Easter uprising.[60] Comparison of Sir John Arkwright's "O valiant hearts" with two other famous hymns of the post-war period and with Kipling's reveals a wide spectrum of attitudes to war and the nation.

Kipling puts to idolatrous use the Old Testament myth of the Chosen People. The Lord of the far-flung British battle-line has entrusted His people with "Dominion over palm and pine." Here Kipling goes back further, to the divine commitment of the earth to Adam. The "ancient sacrifice" required of man, a "humble and contrite heart," is set forth in the 51st Psalm and a verse in Isaiah.[61] The prophet denounces the vain sacrifices of the idolater, concluding: "When thou criest, let thy companies deliver thee; but the wind shall carry them all way; vanity shall take them: but he that putteth his trust in me shall possess the land, and shall inherit my holy mountains" (Isa. 57. 13). Kipling alludes to other Old Testament books, but nowhere to the New Testament. He adapts pre-Christian biblical teachings: the distinction between God's holy nation and the heathen that put their trust in cannon and shrapnel, the boasting Gentiles outside a Law that is at once the Law of Moses and Kipling's own Law of the Jungle (that is, of tribal survival) fashioned from the teachings of Darwinian biologists.

To say this is not to disparage either Kipling's Hebraic teaching or his Hellenic warning against tribal hubris. But for its contemporary allusion, to the "lesser breeds," his poem conveys far more sober wisdom than does the ritualese rant of "O valiant hearts," an elegy based on the Last Supper and the Arthurian romances. Arkwright's text, though still sung at some Remembrance Day services, is otherwise so little known as to need quoting in full:

> O valiant hearts, who to your glory came
> Through dust of conflict and through battle flame,
> Tranquil you lie, your knightly virtue proved,
> Your memory hallowed in the land you loved.
>
> Proudly you gathered, rank on rank, to war,
> As who had heard God's message from afar:
> All you had hoped for, all you had, you gave
> To save mankind—yourselves you scorned to save.
>
> Splendid you passed, the great surrender made,
> Into the light that never more shall fade:
> Deep your contentment in that blest abode
> Who wait the last clear trumpet-call of God.
>
> Long years ago, as earth lay dark and still,
> Rose a loud cry upon a lonely hill,
> While in the frailty of our human clay
> Christ, our Redeemer, passed, the self-same way.
>
> Still stands His cross from that dread hour to this,
> Like some bright star above the dark abyss;
> Still, through the veil, the victor's pitying eyes
> Look down to bless our lesser Calvaries.

> These were His servants, in His steps they trod,
> Following through death the martyred Son of God:
> Victor He rose; victorious too shall rise
> They who have drunk His cup of sacrifice.

> O risen Lord, O Shepherd of our Dead,
> Whose cross has brought them and Whose staff has led—
> In glorious hope their proud and sorrowing Land
> Commits her children to Thy gracious hand.[62]

Sir John Arkwright knows the eucharistic rites and hymnody, as witness his allusion to Conder's "blest cup of sacrifice"[63] and his typology of Christ as Shepherd leading the chosen flock with His staff. His elevation of fallen officers, presumably, to models of "knightly virtue," each scorning self-preservation, is more forgivable than his idolatrous parallel of each with Christ. Even as he deprives the Cross of personal relevance by comparing it to a "bright star," he mythologizes the squalid butchery in France into a million "lesser Calvaries" and the recruiting drives to "God's message from afar." Evidently familiar with orthodox theology, as witness the dual motifs in the third stanza of the instant passage into unfading light and the long rest pending the Last Trump, Arkwright transforms Christ into a Shepherd of the dead, thus banishing Him from the post-war world of the living. But his subtlest (or least realized) touch of idolatry is his metamorphosis of the "proud and sorrowing Land" into the willing mother who commits her children to Christ. Orthodox hymns like "For all the saints" were misapplied in Remembrance services, but "O valiant hearts" was never anything but idolatrous. Wonder is that it endured so long before a common revulsion consigned it to obscurity. Ironically, this beatification of dead British soldiers was sung to a tune by Gustav Holst, a composer of German descent. It appeared in a grammar-school hymn-book as late as 1937.[64]

The more reflective and genuinely Christian lyrics of Sir Cecil Spring-Rice and Clifford Bax remain in common use. At the end of 1917 the former was suddenly recalled from his post as Ambassador in Washington, where he had served throughout the war. Soon after a farewell call on President Wilson, he added a new first verse, beginning "I vow to thee, my country" to two stanzas on heaven composed in 1911. The complete poem, embodying his realization that service to an earthly country may pass forgotten and needs therefore to be underpinned by love of the heavenly land, came into use as a hymn seven years later, under the heading "The Two Fatherlands," reaching its pinnacle of fame when sung at the royal wedding in 1982. By coincidence it too was set to a tune from Gustav Holst's "Planets" entitled "Thaxted," the village where Holst had composed the suite.[65] In his architecturally renowned village church the Rector of Thaxted, Conrad Noel, was later to hoist the Red Flag and denounce imperialism lock, stock, and barrel, rather than taking the balanced view of Spring-Rice.

Though chastened by his inconsiderate recall, the author makes a patriotic commitment only just short of idolatry, offering a "love that asks no question" but "makes undaunted the final sacrifice." His line on heaven as "another country, I've heard of long ago," in the second verse, is the more revealing for having been written three years before the war. Literally it means only that he was brought up a Christian, but his next line "Most dear to them that love her, most great to them that know" leaves open the possibility of disbelief. His personal patriotic commitment in the first has no true correlative in the subsequent verses. None the less, his concluding lines reconcile objective awareness of a heaven no longer universally believed in with the missionary hope and inwardness that were the legacy of the Wesleys:

> Her fortress is a faithful heart, her pride is suffering;
> And soul by soul and silently her shining bounds increase,
> And her ways are ways of gentleness and all her paths are peace.

To this extent, the Learned and Popular traditions meet in this admirable hymn.

In 1918 Clifford, brother of the composer Arnold Bax, wrote "Turn back, O man, forswear thy foolish ways." Aptly set to a Genevan psalm tune dating from before the development of either English hymnody or nationalism, it also expounds a religion of inwardness, in contrast to the "tragic empires" that rise age by age to fulfil dreams of power. Partly because of an intrinsically difficult ruling idea, and partly, no doubt, because of an obscure allusion in its opening verse,

> Yet thou, her (earth's) child, whose head is crowned with flame,
> Still wilt not hear thine inner God proclaim—
> "Turn back, O Man, forswear thy foolish ways."

this hymn has never been so popular as "I vow to thee," but its best days may be to come, for the refrain that with variations echoes throughout the remaining stanzas, "Earth might be fair, and all her people one" represents the only dream mankind can afford to fulfil. If a dream of terrestrial happiness, it originated in the prophecy of Micah and had an analogue in the vision of "Solomon," author of the earliest known Christian hymn-book. The dream of world-conquest, implies Bax, leads but to suffering and disappointment, and only when man has awakened from his "haunted sleep" can "God's whole will be done."[66]

A relativist critique would doubtless represent Kipling and Arkwright as living in religio-patriotic dreams from which two world wars have awakened us, Spring-Rice and Bax as voicing the awareness of the more thinking among the English establishment that the days of Empire were numbered. Speaking in Ottawa not long before his sudden death, Spring-Rice embodied in two symbols a truth that I believe mankind must learn if his dominion over this planet is to continue. Contrasting the civilizations of Egypt and Assyria, founded on fear and absolute power, with Christian civilizations having as their often unrealized ideal self-sacrificing love and service, he pointed to their respective emblems as being the Scourge and the Cross.[67]

APPENDIX (see note 24)

Wesley's Text

Soldiers of Christ, arise,
   And put your armour on,
Strong in the strength which God supplies
   Through his eternal Son;
Strong in the Lord of Hosts,
   And in his mighty power,
Who in the strength of Jesus trusts,
   Is more than conqueror.

Stand then in his great might,
   With all his strength endued;
But take, to arm you for the fight,
   The Panoply of God:
That having all things done,
   And all your conflicts pass'd,
Ye may o'ercome, through Christ alone,
   And stand entire at last.

Stand then against your foes,
   In close and firm array:
Legions of wily fiends oppose
   Throughout the evil day:
But meet the sons of night,
   But mock their vain design,
Arm'd in the arms of heavenly light,
   Of righteousness divine.

Leave no unguarded place,
   No weakness of the soul;
Take every virtue, every grace,
   And fortify the whole:
Indissolubly join'd,
   To battle all proceed;
But arm yourselves with all the mind
   That was in Christ, your Head.

Abbreviated Text

Soldiers of Christ, arise,
   And put your armour on;
Strong in the strength which God supplies,
   Through his eternal Son;

Strong in the Lord of Hosts,
   And in his mighty power;
Who in the strength of Jesus trusts
   Is more than conqueror.

Stand then in his great might,
   With all his strength endued:
And take, to arm you for the fight,
   The panoply of God.

From strength to strength go on,
   Wrestle, and fight, and pray;
Tread all the powers of darkness down,
   And win the well-fought day.

That having all things done,
   And all your conflicts past,
Ye may o'ercome, through Christ alone,
   And stand entire at last.
            (*MHB* 1933)

15

IDOLATRY AND RELIGION IN DECLINE

> *The Sea of Faith*
> *Was once, too, at the full, and round earth's shore*
> *Lay like the folds of a bright girdle furl'd.*
> *But now I only hear*
> *Its melancholy, long, withdrawing roar,*
> *Retreating, to the breath*
> *Of the night-wind, down the vast edges drear*
> *And naked shingles of the world.*
>
> Arnold, "Dover Beach"

What constitutes an idol once endowed with supreme value can legitimately claim our affections. A monarch or president represents the order without which civilization disintegrates, while school and family establish interior and social harmony. The natural order humankind despoils at its peril. Yet viewed as its own end, each becomes an idol. A pope or king owns subjection to a higher Sovereign, a premier or president to the law, parents to the mores and, depending on their belief, the religion of their society. That rulers of every kind have sought power as an end requires no demonstration. Even the family, however sanctified by sacred books, can to the general detriment become its own end, as witness the mismanagement of a state or enterprise by a clan.

Without doubt late Victorian and Edwardian hymnody, notably for the young, encouraged the improper veneration of the nation-state, yet there was a world of difference between its presumption that God had chosen Britain as an instrument to spread His Kingdom and the worship of Hitler as incarnating a national will subject to no higher law, or the current adoration of "Mother Russia."

Some poets of the Learned tradition, to be sure, endorsed the social hierarchy as divinely sanctioned, as implicitly did many of the Popular tradition who consoled the poor with visions of future happiness. After the mid-nineteenth century, neither group idolized the family structure, but both intensified and further sentimentalized the Romantic cult of the child. Hymnals of the Learned tradition, with some for the first elementary schools, fostered the companion cult of Nature that continued to flourish after the First World War when other secular cults—of nation, social hierarchy, child, and school—were dying out or taking more acceptable forms. Among the populace at large, hymn-singing, like worship itself, was confined to the school assembly, yet compilations both for adults and for children represented a poetic taste more catholic and more fastidious than that of any age in England since those of the monastic orders.

A cult may be termed idolatrous when it violates one of two principles, contingency and delegation. The Christian or any other nation that worships a transcendent deity must acknowledge its own dependence, even that of the natural and cosmic order, upon the Creator, and the power of parents or rulers as deputed by Him, whether directly or by election.

Between the wars patriotic hymns declined in proportion and suffered a change of tone and focus. The nation, its confidence eroded by the slaughter and subsequent unemployment, ceased by degrees to presume itself either self-sufficient or divinely sanctioned to rule and evangelize vast regions of the earth. In the quickly established Remembrance Day convention, hymns and prayers commemorated fallen members not so much of the nation as of the social community. The perfervid patriotism of a previous era can be glimpsed in some lyrics reprinted in *Songs of Praise* (1925, 1931) and some school hymnals.

> What heroes thou hast bred,
> England, my country!
> I see the mighty dead
> Pass in line . . .

declares G.K. Menzies, ready to give his all for this "Mother."[1] More typical, however, is the elegaic sadness, redolent of Elgar's Cello Concerto (1922), that pervades the liturgy for Remembrance Day in the Harrow County Grammar School hymnal of 1923. After Binyon's poem "For the Fallen" come "O God, our help in ages past," the "Benedictus" and a prayer to the God who has "sheltered," "redeemed," "spared," and "helped" the nation "to this hour." Then follow the opening three verses of "For all the Saints," the reading of the names of casualties, a thanksgiving for their example, the Two Minutes' Silence, Last Post, and Reveille. The ensuing prayer for grace to follow "the path of courage and self-sacrifice," for hearts to "feel for the suffering and oppressed" and for devotion to "Truth and Righteousness" remains above criticism. When, however, the hymn resumed at "O blest communion, fellowship divine" and the service concluded with the Collect for All Saints ("O Almighty God, who has knit together Thine elect in one communion and fellowship in the mystical body of Thy Son. . . . "), and the National Anthem, many a boy must have imagined saints in khaki raiment marching in columns of four.[2]

Yet the prevailing mood is elegaic, a calling of bugles from sad shires. Exultant military hymns of an earlier day, headed "Soldiers of Christ," pertain to other services. "Fight the good fight" follows its source-text in the service for "St. Paul's Day" (p. 41). Laurence Housman's "Lord God of Hosts," sung on St. George's Day to the tune of "Eternal Father, strong to save" and resolving to make England a "land acceptable" to God, is anything but jingoistic. Even the psalm verse for Commonwealth Day, "Blessed is the nation whose God is the Lord; and the people he hath chosen for his own inheritance" (Ps. 33.12), and National Anthem, are accompanied by the restrained early Victorian "Lord, while for all mankind we pray" and German "Now thank we all our God." Only the Trafalgar Day devotion is idolatrous. When singing Kipling's "Recessional" boys might well have envisaged Napoleon's men as among "lesser breeds," and when singing "Lord of our life, and God of our salvation" envisaged "hungry billows" curling not around the Church but around Nelson's ships.[3]

The strange brew of apocalyptic radicalism and nationalism stirred up in pre-war Broad Church hymnals still simmered in *Songs of Praise*, but with more of the former. Under "Social Service" (173-84) poets protest abuses from slavery to laissez-faire economics. Blake finds it unholy to see "so many children poor" (174); the pacifist Whittier urges each to enfold his "brother" man (176); yet Shelley proclaims that "The world's great age begins anew" (180), Kingsley that the "day of the Lord" is "at hand" (179). In the more balanced "O God of earth and altar," Chesterton laments the faltering of "earthly rulers" and division of people by "walls of gold," "swords of scorn," above all by pride and "lies." He calls mainly, however, for social and organic unity:

> Tie in a living tether
> The prince and priest and thrall,
> Bind all our lives together,
> Smite us and save us all (177).

The recurrent archaisms "thrall," "ire," and above all "sword" must regrettably confine this admirable assertion of the social gospel to the age of William Morris or the later Tennyson.

The widespread influence of G.W. Briggs' enlarged version of *Songs of Praise* (1931) upon compilers for schools perpetuated this strain of chivalric patriotism. As mentioned in Chapter 14, "O valiant hearts" appeared in a school hymnal as late as 1937.[4] A precursor of *Songs of Praise*, E.M. Palser's *New School Hymnal* (1913), in use long after its time, carries a statement by Julian that reads like an epitaph on Victorian civilization. The ideal school hymnal will "express . . . on the one hand the sense of dependence . . . frailty . . . penitence . . . purity and the high vision of heaven"; on the other "steadfastness, resolve, the facing of odds, the warrior and chivalrous aspect of the Cross, the thrilling memory of prophet and apostle, saint, hero and martyr." Its further keynote should be "praise and jubilation" at the "majesty of God's creation" and "God-given beauty of human life." Julian invokes the Learned tradition in calling for a hymnal "designed for a community drawn from the higher ranks," "full of culture," and "thoroughly edited," as regards "purity of text," "exact indication" of source and author, "effective grouping," "full indexes," and one showing a high degree of "imagination and poetic form."[5] The patriotic or any other vein of hymnody flourished between the wars mainly by continuance of the Learned tradition, which now identified the nation less with an imperial than with a cultural heritage.

Robert Bridges' *Yattendon Hymnal* (1899) represents the most conscious endeavour to merge worship with literary culture. Depressed by the undiscriminating attention paid in Julian's *Dictionary of Hymnology* to poetically worthless lyrics as well as to great hymns, Bridges introduced treasures from the seventeenth-century poets that took their place in the canon of English hymnody. Though the book itself was to remain a collector's item, its influence upon compilers can scarcely be exaggerated.

Percy Dearmer did hymnody an equal service by enlisting Ralph Vaughan Williams as musical editor of the *English Hymnal* (1906), which in time endowed all denominations with superb lyrics and tunes. Dearmer and Williams, T.S. Eliot, and Benjamin Britten, among others, made the Anglican Church a patron of the arts like no spiritual organization in Britain since the high Middle Ages. By recruiting Martin Shaw as musical co-editor (with Vaughan Williams) of *Songs of Praise*, Dearmer further enriched the store of melodies, but by then needed a Bridges to subdue a craving for relevance that prompted such mischoices as "With wonderful deathless ditties / We build up the world's great cities" (*SP* 184).

Having largely, as Coleridge and Thomas Arnold hoped, evolved into the nation's spiritual antenna, the Church of England between the wars became almost a phantom, for to what extent even Bridges, Williams, or Britten believed the central Christian tenets remains in doubt. Like Thomas Hardy as poet (as distinct from the novelist), or the littérateurs so ready to denounce the *New English Bible* and experimental liturgies, they represented a strain of authors and composers more Anglican than Christian. Together with the British Broadcasting Corporation, the Shakespeare and National theatre companies, and the British Museum, the great cathedrals of the Anglican Church form a major portion of the nation's cultural heritage, but what the half-instructed thousands who drift through them actually believe or gather has become increasingly uncertain.

In his preface to *Songs of Praise* Dearmer affirmed that if the churches were "to recover during the present century the ground . . . lost during the last" much would depend on the hymn-books used and "the way hymns are chosen." He and his co-editors hoped to bring hymn lyrics and tunes into the mainstream of English culture. Noting that from the appearance of the *English Hymnal* six important collections had but fifty items in common, they tried to match some "two hundred really fine" lyrics in common use with equally distinguished settings. They also resolved to avoid the common practices of restricting to Christmas and Easter those on the "glorious message" of the Incarnation and Resurrection while using penitential items throughout the year, and of overworking sentimental Victorian vesper hymns. In consequence, the forty initial titles on times and seasons were followed by a mere sixty on the liturgical calendar, while the "General" section included scores of items normally prescribed for the greater festivals.

In merging the liturgical with the calendar year and sacred with civil themes (after the section on the "Communion of Saints" came one on "Social Service"), so blending the hymnal with the anthology, Dearmer had been preceded by E.H. Palser, whose school collection had indeed carried no lyrics on the Sacraments or Last Things and very few on the Crucifixion. Palser had employed the author's non-sacramental refrain to "For the beauty of the earth" to make that eucharistic hymn a nature poem. He had also placed festive hymns like "As with gladness men of old," under the general heading "Praise." An English master at Westminster School, Palser introduced lyrics by Herbert and Vaughan, and quoted Tennyson on "Holy! holy! holy!" as in devotion and "purity of language" the "finest [hymn] ever written," and Arnold on "When I survey the wondrous Cross" as "the finest in the language." Like Dearmer, he tried to incorporate the best hymns into the canon of English poetry.

The price of this and the search for social and educational relevance—as in headings like "Christian Warfare" or "Perseverance, Work, Strife"—was the loss of that mythic sequence of Creation, Fall, Redemption, and Last Things so familiar in earlier church and public-school hymnals. In many instances religious verse was appropriated to the service of the school or of "National and Civic" institutions.[6]

The mythic sequence, or liturgical calendar, survived best in service-books for the great public schools: Winchester (1928), Harrow (1927), and Eton (1937). In its austere liturgical scheme and numerous texts in Latin, the Winchester collection (a revision of that issued in 1910) suggests that worship in the College chapel had changed little since the high Victorian era. Yet even in this Anglo-Catholic selection many items came from Watts,

Wesley, and the Evangelicals. The Eton College hymnal, based upon *Hymns Ancient and Modern* and *Songs of Praise*, could have served any "central church" Anglican cathedral. As compared with its late Victorian predecessor (1895), the Harrow collection carried few memorials of saints or pupils dying while at school, but a number of Remembrance Day hymns. If in general less "churchy," it showed a distinct muting of tone in its "National" section, the "Recessional" being outweighed by the unchauvinistic "Jerusalem," "Rejoice, O land, in God thy might" and "Judge eternal . . . " of Blake, Bridges, and Scott Holland. Even Kipling's "Land of our birth," a doctrinally unexceptionable specimen of "manly" Edwardian verse designed to inculcate the boy scout (and Christian) virtues of cleanliness, chastity, compassion, and obedience to conscience, has a refrain

> Land of our birth, we pledge to thee
> Our love and toil in the years to be;
> When we are grown and take our place
> As men and women with our race.

unworthy of its poet, yet indicative of the shift of focus from the nation's mission of conquest and conversion to its heritage and traditions. Some lines by Bridges reprinted in the Eton book further illustrate that shift:

> In thee our fathers trusted and were saved,
> In thee destroyed thrones of tyrants proud;
> From ancient bondage freed the poor enslaved;
> To sow thy truth poured out thy saintly blood.

While "The King, O God, his heart to thee upraiseth; / With him the nation bows before they face" (246) celebrates a "plenteous nation" still by divine fiat its "power extending," this and a subsequent stanza on intellectual integrity, courage, joy, and "faith beyond the grave" imply commitment to Christian democracy rather than tribal superiority.[7]

The best hymnals for girls conveyed a feeling more for the nation's literary than its social or imperial traditions. They had also become more orthodox. The *Cheltenham Ladies' College Hymnal* (1919),[8] with its range of mainstream Anglican, Catholic, and Dissenting hymnody, exuded a very different strain of piety from the liberal-Protestant enthusiasm of Miss Beale. While the distribution of boarding houses throughout the town ruled out Sunday communion hymns, the orthodox yet ecumenical flavour may be seen in this sample:

124 Lord Jesus, think on me (early N. African)

   16 O blest Creator of the light (early Latin)
   38 Come, O Creator Spirit, come (early medieval)
   49 Captains of the saintly band (Gallican)
   11 All my heart this night rejoices (German, 17th century)
   21 Come let us to the Lord our God (Scots Paraphrase)
    3 Ye servants of the Lord (Congregational)
   56 Forth in thy name, O Lord, I go (Wesleyan)
   37 The head that once was crowned with thorns (Evangelical)
   73 Alleluia, sing to Jesus (Anglo-Catholic)
  128 My God, how wonderful thou art (modern Catholic)
  125 Lord of all being, throned afar (American Unitarian)

Anglican orthodoxy and poetic taste attained their joint apotheosis in the finest public school hymn-book I know, that for St. Paul's Girls' School (1929).[9] Sequences for morning service and the liturgical year bring before singers the mythos or sacred story, indeed the entire spectrum of objective worship. In place of "Awake, my soul, and with the sun" or "Christ, whose glory fills the skies," the chaplain could select, inter alia, Bright's "At thy feet, O Christ, we lay / Thine own gift of this new day" (6), Newman's simple and touching version of an Ambrosian hymn "Now that the sun is beaming bright" (9), a literal translation of "Iam orto lucis sidere" or an unsentimental meditation "O Father, hear my morning prayer" (10) that epitomizes a quietist counter-melody to the book's Anglo-Catholic certitude. Let something of good be born in the singer "as the moments fly"; let the hours carry her a little "farther from the world" and "nearer thee."

At Christmas-tide, the chaplain could choose from a sprinkling of Latin carols and a whole range of medieval, Gallican, Anglo-Catholic, Evangelical, and other classics, from "Hark, a thrilling voice is sounding" (17) to "It came upon the midnight clear" (24), or "In the bleak mid-winter" (22). The alphabetically arranged "General" hymns, however, best exemplify that drawing upon the English and Latin poetic heritage that had been the raison d'être of the *Yattendon Hymnal*. Lyrics by Herbert, Vaughan, and Wither, "Let all the world in every corner sing" (145), "My soul, there is a country" (154), and "Come, O come in joyous lays" (114) are balanced by "All creatures of our God and King" (205), "City of God" (206), and Helen Waddell's beautiful translation of Abelard's "O quanta qualia" (208), published in that very year.[10] This came in a supplement to a collection originally designed to end with "And did those feet," the National Anthem, "I vow to thee, my country," "What heroes thou hast bred, / England, my England," and the School Song (199-202). Presumably these were aired for the annual prize-giving rather than Remembrance Day, since "O valiant hearts" figures among items for All Saints-tide.

Editors of the widely used *Public School Hymn Book* (1919) reacted not only against the pietism and death consciousness but against the idealism and nationalism of the pre-war generations. Thus "Weary of earth and laden with my sin" and "I heard the voice of Jesus say," vanished with "Soldiers of the Cross," "O merciful and holy," and the Boer War lyric "From homes of quiet peace." A patriotically inclined headmaster still had available the "Recessional," "Lord of the brave," and a plenitude of other suitable hymns.

Twenty years later, two further trends were evident in the hymnal for Worksop College, a school mainly for future army officers.[11] Though even more Anglo-Catholic than those for Winchester and St. Paul's, it carries lyrics by G.W. Briggs, editor of the orthodox enlargement of *Songs of Praise*. His commemoration hymn "Our Father, by whose servants / Our house was built of old" (103) treats the school itself as a venerable house of God, wherein present scholars who "reap" what their predecessors "have sown" themselves store up a "harvest" to be "garnered" by "ages yet unknown." An obscure hymnist named Dugmore (1843-1925) praises God as Creator of the "changeful beauty" of hill, vale, and ocean, that has inspired poets, painters, and musicians.[12] The arts and crafts having attracted even fewer hymnists of talent than have nature and tribal loyalties, in the hands of a more gifted poet Dugmore's vision might have served modern Christians better than most nature hymns.

A better poet, Joyce Anstruther ("Jan Struther"), composer of several well-known hymns for both children and adults, exemplifies appropriate "naturing" of the mythos by employing for her Easter carol "High o'er the lonely hills" the springtime greening of hill and vale as an analogy of the Resurrection.[13] In the hymnal for Ashford Grammar School (1937), appeared this (No. 37) and an adaptation of "Rejoice, the Lord is King" that illustrates naturing beyond the threshold of idolatry. Its first verse merely substitutes "Children" (rejoice) for "Mortals," but thereafter all but the refrain is rewritten in natural instead of mythic terms. God sends "wintry north-winds" and "thick showers of snow" to protect the "infant grain," "wakes the genial spring" and in due season "fills the golden ear." By the end a quite different future awaits mankind from that envisaged by Wesley, for

> Ye years, and months, and days,
> Bring in the eternal reign
> Of love and joy and praise (87)

implies an earthly paradise, the elements of death, apocalypse and judgment having vanished.[14] Fortunately, this lyric never took root, but arguably reverence for the life-cycle and ecology constitute the real religion of our time. The natural world viewed in a religious light had, however, been a central concern of poets since Wordsworth and Keble, and never more so than during the Edwardian and Georgian eras spanned by the career of Walter de la Mare.[15]

In hymns as in secular lyrics, naturalism went hand-in-hand with social idealism, and a would-be pacifism. Thus in the Ashford book, the naturalized Wesleyan hymn appears opposite "Ring out, wild bells" (88) in which Tennyson yearns for "nobler modes of life" than commercialism, party politics, or warfare. Between the wars at least six collections intended for or used in day-schools reprinted "These things shall be," a late Victorian attempt to secularize the prophet Micah's vision that nations shall make war no more.[16] Its final vision of "new arts" blooming in an earthly paradise reminds us how seriously the secular utopias of William Morris and H.G. Wells were taken by countless students before the Second World War. In hymns, at least, the genuinely Christian internationalism of "In Christ there is no East nor West" has outlasted both Broad Church and secular idealism.

Nature lyrics could fit into so orthodox a hymnal as that for the Girls' High School, in the cathedral city of Wakefield, without secular implication.[17] In a double-page spread (Nos. 9-11) "All things bright and beautiful," "And did those feet," and a Victorian nature lyric, "Angels holy, high and lowly" just within the bounds of immanentist theology, together convey a desire to restore the land to its pristine beauty and its inhabitants to the divine image. In "Angels holy" (1840), however, J.S. Blackie anticipates the Unitarian James Martineau's formula for modern devotional poetry[18] by shifting from angelic to earthly praise, by describing oceans, mountains, rivers, and fountains on earth and "starry temples" above. His post-romantic version of the "Benedicite" concludes with each voice singing its "free song" in praise of its "mighty Lord," with no mention of Christ or any life to come. But this otherwise old-fashioned hymn-book, which included, for example, Watts' "Christ hath a garden walled around" (22), supplies those elements of the mythos.

The Learned tradition was brought to bear upon the mass of children mainly in offshoots of *Songs of Praise*. One of the earliest and best remained in use throughout the city and county of Leicester from the mid-twenties until long after the shift to comprehensive schools in the 1950s. After editing *Songs of Praise Enlarged*, G.W. Briggs went on to produce innumerable school hymnals for Oxford University Press. Some local authorities produced their own hymnals, of which the best I have seen was compiled for Wolverhampton by an interdenominational committee of local clergy. In addition, Oxford University Press issued hymnals for junior elementary and church schools.[19] Independent or direct grant grammar schools often used the decidedly orthodox *Public School Hymn Book*.

Of two neo-Victorian selections for elementary schools by educational publishers, neither truly exemplified the Popular tradition. The *School Hymn Book* issued by Evans in 1920 apparently had some success, since a reprint came out forty years later.[20] It abounds in pseudo-romantic nature lyrics, patriotic hymns, and the sentimental ditties on childhood that called down Percy Dearmer's wrath at the "mass of hymns" by "excellent didactic persons, who often betray themselves by harping on the word 'little' till it becomes almost an expletive; and who put into the mouth of the unsuspecting adolescent words which express not what the child is but what they fancy a child ought to be."[21] To be fair, as alternatives to "God make my life a little light" (61), "Jesus, Friend of little children" (92) or "God who hath made the daisies" (31) children could have sung the non-sacramental version of "For the beauty of the earth" (36), some unexceptionable psalm paraphrases and standard hymns or carols for Christmas and Easter, morning and evening. Lyrics deemed too "passionate," "gloomy," or "terrifying" for children were omitted. Without "Rock of Ages" little remains of the Popular tradition save patriotic songs given undue prominence by being placed immediately after those for morning and afternoon service: "God bless our native land" (27), "Now pray we for our country" (23), Kipling's "Recessional" and "Land of our birth" (26, 28). But a thanksgiving for Victoria's reign (24) and a petition for "Lands across the sea" that fly "the flag of Britain" (25) must have lapsed into desuetude.[22]

A school hymnal issued by E.J. Arnold in 1922[23] carries a few non-military "national" hymns but mainly consists of texts standard among all "who regard the truths of religion from different standpoints." A single letter of the index subsumes Newman's "Lead, kindly Light" (12), Herbert's "Let all the world in every corner sing" (101), Milton's "Let us with a gladsome mind" (100), Wesley's "Lo! He comes . . . " and "Love divine" (24, 138), the didactic "Little drops of water" (70) and devotional "Loving Shepherd of Thy sheep" (81).

Whether or not these commercial publishers would have taken a chance on Jan Struther's quickly popular "Lord of all hopefulness, Lord of all joy" (1931), reprinted in the Junior Schools book,[24] no new selection by a commercial house survives in major library collections. Evidently, notwithstanding the handsome royalties earned by Briggs,[25] educational publishers did not consider the school hymn-book a commercial proposition.

In what ways did the inter-war school hymn-books, inspired by the Learned tradition, differ from those for the first elementary schools, inspired by the Popular? In a nutshell, they emphasized the mythos (specifically the Nativity), revered the natural world as a manifestation of Providence, and excluded all reference to social class. The later books instil an ethic valid for children of all ranks; their precursors one valid for the children of toil, sickness, and want. But the reader who knew nothing of the Great Depression would gather from, for example, the Oxford school collections that during the 1930s all children lived in prosperous southern villages or country towns, for no hymns address the condition of those in the industrial north whose fathers might be unemployed.

The Leicester area, being spared the mass unemployment that ravaged even the West Midlands, could be equated with the South. In the Leicester(shire) and Oxford hymnals, the Learned tradition supplies a core of objective and mythic hymns, from "All people that on earth do dwell" to "O come, O come Emmanuel," the Oxford junior school book being notably rich in carols. Yet some of its texts treat man as part of a natural order, as in E. Brailsford's

> All things which live below the sky
> Or move within the sea,
> Are creatures of the Lord most high
> And brothers unto me. (16)

This Franciscan sentiment, here developed into avowals of fellow feeling for robin, swallow, gull and wren, shows why "All creatures of our God and King" (14) is among the most beloved modern hymns. The brotherhood of all creatures supplanted the more ancient principle of analogy, of Nature-as-divine-revelation, because of the need to reconcile Christianity with evolution, to meld the notion of a divinely ordained Chain of Being with that of a continuum between species. This religion of nature vies with ecology and the veneration of the arts as the real religion of modern man. No lyric of modern origin, however, approaches in quality Keble's "There is a book . . . " (25), let alone those of Prudentius or Fortunatus. Beside

> The works of God above, below,
> Within us and around,
> Are pages in that book, to show
> How God himself is found.

and

> The moon above, the Church below,
> A wondrous race they run;
> But all their radiance, all their glow,
> Each borrows of its sun.

even Brailsford's lyric or the still popular "Summer suns are glowing" (Leicester, 182) want poetic substance. The absence of both the Hebraic trope of earth as the divine handiwork and the Darwinian image of life as struggle has reduced the nature-hymn to banality. The best verse on earth as man's home, not his place of exile, is to be found in the secular anthologies.

In this century, hymnists have found God more immanent in the human vocation and psyche than in nature. In "Lord of all hopefulness" children trust to encounter Christ, "skilled at the plane and the lathe," in their school work, in the joy of morning and peace of bedtime. More directly, in "Lord of health, thou life within us," Dearmer combines the trope of Christ the Liberator with a Goethean theme of the Spirit as life-force that once released by Christ, "leaps and glows" within.[26] The child who sings the concluding line "Till to thy far hills we rise" might be forgiven for confusing an old *topos*, the holy mount of Heaven, with the modern image of mountaineering as a means of self-transcendence. By removing death from the normal experience of children, the extension of the life-span has conferred supreme value upon this life, formerly presented to children as a condition of exile from their true home. This accommodation to life on earth has conditioned state school religion and also largely explained the shift of focus from the Passion to the Nativity, for to singers and hymnists of the eighteenth century the sacred mystery was death, and to those of the earlier twentieth it was birth. Not coincidentally, the former cult preceded a decline in juvenile mortality resulting from medical and social improvements; the latter accompanied a decline in the birth-rate accelerated by contraception.

The following comparison of the Leicester, Wolverhampton (*Wulfruna*) and *English School* (1939) hymn-books will involve categories of hymns employed in Chapter Five.[27] Leicester alone includes: (1) Victorian praise hymns of a unitarian cast ("Immortal, invisible . . . ," "Immortal love, for ever full"); (2) triumphal Christ-hymns ("At the name of Jesus," "See, the Conqueror mounts . . . "); (3) Holy Spirit: "Breathe on me, Breath of God" and (surprisingly), "Come down, O Love Divine"; (4) Wesleyan devotional hymns ("Love Divine . . . ," "O for a thousand tongues . . . "); (12) nature lyrics either secular ("I learned it in the meadow path") or analogical, as in Heber's "I praised the earth, in beauty seen," where earth is God's "ruined" handiwork;[28] (15) patriotic hymns, especially responses to the American Civil War and First World War ("Once to every man and nation," "I vow to thee . . . ," "Turn back, O man . . . "); together with a few poems unsuitable for singing ("Ring out, wild bells").[29]

Wolverhampton alone carried: (1) older praise hymns ("Give to God immortal praise"); (2) passion lyrics that were collectors' items (e.g., a seventeenth-century version of "Vexilla regis"); (4) some devotional lyrics

("Jesus, thou joy of loving hearts"); and a few on death and heaven ("Nearer, my God, to Thee").[30]

Both had (1) further paeans to the Creator ("Eternal Ruler of the ceaseless round"); (2) further triumphal lays ("Crown him with many crowns," and "Hail the day that sees him rise"); (3) one or two invocations ("Gracious Spirit, dwell with me"); (4) famous devotional ("How sweet the name . . . ," "Rock of Ages") and (10) reflexive hymns ("Glorious things of thee are spoken") that were all omitted from the *English School* collection, together with some consecrating day or evening (11) ("Forth in thy name . . . ," "At even, ere the sun was set"), and nineteenth-century favourites (7) on the journey through darkness ("Lead, kindly Light," "Through the night of doubt and sorrow"); (8) death ("Abide with me") and (9) heaven ("Jerusalem the golden").[31] The extreme of objective hymnody was reached in the *Oxford Book of School Worship*, whose editors also omitted "Jesu, Lover" and "Rock of Ages" as unsuitable for children.

The *English School* compilers alone chose some popular carols ("Good King Wenceslas") or nativity hymns ("Angels from the realms of glory") but more that were collectors' items ("As Joseph was a-walking"). Whether in selecting Victorian and earlier children's hymns ("Jesus, tender Shepherd," "I sing th'almighty power of God") or adult praise and mythic hymns, ("Bright the vision that delighted," "Lo! he comes . . . "), their first concern was poetic quality. Nevertheless, Newton's "Kindly spring again is here" was among the more specifically religious of a large number on the natural seasons.[32] With the Leicester books, they shared further nature lyrics (" 'Tis winter now, the fallen snow," "All things bright and beautiful"), some mission hymns ("City of God," "Hills of the north"), a few choice items for Christmas ("O sola magnarum urbium" in different versions), and one or two Victorian texts with a patriotic theme or implication ("Lord, while for all mankind . . . ," "The day thou gavest . . . ").[33] With the Wolverhampton compilers they shared mainly older hymns of praise but a few older ones on the Nativity, Resurrection, and Holy Spirit ("The first Nowell," "Christ the Lord is risen today," "Veni Creator Spiritus").[34]

Some fifty items appear in all three and also in the Oxford book for junior schools. Of these, some two-thirds were not listed by Routley as among the fifty-three favourite hymns of the English people,[35] a number being seasonal ("Christians, awake," "Ride on, ride on . . . "). Bearing in mind his list probably reflected the taste of older generations, we note among year-round items not there but in all three school books: (1) praise hymns by Herbert ("Let all the world . . . ") and Milton ("Let us with a gladsome mind") and what might be styled (12) sacramental nature lyrics ("All creatures of our God and King," "For the beauty of the earth") evoking that cheerful reverence for life most characteristic of modern school worship. In the same vein, "Summer suns . . . " and "There is a book . . . " survive in all the school books.[36]

By contrast, the following that appear neither in the *English School Hymn Book* nor in Routley's list point to obsolescent themes and images:

(1) God that madest earth and heaven
How shall I sing that majesty/Which angels do admire . . .

(2) The golden gates are lifted up

(6) Onward, Christian soldiers
The Son of God goes forth to war

(7) Children of the heavenly King
O happy band of pilgrims

(9) There is a land of pure delight
Who are these, like stars appearing . . .

(10) Come, let us join our cheerful songs/With angels round the throne

(11) Sun of my soul, thou Saviour dear[37]

The themes in abeyance were the triumphal Ascension, celestial hierarchies, and guardian angels; the images in decline reflect the old-world view of instantaneous creation and of this life as a pilgrimage or exile's return. With these might be counted a further motif found only in the Leicester and Wolverhampton books, the life of personal devotion to Christ, could we distinguish obsolescence from the weeding out of lyrics too intense for children. With some exceptions of the highest musical and poetic quality, the seventeen listed by all the school compilers and by Routley enjoin an activist, "healthy-minded" religion more concerned with embracing this life than being delivered from it:

Praise
(1) O worship the King
Praise, my soul, the King of heaven
Praise the Lord! ye heavens adore Him
Praise to the Lord, the Almighty, the King of creation

Providence
God moves in a mysterious way
Now thank we all our God
All people that on earth do dwell

Trinity
Holy! holy! holy! Lord God Almighty

(2) There is a green hill far away
     When I survey the wondrous Cross

(5) Jesus shall reign where'er the sun

(6) Fight the good fight with all thy might

(7) "Who would true valour see" or "He who would valiant be"

(9) For all the saints, who from their labours rest
     Ye holy angels bright

(11) Glory to thee, my God, this night
     New every morning is the love

(12) Come, ye thankful people, come
     We plough the fields and scatter

The swings away from nationalism and from the sentimentalizing of nature and childhood also affected hymnals for church schools. The huge *Methodist School Hymnal* of 1911 had plugged military imagery and the child's "littleness." Even the great hymnologist Julian joined in the cult of the Christ-child "meek and gentle" (198), while another poet thrust before children an effeminate "Shepherd / Wiping every tear" who folded children in his "bosom" like any Victorian mother (222). But from a collection so comprehensive the head teacher or Sunday-school superintendent could choose songs evoking almost any kind of devotion. "Grant us, O our Heavenly Father" by Thring (307) presents a serene upper-class Anglican view of life-as-service alongside the blinkered view imputed to lower-class children in "The wise may bring their learning" (308), where they are told to please God by performing their "little duties" in home and school. Again, Thring's professional-class conception of work as "sweet" and blest with "quiet rest" (589) appears alongside "Sons of labour, dear to Jesus" (588), which exhorts working people to bear with "brave hearts" the "pain" of their daily return to "duty." The confusion not merely of class-consciousness but of sacred and secular ideals comes to a head in the juxtaposition of the agnostic Clough's "Say not the struggle nought availeth" (598) with a lyric asking help to bear a "brother's load" and see the divine image in "hungry man and shoeless bairn." (597). The senior school head could have prescribed a repertoire of Methodist or general Christian classics, while any sensitive junior school teacher could have left unsung those arch and inane ditties that exhort "tiny pilgrims" to hear "little birds" or ask a "Little beam of rosy light" why it shines.[38] The latter had to search hard, however, for traces of the Crucified Christ.

In the post-war selection (1923)[39] ethical and natural piety can be discerned. In "I thank thee, Lord, for life" (11) the child returns thanks for keenness of mind and sense, for health, and for being saved by home and work from "self and greed," and the "dark curse of idle days." Vagueness regarding the future life (a "star" of hope) appears both here and in the more orthodox "Lord, Thy children, lowly bending" (18), which depicts angels singing at the Nativity but does not look beyond present worship in "this hallowed place." Likewise, "Singing from the mountain spring" (25) describes birds and spring growth, while merely hinting at a future life in "Sing on till the break of day." Even one presenting an image of the Spirit's light shining on the "holy page" of scripture looks no further than the daily struggle to "choose the right" (8). For that purpose one poet seeks the "fellowship divine" but enjoys the "atmosphere of heaven" in the church service. The really supernatural hymns convey the military image of life as a march behind "our Captain" to "realms of light," or else the Victorian domestic ideal, as when "Afric's sons" and the "teeming millions" of Asia assemble "with the family complete to sing the heavenly chorus."[40]

Not until after the Second World War did an editor rejoice, in the *School Hymn Book of the Methodist Church*,[41] at the disappearance of "unreal," "morbid and sentimental" lyrics in favour of those evincing the "growing care" for "theological" and "moral" implications. While not free of inane verse on God in Nature or well-meant but feeble efforts to relate Christianity to working-class life, this collection offers both a more orthodox, and a more adult version of the Christian faith and life. None of the many hymns on work has caught on like "Forth in thy name" or "Teach me, my God and King," for religious meaning, poetic quality and popular appeal elude the hymnist hot for relevance. The best in this kind, Geoffrey Studdert-Kennedy's "When through the whirl of wheels" (447),[42] treats engines and flaring furnaces as symbols of God's "boundless energy" and Second Coming. When in labour's "sweat" and "sorrow" the "sunshine of the great tomorrow" flames, Christ will come "in workman's jacket as before," to sweep the shavings from earth His "workshop-floor." As the Industrial Age passes into history, the closure of mines and steelworks must render daily more ephemeral this brave attempt to bridge the gap between the handicraft or pastoral metaphors of the New Testament and modern working-class life. The impersonal work and multinational corporations of the Computer Age seem even more difficult to suffuse with the glow of divine vocation.

In the Congregational book *School Worship* (1926),[43] running heads excerpted from the General Thanksgiving counterbalance the secular emphasis of, for instance, the section on "Loyalty and Friendship," subdivided into "Home and Friends," "The School," "Our Nation and Fellow-Countrymen" and, finally, "Church and Missions." Universalist

mission hymns and patriotic songs survive here from the pre-war generation, as do some egregious Victorian treatments of Christ as model child and
infantile lyrics on heaven in an abridgement for juveniles of the *Scottish
Church Hymnary* (1928).[44] Despite a few Victorian survivals ("Do no sinful
action" (97) or "Jesus, Friend of little children" (87)) the *Scottish School
Hymnary* of 1959[45] reverts to an eighteenth-century stateliness and
transcendence. But for a handful of military or didactic hymns it is
indistinguishable from any good adult hymnal in the Learned tradition. It
directs devotion toward a "healthy-minded" image of the Father instead of
a lachrymose or effeminate figure of the Son. Its patriotic effusions are
more social and moral than militant.

The Popular tradition lingered until after the Second World War in
extreme Protestant and in Roman Catholic hymnody for the young. Its
survival in Baptist and pentecostal collections may be taken for granted, but
Hymns for Catholic Schools (1949), the result of a survey by a Catholic
headmaster,[46] shows that the many thousands educated in Catholic schools
continued to absorb a religious culture quite distinct from that of the
"highest" Anglican public schools. More objective yet warmer and more
sentimental than Anglo-Catholicism, this culture is best described as
Catholic-evangelical. Beside "Adeste fideles" stands "See, amid the winter
snow" (5-6), beside "Ave verum corpus" stands "Jesu, gentlest Saviour"
(35-6), and beside "Ave maris stella" stands [upon] "What a sea of tears and
sorrow / Did the soul of Mary toss" when beholding the Crucifixion (70-1).
For good or ill, the youthful singer dwells completely within the Catholic
myth, his England St. George's land, his exile that of a Catholic in a
Protestant society, his heart set upon the Babe and the Crucified, his
struggle against temptation and doubt aided by his Lady, his patron saint
and his guardian angel. Not for nothing did the headmistress who informed
me of this hymnal and the Roman Catholic medievalist J.A.W. Bennett[47]
express admiration for the Methodist hymns. The warmer devotion
cherished by Newman after his conversion resembled that of the Wesleys he
despised, the cults of the Precious Blood and Sacred Heart having arisen in
the age of Pietism and the Evangelical revival.

The Nativity items (15 out of 113) typify the split of sensibility between
traditional objective mythology and modern subjective pietism. The use of
analogy by the Elizabethan martyr-poet Robert Southwell is (in no
derogatory sense) naïve. In "The first Nowell" (*not* the popular carol), upon
beholding the Babe tremble with cold in "homely manger," he exhorts us to
ignore the poor surroundings:

> This stable is a prince's court,
> The crib his chair of state;

The beasts are parcel of his pomp,
The wooden dish his plate.

The persons in that poor attire
The royal liveries wear;
The Prince himself is come from heaven,
This pomp is prized there. (13)

We are not to identify with Christ the "little pilgrim" (a term later hymnists used of the child-worshipper), but to kneel and adore.

By contrast, Faber ululates over this "Dear Little One" like a mother in some Victorian best-seller, detecting "sorrow and love" in the sleeper's "faint and feeble" cry. Having proclaimed the Babe divine, he yearns to "spread" His love among "forgetful men" (14).[48] Here we see a change from adoration to self-conscious participation in the work of redemption that Faber doubtless caught from Protestant passion hymns before his conversion. We must distinguish this resolved participation from the sorrow and love that the Crucified Christ draws from medieval and modern beholders in the "Stabat mater" or Faber's own "O come and mourn with me" (16-17, 18). Notably another Victorian hymnist, as Prodigal Son, admits having forfeited his claim to enter heaven, where saints rejoice in a "boundless sea of love" recalling the womb symbols of Wesley or Toplady.[49]

In three respects this collection of hymns frequently sung in Catholic schools differs from those of the Popular tradition and those reflecting the consensus in late Victorian Sunday-schools. First, the Latin and translated texts for the greater festivals—"Victimae Paschalis," "Veni Creator Spiritus," and "Veni sancte Spiritus"—maintain something of the Learned tradition. Second, even enthusiastic hymns to the Blessed Sacrament require the child to identify with a Saviour incarnate in historical time and objectively present upon the altar; only those to the Sacred Heart and Precious Blood require him to adore an imagined object. For all the strictures of Ronald Knox,[50] their enthusiasm appears identical with the warmth of Catholic worship that appealed to Newman and his fellow converts from the coldly formal Anglicanism of Oxford colleges. Thirdly, even its most sentimental hymnody remains uncorrupted by the Victorian cult of childhood. This opening stanza, for instance, attributes "littleness" to the Babe, not the worshipper:

Little King, so fair and sweet,
See us gathered round Thy feet;
Be Thou Monarch of our school,
It shall prosper 'neath Thy rule.

> We will be Thy subjects true,
> Brave to suffer, brave to do,
> All our hearts to Thee we bring,
> Take them, keep them, little King. (39)

Execrable as is this jingle, or later verses on Christ as "Playmate," "Teacher" or parent figure calling the dying child home for "holidays," the theology and orientation remain orthodox and traditional. Cult of the Virgin apart, the school hymnody of the Catholic revival can be taxed with sentimentalism and poverty of diction, but never with the cults of nature, home, class, or country.

16

CONCLUSION

And for all this, nature is never spent;
There lives the dearest freshness deep down things
Gerard Manley Hopkins, "God's Grandeur" (1877)

Hymns and the Christian "Myth" traces the changing ways in which hymns represented the divine nature and the human prospect, and how English hymns have recorded human responses to the divine self-giving. Their re-enactment within the psyche of the mythos, or sacred story, of man's redemption was indispensable for the imitation of Christ in the "social gospel" of redemptive activity within this world. The present book has remarked the intrusion into hymnody of secular themes and attitudes, the transference of religious veneration to the idols of family, class, and tribe, the projection of transcendence upon nature and the nation-state. Before considering the hymn's present and future, we should recall the main features of its past.

Objective hymns and also those termed "reflexive," that is, concerned with the act of worship, appear in the New Testament, subjective and reflexive ones in the earliest known Christian hymnal, the *Odes of Solomon*.[1] During the first quarter of the Christian era the suppression of subjective lyrics and incorporation of the other types into the Byzantine and Benedictine liturgies virtually eliminated popular hymn-singing. In Byzantium, poets depicted a heavenly hierarchy parallel to the earthly, addressing God as cosmic Emperor and their sovereign as divinely ordained. In the West, as Roman authority crumbled, monastic poets bore in mind the aspirations and temptations of the celibate life, extending their voluntary exile to the whole state of fallen man. The veneration of God the Father being the main object of psalmody, the mythos of the Son's advent, incarnation, crucifixion, resurrection, and ascension, together with the coming of the

Class and Idol in the English Hymn

Holy Spirit, formed the subject-matter of innumerable hymns, those in Latin being devoted more to the Crucified, those in Greek more to the Risen Christ.[2]

In the Latin church, subjective and even erotic devotion returned during the high Middle Ages in lyrics to the Virgin and Child. Meantime objective hymnody focused on the collective plight of man facing the Last Judgment, supposedly at the end of the first millennium, then by apocalyptic numerology about 1260, and finally during the fourteenth century, as the feudal and ecclesiastical structures began to collapse. In the thirteenth century, the new dogma of transubstantiation and consequent devotion to the Blessed Sacrament created a demand for reflexive hymns.[3] In that century the continuing spate of passion lyrics treating Christ as source and object of every longing, as King, Soldier, Knight, Lover, or Victim (though not yet Friend),[4] that had sprung from the homeless heart of the celibate, seems to make nonsense of the Marxist critique of religion as the "spirit of spiritless conditions," for was not the time of Abelard or Bernard the very climax of medieval Christian civilization? A criticism more difficult to refute is that the mythos so saturated the consciousness of Christendom as to drive out that awareness of nature (based though it was on Old Testament poetry) in late Roman hymns by Prudentius and Fortunatus.[5] The answer to the charge that prepossession with the heavenly story led Western man to neglect his responsibility to the earth lies neither in hymnals nor in collections of secular nature lyrics (though many came from religious houses) but in the tillage and forestry of Benedictine monks and lay brethren.[6]

The influence of Luther upon English hymnody was delayed until the Wesleyan revival. That of Calvin had kept hymn-singing out of services until the late seventeenth century, when Watts and his precursors introduced psalm-based, then original hymns to Dissenting congregations.[7] Upon returning from exile in Geneva, the Elizabethan reformers established a Calvinistic and Hebraic cult of a patriarchal divinity, a heavenly King who ruled His people through their earthly sovereign, as in ancient Byzantium. Hymnists from the Anglican George Wither to the Independent Watts portrayed their nation as God's second Israel, or consecrated people, a concept that was to inspire missionary hymns from "Jesus shall reign where'er the sun" to "Onward, Christian soldiers."

The exclusion from Anglican services not just of Wesley's hymns but of those by the Calvinist Evangelicals Cowper and Newton set up a division between devotional and liturgical singing, the one liable to become intemperate and egocentric, the other formal and restrained to the point of coldness. Inevitably the former characterized popular worship, out of doors or in the Methodist chapel, the latter genteel worship in cathedral, or college, or simpler services in the squire-dominated village church. The

Popular and Learned traditions, though they came together in the late nineteenth century, have diverged again as the rift has widened between mainstream and pentecostal churches. The Wesleys and Cowper, indeed, most poets in the Popular tradition, wrote lyrics popular by destination, distinguishable from the Gospel songs of Sankey by a higher order of imagination and craftsmanship. Only Primitive Methodist outpourings in the hard times of the early nineteenth century, together with negro spirituals, can be termed popular by origin. Since the one repeats insistently the motif of imminent Apocalypse when revolution has been stillborn, the other that of Exodus to a celestial Promised Land when earthly hope appears foredoomed, do hymn lyrics voice only the thankfulness of the comfortable or the longings of the homeless? Does man make God in the likeness of the time, to quell the rebellious, stir the zealous into teaching natives their conqueror's religion, reinforce father's authority, sanctify mother's tenderness, bless their child's obedience, cozen the masses into submission and prompt the children of wealth and privilege to expiate their guilt in social service? Has man "built him fanes of fruitless prayer," and bent his knee before the void?[8]

If, as Marx alleged, religion is no more than the "heart of a heartless world," the "spirit of spiritless conditions," what can endow a society with heart, or breathe spirit into a suburban or working environment? Any answer must take into account what is believed or assumed transcendent. In every coherent culture, the sense of obligation, or "ought," at times of crisis overrides considerations of personal gain or safety. Where no higher principle controls the lust for power or profit, inhumanities abound and drudges tramp on leaden feet, or else the community falls apart. The saving grace of Marxism, its gift and spur to Christianity, lies in its sense that the hungry should be filled with good things and the mighty put down from their seats. Its tragedy lies in the readiness of ideologues and despots to deny the transcendence that enjoins compassion upon the proud, and constrains the powerful who would act out their dreams and abstractions to learn of the humble and meek. As between those slave labourers of the American South who knew a higher Being and those captives in Stalin's Russia who knew none, which were the more dispirited? In this century what immeasurable suffering has resulted from the attribution of sacredness to the nation-state and of divine power to the self-consecrated dictator?

Compared to a Hitler or Stalin, those ever-changing idols of the young, "pop" singers, do little harm. Many have, like the Beatles, given utterance to something very like the "religionless Christianity" of the late John Robinson's *Honest to God*: a cult of neighbourly and erotic love, classless, raceless, and non-violent, disowning dogma and institution. It is tempting to identify this with folk lyrics popular by origin, and the cults of fundamentalist singers with those popular by destination, but in each case the cults, being fostered by record companies, are too intertwined to unravel. What political and musical idols alike proclaim is the inability of the mass of mankind to live without myths and hero figures. A demythologized religion appears doomed to remain both songless and devoid of mass appeal. If not Christ, then the people's hero; if not the Exodus and Resurrection, then the Long March of Mao Zedong or the tale of the singer's rise to stardom.

The other pole of the Marxist critique, that religion invents a home for the homeless, deserves scrutiny. It could be argued that Popular hymnody voices the aspirations of the dispossessed, of mill-hands and miners during the Industrial Revolution, of black slaves during the reign of King Cotton, even of those who resort to the certainties of fundamentalist religion when displaced from work by the computer. In "Learned" hymnody, by the same token, the fortunate offer thanks and praise qualified only by their human subjection to death and emotional, or less often, physical suffering. In early and medieval liturgies, however, hymns unmistakably objective and "Learned" consecrate the voluntary homelessness of monk or nun while lamenting mankind's exile from his true homeland. In the early twentieth century, hymnals enjoined a more unquestioning attachment to nature and country upon children of the populace than upon those of its rulers. Spiritually, Christianity requires all its adherents to leave home, as Christ did the Apostles. All who would enter the Kingdom of Heaven must leave behind their passports, bank-books, and degree certificates, having at their baptism accepted rebirth into a classless and timeless society capable of using or fulfilling whatever talents they possess.

However Christian charity may shine in the lives of priest, minister, monk, or nun, we no longer esteem the clerical above the secular vocation, nor the celibate above the married state. Both the conventual discipline and the Wesleyan one modelled upon it had the unintended effects of conferring prosperity. Even on Marxist assumptions, the examined and ordered life of monk or convert must be preferred to the despair, degradation, and consequent alcoholism that Wesleyans and Evangelicals did so much to counteract. In their different ways, apostles from St. Benedict to Wesley established centres of order amid chaos, the work attributed to the Spirit in Genesis. Civilization was enriched by the handiwork and learning of monks and nuns, as it was later by the commercial and domestic integrity of Methodists and Evangelicals, no less than by their much-vaunted social reforms.

The cruelties and hypocrisies so pilloried by anti-Catholic or anti-Evangelical novelists, like those of Christendom in general, stemmed from attachment to power, possessions, class, tribe, or even family, in the guise of detachment; from the projection of transcendence upon ideologies, social institutions, or natural affections. In past ages, hysterical or sadomasochistic compulsions have conditioned not a few ascetics, mystics, and even poets to a hatred of "Brother Ass" the body, of nature and its creatures, that now seems more Gnostic or Manichean than Christ-like. In *Man and the Natural World* Keith Thomas assembles a sad catalogue of literary aspersions upon wild creatures (consider the former significance of words like "bestial" or "brute") but is at pains to point out exceptions in authors so early as Chaucer or the fifteenth-century mystic Margery Kempe, in whom the sight of a horse ill treated inspired visions of Christ being scourged. His citations show beyond doubt that our ancestors of the Tudor and Stuart eras linked the ferocity of animals and insects with the Fall and holiness with the slaying of the beast within.[9] Notwithstanding the condemnation by Puritans, and Evangelicals like Cowper, of cruel sports involving animals, and the contribution of rural clergymen to natural history,[10] Christian colonists, Catholic or Protestant, ravaged the natural environment and its creatures in the Americas as native Indians had not, and even now the insensitivity of right-wing governments influenced by fundamentalism appears more than coincidental. The antithesis between the Judaeo-Christian mythos and ethic and nature cuts so deep as to bring into question the compatibility of those religions with an enlightened or humane attitude to the natural world. Our post-Darwinian tendency to regard ourselves as governed by the same necessities as other mammals and subject to the same extinction threatens the very foundation of Christianity: belief in God as the Creator, Redeemer, and Sanctifier.

If the Christian faith dies, its archetypes, like classical and Norse myths before them, will disappear into the poet's compost heap, its lyrics survive like the Homeric hymns as relics of arcane devotion. Not long ago a scholar famed for his work on wartime writing congratulated me on choosing for dissection a "dead literary form." So it must appear to anyone ignorant of the torrent of hymns since the mid-sixties, especially if he grew up during the sterile decades after the First World War. If generation lag, as I have shown, preserved the faith in compilations for the young, it preserved his assumption of the hymn's demise against evidence to the contrary.

To determine the number of new hymns, or even new hymnals, during the past twenty years would make an interesting joint project for an Englishman and an American, each resident near one of the great publishing centres and skilled in computer programming. With new texts and collections still pouring from the presses, to hazard an opinion upon the great hymns of the late twentieth century would be premature. Even to prophesy that, in the shrunken state of mainstream churches, their poets will not become household words, is to risk being silenced by the advent of a new Watts,

Wesley, or Fortunatus to outdo even a Sydney Carter, Fred Kaan, Fred Pratt Green, or Brian Wren, not to mention their North American counterparts. While using a number of new lyrics in church and at hymn society conferences on both continents, I have noticed some general directions.

The first is a striving toward oneness, both of churches and of nations. Now that most major denominations, in North America, at least, use a common lectionary extending over three years of services, the first hymn cycle, a modern parallel to the Breviary, has begun to appear.[11] New hymns consequently tend to stress such beliefs and attitudes as Christians have in common not only with each other but with Jews. The final chapter of my previous book illustrated the unitarian tendency of nineteenth- and early twentieth-century hymns. One of many now popular texts by members of the St. Louis Jesuits, "Be not afraid," recapitulates an assurance common to Christians and Jews: "You shall cross the barren desert, / but you shall not die of thirst," reserving distinctively Christian language for the final verse from the Beatitudes, "Blessed are your poor, / for the kingdom shall be theirs."[12] That verse illustrates not so much a tension as an intended ambiguity especially prevalent in present-day Roman Catholic and Anglican social teaching, with its endorsement of non-violent change in favour of the underprivileged.

The late twentieth-century hymnist of whatever denomination encourages singers to Christianize rather than turn their backs upon the world. When writing on human rights, in "For the healing of the nations," Fred Kaan calls for a "just and equal sharing / of the things that earth affords" through a "life of love in action." His list of attitudes that kill "abundant living": pride of "status, race or schooling, / dogmas keeping man from man" condemns as divisive not only doctrinaire religious teaching but the class-consciousness and nationalism that were the backbone of the British and other European peoples from about 1870 to 1945. If this plea by Kaan appears secular-humanist, his lyric headed "Into the World" ("Lord, as we rise to leave the shell of worship") describes Christians as "called to the risk of unprotected living" and pleads for "the nerve to lose our life to others," before asking the "Lord of all ages" to lead His church "through death to resurrection."[13]

In the same way, a lyric such as Brian Wren's "There's a Spirit in the air"[14] celebrates a love revealed in Christ "living, working, in our world," treating of both the literal and sacramental meal, and of the Spirit as inspiration in the "fight" to feed the poor, house the homeless, and befriend the stranger. One great difference between mainstream and pentecostal Christians lies in their attitudes to this social gospel of non-violent social and economic change in favour of the poor and the oppressed.

Likewise the present-day hymnist will either try to reconcile natural evolution and the present-day cosmos with an immanentist or transcendent view of God, or else represent the Creation as though the literal truth of Genesis had never been questioned. The apparent contradiction between two successive lyrics by the same author that were intended to accompany readings from the lectionary illustrates the difficulty of generalizing. The first, "Wind who makes all winds that blow" treats the Holy Spirit as immanent in literal wind and fire, in gales on earth, and "suns around which planets turn," while the second, "The Lick of the tide, the lunge of the storm," contrasts the unchangeable love of God with the ceaseless and apparently purposeless processes of natural growth, decay, and erosion.[15]

What might be called the creationist hymn cannot certainly be identified with pentecostal fundamentalism. Peter Davidson's "The Singer and the Song," which celebrates the origin of the cosmos as God's "Song" following a divine "dream," by which "light pierced the darkness and rhythm began," like Bert Polman's "In the beginning was the Word eternal," avoids any scriptural detail a scientist or liberal theologian might question.[16]

If the new hymnody reconciles different religious traditions, classes, and nationalities, accommodating both an evolutionary and a creationist view of nature, both ceaseless change and a divine presence to fill the immense void of the cosmos and the emptiness of the human heart, upon what do its authors and composers turn their backs? In almost every instance, they avoid the sentimentalism so long associated with popular hymnody. Words and tunes alike have a strong, assertive, or as we now say "upbeat" tendency. Thirty years ago an Anglican priest told me that he dared not drop a glutinous Victorian lyric to the Blessed Virgin lest he lose half the women in his congregation. Choir members visiting an old people's home can be asked to sing, often for the first time, outworn hymns they find embarrassingly self-centred and sentimental. Many lyrics associated with charismatic worship repel by their simplistic reiterations, also couched in the first person singular, but sentimental they are not. In the new hymnody, the gap between men and for women, like that between adults and for children, continues to close.

"There's a Spirit in the air," which illustrates several of these tendencies, happens to have a four-part setting.[17] A great many recent lyrics, however, are sung in unison. The main reason for the preponderance of unison settings is doubtless the shortage of trained singers. It has the effect, nevertheless, of diminishing gender-consciousness. In English-speaking lands the church that requires men to sit on one side and women on the other is now a rare anachronism, but many German congregations have always sat in four groups—sopranos, altos, tenors, and basses. Unison setting accords with the tendency of modern composers, choral or orchestral, to distribute snatches of melody among the different voices or parts, rather than giving the melody predominantly to the higher voices or instruments. Unison settings cannot, therefore, be attributed to a single cause. Their effect, however, is to blur distinctions not only between male and female but between a trained choir and untrained congregation. For the foreseeable future, unison melodies will continue to suit the capacities of congregations rather than choirs, dropping in pitch to accommodate male voices rather than acquiring the elaboration of the Gregorian chant intended for monastic singers who, whatever their musical abilities, sang seven times daily.

One more distinction fast being obliterated is that between secular and church tunes or even lyrics. A generation or more ago, when churchgoing seemed almost confined to the managerial and professional classes, the real religious feelings of the younger generation were expressed in anti-war lyrics of the Beatles and other groups, that endorsed love, whether sexual or asexual. The incursion of the guitar into church worship, and the immense influence of "pop" and folk tunes, seems to have been paralleled by a muting of the anti-Christian sentiments in popular lyrics, and an increasing association of the mainstream churches with outsiders and order-receivers, rather than with insiders and order-givers. A growing insecurity, as economic competition and technological change dislodge even the skilled and educated, brings once-comfortable worshippers face to face with the reality so plain to earlier generations of Christians, that notwithstanding our increased life expectancy, here we have no abiding city.

From among Albert Bayly, Sydney Carter, Timothy Dudley-Smith, Fred Pratt-Green, Kaan, Wren, and a hundred others who have poured out new hymns for adults within the past two decades, perhaps no Watts or Wesley will arise, for history runs off no reprints. As beyond question the hymn survives, so lives the God once declared dead by existentialist writers and philosophers, and lives not merely in the bigotry of Islamic or Christian fundamentalists.

To speculate on the future of the Christian faith and institutions is outside my scope, but if hymn lyrics of the late twentieth-century revival are to establish themselves in the collective unconscious as did "Abide with me" in Britain or "Amazing Grace" in North America, their authors must surmount two enormous hurdles.

First, they must make headway against tides of ignorance and indifference that have built up over generations not only among the populace at large but in the alumni of schools with traditions of worship. While nearly every independent boarding- or day-school included in my recent survey reported using a hymnal, usually *Hymns for Church and School*, *Hymns Ancient and Modern*, or some version of *Songs of Praise*,[18] at many the morning chorus sounds thinner than it did. At one famous day-school during the 1960s so few boys joined in singing the morning hymn that the headmaster seriously considered eliminating it. A staff-student committee ensured its survival by drawing up a list of forty texts from *Songs of Praise* to be used regularly, and some dozen occasionally, then placing a specially trained choir in the centre of the hall. A member of that committee who became head of another school found upon arrival that hymn-singing had ceased, and revived it by producing a booklet of some thirty classics.[19] In the municipal schools of Wolverhampton, once served by that town's excellent school hymnal, "the singing of hymns," to quote the Director, "forms a much less regular part of school assemblies than was once the case." Its continuance in largely suburban and rural Leicestershire suggests environment and to a lesser degree class as determinants.[20] The industrial West Midlands, always a difficult area for clergy, has absorbed vast numbers of Hindus and Muslims. Yet even in a well-known west-country Methodist school the headmaster reported a baffling lack of enthusiasm for the morning hymn.[21] In all probability, the more durable of "pop" lyrics have in the young replaced hymns as vehicles of folk wisdom and morality.

Efforts to counteract this tide have taken two main forms, Popular-by-destination and Learned. In both church and school, with some success, clergy and teachers have encouraged the use of instruments and idioms familiar to the under-thirty-fives. Alternatively, they have discontinued the use of subjective devotional lyrics in favour of those more objective and doctrinal. This was the conscious endeavour both of the revisers of the Scottish *Church Hymnary* (1973)[22] and of the compilers of two selections for the grammar schools discussed earlier, on the assumption that students would more readily sing lyrics of restrained tone and collective viewpoint, or objective praise-hymns, than "Rock of Ages" or "Abide with me." The staff-student committee even excluded "When I survey the wondrous Cross." Among items selected by all the parties concerned were "Through the night of doubt and sorrow," "He who would valiant be," "O worship the King," and "O come, all ye faithful."

Nevertheless, just as by generation lag teachers brought up in the faith kept hymn-singing going among pupils who worshipped nowhere but at school, so by the same token teachers not so reared cannot but transmit their own scepticism or even ignorance. Some examinees in English at Cambridge were reported recently to have listed Aesop among authors of the Bible, at best a mark of irreverence.[23] A West Midland Methodist minister found his task harder in the 1980s than thirty years earlier, since at that time the sceptic knew what he was denying, whereas today young people no longer knew what was meant by "God."[24] Similar stories could be told in other

English-speaking countries, yet the tide of faith appears so far to have receded less in North America than in Britain.

The modern hymnist's other difficulty is to find coherent and meaningful imagery. If writing for the mainstream churches, in which the Learned tradition predominates, he has to cope with the cleavage between orthodox and modernist. Anglicans, in particular, range from "classical" Christians who find no difficulty in singing hymns steeped in the male-oriented, hierarchic language of the Scriptures to liberals who might envisage Christ as no more than the last and greatest Hebrew prophet, and so endorse little or nothing of the mythos of the Risen Christ. While some late Victorian hymns imply a deity more unitarian than triune, few singers even now would respond to hymnody that treated of a merely human and mortal Jesus. The lapse of time between the "Magnificat" and hymn texts on the relief of poverty and suffering supports the contention by John Hick and his fellow essayists that the "Myth of God Incarnate" deflected attention from the implementation of Christ's ethical teaching. In Dudley-Smith's inspiring paraphrase of the "Magnificat" the refrain line "Tell out, my soul, the greatness of the Lord" and the keynote of praise overlay the social strain, which is confined to "Proud hearts and stubborn wills are put to flight, / the hungry fed, the humble lifted high." By an even stronger tilt, however, Kaan's "Sing we a song of high revolt," headed "Magnificat Now," concentrates upon God's disowning of the proud, exaltation of the poor and satisfying "with bread and cup" the hungry of many lands. Sacramental is presented as inseparable from literal sustenance but finally God "calls us to revolt and fight / with him for what is just and right, / to sing and live Magnificat / in crowded street and council flat."[25] The first paraphrase might be criticized for upholding Anglican Establishment values, the second for endorsing Nonconformist left-wing ones. The struggle for social justice, however, requires a vision of the cosmos and its Creator that exposes the folly of our selfish and short-sighted quests for wealth or power, whether individual, corporate, national, or ideological.

In a hymn on "The Claims of Love," George B. Caird condemns those futile strivings, insisting that "We are thy stewards; thine our talents, wisdom, skill," our "only glory" to fulfil that trust. "Make us, thy children, free from greed and lust for power, / Lest human justice, yoked with man's unequal laws, / Oppress the needs and neglect the humble cause."[26] The rarity in medieval hymnody of that reverence for the majesty and beauty of creation so evident in the Psalms and the verse of Prudentius and Fortunatus implies a lack of interest in man's stewardship of the earth and its creatures that was consistent with the preoccupation of the uneducated or undevout with survival or pleasure, and of the educated devotee with the mythos and inner life.

No doubt the new resources and principles revealed by explorers and scientists were prerequisite for any conviction of man's ability to improve his lot by organized effort, as distinct from piecemeal relief of hunger and disease. Yet modern man, for all his technology, remains tragically incapable of civilized conduct on the basis of abstract ideas. The will and imagination needed for vigorous action seem capable of being aroused only by concrete images of myths and heroes. How otherwise can we explain the savagery let loose by revolutionary ideologies in France and the Soviet Union and by a right-wing ideology in Nazi Germany, or the irresolution of democratic Britain until led by a hero-figure who was himself inspired by a quasi-historical myth, the empire of the free? Admittedly the originating myth of God's covenant with the first Israel has enabled the Jewish community to retain its identity against incalculable odds, but without the Resurrection and consequential prospect of life beyond death, no such longevity could be predicted for the Christian churches.

The sacred poet must steer between a demythologized religion that rests upon a foundation of sand and the no less stultifying fundamentalism of those churches and evangelists that gain converts (and sometimes wealth) by proffering illusory certainties. The religion which refuses to accommodate itself to scientific discovery and biblical criticism can no more inspire the artist of originality and talent than it can the intellectual. Nor can one that remains fixated upon conversion, world-denying devotion, and personal salvation. To require this fixation is to restrict the poet to the simplistic jingles of much charismatic hymnody, or the reiteration of worn-out passion tropes.

That the hymn should be scriptural goes without saying, yet puts the modern poet in a quandary. By what images can he replace the King of Heaven now that kings have all but vanished from the earth, or the Good Shepherd when much of the earth's population lives in cities? Can heaven itself, or its Creator, inspire the singer as they did when the cosmos was a three-storey tenement and creation literally instantaneous? Though God as "Lord" connotes not feudal order but voluntary submission to Christ, can "King," "Lady," or even "sovereign" and "humble" have religious meaning now that hereditary hierarchies have almost everywhere given way to societies, democratic or totalitarian, that are in principle classless?

G.W. Briggs' impeccably scriptural hymn "Christ is the world's true light" exposes this difficulty about imagery. Christ is "captain of salvation" and "daystar . . . of every man and nation" in whom "all races meet," forgetting "ancient feuds." When Christ, the "Prince of Peace," is "throned as Lord," men will "To ploughshare beat the sword, / to pruning-hook the spear." For these images the hymnist draws upon an outdated cosmology and obsolete weapons and implements, not to mention male hegemony.[27]

Again, the grounding of the Parables in a society of shepherds, farmers, and fruit-growers needs no demonstration. The symbols of bondage that inspired the negro spirituals came from the Old Testament narratives of the Exodus and captivity in Babylon, but the miners, even the mill operatives, who flocked to hear John Wesley had not lost contact with the life of sheepfold, barn, and country road. Until very recently, even secular poets have usually grown up in a village or garden suburb.

Now that more poets come from industrial areas, images drawn from the factory or mine are already being outdated by the new technology, which will in the foreseeable future make nonsense not only of the imagery of toil but, for most people, of any single vocation or career. In his now-famous hymn "God of concrete, God of steel," Richard Jones avoids this pitfall by consecrating as "the Lord's" the infrastructure of present-day civilization, its wheels, pylons, girders, rails, motorways, and satellites. Having swallowed this bold innovation, singers may soon find "steam" and "atom" relics of outdated technology. In the latter verses, moreover, science and religion co-exist somewhat unconvincingly in "Lord of science, Lord of art . . . of map and graph and chart . . . of physics and research" but also "Bible . . . Church . . . sequence and design." Finally, the poet celebrates the "world of love" in traditional religious terms. God's "glory fills the earth," "Loosed the Christ with Easter's might, / Saves the world from evil's blight," and "Claims mankind by grace divine."[28]

Many of the great biblical symbols, nevertheless, retain their relevance: the inward voice heard in the whirlwind, the mighty wind and tongues of flame, the seed that falls on fruitful soil and house founded on a rock, and even the celestial city, though not its jewellery and accoutrements. As the poets struggle to express the biblical notion of Fatherhood, and accommodate their religion to sexual equality, their reluctance to address God the Holy Spirit is the more surprising. The medieval masterpieces "Veni Creator Spiritus" and "Veni sancte Spiritus" foreshadow not merely that inner realization of and active response to the Passion and Incarnation that were to inspire the poetry of the Evangelical and Catholic revivals, but the modern awareness of the divine as ground of our being, and of nature as a sacrament. If we moderns can point to anything as the substance that endures in defiance of Marxist or Freudian reductionism, outlasting all social systems and surviving all revolutions, it is surely that irrepressible power of renewal, that inexhaustible fertility, latent in the natural world and its Creator and ground. Though but yesterday Christian faith and praise seemed dead, today they live.

Sydney Carter's "Lord of the Dance," though apparently based on a title for the Buddha, represents both the age-old Christian mythos and the natural piety underlying our ecological movement. Neither a medievalist nor a sacramentalist, but a Quaker, Carter weaves his great lyric around the figure of the cosmic dance, which goes back to Dante and before him to the prophet Samuel.[29] The dancer is at once the Creator Spirit who danced "in the morning / when the world was begun" and Christ who "danced on the earth." Alluding adroitly to the scribes and pharisees who were piped to and would not dance (Luke 7.32), the divine dancer performs healing miracles on the sabbath, is arrested and crucified, but resurrected otherwise than in the Gospels.

> But I am the dance
> and I still go on:
> They cut me down
> and I leap up high;
> I am the life
> that'll never, never die;
> I'll live in you
> if you'll live in me. . . .

Like an earlier Christian poet quoted in the epigraph to this chapter, Carter gives a Christian meaning to the self-renewing power of nature. But whereas Hopkins ascribed that power to the Holy Spirit "o'er the bent world brooding / On ah! bright wings," Carter asserts it in place of the supernatural and apocalyptic events that follow the death on the Cross. His Lord of the Dance, in short, is "the dancer and the dance" in the sense of being at once Creator, Redeemer, and cosmos.[30]

The success of hymns in winning hearts depends on no accidents of four-part harmony, obsolescent in sacred as in secular music, for many of the grandest Christian hymns date from the ages of plainsong. Nor can it depend upon images and idioms bound up with obsolete social structures or cosmologies. It depends upon the capacity of theologians and poets to voice the inchoate longing of humankind to become one, to melt down its weapons and with the scrap forge a civilization more imbued with the divine Spirit. The earliest Christian hymnal depicted the faith as a flooding river destined to overspread the earth, its Founder as a liberator striking chains from the dead, and His teaching as the true light now shining from the faces of His disciples to dispel this world's vanity and folly.[31] In this and future ages, when humankind faces a choice between tribal or ideological feuding and its own self-induced apocalypse, only a religion and poetry couched in collective terms can have meaning. The believer can no longer afford to pursue his own salvation and let the world go to the devil. Nor can he follow the Gadarene swine of bigotry and intolerance, whether sectarian, nationalistic, or ideological.

Within the past few years it has been my privilege to see performances from Munich and Vienna of Bach's B Minor Mass and Christmas Oratorio. How moving, and how exuberant was the singing of men, women, and boys too young to recall the sinister idolatry that had possessed their parents' generation, threatening to plunge all Europe into a second dark age. Bach and Handel set the teachings of the scriptures in the musical idiom and with the musical resources of their time, as do the poets and composers responsible for the surge of new hymns and tunes. If the light of divine and human love shine not in the darkness of this century, then indeed, as says the great hymn to the Spirit, "Veni, sancte Spiritus":

sine tuo numine	Without Thy divine power,
nihil est in homine,	Nothing is in humankind,
nihil est innoxium.	Nothing is free from evil.[32]

No translation has conveyed the force of "numen," the divine instress of Spirit failing which the heart and imagination become as Samuel Beckett's ash-cans or T.S. Eliot's empty cisterns and exhausted wells,[33] and a once coherent civilization becomes eroded by a thousand trivialities and corruptions.

APPENDIX

		Class	Reprints	First line
A	*60-plus*	4	81	Glory to thee my God this night, 57 (1695)
				(All praise to thee, my God this night, 24)
		11	79	Awake my soul, and with the sun (1695)
		4	77	Jesu, Lover of my soul, 40 (1740)
				(Jesus lover of my soul, 37)
		2	73	Hark the Herald Angels sing (1739)
		1	72	God moves in a mysterious way (1779)
		4	70	Rock of Ages cleft for me (1775)
		1	70	O God our help in ages past, 51 (1719)
				(Our God, our help in ages past, 19)
		1	70	Holy, holy, holy, Lord God Almighty (1827)
		1	68	New every morning is the love, 42 (1827)
				(O timely happy, timely wise, 26)
		5	67	Jesus shall reign wher'er the sun (1719)
		6	66	Soldiers of Christ, arise (1742)
		5	64	From Greenland's icy mountains (1827)
		2	64	When I survey the wondrous cross (1707)
		1	61	All people that on earth do dwell (1561)
		9	61	Come let us join our cheerful songs (1707)
		1	60	Let us with a gladsome mind (1623)
B	*48-59*	2	59	Rejoice the Lord is King (1746)
		4	58	How sweet the name of Jesus sounds (1779)
		3	58	Our blest redeemer ere he breathed (1829)
		2	57	Hail to the Lord's anointed (1821)

	11	57	Lord dismiss us with thy blessing (two hymns, 1773, 1850)
	11	57	Sun of my soul, thou saviour dear (1827)
	9	55	There is a land of pure delight (1707)
	2	54	Christ the Lord is risen to-day (1739)
	1	54	Now thank we all our God (1647, trans. 1863)
	2	53	As with gladness men of old (1861)
	1	52	Before Jehovah's awful throne (1719)
	8	52	Abide with me, fast falls the eventide (1847)
	5	52	Thou, whose almighty Word (1813)
	8	51	Nearer, my God, to Thee (1841)
	2	51	Lo! He comes, with clouds descending (1758)
	6	51	The Son of God goes forth to war (1827)
	7	50	Children of the heavenly King (1742)
	1	49	Praise, my soul, the King of Heaven (1834)
	7	48	Lead us, Heavenly Father, lead us, 37 (1821) Lead us, Heavenly Father, 11
	11	48	Christ whose glory fills the skies (1740)
	6	48	Onward, Christian soldiers (1864)
C 40-7	4	47	I heard the voice of Jesus say (1846)
	1	47	The spacious firmament on high (1712)
	2	46	Brightest and best of the sons of the morning (1827)
	1	46	Eternal Father, strong to save (1861)
	9	46	Jerusalem, my happy home (1601)
	1	46	Praise the Lord! ye Heavens adore him (1797?)
	4	46	When all thy mercies, O my God (1712)
	9	45	Jerusalem the golden (12 cent., trans. 1851)
	2	45	Hark, the glad sound, the Saviour comes (1755)
	10	45	Ye servants of the Lord (1755)
	2	45	Songs of praise the angels sang (1819)

3	44	Come, Holy Ghost, our souls inspire (9 cent., trans. 1627)
2	44	All hail the power of Jesus' name (1779)
7	44	Guide me, O thou great Jehovah (Redeemer) (1745, trans. 1771)
10	44	Glorious things of thee are spoken (1779)
2	44	There is a green hill far away (1848)
3	43	Come, Holy Spirit, come (1759)
7	43	O God of Bethel, by whose hand (1755, alt. 1781)
7	43	Lead, kindly Light, amid the encircling gloom, 23 (1833)
		Lead, kindly Light, 20
7	42	Jesus calls us: o'er the tumult (1852)
4	42	The King of love my shepherd is (1868)
10	41	For the beauty of the earth (1864)
2	41	Hail the day that sees Him rise (1739)
4	41	There is a fountain filled with blood, 27 (1779)
		There is a fountain fill'd with blood, 14
13	41	Gentle Jesus, meek and mild, 27 (1742)
		Lamb of God, I look to thee, 14
15	40	God bless our native land (1836)
7	40	O happy band of pilgrims (1862)
2	40	O come, all ye faithful (1744, 1793, trans. 1841)
4	40	Just as I am without one plea (1838)
D *30-9* 1	39	From all that dwell below the skies (1719)
4	39	My faith looks up to thee (1830-1)
8	39	For ever with the Lord (1835)
7	39	O Jesus, I have promised (1868)
4	39	Hark, my soul, it is the Lord (1779)
4	39	Prayer is the soul's sincere desire (1819)
6	39	Stand up, stand up for Jesus (1858)
7	38	Forth in thy name, O Lord, I go (1749)
12	38	There is a book, who runs may read (1827)
1	38	O worship the King (1833)

12	38	We plough the fields, and scatter (1782, trans. 1861)
11	37	At even, ere the sun was set (1868)
2	37	It came upon the midnight clear (1850)
4	37	Now the day is over (1867)
4	37	O, for a heart to praise my God (1742)
2	37	Ride on, ride on in majesty (1827)
6	37	Fight the good fight with all thy might, 20 (1863)
		Fight the good fight, 17
10	36	Jesus, where'er thy people meet (1779)
4	36	Through all the changing scenes of life (1696)
7	36	Oft in danger, oft in woe (1827)
2	36	Once in royal David's city (1848)
2	35	All glory, laud, and honour (c. 820, trans. 1851, alt. 1861)
12	35	Come, ye thankful people, come (1844)
2	35	Love Divine, all loves excelling (1747)
4	35	O for a thousand tongues to sing (1739)
7	35	Thine for ever! God of love (1847)
2	34	Come, thou long-expected Jesus (1744)
13	34	Blest are the pure in heart (1827)
2	34	Jesus Christ is risen to-day (14 cent., trans. 1708)
4	34	Saviour, blessed Saviour (1862, alt. 1868)
4	33	I lay my sins on Jesus (1834)
10	33	The Church's one foundation (1866)
4	33	Saviour, when in dust to thee (1839)
9	33	Bright the vision that delighted (1837)
4	33	Sweet the moments, rich in blessing (1757, alt. 1770, 1854)
12	33	Summer suns are glowing (1871)
7	33	Through the night of doubt and sorrow (1859, trans. 1867)
15	33	God save our gracious King, 21 (1744, alt.)
		God save our gracious Queen, 12
13	32	By cool Siloam's shady rill (1827)
2	32	Art thou weary, art thou languid? (1862)

10	32	O day of rest and gladness (1862)
4	32	Father, whate'er of earthly bliss (1776)
4	32	One there is above all others (1779, alt. 1867)
2	31	Crown him with many crowns (1851)
8	31	Brief life is here our portion (12 cent., trans. 1851, alt. 1861)
4	31	O for a closer walk with God (1779)
7	31	'Forward' be our watchword (1844?)
3	31	Gracious spirit, dwell with me (1855)
9	31	There is a happy land (1843)
1	31	The Lord my pasture shall prepare (1712)
4	31	O thou to whose all-searching sight (1725, trans. 1738)
2	31	When, his salvation bringing (1830)
6	30	Brightly gleams our banner (1860)
4	30	Come, my soul, thy suit prepare (1779)
4	30	Come unto me, ye weary (1867)
3	30	Gracious spirit, Holy Ghost (1862)
2	30	Hark, the song of jubilee (1818)
1	30	My God, how wonderful thou art (1849)
7	30	My God, my Father, while I stray (1834-9, four texts)
14	30	Lord, thy word abideth (1861)
4	30	Jesus the very thought of thee (12 cent., trans. 1849)
1	30	O Thou from whom all goodness flows (1791)
12	30	Fair waved the golden corn (1851)
12	30	O Lord of heaven and earth and sea (1862)
2	30	While shepherds watched their flocks by night (1696)

II ANALYSIS OF HYMNS WITH 40-PLUS REPRINTS

Class	Pre-1800	Post-1800	Total
1 (Father)	8	3	11
2 (Son)	7	6	13
3 (Spirit)	2	1	3
4 (Devotion)	5	3	8
5 (Mission)	1	2	3
6 (Military)	1	2	3
7 (Pilgrimage)	3	4	7
8 (Death)	0	2	2
9 (Heaven)	3	1	4
10 (Worship)	2	1	3
11 (Time)	4	3	7 ("Lord, dismiss us" counted once in each column)
12 (Nature)	0	0	1
13 (Ethic)	1	0	
14 (Bible)	0	0	
15 (Patriotic)	0	1	1

III ANALYSIS OF HYMNS WITH 30-39 REPRINTS

Class	Pre-1800	Post-1800	Total	Grand Total	Pre-1800	Post-1800
1	3	2	5	16	11	5
2	3	10	13	26	10	16
3	0	2	2	5	2	3
4	8	7	15	23	13	10
5	0	0	0	3	1	2
6	1	3	4	9	2	5
7	1	6	7	14	4	10
8	0	2	2	4	0	4
9	3	2	5	9	6	3
10	1	1	2	5	3	2
11	0	2	2	9	4	5
12	0	6	6	6	0	6
13	0	2	2	3	1	2
14	0	1	1	1	0	1
15	1	0	1	2	1	

Grand total is of hymns in each category reprinted 30 or more times.

IV COMPARISON OF 100 TEXTS MOST REPRINTED IN
"LEARNED" AND "POPULAR" HYMNALS

In the following tables, the figures refer to the number of recurrences. "No" in the final column denotes non-appearance among texts listed 30 or more times in the main computer search. (L = Learned, P = Popular)

A Texts in *first* quartile of each set of 100 texts

	L	P	Class
Rock of Ages	34	7	4
Hark! the herald angels	33	8	2
Soldiers of Christ, arise	32	7	6
God Moves in a mysterious way	31	7	1
From Greenland's icy mountains	31	6	5
Christ the Lord is risen today	28	8	2
There is a land of pure delight	28	6	9
How sweet the Name	27	6	4
Thou whose almighty Word	27	6	5
Rejoice, the Lord is King	27	6	2

B Texts in *first* quartile of "Learned" list and *last* of "Popular"

	L	P	Class
Lord, dismiss us (2 texts)	31	4	11
Come, Holy Ghost, our souls inspire	30	4	3
Let us with a gladsome mind	27	4	1

C Texts in *first* quartile of "Learned" list and *middle* quartiles of "Popular"

	L	P	Class
Lo! he comes, with clouds	31	5	2
Our blest Redeemer	28	5	3

D Texts in *last* quartile of "Learned" and *first* of "Popular" list

	L	P	Class
Guide me, O Thou great Jehovah	18	6	7
Lead us, heavenly Father	17	6	7

E Texts in *middle* quartiles of "Learned" and *first* quartile of "Popular"

	L	P	Class
Jesu, Lover of my soul	22	7	4
Ye servants of the Lord	21	7	10

F Texts in *middle* quartiles of each list

	L	P	Class
Jerusalem the golden	25	5	9
Before Jehovah's awful throne	24	5	1

	L	P	Class
O God of Bethel	24	5	7
I heard the voice of Jesus	23	5	4
Songs of praise the angels	23	5	2
Nearer, My God, to Thee	23	5	8
For ever with the Lord	21	5	8 No
Jerusalem, my happy home	21	5	9
Children of the heavenly	20	5	7
Glorious things of thee are	20	5	10
When all thy mercies, O my	20	5	4

G Texts in *middle* quartile of "Learned" and *last* of "Popular"

Abide with me	22	4	8
Glory to Thee, my God, this night	22	4	11

H Texts in *last* quartile of "Learned" and *middle* of "Popular"

All hail the power of Jesu's	17	5	2
O day of rest and gladness	17	5	10
Come, ye thankful people	16	5	12

I Texts in *first* quartile of "Learned" and *not* among 100 in "Popular" list

Awake, my soul, and with the sun	11
When I survey the wondrous Cross	2
Sun of my soul	11
All people that on earth do dwell	1
Come, let us join our cheerful songs	9
Holy! holy! holy! Lord God Almighty	1
Jesus shall reign where'er the sun	5
Hail to the Lord's anointed	2
As with gladness men of old	2
Praise, my soul, the King of Heaven	1
Now thank we all our God	1

These predominantly objective and mythological hymns are most indicative of the Learned tradition.

J Texts *not* in "Learned" list and in *first* quartile of "Popular"

Another six days' work is done	10 (9?)
Jesus, I love Thy charming name	4 No
Glory to God on high	1 No
Father of mercies, in Thy word	14 No
Do not I love thee, O my Lord	4 No

	L	P	Class
Dear refuge of the weary soul			4 No
Blow ye the trumpet, blow			2 No
It is not death to die			8 No
One there is above all others			4
O for a closer walk with God			4
O happy day that fixed my choice			4 No

Less certainly, the above indicate world-and-life-denying pietism in the Popular tradition.

V ANALYSIS OF PUBLIC SCHOOL HYMNALS (CHAPTER 11, NN. 45-8)

A. Found in at least four (n. 45)

Abide with me; fast falls the eventide
All people that on earth do dwell
As pants the hart for cooling streams
As with gladness men of old
Awake, my soul, and with the sun
Before Jehovah's awful throne
Blest are the pure in heart
Bread of heaven, on thee we feed
Brief life is here our portion
Brightest and best of the sons of the morning
Call Jehovah thy salvation
Children of the heavenly King
Christ the Lord is risen today
Christ, whose glory fills the skies
Christian, seek not yet repose
Come, Holy Ghost, our souls inspire
Come, let us join our cheerful songs
Come, let us join our friends above
Come, O thou Traveller unknown
Dies irae (a translation of)
Father! by thy love and power
Forth from the dark and stormy sky
Glorious things of thee are spoken
Glory be to Thee, my God, this night
Go to dark Gethsemane
God moves in a mysterious way

God the Lord a King remaineth
Great God, what do I see and hear?
Hail the day that sees Him rise
Hail to the Lord's Anointed
Hark, the glad sound! the Saviour comes
Hark the herald angels sing
Holy, holy, holy! Lord God Almighty
Hosanna to the living Lord
Jerusalem, my happy home
Jerusalem the golden
Jesus Christ is risen today
Jesus lives! no longer now / thy terrors now
Jesu(s), Lover of my soul
Lead us, heavenly Father, lead us
Lo! He comes, with clouds descending
Lord, behold us with Thy blessing
Lord, dismiss us with Thy blessing
Love Divine, all love(s) excelling
My God, and is Thy table spread
Nearer, my God, to Thee
New every morning is the love
Now thank we all our God
O for a heart to praise my God
O God of Bethel, by whose hand
O God, our help in ages past
O God, unseen yet ever near
O sacred head, surrounded / sore wounded
O Thou from whom all goodness flows
"O timely happy, timely wise" (see "New every morning . . . ")
O worship the King
Oft in danger, oft in woe
Our blest Redeemer, ere He breathed
Praise, my soul, the King of heaven
Praise the Lord! ye heavens adore Him
Rock of Ages, cleft for me
Round the Lord in glory seated
Saviour, again to Thy dear name we raise
Saviour, when in dust to Thee
Soldiers of Christ, arise
Sun of my soul, Thou Saviour dear
"Take up thy cross," the Saviour said
The Lord my pasture shall prepare

The Son of God goes forth to war
The strain upraise of joy and praise
Thine for ever! God of love
Thou art gone up on high
Thou whose almighty Word
Three in One, and One in Three
Through all the changing scenes of life
Thy way, not mine, O Lord
We saw Thee not, when Thou didst tread
When gathering clouds around I view
When God of old came down from heaven
When I survey the wondrous Cross

B. Found in three (n. 46)

Angels, from the realms of glory
As now the sun's declining rays
At even, ere the sun was set
Blest be Thy love, dear Lord
Captain of Israel's host, and guide
Deck thyself, my soul, with gladness
Ein feste Burg (a translation of)
Father, whate'er of earthly bliss
Guide me, O Thou great Jehovah
Hark, the song of jubilee
How sweet the name of Jesus sounds
Jesus shall reign where'er the sun
Just as I am, without one plea
Lord, in this Thy mercy's day
Lord of mercy and of might
Lord of the worlds above
Lord, thy word abideth
Lord, when we bend before Thy throne
O come, all ye faithful
O Father, who didst all things make
O Lord, how happy we should be
O Saviour, is Thy promise fled?
Pleasant are Thy courts above
Rejoice, the Lord is King
Saviour, breathe an evening blessing
The eternal gates lift up their heads
The Lord of might from Sinai's brow

The radiant morn has passed away
The sun is sinking fast
Thou art the way; by Thee alone
Veni, sancte Spiritus
When all Thy mercies, O my God
Where high the heavenly temple stands
Ye boundless realms of joy
Ye servants of God

C. *Found in Cheltenham (1890), Harrow (1895), and Public School (1904)*
(n. 47)

A few more years shall roll
Abide with me; fast falls the eventide
According to Thy gracious word
All glory, laud and honour
All people that on earth do dwell
All praise / Glory to Thee, my God, this night
And now, O Father, mindful of the love
Art thou weary, art thou languid
As pants the hart for cooling streams
As with gladness men of old
At even, ere the sun did/was set
At Thy feet, O Christ, we lay
Awake, my soul, and with the sun
Before Jehovah's awful throne
Before thine awful presence, Lord
Blest are the pure in heart
Bread of the world in mercy broken
Brief life is here our portion
Brightest and best of the sons of the morning
Children of the heavenly King
Christ the Lord is risen today
Christ, whose glory fills the skies
Christian, seek not yet repose
Christians awake, salute the happy morn
Come, Holy Ghost, our souls inspire
Come, let us join our cheerful songs
Come, let us join our friends above / Let saints on earth in concert sing
Come to a desert place apart
Conquering kings their titles take
Ein feste Burg (a translation of)

Eternal Father, strong to save
Father, before Thy throne of light
Father, let me dedicate
Father of heaven, whose love profound
Father, whate'er of earthly bliss
Fight the good fight with all thy might
Forth in Thy name, O Lord, I go
From Greenland's icy mountains
Go to dark Gethsemane
Go, when the morning shineth
God moves in a mysterious way
Gracious Spirit, Holy Ghost
Great God, what do I see and hear
Guide me / us, thou great Jehovah
Hail to the Lord's anointed
Hark! a thrilling voice is sounding
Hark, the glad sound! the Saviour comes
Hark, the herald angels sing / —how all the welkin rings
Hark! the song of jubilee
Here, O my Lord, I see Thee face to face
Holy, holy, holy, Lord God Almighty
How sweet the name of Jesus sounds
I heard the voice of Jesus say
In the hour of trial
It came upon the midnight clear
Jerusalem, my happy home
Jerusalem the golden
Jesu, lover of my soul
Jesus calls us o'er the tumult
Jesus Christ is risen today
Jesus lives! no longer now / thy terrors now
Jesus shall reign where'er the sun
Lead, kindly Light, amid the encircling gloom
Lead us heavenly Father, lead us
Lo! He comes with clouds descending
Lord as to Thy dear cross we flee
Lord, behold us with Thy blessing
Lord, dismiss us with Thy blessing
Lord, in this Thy mercy's day
Lord, we thank Thee for the pleasure
Lord, when we bend before Thy throne
Love divine, all love(s) excelling

My God, my Father, while I stray
Nearer, my God, to Thee
New every morning is the love
Now thank we all our God
Now the labourer's task is o'er
O come all ye faithful
O God of Bethel by whose hand
O God of truth, whose living word
O God our help in ages past
O God, unseen yet ever near
O happy band of pilgrims
O Jesu, Thou art standing
O Lord of heaven, and earth, and sea
O Son of God, our captain of salvation
O Thou from whom all goodness flows
O Thou, who makest souls to shine
Oft in danger, oft in woe
Onward Christian Soldiers
Our blest Redeemer, ere He breathed
Our day of praise is done
Praise, my soul, the King of heaven
Prayer is the soul's sincere desire
Ride on, ride on in majesty
Rock of Ages, cleft for me
Saviour, again to Thy dear name we raise
Saviour, when in dust to Thee
Soldiers of Christ, arise
Songs of praise the angels sang
Sun of my soul, Thou Saviour dear
Sweet Saviour, bless us ere we go
"Take up Thy cross," the Saviour said
The Church's one foundation
The day is past and over
The head, that once was crowned with thorns
The King of Love my shepherd is
The saints of God, their conflict past
The Son of God goes forth to war
The spacious firmament on high
The strife is o'er, the battle done
There is a book, who runs may read
There is a land of pure delight
Thine arm, O Lord, in days of old

Thine for ever, God of love
This is the day of light
Thou art gone to the grave; but we will not deplore Thee
Thou art gone up on high
Thou art the way; by Thee alone
Thou, whose almighty word
Three in one and one in three
Through all the changing scenes of life
Through the day, Thy love has spared us
Through the night of doubt and sorrow
Thy way, not mine, O Lord
We plough the fields and scatter
We saw Thee not, when Thou didst come / tread
We sing the praise of Him who died
Weary of earth and laden with my sin
When all Thy mercies, O my God
When God of old came down from heaven
When I survey the wondrous cross
Who are these like stars appearing
Who shall ascend to the holy place

D. Found in at least three of earlier group (n. 48)

As now the sun's declining rays
As the hart the brooks desireth
Blest be Thy love, dear Lord
Bread of heaven, on Thee we feed
Call Jehovah thy salvation
Captain of Israel's host, and guide
Dies irae (In Latin or English)
Father, by Thy love and power
Forth from the dark and stormy sky
Glorious things of thee are spoken
God the Lord a King remaineth
Hosanna to the living Lord
Jesu dulcis memoria (translation of)
Lord of mercy and of might
Lord of my / our life, whose tender care
Lord of the worlds above
Lord, pour Thy Spirit from on high
Lord, shall Thy children come to Thee
Lord, Thy word abideth

My God, and is Thy table spread
O Father, who didst all things make
O for a heart to praise my God
O God of hosts, the mighty Lord
O Lord, how happy we should be
O sacred Head, surrounded / sore wounded
O Saviour, is Thy promise fled?
O Thou, to whose all-searching sight
O worship the King
Pleasant are Thy courts above
Praise the Lord, ye heavens adore Him
Praise to the Lord, the Almighty, the King of Creation
Rejoice, the Lord is King
Round the Lord in glory seated
Saviour, breathe an evening blessing
Spirit of mercy, truth and love
The eternal gates lift up their heads
The Lord my pasture shall prepare
The Lord of might from Sinai's brow
The radiant morn hath passed away
The roseate hues of early dawn
The Son of God goes forth to war
The strain upraise of joy and praise
Veni, sancte Spiritus (Latin or English)
Wake, wake (O wake) for night is flying
We thank Thee, Lord, for this fair earth
When gathering clouds around I view
Where high the heavenly temple stands
While shepherds watched their flocks by night
Ye boundless realms of joy

ABBREVIATIONS

AM	*Hymns Ancient and Modern* (London: Clowes). Date refers to edn.
AMR	*Hymns Ancient and Modern Revised* (1950 edn.)
AV	Authorized Version (King James Bible)
BCP	Book of Common Prayer
Breviary	*Hours of the Divine Office* (Collegeville, MN: Liturgical Press 1963)
CH	*Congregational Church Hymnal*, ed. George Barrett. (London: Congregational Union 1884)
Coll. P.	*A Collection of Hymns for the Use of People Called Methodists*, ed. Frank Baker, Vol. 7 in *Works of John Wesley*, ed. Franz Hildebrandt and Oliver A. Beckerlegge (Oxford: Clarendon Press 1983)
Coll. P. (1830)	*A Collection . . . with a Supplement* (London: Wesleyan Conference Office 1830)
EH	*English Hymnal* (London: Oxford University Press 1906, rev. 1933)
GHC	*Gospel Hymns Consolidated* (Toronto: Copp, Clark and Co. 1883)
H.B.	Hymn Book
HCM	*Hymns and the Christian "Myth"* (Vancouver: University of British Columbia Press 1986)
HG	Erik Routley, *An English-Speaking Hymnal Guide* (Collegeville: Liturgical Press 1979). Figure refers to entry number.
HSGBI	*Bulletin* of Hymn Society of Great Britain and Ireland
Julian	John Julian (ed.), *A Dictionary of Hymnology* (2nd edn. 1907, rpt. New York: Dover 1957). i or ii refers to column, e.g., 365 i, page 365, left column.
OH	John Newton, William Cowper, *Olney Hymns* (3 vols., Olney 1779), edn. used, Edinburgh: Ritchie 1854
PCH	Erik Routley (comp.), *A Panorama of Christian Hymnody* (Collegeville: Liturgical Press 1979). Unless page number shown, figure refers to item number, as in a hymnal.

Ps.	Psalm
SSU	Sunday School Union (combined Methodist-Congregational, locally organized)
Watts *DS* and *MS*	Isaac Watts, *Divine Songs*, with *Moral Songs*, attempted in Easy Language for Children (London 1715)
Watts, *Hymns*	—*Hymns and Spiritual Songs* (3 vols., London 1707, 1709)
Watts, *Psalms*	—*Psalms of David Imitated* (London 1719)
Watts, *Works*	—*Works of the Reverend and Learned Isaac Watts, D.D.*, ed. George Burder (6 vols., London: J. Barfield 1810)

NOTES

Unless the page is indicated, numerals for hymn-books refer to hymn numbers.

NOTES TO PREFACE

1 Matthew Arnold, "The Study of Poetry," an introduction to T.H. Ward's *English Poets* (1880), rpt. in *Essays in Criticism*, 2nd series (London: Macmillan 1888), 2-3.
2 Arnold, *Culture and Anarchy* (1871), Ch. 3, in *Works of Matthew Arnold*, 15 vols. (London: Macmillan 1903-4), VI, 92.
3 R.L. Greene, *Early English Carols*, 2nd edn. (Oxford: Clarendon 1977), cxviii ff.

NOTES TO CHAPTER ONE

1 Thomas Hardy, *Far from the Madding Crowd* (London: Macmillan 1974) 31.
2 Lionel Adey, *Hymns and the Christian "Myth"* (Vancouver: University of British Columbia Press 1986). Hereafter *HCM*.
3 Isaac Watts, *Hymns and Spiritual Songs*, 3 vols. (London 1707, 1709), II, No. 22.
4 *Works of the Reverend and Learned Isaac Watts, D.D.*, ed. George Burder, 6 vols. (London: J. Barfield 1810), IV, 255.
5 *New Congregational Hymn Book* (London: Congregational Union 1859); the same,

with *Supplement* (1874). On Congregational hymnals, see Louis F. Benson, *The English Hymn: Its Development and Use in Worship* (Richmond: John Knox Press 1962, originally 1915), 453ff. On public and elementary school hymnals, see Chapters 11 and 9 below.
6 Norman Longmate, *The Workhouse* (London: Temple Smith 1974), 68-9. See also Ian Anstruther, *The Scandal of the Andover Workhouse* (London: Geoffrey Bles 1973), passim.
7 Owen Chadwick, *The Victorian Church*, 2 vols. (London: A. and C. Black 1966), II, 250.
8 Desmond Bowen, *The Idea of the Victorian Church* (Montreal: McGill University Press 1968), 5-6.
9 Hannah More, cited in Ford K. Brown, *Fathers of the Victorians* (Cambridge: Cambridge University Press 1961), 190: "To teach them [the poor] to read, without giving them principles, seems dangerous; and I do not want to teach them to write, even in my weekly [evening] schools." But Thomas Walter Laqueur, in *Religion and Respectability: Sunday Schools and the Working Class Culture, 1780-1850* (New Haven and London: Yale University Press 1976), 103-7, says that "Almost all Sunday schools taught writing," especially if Dissenting. Thus, "after decades of official opposition, 61 of 68

New Connexion Methodist schools taught it, as did nearly all those run by Primitive Methodists and Unitarians, but only 8 of 40 Baptist schools.''

10 E.P. Thompson, *The Making of the English Working Class* (New York: Pantheon Books 1964), 354: "[As churches supported no other reform movements] one comes to suspect less a . . . social conscience than a desire to disarm criticism.'' Donald Davie, in *A Gathered Church: The Literature of the English Dissenting Interest, 1700-1930* (London: Routledge 1978), 58, asserts: "bending all energies towards one definable objective—after the slaves were emancipated it became, significantly, foreign missions—had the perhaps intended effect of stifling all protests at more pervasive and inflammable injustices, nearer home.''

11 Bowen, 64.

12 Ibid., 249.

13 Hardy, loc. cit.

14 Flora Thompson, *Lark Rise to Candleford* (Harmondsworth: Penguin 1973; orig. publ. Oxford University Press 1939), 212.

15 Horton Davies, *Worship and Theology in England*, 5 vols. (Princeton: Princeton University Press 1961-75), III, 227.

16 On T.T. Lynch and "Rivulet" controversy, see Chadwick, I, 405-6; Benson, 454-5.

17 On this reference by T.S. Eliot in *After Strange Gods*, and F.R. Leavis' refutation of the implied lack of cultural tradition, Davie (93-4) concludes that "what went on in the Eastwood Congregational Church" or what Mrs. Lawrence "transmitted" remain unclear. On late Victorian Congregational Sunday school hymnody see Chapter 10 below.

18 William Hale White ("Mark Rutherford"), *The Revolution in Tanner's Lane*, 8th edn. (London: T. Fisher Unwin 1890), 95-6.

19 Watts, *Psalms of David Imitated* (London 1719), Ps. 67, headed "The Nation's Prosperity and the Church's Increase," printed in *Works*, IV, 174 with end-note: "Having translated the scene to . . . Great Britain, I have borrowed a devout . . . wish for the happiness of my native land from Zech: ii, 5 and offered it up in the second stanza, 'I will be a wall of fire round about, and will be the glory in the midst of her'.''

20 Harry Escott, *Isaac Watts: Hymnographer, A Study of the Beginnings and Develop-*

ment of the English Hymn (London: Independent Press 1962), 20ff.

21 See Davie, 65. Davie (61) notes editor as the hymnist Josiah Conder (cf. Julian, 256i) but regards Hall and "associates" (80) as primary influences.

22 Hugh McLeod, *Class and Religion in the Late-Victorian City* (London: Croom-Helm 1974), 26-7.

23 Bernard Semmel, *The Methodist Revolution* (New York: Basic Books 1973), 59-60, 112.

24 Ibid., 114, 117. Robert Currie, *Methodism Divided: A Study in the Sociology of Ecumenicalism* (London: Faber 1968), 56-60, 68-9.

25 Ronald Knox, *Enthusiasm: A Chapter in the History of Religion* (Oxford: Clarendon Press 1962), 448-9.

26 On Wesleyanism as appealing to the lower classes (and Evangelicalism to the middle) see Davies, III, 268; E.P. Thompson, 379 ("uprooted and abandoned"), 391 ("among working-class movements"), but 394 (among "new elite" of manufacturers); McLeod, 33, claims 52 per cent of Wesleyans in Bethnal Green were "manual workers.''

27 Robert F. Wearmouth, *Methodism and Working Class Movements of England, 1800-1850* (London: Epworth Press 1937), 168. Sandra S. Sizer, in *Gospel Hymns and Social Religion: The Rhetoric of Nineteenth Century Revivalism* (Philadelphia: Temple University Press 1978), 66-7, notes ecclesiastical concern re "disruptive" New England camp meetings.

28 Borrow cited in Joseph Ritson, *The Romance of Primitive Methodism* (London: Dalton 1909), 273. Julia Stewart Werner, *The Primitive Methodist Connexion: Its Background and Early History* (Madison: University of Wisconsin Press 1984), 19, 155-7, 159.

29 On *Small H.B.*, see H.B. Kendall, *Origin and History of Primitive Methodism*, 2 vols. (London: Dalton, n.d.), II, 2, but cf. Davies, III, 144-5, and Julian, 730 i.

30 *Large Hymn Book for the Use of Primitive Methodists* (1825), 1841 edn. (kindly loaned by Rev. F.S. Pritchard, but not in British Museum Catalogue), Preface, vi-viii. Cf. continuum from United States revivals of 1857-8 and 1870s to Graham's, traced in Sizer, 153-8, and in William G. McLoughlin, jr., *Modern Revivalism:*

Charles Grandison Finney to Billy Graham. On Bourne and Finney, see Werner, 175.

31 On songs, see Ritson, 270, Kendall, II, 32-3, Werner, 149; on unrest and Primitive Methodism, see Semmel, 137, Werner, 167-76, and on singing as outlet for anger, see Ritson, 283-4.

Disagreeing with Semmel ("most missionary effort where most Luddism"), Werner finds inconsistencies between adjoining towns. On sect and agricultural riots, see E.J. Hobsbawm and George Rude, *Captain Swing* (London: Lawrence and Wishart, 1969), 65, 86, and esp. 186 ("riot and dissent" too coincident "to be wholly accidental"), 289 (religion as "passive response to defeat"). Sizer, 75, 191, notes fear in 1820s of unrest spreading from Europe via revivalists.

32 J.F.C. Harrison, *The Second Coming: Popular Millennarianism, 1780-1850* (London: Routledge 1979), 222-3: "millennarian ideology of [social] change" was attractive to "domestics, engravers, shopkeepers" and a threat to the Anglican Establishment.

33 [Rev. C. Shaw], *When I Was a Child: Memories of an Old Potter* (London: Methuen 1903, rpt., Wakefield: S. and R. Publishers 1969), 169, 172-8. Werner, 148, 156-7.

34 Chadwick, I, 389-91.

35 On dying Toplady's refusal to retract his attacks on John Wesley, see Knox, 502.

36 Chadwick, I, 449, 454, 456-7.

37 Wesley stipulated in 1768, 1781, and 1783 that all boys board from age 8 to graduation without holidays or play, be continuously supervised, and rise at 4 A.M. for prayer. In *Works of John Wesley*, 14 vols. (Grand Rapids: Zondervan 1958-9, rpt., London: Methodist Conference 1872), XIII, 283-302.

38 Knox, 502.

39 Calvinist authority figures in childhood scenes of Dickens, *Dombey and Son* (1848), *David Copperfield* (1850), *Bleak House* (1853), *Great Expectations* (1860); Rev. Branderham and servant Joseph in Emily Brontë, *Wuthering Heights* (1847); Pitt Crawleys and Rev. Bartholemew Irons (Ch. 33) in Thackeray, *Vanity Fair* (on possible model, Joseph Irons, see Ch. 3 below); Blake, *Songs of Experience* (1794).

40 Marian Ann Evans ("George Eliot"),

Middlemarch (1871), Ch. 70 (Harmondsworth: Penguin 1965), 758.

41 B.K. Cunningham (1909), cited in Davies, III, 219.

42 Davie, *Gathered Church*, 58-9, 81, 141-3.

43 McLeod, 219.

44 Chadwick, I, 366.

45 Bowen, 23-7; Chadwick, II, 241ff.

46 Chadwick, II, 287. Werner, 78, 85, 128-30, 173.

47 Chadwick, I, 367-8.

48 *Bleak House*, esp. Ch. 16; Elizabeth Gaskell, *Mary Barton* (1848), *North and South* (1854-5) passim.

49 Jane Austen, *Emma* (Edinburgh: J. Grant 1911, originally 1816), 124-5, but generally in Ch. 10 and in allusions to Mr. Knightley's acts of charity.

50 Henry Moseley, cited in Harrison, xiii-xiv.

51 E.g., Martineau and Johnson families, prominent in Birmingham and Leicester respectively in late nineteenth and twentieth centuries.

52 Bowen, 335.

53 E.g. that of Rugby School mission in East End of London.

54 Chadwick, II, 226.

55 Ibid., 229.

56 Ibid., 227.

57 McLeod, 33.

58 Chadwick, II, 232.

59 Ibid., 235-7.

60 Loc. cit.

61 McLeod, 29.

62 Charles Booth, *Life and Labour of People in London*, 7 vols. (London: Macmillan 1902), VII, 124.

63 McLeod, 42-3; Booth, 424: "Throughout London the female sex forms the mainstay of every religious assembly. . . . Otherwise the . . . distinctions are . . . of means." "Fashionable" areas have "prosperous," well-attended churches, "middle class" ones "vigorous . . . religious development . . . with active social life"; working class ones [in] "organized religion a comparative blank," poorer ones "missions," the "task . . . the more hopeless" the worse the slum.

64 Bowen, 258-9; Chadwick, II, 120.

65 Alasdair MacIntyre, *Secularization and Moral Change* (London: Oxford University 1967), 66-7.

66 David Newsome, in *Godliness and Good Learning: Four Studies on a Victorian Ideal* (London: Murray 1961), regards the

ideals of Hughes, Kingsley, and Leslie Stephen as being "thirty or forty years later . . . the creed of a typical housemaster" (216); cites the view of Thring (Uppingham) that a school should educate all its pupils against that of Arnold (Rugby) that a schoolmaster's "first, second and third duty" was to "get rid of unpromising subjects" (220); and claims that "the ideal of godliness and good learning killed itself by its excesses" (231). Dickens portrays "excesses" in curriculum of Paul Dombey and "ideal" in school of *David Copperfield*, Ch. 16, based on King's School, Canterbury.

67 Ernest Belfort Bax, *Reminiscences and Reflexions of a Mid and Late Victorian* (London 1918), cited in Susan S. Tamke, *Make a Joyful Noise unto the Lord: Hymns as a Reflection of Victorian Social Attitudes* (Columbus: Ohio University Press 1978), 200-1.

68 Watts, *Works*, IV, 428.

69 Ibid., 447.

70 Albert Edward Bailey, *The Gospel in English Hymns: Backgrounds and Interpretations* (New York: Scribner's 1950), 51.

71 Conclusion of Ps. 72 (First part), in Watts, *Works*, IV, 179. Full text in *PCH* 43.

72 Philip Doddridge, *Hymns Founded upon Various Texts in Scripture*, ed. Job Orton (London 1793), No. 198 ("See Israel's gentle Shepherd stand"): "If Orphans they are left behind, / Thy Guardian-care we trust; / That Care shall heal our bleeding hearts / If weeping o'er their Dust." Cf. No. 211 ("The King of Heaven his Table spreads"): "Ye hungry-poor that long have strayed / In Sin's dark Mazes, come: / Come from the Hedges and Highways, / And Grace shall find you room." However scriptural and metaphorical, these lines indicate social concern, on which see also *HCM*, 117-18, 165-6.

73 Doddridge, *Hymns*, Nos. 84, 140, 369, 156.

74 McLeod, 179-80.

75 Levin L. Schücking, *The Puritan Family* (1929), trans. Brian Battershaw (New York: Schocken Books 1970), 56-7.

76 Philippe Ariès, *Centuries of Childhood* (L'Enfant et la vie familiale sous l'ancien

Régime), trans. Robert Baldick (London: Cape 1962), 335-6.

77 Ibid., 94-9.

78 Davies, IV, 193.

79 Cf. E.P. Thompson, 354-5, 359ff. on endorsement of Methodist ethos in Andrew Ure, *Philosophy of Manufactures* (1835).

80 Respectively Mandell Creighton, re 1890-1914, cited in Bowen's Preface; Chadwick, II, 322, re 1868-1921.

81 Knox, 592.

82 Especially Blake, *Songs of Innocence* (1789), *Songs of Experience* (1794); Coleridge, *Christabel* (1797, 1800), "Frost at Midnight" (1798); Wordsworth, "Ode on Intimations of Immortality from Recollections of Early Childhood" (1802, 1806-7).

83 See Peter Coveney, *The Image of Childhood in Victorian Fiction* (Harmondsworth: Penguin 1967), 240-7, also prefatory poem and conclusion of Charles Lutwidge Dodgson ("Lewis Carroll"), *Alice's Adventures in Wonderland* (1865) and prefatory poem of *Alice Through the Looking-Glass* (1872).

84 Condensed from Davies, III, 229-30.

85 Samuel Butler, *The Way of All Flesh* (1903), Ch. 49. On swoons, etc., at Wesley's meetings, see Knox, 521-5.

86 Chadwick, I, 67-8.

87 John Keble, *The Christian Year: Thoughts in Verse for Sundays and Holy-days Throughout the Year* (London: Oxford University Press 1914, orig. ed. 1827), 42-3. On Keble's Lectures on Poetry, see Georg B. Tennyson, *Victorian Devotional Poetry: The Tractarian Mode* (Cambridge, MA: Harvard University Press 1981), 56-69.

88 Davies, III, 119.

89 Chadwick, I, 517.

90 Alfred Lord Tennyson, *In Memoriam* (1850): Prologue, then poems 2, 106, and 131 (esp. ll. 121-44).

91 McLeod, 155, 229-31; *School Hymns with Tunes . . . Supplementary to "Church Hymns"* (London: Bell 1892).

92 Ibid., 284-6.

93 Ibid., 285.

NOTES TO CHAPTER TWO

1 Cited in Barbara Kiefer Lewalski, *Protestant Poetics and Seventeenth-Century Lyrics* (Princeton: Princeton University

Press 1979), 33. Karl Marx, "Toward the Critique of Hegel's Philosophy of Law," cited in Saul K. Padover, *Karl Marx: An Intimate Biography* (New York: New American Library 1980), 29-30.

2 Ibid., 86ff.

3 Ibid., 87, 91, 92, 99 respectively.

4 Ibid., 8-12.

5 George Burder, *A Collection of Hymns from Various Authors, intended as a Supplement to Dr. Watts' "Psalms and Hymns"* (London: 14th edn. 1811, originally 1784).

6 This and succeeding comments based on J. Ernest Rattenbury, *Wesley's Legacy to the World* (London: Epworth Press 1928), and *The Evangelical Doctrines of Charles Wesley's Hymns* (London: Epworth Press 1941).

7 E.g., "Jesu, Lover of my soul" and "Thou Shepherd of Israel"; see Rattenbury, *Evangelical Doctrines*, 71.

8 Fuller analysis in Rattenbury, *Evangelical Doctrines*, 74ff.

9 *Works*, II, 125 (1748); III, 268 (1766); 285 (1767).

10 Ann Frank, *Diary*; Alexander Solzhenitsyn, *Gulag Archipelago*, passim.

11 I.e., working upon hearts; cf. quotations in Knox, *Enthusiasm*, 492.

12 Rattenbury, *Evangelical Doctrines*, 292-3, 72-84.

13 Bernard Lord Manning, *The Hymns of Wesley and Watts: Five Informal Papers* (London: Epworth Press 1942), 14, a judgment called "reprehensible" in Madeleine Ford Marshal and Janet Todd, *English Congregational Hymns in the Eighteenth Century* (Lexington: Kentucky University Press 1982), 6.

14 *Methodist School Hymnal*, 1911, discussed in Ch. 13 below.

15 Originally in Charles Wesley, *Hymns and Sacred Poems*, 1749, "Before Work," cf. Routley *HG* 208: "perhaps the first and greatest of weekday hymns." Full text in *PCH* 67 and *EH* 259.

16 Even E.P. Thompson (*The Making of the English Working Class*, 354), attributes this to "the younger leaders of Methodism," esp. Jabez Bunting (374), rather than the Wesleys.

17 In order, as listed: Samuel Medley (1785), No. 507 in David Denham, *Saints' Melody* London (1837) (entirely metaphorical use);

Joseph Hart (1759), John Rippon, *A Selection of Hymns from the Best Authors Intended as an Appendix to Dr. Watts' "Psalms and Hymns"* (London 1787), Comprehensive Edition, 1844, 115; John Newton, *Olney Hymns* (Olney 1779), III, 92, "Before Sermon" (primarily metaphorical, but n.b. poverty of villagers); Anne Steele (1776), No. 144 in John Ash and C. Evans, *Collection of Hymns for Public Worship* (Bristol, 1769); Joseph Stennet (1732), Denham 1025 (n.b. rest, water, and purification motifs in "In heaven from all their toil and pains, / Where seas of joy eternal flow, / Without a taint of mortal woe"); James Montgomery (1819); Newton, *OH* III 59 and Denham 95; No. 245 in (William) *Gadsby's Hymns* (Manchester, 1814) and Denham 690, under "Christian Experience" (unlisted by Julian but n.b. pilgrim motif of "With dangers thick on every hand, / But Jesus guides us through the vale"; cf. Mrs. Gamp on life as "piljin's projiss of a wale" in *Martin Chuzzlewit*).

18 On Particular and General Baptist services see Davies, III, 43-7, 124-36.

19 Cf. alternative title "Odes of Rest" in James H. Charlesworth's introduction to his translation of *Odes of Solomon* (Oxford: Clarendon Press 1973, rpt. Scolar Press 1977); St. Augustine, *Confessions* I i.

20 John Agg, *Collection of Hymns for Public Worship* (Evesham 1795), McGill University Library.

21 I.e., Gothic novels. William Wordsworth, Preface to 1802 edn. of *Lyrical Ballads* (5th edn. London: Methuen 1924), 13.

22 Joseph Scriven "What a Friend we have in Jesus!" (c. 1855), Canadian hymn widely known owing to use by Moody and Sankey. Cf. Newton's reproach with 2 Sam. 16. 17.

23 (J. Newton) *Twenty-Six Letters on Religious Subjects* (London: Oliver 1774), Letter xxii, "On the Advantages of a State of Poverty" (170-1).

24 Probably Deut. 24. 18.

25 Paul Fussell, *The Great War in Modern Memory* (New York: Oxford University Press 1979), 118-19.

26 Gilbert Thomas, *William Cowper and the Eighteenth Century* (London: Allen and Unwin 1948), 176.

27 E.P. Thompson, 378-9.

28 *Hours of the Divine Office* (Collegeville, MO: St. John's University 1963), 3 vols., I, 158 (Aurora); 1608 (O sol).

29 *OH* III, 1-5: "Solemn Address to Sinners," e.g., No. 2: "Stop, poor sinner . . . think. . . . (lest) you drop / Into the burning lake"; No. 4 (Prepare to meet God): "the rich, the great, the wise / Trembling, guilty, self-condemned, / Must behold the wrathful eyes / Of the Judge they once blasphemed."

30 George Eliot, *Adam Bede*, Ch. 3 (principle), 15 (practice by Dinah).

31 Thompson, 388, gives Methodist membership as 60,000 in 1789; 90,000 in 1795; 107,000 in 1805; 154,000 in 1811; 237,000 in 1827, showing greatest increase *after* period of 1790s when revolution most likely, with inference that turning to apocalyptic faith ("chiliasm of despair") represented inability of workers to change social structure.

32 Wearmouth, *Methodism and the Working Class . . .*, 224.

33 Brown, *Fathers of the Victorians*, 187-8, 375, 436-7. Davie's hostile assessment of Wilberforce (*Gathered Church*, 57) oversimplifies Brown's view.

NOTES TO CHAPTER THREE

1 William Hunter (Irish-born American Methodist-Episcopal), *Minstrel of Zion* (1845), rpt. *Methodist Scholar's Hymn Book* (London 1870), *Book of Sacred Songs for* (London) *Board Schools* (1873), (Huddersfield) *School Board Hymn Book* (1873), etc.

2 R.L. Greene (ed.) *Early English Carols*, cviii.

3 *A Collection of Hymns for the Use of People called Methodists* (London: Wesleyan Conference Office 1830), "Additional Hymns" (Nos. 540-60); "Supplement" (561-769). Nos. 526-39, for Methodist Societies, were added in John Wesley's lifetime.

4 Sister Mary Edward, headmistress of former St. Dominic's School, Stoke-on-Trent, found Catholic hymnody "disjointed and fragmented" by contrast with Anglican. Her school, founded in 1857, had used hymns only from 1930s, and she remarks absence of congregational hymn-singing tradition even now (letter, 3 March 1980).

5 Benson, *English Hymn*, 353. Julian (331-

43) lists 42 in 1800-20, 40 in 1821-50, and 43 in 1851-60.

6 The Injunctions of Elizabeth allowed free use of a hymn or "such like song" before and after Morning and Evening Prayer (Julian, 346ii). James I licensed George Wither's *Hymns and Songs of the Church* (1623) (Julian 1289-90).

7 See Routley, *PCH* 38 and No. 91, who substitutes Nathaniel Micklem's rendering of Zech. 13: 1 ("There springs a fountain, where for sin. . . . ").

8 Erik Routley, *Hymns and Human Life* (London: Murray 1952), 81. See Lowther Clarke, "One Hundred Years of 'Hymns Ancient and Modern'" (London: Clowes 1960), 17, on Archbishop's acceptance of dedication, and Julian, 503ii.

9 Stanza 1, Advent II, *Heber's Hymns, Written and Adapted to the Weekly Church Services of the Year* (London: Murray 1827).

10 Advent IV and III.

11 Epiphany III ("Lord! whose love is power excelling") and IV.

12 Routley (*PCH*,45) implies contrary, including Heber with Montgomery among "Romantic" hymnists, instancing "I praised the earth, in beauty seen." He curiously judges "Bread of the world" a "Communion hymn but hardly a eucharistic one," presumably because of emotionalism and lack of scriptural reference.

13 James Martineau (ed.), *Hymns of Praise and Prayer* (London 1874), xiv.

14 Discussed as such in Tennyson, *Victorian Devotional Poetry*, 74ff.

15 *AM, AMR* 4: "New every morning"; *AM, AMR* 18: "Hail, gladdening light" (trans. *Phos hilaron*); *AM, AMR* 24: "Sun of my soul"; *AM* 67, *AMR* 536 "Word Supreme, before creation"; *AM* 143, *AMR* 144: "Lord, in Thy Name Thy servants plead"; *AM, AMR* 154: "When God of old came down from heaven"; *AM, AMR* 168: "There is a book, who runs may read"; *AM* 213: "A living stream, as crystal clear"; *AM* 261, *AMR* 335: "Bless'd are the pure in heart"; *AM* 350: "The voice that breathed o'er Eden"; *AM* 581: "Lord of Life, Prophetic Spirit."

16 "Hues of the rich, unfolding morn," *Christian Year*, 3-5: "Morning."

17 William Wordsworth, *The Prelude, or Growth of a Poet's Mind* (1805) X, 140-4: "called upon to exercise their skill / Not

in Utopia . . . / But in the very world . . . of all of us,—the place in which, in the end, / We find our happiness, or not at all!'' (unchanged in 1850 text).

18 '' 'Tis gone, that bright and orbed blaze,'' 5: ''Evening.''

19 ''Ode on Intimations of Immortality . . . ,'' 1-2.

20 Pp. 92-3: ''Whitsunday.''

21 P. 453: ''Harvest.''

22 Keble, *Christian Year*, 42-3: Septuagesima.

23 P. 455: ''Holy Matrimony.''

24 Pp. 156-8: ''The Purification.''

25 *Paradise Lost*, I, 17-18.

26 Søren Kierkegaard, *Purity of Heart Is to Will One Thing* (1846), trans. Douglas Steere (London: Collins 1961), passim.

27 E.g., in H.M. Butler (ed.), *Hymns for the Chapel of Harrow School* (4th edn., Harrow: Wilbee 1881), and *A Selection of Hymns and Carols . . . for Use in Preparatory Schools* (Winchester: privately printed 1894, as supplement to *AM*).

28 Keble, *Sermons Academical and Occasional* (Oxford: Parker 1848), 129-48, printed in *Christian Year* (Oxford University Press ed. cit.).

29 *Collection of Hymns and Anthems Used in St. Andrew's Chapel, Aberdeen* (18th edn.: Aberdeen 1836).

30 *Hymns Selected from Most Approved Authors for Use of Trinity Church, Boston* (Boston: Munroe, Francis, Parker 1808).

31 *Hymns of the Protestant Episcopal Church of the United States of America*, with Additional Selection by Rev. C.W. Andrews (Philadelphia: Hooker 1845). Text on 140, ''O Lord, Thy work revive,'' ascribed to Thomas Hastings but not in Julian 494-5 (q.v.). This and Kelly, ''The Gospel comes'' (143) occur in Andrews' supplement, more Calvinistic than main hymnal, which follows liturgical calendar until section on ''Christian Life'' (96ff.) where several texts on Last Judgment. Anglican-evangelical, Methodist and Dissenting texts passim. On American hymnody, see Benson, 358-431.

32 Doddridge, *Hymns*, No. 198 (on Mk. 10.14): ''See Israel's gentle Shepherd stand.''

33 No. 211: ''The King of Heaven His table spreads.''

34 E.g., No. 111: ''Mark the soft-falling snow.''

35 Preface.

36 *The Church Psalmist, or Psalms and Hymns for Public, Social and Private Use of Evangelical Christians* (Philadelphia: 1847, originally New York 1843), viii. On history, see Benson, 384. On Beecher, see Sizer, 21-2.

37 Benson, 375-6, re Asahel Nettleton (ed.), *Village Hymns for Social Worship, designed as a Supplement to Psalms and Hymns of Dr. Watts* (New York: Sands 1840), original Preface (1825). No. 41 by Lee: ''An angry God, a Judge severe''; 39: ''How great, how terrible that God''; cf. 237 with 241: ''an impartial survey take, / Is Jesus formed and living there? [in the heart],'' and predilection of U.S. corporations for ''objective'' external assessments. Sizer notes (67) that Nettleton produced hymnal on his initiative owing to committee's slowness in producing counterblast to Revival hymnody.

38 Archibald Alexander (ed.), *A Selection of Hymns Adapted to Devotions of the Closet, Family and Social Circle* (New York: Leavitt 1831), v., cf. R.W. Dale's Preface to *The English Hymn Book* (London: Hamilton, Adams 1874): ''Let me choose the Hymns and I care not who writes the theology.''

39 *A Choice Selection of Hymns and Spiritual Songs for . . . Prayer, Conferences and Camp Meetings* (Windsor, VT 1827).

40 Story in Ritson (265), who remarks (263) ''dominant note of battle and conquest'' in ''hymns and tunes carried through villages.'' Cf. defensive posture in hymn-quotations with Sizer (42ff.) on decline of ''aggressive activism'' after 1820s. Originally ''I scorn to fear,'' as in Werner, 149.

41 Popularity attested in Kendall, II, 11.

42 Nos. 5-6 in *Small Hymn Book*, 80 in *Large . . .* (bound together).

43 In *Small Hymn Book*, the 154 items, all for Camp Meetings, are poetically inferior but more dramatic, e.g., ''Holy War'' and ''Dying Pilgrim'' (3-6), ''Scripture Fulfilling'' (25-7), ''Alarm to Sinners'' and ''Millennial'' (49-51). *Large* H.B. differs from *Coll. P.* (1830) in Calvinistic emphasis on divine majesty and simpler headings, e.g. ''Inward Religion'' for ''Inward and Formal . . . ,'' ''Prayer and the Fight of Faith'' for ''Believers Fighting,'' ''Believers Interceding for the World.''

44 Werner (149) finds heaven predominant, and notes promise of status. James

Obelkevich, in *Religion and Rural Society: South Lindsey, 1825-75* (Oxford: Clarendon 1976), 232, notes objective theology of heaven, communion with departed, and (236) "large proportion of the *Primitive Methodist Magazine* . . . devoted to obituaries," further indicating status conferred by membership.

45 *When I Was a Child*, 136.

46 Rev. R. Jukes, Primitive Methodist, Manchester, cited in Kendall, II, 33.

47 Lytton Strachey, *Eminent Victorians* (2nd edn., London: Chatto 1921), 13.

48 *When I Was a Child*, 7. Cf. dying member, "I feel religion to be blessed reality. It has not all been noise." (cited in Obelkevich, 220).

49 View formed from reading Shaw, Ritson (83ff.) and Wearmouth (*Working Class*) and from experience of former P.M. families in Durham coalfield, but confirmed by Werner who (175) claims sect helped poor in "transition from the old world to the new."

50 Julian, 730ii, re Rev. John Flesher, a "great preacher" who protested "unfitness" for task (Kendall, I, 370), but "freely altered or re-made" 225 of 852 texts to "strengthen the copyright": Editor's Preface to *Primitive Methodist Hymn Book* (London: R. Davies 1854).

51 No. 523, C. Wesley: "I and my house will serve the Lord" (*Coll. P.*, 472, headed "For Masters," i.e., for household with servants). No. 522, Bourne (1829): "O Righteous Father, Lord of all." No. 531 (as in 1887 P.M. Hymnal), "With gratitude, O Lord, I see." No. 526: "Soon as the morn with roses" 531, 532 not listed in Julian.

52 Joseph Irons, *Zion's Hymns, Intended as a Supplement to Dr. Watts' "Psalms and Hymns," for Use of . . . Congregation at Grove Chapel, Camberwell* (3rd edn., London 1825). On use, see Julian, 571.

53 Robert Hall, jr., on whom see Davie, *Gathered Church*, 61-5, died in 1823. While agreeing with Davie (89), that Spurgeon preached to "the poorest of the poor" and that early 19th-century Baptist clergy ranked below Congregational (84), I base judgment re class on Booth, VII, 133 (cited in n67 below) and 139ff.

54 General Baptists of Leicestershire and Yorkshire, influenced by Methodists, "believed in Christian song" (Julian 111).

55 (1787). William Gadsby, *A Selection of Hymns for Public Worship* (Manchester 1814), "used exclusively by . . . more highly Calvinistic . . . Baptist churches" (Julian, 113).

56 E.g., "A beggar poor, at mercy's door" (Gadsby 378) (Denham 507), "Come, ye sinners, poor and wretched" (723) (Denham 416), "We travel through a barren land" (245) (Denham 690).

57 "Hymns marked C.W. were composed by that good and gracious man Charles Wesley" in whose hymns the "life and breathing" are "not . . . even approached by Watts." John Gadsby, Preface to *Gadsby's Hymns*.

58 Cf. Sizer, 31-2, 126-8 (hymns), and 105-6 (similar themes in American popular novels).

59 Supplement, Nos. 90, 91 (Erskine), 94, 95, 96.

60 Julian, 112i, specifies thirty years from publication of Steele's *Poems* . . . (1760). Charles Haddon Spurgeon (ed.), *Our Own Hymn-book: A Collection of Psalms and Hymns for Public, Social and Private Worship* (London: Passmore and Alabaster 1869).

61 Henry Ward Beecher (ed.), Preface to *Plymouth Collection of Hymns and Tunes* (New York: Barnes 1855), on whose importance see Sizer, 149. On contrast of scholarly Baptists and populists, see Davie, *Gathered Church*, 64-6, 79-80, 88-90. On Spurgeon and extramural services, see Davies III, 333ff.

62 *HG* 185. In Burder's collection: "The Saviour, O what endless charms" (117); "Dear Refuge of my weary soul" (40); "Thou only Sov'reign of my heart" (57); "Ye mourning sinners, here disclose" (74), on sickness.

63 Full version No. 289 of *Hymnal for Use in Congregational Churches* (1897), rpt. of *Presbyterian Hymnal* (Philadelphia 1895), both ed. Louis F. Benson. *PCH* 271 omits verse on "wretched sons of want."

64 Text No. 555 in *The Hymn-Book Annotated* (Toronto: Oxford University, 1939). Some versions, e.g., No. 376 in *The Hymnary* (Toronto: United Church of Canada Publishing House 1930), have "kindred minds."

65 On three hymns under this title, see *HG* 313. Medley's text is No. 555 in *Hymn-Book Annotated*.

66 Booth, VII, 124: "the attitude . . . of the Baptists brings with it a too obtrusive piety . . . the material out of which hypocrisy weaves her hateful cloak" and which (136) "favoured cant." Pietistic language illustrated 183-90. Booth notes strong congregational bond (126-8) but that Baptists too often view poverty as "the result of sin or self-indulgence" (133).

67 Davie, 89, on Spurgeon's "histrionics and sentimentalism in the pulpit," "vulgarities" that "led him to misinterpret . . . Scriptural text and . . . doctrine" and "disastrous . . . ministry, and . . . influence." Booth, 133: " 'Tabernacles' . . . within easy access . . . of the lower middle and upper working classes, from whom, . . . with some of strictly middle class, the congregations are drawn."

68 Editor's Preface.

69 Cf. Evangelical benevolent societies listed in Brown, 329-40, with their apparent absence from American revivals described by Sizer. Evidently later revivalists encouraged individual, not organized, beneficence.

70 Denham No. 739 ("Homegoing"), 740 ("Home, sweet"), 1013 ("Happy home") and "Comprehensive Rippon" (London 1844), 12th edn. of *Selection*. Nos. 1149, 1152 treat home as metaphor for heaven. Cf. Spurgeon, Nos. 849-53: "This is not my resting place" (Bonar), "We've no abiding city" (Kelly), "What is life? 'Tis but a vapour" (anon.), "Come, let us join our friends above" (Wesley).

71 No. 345: "Come Lord! and tarry not."

72 Respectively: "Father, whate'er of earthly bliss"; "O Lord! my best desires fulfil''; "My God and Father, while I stray"; "O how I long to reach my home"; "For ever with the Lord" (Montgomery); "My rest is in heaven—is not here"; "This is not my place of resting."

73 Spurgeon allots 63 texts to Death, Burial, Resurrection, Heaven, and Hell, 34 to Christ's life, death, and rising. Conversely, of 23 for Revivals and Missions none have imperialist or patriotic theme. Spurgeon's congregation "poorest of the poor" and "probably the largest in Christendom" (Davie, 89, 88).

74 *Domestic Praise* (Manchester 1850), Preface: "singing of hymns . . . an agreeable introduction to the morning and evening worship of the family" [especially with] "Christian friends" more compatible with Nonconformity than *The Evensong . . . Selection of Hymns and Chants for Family Worship*, ed. W.H. Birch (London n.d.), which has items by Watts and Doddridge but provides for Sunday and weekday services in Tractarian mode and has *Te Deum* and 3 psalms.

75 Cf. *Domestic Praise*: "Oh for the all-reviving grace . . . We tread the very verge of doom" (94); "Death rides on every passing breeze . . . shall earth our hearts engage / And dreams of days to come? . . . Turn! Christian, turn! thy soul apply / To truths divinely given" (95); "When I can trust my all with God" (51). *Evensong* has sentimental evening hymns, e.g., "Sun of my soul" (25); "Saviour, breathe an evening blessing" (23).

76 Full title *Hymns for Public Worship of the Working Men's Christian Association* (London 1872, private printing). *Letters of Gerard Manley Hopkins*, ed. C.C. Abbott (3 vols., London: Oxford University Press 1935), I, 27-8.

77 E.g., "Soldiers of Christ, arise" (189); "A charge to keep I have" (190); "There is a fountain opened wide" (sic) (97); "For ever with the Lord" (197); "My rest is in heaven" (192).

78 Posthumously published in Ebenezer Elliott, *More Verse and Prose* (1850), first as a hymn in *Congregational Church Hymnal*, ed. George Barrett (London: Congregational Union 1887) with "famous" tune (*HG* 812).

79 See Basil Willey, *Nineteenth Century Studies: Coleridge to Matthew Arnold* (London: Chatto 1949), 44, 47-8, 49, 54, 56; A. Owen Barfield, "Form in Art and Society" (1951), in *The Rediscovery of Meaning and Other Essays* (Middletown: Wesleyan University Press 1977), 217-27.

80 Bryan R. Wilson finds seven beliefs common to Third World religious movements of protest: (1) value and need of conversion; (2) divine destruction of existing order; (3) withdrawal, solitary or communal; (4) religious understanding (*gnosis*) as means of salvation; (5) magic; (6) reform under divine guidance; (7) utopian reconstruction (*Magic and the Millennium*, cited in Harrison, *Second Coming*, 8-9). Nos. 1 and 2 observable in Wesleyan and

Primitive Methodism; No. 3 among Adventists, Plymouth Brethren and, to a degree, Baptists (cf. early monasticism); No. 4 in Catholic and Calvinist churches; No. 6 in Liberal Protestant movements and No. 7 in French and Marxist revolutions, but tempered by social environment.

81 Best verse of "Hugh McDiarmid" and William Morris in Scots and neo-medieval diction.

82 See *Comus*, ll. 768-76.

83 *The Sailor's Hymn Book*, ed. T.C. Finch, for British and Foreign Sailors' Society (London: Ward 1850 edn.). E.g., "I'm on a foreign coast . . . Pilot Divine, appear" (278); "In the wild waste of waters . . . / How delightful to think that my Saviour is here" (number unrecorded, *mea culpa*). Many of 500 texts on model of "Come ye sinners, poor and wretched."

84 *Soldiers' Hymn Book* (Aldershot comp. and pub.: Aldershot Mission Hall and Soldiers' Institute 1869). Alphabetical arrangement. No. 292: "We are but strangers here, / Heaven is our home" transposed from "I" and "my."

85 *The Soldier's Book of Hymns*, Compiled by an Officer, C.H.M. (n.p. 1863). Format: Christian's Life; Christ's Army; Calls to Arms; Exhortations; Watchfulness and Endurance; Hymns of Faith, Supplication, Praise, Comfort; Holy Communion; Sunday Morning and Evening; The Queen; The Nation; When Going on Active or Foreign Service; In Time of Trouble . . . Sickness . . . Hour of Death; Funeral Hymns; Heaven. Compiler trusts that "my comrades may be strengthened in performing the duties and bearing the trials of their profession as faithful soldiers of Jesus Christ our Saviour and of Her most gracious Majesty the Queen" (Preface), evincing ruling-class ethos.

NOTES TO CHAPTER FOUR

1 R.W. Dale, Editor's Preface, *English Hymn Book* (London: Hamilton, Adams; Birmingham: Hudson 1874); Negro spiritual; *They Stand Together: Letters of C.S. Lewis to Arthur Greeves, 1914-63*, ed. Walter Hooper (London: Collins 1979), 316 (Owen Barfield speaking of Lewis and others).

2 *Psalms, Hymns, and Passages of Scripture for Christian Worship* (London: Partridge and Oakey 1853), Nos. 1-205 psalm versions, mainly by Watts; among 900 texts at least 16 by C. Wesley; among translations "Creator Spirit, by whose aid" (394), "Day of wrath, that awful day" (393), "Thou hidden source of calm repose" (335), "Commit thou all thy griefs" (565), and "Thou hidden love of God" (586).

3 From *OH* "Glorious things . . . " (107), "God moves in . . . " (238), "O for a closer walk . . . " (517); Heber's *Hymns* "Bread of the world . . . " (729), "Brightest, and best . . . " (273), "From Greenland's . . . " (842), "Holy, holy, holy . . . " (441); Keble, *Christian Year* "O timely happy . . . " (744), "There is a book . . . " (234); Grant, "O worship the King" (144); Lyte, "Praise, my soul . . . " (142), "Abide with me . . . " (883), only composed in 1847; Adams, "Nearer my God . . . " (520).

4 Cf. George MacDonald's expulsion from Congregational ministry (1853) for denying eternal punishment.

5 "When I survey . . . " (712), "The head that once . . . " (371), "Ride on . . . " (297).

6 On controversy re alleged deism in T.T. Lynch, *The Rivulet: A Contribution to Sacred Song* (1855), see Benson, 454-6.

7 Of 90 on Christ, 27 page-indexed A-H are: "All hail, incarnate God" (430), "All hail the power of Jesus' name" (177), "And will th' eternal King" (298), "And will the Judge descend" (572), "Ascend thy throne, Almighty" (370), "Blessed Redeemer, how divine" (244), "Christ our passover is slain" (186), "Christ the Lord is risen today" (141), "Come thou Almighty King" (643), "Come, thou long-expected Jesus" (162), "Come, ye that love the Saviour's name" (175); then six to Christ as "Dear Saviour" (515, 244, 81, 272, 440, 365), and "Dear Shepherd of thy people" (340); "Ere Christ ascended to his throne" (454), "Gentle Saviour, look on me" (524), "Hail, mighty Jesus, how divine" (77), "Hail, thou once-despised Jesus" (75), "Hark, the herald angels . . . " (130), "Hark, 'tis our heavenly Leader's . . . " (328), "He dies! the Friend of sinners" (474), "He lives; the great Redeemer" (152), "Hosanna, Christ" (620). The ex-

ceptions, devotional hymns, mostly in 35 to "Jesus," but n.b. "J. is our great salvation" (p. 118), and "J., mighty King in Zion" (449).

8 1.64 per cent 16 texts, Nos. 33, 36-7, 39, 40-3, 397, 399, 417, 455, 513, 533; 0.3 per cent Nos. 2, 22, 28; 1.03 per cent 10 texts, Nos. 160, 170, 171, 172, 347, 374, 516, with 113, 114, 431 on "Friend," but judgment difficult as Nos. 33-169 headed "Love of Christ."

9 769 texts, some on more than one theme. Numbers after virgule (/) refer to 1830 Supplement.

Birth: Nos. 220, 605; Miracles (objective): 32, 146, / 612; (subjective): 1, 2, 40, 107, 109, 114, 135, 166, 219, 224, 305, 370, 398, / 611 (part); Example: 127 (part), 212, 213, 364, 436, 442, 447, 459, 471, 504; Resurrection/Ascension: 86, 463, 553, 554, / 627, 628, 629, 630, 631, 632, 633.

Passion/Crucifixion: (objective) 22, 228, 545, / 613, 621, 625 (part), 760; (subjectively applied) 9, 23, 24, 29, 35, 123, 128, 151, 160, 168, 175, 181, 184, 186, 228, 237, 362, 371, 373, 422, 433 (part), 453 (applied to country), 548, and 549 (eucharistic), / 619, 759.

Atonement: (objective) 9, 27, 28, 29, 33, 36, 122, 127 (part), 149, 157, 162, 190, 201, 202, 207, 215, 257, 345, 380, 400 (part), 436, 439, 546, and 547, and 551 (eucharistic), / 614, 616, 618, 754; (subjective) 3, 4, 14, 20, 84, 96, 102, 106, 114 (refrain), 150, 174, 180, 189, 217, 279, 330, 338, 346, 349, 375, 414, 443, / 622.

Judgment: (objective) 43, 44, 46, 54 (part), 55, 56, 57, 58, 59, 61, 62, 63, 64, 65, 66, *67*, *75*, 80, 81, 132, 176, 280, *536*, *555*, *557*, / 717, 729; (realized eschatology) 103, 318. (Italicized nos. respectively on expectation, seeing in heaven, second coming (2), worship of Lamb.)

Incarnation (doctrine): 31, 185 (part), 194, 195, 197, 220, 231 (part), 262 (part), 281, 336, 337, 400 (part), / 565, 601, 602, 603, 608, 609, 661; (subjectively applied) 18, 101, 141, 153, 172, 193, 208, 300, 303, 327, 343, 353, 379, 382, 383, 385, 399, 413.

Most items in Supplement by Charles Wesley, but preponderance of subjective hymns on Sacrifice and objective ones on Judgment in Nos. 1-560 indicates John Wesley's principles of selection.

10 Clarke *One Hundred Years* . . . , 38, re

Edward H. Bickersteth (ed.), *A Hymnal Companion to the Book of Common Prayer* (London 1870), based on a collection of 1858. My quotations from 1878 edn. (rpt. Longmans 1919). On *AM* editors' policy, and granting of permission in 1876, see Susan Drain, "An 'Incomprehensible Innovation': The Application of Copyright Law to Hymn Publishing in the Church of England, 1860-80," *Publishing History* 15 (1984), 65-90.

11 Respectively *AM* (1868) 1, *HC* (1870) 1; *AM* 5, *HC* 6; *AM* 6, *HC* 8; *AM* 10, *HC* 11*; *AM* 11, *HC* 12; *AM* 14, *HC* 9; *AM* 276, *HC* 12; *AM* 17, *HC* 18; *AM* 279, *HC* 193 (*"All praise. . . .). Clarke (32) calls *AM* "a Tractarian manifesto" yet lists only "Now my tongue, the mystery telling," "Thee we adore, O hidden Saviour"; "My God, and is thy table spread"; "Bread of Heaven, on thee we feed,", and "O God unseen, though ever near," only the last originally Anglican.

12 *AM* 86, *HC* 122; *AM* 10, *HC* 138.

13 *AM* 221, *HC* 56; *AM* 394, *HC* 52; *AM* 11, *HC* 9.

14 *AM* 310, *HC* 102.

15 *AM* 217, *HC* 88.

16 *AM* 2, *HC* 3; *AM* 263, *HC* 254; *AM* 222, *HC* 393.

17 Figures by Clarke, in article "One Hundred Years of *Hymns Ancient and Modern*," in *The Hymn*, Vol. 12 (1961), 29-30, and Ibid., 34, 60, citing Henry Twells, who reported to Convocation of 1892 that 10,237 churches used *AM*, 1,144 *Church Hymns*, and 1,420 *HC*.

18 Principle of alteration defended in Preface to *AMR* (1950), vii.

19 *People's Hymnal*, comp. R.F. Littledale (London: Joseph Masters 1867), quotations from Preface.

20 Clarke, 19, cites article in *Christian Remembrancer* (1851) on "new Roman Catholic fashion of singing," especially "O Paradise."

21 *Hymns for London Mission*, by Compilers of "Hymns Ancient and Modern" (London: Clowes 1874).

22 *Encyclopedia Britannica*, 15th edn. 27: 225ff., "Servitude."

23 Based on Paula Maulstby, on "Black Hymnody," at conference of International Association of Hymnologists and Hymn Societies of Great Britain and America, Oxford, August 1981.

24 Comment of my (German-born) research assistant Mrs. Maria Abbott, borne out by Moravian hymns discussed in *HCM*, Chapter 11.
25 *PCH*, pp. 156-7.
26 Tamke, 203.
27 Tamke, 4, 183, n. 12 cites publishers and J. Edwin Orr's *Second Evangelical Awakening* (London 1949), 261 for overall sale of 90,000,000 copies of Sankey's hymnals by 1949, and David P. Appleby's *History of Church Music* (Chicago 1965), 143, for 80,000,000 in England in first fifty years. However inconsistent, figures prove the point.
28 Text used, *PCH* 391.
29 Julian discusses only one lyric by Moody (994) but many tunes by Sankey. In *Sacred Songs and Solos, with Standard Hymns*, comp. and sung by Ira D. Sankey.
30 No. 68 in *Sacred Songs, and Solos*, No. 124 in *Gospel Hymns Consolidated* (Toronto: Copp & Clark 1883), No. 444 in *Hymnal Companion* (1878).
31 *GHC* 92, by F.H. Huntington (Julian, 544).
32 *Sacred Songs . . .* 9; *Gospel Hymns . . .* 204.
33 *PCH* 392.
34 Respectively *PCH* 393, *SS* 28, *GHC* 90 and 345, lyric by Ellen H. Willis.
35 *PCH* 394 and elsewhere, e.g., Reynolds (comp.) *A Joyful Sound* (New York: Holt, Rinehart, Winston 1978), No. 143.
36 *EH* 583 (!), *SS* 14, *GHC* 37, and *PCH* 678 (!).
37 J. Scriven, published anon., 1865 (*HG* 794).
38 *PCH* 396.
39 "Mark Twain" (Samuel Clemens), *Huckleberry Finn*, Chapters 19, 25, 26.
40 "William" books by Richmal Crompton. British Library lists 44 titles by Richmal Crompton Lamburn from 1922 to 1965, nearly all London (Newnes).
41 *PCH*, 157: "Fanny Crosby . . . said to have composed more lyrics than Charles Wesley, but . . . when you have seen one you have seen them all. Ira D. Sankey . . . composed relatively few, and his style had a . . . homespun innocence that often avoided sheer platitude . . . P.P. Bliss was more prolific, and less inventive."
42 *SS* 7, *GHC* 158.
43 *GHC* 171. On ultimate source, Ps. 18. 2, see David L. James, "Hightower's Name:

A Possible Source," *American Notes and Queries* 13 (Sept. 1959), 4-5.
44 *PCH* 395.
45 *PCH* 390.
46 James Martineau, *Hymns of Praise and Prayer* (London 1874), Preface, and *Odes of Solomon*, discussed in *HCM*, Chapters 1 and 3.
47 *PCH*, 157: [Gospel Songs designed as] "ministry to immaturity."
48 *SS* 25, *GHC* 4, *EH* 580 (!).
49 *AM* (1875) used as several texts written since 1868.
50 "Eternal Father" *AM* 370, *HC* 533; "Lord behold . . . " *AM* 576 and most school hymnals, but not in *HC*.
51 Frank Colquhoun, *Hymns that Live: Their Meaning and Message* (London: Hodder & Stoughton 1980), 291ff.
52 John 10.11-15.
53 C.S. Lewis, *Surprised by Joy* (London: Bles 1955), passim.

NOTES TO CHAPTER FIVE

1 Letter from Dr. Erik Routley to author, 20 March 1980.
2 E.g., Routley, in *Hymns and Human Life*, 270ff., employs lists of hymns sung in Westminster Abbey on national occasions to establish a canon of "national anthems."
3 Ibid., *H.G.* and David W. Perry, *Hymns and Tunes Indexed by First Lines and Tunes* (London: Hymn Society of Great Britain and Ireland and Royal School of Church Music 1980), all compiled from current English hymnals.
4 School-hymnal surveys in Chapters 10, 11, and 12.
5 *One Hundred Hymns for Special and Schoolroom Services, Cottage Meetings, Family Worship, and Private Devotion* (London: Rivingtons 1861), ed. by a "lay member" probably of All Souls, Marylebone. *A Hundred Hymns Selected by Readers of "Sunday at Home" as the Best in the English Language* (2nd edn., London: Religious Tract Society 1888). Rev. James King, *Anglican Hymnody . . .* 325 Hymns of the Highest Merit According to . . . the Whole Anglican Church (London: Hatchard 1885). *One Hundred Hymns for Schools* (London: Oxford University Press 1956), editor anon.

6 *HG*, and Perry.

7 See Bibliography.

8 "Praise . . . ": H.F. Lyte (Ps. 103); J. Goss, "Praise My Soul"; "Now . . . ": M. Rinkart; J. Cruger, "Nun danket"; "Rejoice . . . ": C. Wesley (Phil. 4.8); Handel, "Gopsal"; W.C. Dix, alt. *AM* (1868) (Matt. 2.11); C. Kocher, "Dix" (from chorale "Treue Heiland"); S. Baring-Gould (Matt. 16.18 only); A. Sullivan, "St. Gertrude."

9 Cf. analogy in J.H. Gurney, "Fair waved the golden corn" (1851) based on Lev. 2.14. "For the beauty . . . " originally in *Lyra Eucharistica* (1864), as I had to inform a hymnologist who queried my ascription to Eucharist in *HCM*. Only *EH* assigns it thus (*HG* 201).

10 In Bibliography (adult, and public school or collegiate).

11 *Victorian Hymns: Sacred Songs of Fifty Years* (London: Kegan Paul 1887), ed. anon, and dedicated to Queen Victoria. For pessimism, see Tennyson, "Locksley Hall Sixty Years After"; Arnold, "Dover Beach"; Clough, "Easter Day"; Morris, "Love is Enough" et al. Comparable texts in *Victorian Hymns*: W.J. Irons, "Exiles from Paradise, through briar and thorn / We wander now" (33-4); C. Rossetti, "I bore with thee long weary days and nights" (51-2); F. Havergal, "I could not do without thee" (54-6), esp. st. 3; R.C. Chenevix-Trench, "Let all men know that all men move" (79-80), esp. st. 3, "That weary deserts we may tread . . . Through dark ways underground be led. . . . Shall issue out in heavenly day" (birth image); S.J. Stone, "Weary of earth, and laden with my sin" (166-7); J.S.B. Monsell, "When my feet have wandered . . . Out into the desert" (168-70).

12 Samuel Butler, *The Way of All Flesh* (London 1903), Chapter 49.

13 E.g., Denham, 611 ("When . . . "); 857 ("Another . . . "); *Gadsby's Hymns* (1853 edn.), 472 ("When . . . "); 857 ("Another"); "Comprehensive Rippon," 318 ("When . . . "); 857 ("Another . . . ").

14 J. Stennett. My text from *Church Psalmist*, 472.

15 *Church Psalmist*, 495.

16 *Hymnal Companion*, 337.

17 H. Bonar, "I heard the voice of Jesus say," *Hymns Original, and Selected*, 1846 (*HG* 311).

18 J.M. Neale, "Art thou weary, art thou languid," *AM* (1889), 254, in *Hymns of the Eastern Church*, had, as Neale said, "so little of the Greek hymn" in as to be original (*HG* 51).

19 Nos.
   1 Rock of Ages*
   2 Abide with me*
   3 Jesus Lover of my soul*
   4 Just as I am, without one plea*
   5 How sweet the name of Jesus sounds*
   6 My God, my Father, while I stray*
   7 Nearer, my God, to Thee*
   8 Sun of my soul . . . *
   9 I heard the voice of Jesus say*
   10 Art thou weary, art thou languid*
   11 For ever with the Lord*
   12 God moves in a mysterious way
   13 From Greenland's icy mountains
   14 When I survey the wondrous Cross
   15 Lead, kindly Light*
   16 Hark, how all the welkin rings (. . . herald angels sing)
   17 All praise to Thee, my God, this night
   18 A few more years shall roll
   19 Our God, our help in ages past
   20 Our blest Redeemer, ere . . .

Starred items death-oriented or subjectively devotional.

20 Evangelical magazine formerly edited by Mrs. Henry Wood, the novelist.

NOTES TO CHAPTER SIX

1 *Congregational Church Hymnal*, ed. George Barrett (London: Congregational Union 1887); *Primitive Methodist Hymnal* (*PM*), ed. George Booth (London: Dalton 1887); *Hymns Ancient and Modern, for Use in the Services of the Church, with Accompanying Tunes*, eds. W.H. Monk and C. Steggall (London: William Clowes 1889, rpt. 1906); *Scottish Church Hymnary* (Edinburgh 1898); *Baptist Church Hymnal: Hymns, Chants, and Anthems* (B) (London 1900).

2 Exceptions: "All glory, laud, and honour" (Baptist 769, children); "Art thou weary, art thou languid" (*B* 224); "Brief life is here our portion" (Primitive Methodist 561, no. illegible); "Christian, does thou see them" (*B* 421); "For thee, O dear, dear country" (*PM* 562); "Hark, hark, my soul, angelic songs are swelling"

(*PM* 1032); "Jerusalem the golden" (*PM* 563, *B* 469); "Jesus, the very thought of thee" (*B* 174, *PM* 360); "My God, I love thee not because," attrib. St. F. Xavier (*B* 292); "O come and mourn with me awhile" (*B* 112); "O come, O come, Immanuel" (*B* 572); "O happy band of pilgrims" (*B* 439, *PM* 601); "O Paradise" (*B* 445, *PM* 1029); "O Jesu, King most wonderful" (*B* 148); "Praise to the Holiest in the height" (*B* 67, *PM* 230); "Safe home, safe in port" (*B* 459, *PM* 1026); "The Church's one Foundation" (*B* 478, *PM* 717); "The day of Resurrection" (*PM* 113). Being eschatological, and non-sacramental, these were acceptable to "Popular" compilers.

3 E.g., eucharistic hymns of Conder ("Bread of heaven," 493), and Heber ("Bread of the world . . . ," 494) included, those of Aquinas omitted; versions or derivatives of "Veni, Creator Spiritus" (Cosin, 463; Wesley, 213; Hart, 218; Watts, 205; Browne, 208; Caswall, 211) and "O Jesus, I have promised" (380) included but not "Thine for ever . . . "; Watts' "Arise, O King of Grace, arise" (445), "Go, worship at Immanuel's feet" (66), "Shine, mighty God, on Britain shine" (644).

4 Also Crosby "If I come to Jesus" (557), P.P. Bliss "God is always near me" (525), R. Lowry "Shall we gather at the river" (594).

5 *Primitive Methodist Hymnal*, Preface, iii.

6 But Presbyterian comparable to Congregational in number, and range of classic hymns originally British, German, or Latin.

7 Lyte's *Poems, Chiefly Religious* (London: Nisbet and Marsh 1833) show his early preoccupation with death and Platonic idealism, e.g., in "November" (37), "Autumnal Hymn" (60), and "Pilgrim Song" ("My rest is in heaven . . . ," 99), "Stability" (21), all rptd. in *Poetical Works*, ed. J. Appleyard (London: Elliott Stock 1907).

8 *AM* (1889) 229 ("Come"), 252 ("Weary"), latter an early favourite of Bertrand Russell, brought up by Evangelical grandmother. See esp. st. 2, "So vile I am, how dare I stand / In the pure glory of the holy God?", and st. 5, on Jesus "Who found me in the deathly wild / And made me heir of Heaven." Russell, *Autobiography* (3 vols., Toronto: McClelland & Stewart 1967-9), I, 28.

9 *A Study of History*, IV, 52-62, cited in *Arnold Toynbee: A Selection*, ed. W.F. Tomlin (London: Oxford University 1978), 58.

10 Esp. *Alice in Wonderland*, Chs. 3, 8, 10, 11 and *Alice through the Looking-Glass*, Chs. 3, 4, 6, 9.

11 Nos. 92, 29.

12 Full text (*PCH* 234, *EH* 309), as Routley says (*PCH*, 95) "an earnest eucharistic hymn of considerable dignity." See esp. sts. 6-8 and title cum refrain "Our sacrifice of praise." Published in Orby Shipley, *Lyra Eucharistica* (1864) (*HG* 201).

13 "O little Town" (USA, 1866, in hymnal 1874, but in England 1896) in *Scottish* . . . , No. 33, *Baptist* 756 (*HG* 535); "Away . . . " (USA, 1885) in no British hymnal before (Scottish) *Church Hymnary*, 1927 (*HG* 65).

14 Jonathan Gathorne-Hardy, *The Public-School Phenomenon* (London: Hodder 1977, rpt. Harmondsworth: Penguin 1979), 144 exemplifies common core of "simple, stirring" Anglican hymns from *AM*, by "Jesu, Lover of my soul," "God moves in a mysterious way," and "Rock of Ages," but also in all five hymnals examined, and in those for Harrow (1881), Rugby (1885), Uppingham (1874), Cheltenham (1903), and in *Public School Hymn Book* (London: Novello 1903) are: "Abide with me," "Awake, my soul, and with the sun," "Christ, whose glory fills the skies," "Glorious things of thee are spoken," "Lead, kindly Light," "Love Divine, all loves excelling," "New every morning . . . ," "O God our help in ages past," "Onward, Christian soldiers," and "Praise, my soul, the King of Heaven."

15 Quotations respectively from Nos. 649, C. Wesley: "How do thy mercies close me round"; 650, J. Conder: "How shall I follow Him I serve"; 653, C.F. Richter, trans. J. Wesley: "Thou Lamb of God, Thou Prince of Peace"; 654, C. Wesley: "Eternal beam of light divine."

16 E.g., 662, C. Wilson: "For what shall I praise Thee" (sickness, grief); 963, "Abide with me" (death); 36, "God moves . . . mysterious way" (doubt).

17 Nos. 608 (. . . Thy saints), 611, 610.

18 Under "Work and Watchfulness," Nos. 582, R. Heber: "The God of glory walks His round" (re vineyard); 596, J. Montgomery,

"Sow in the morn thy seed" (ministry and teaching); 604, J.S.B. Monsell, "Lord of the living harvest" (mission); 595, C. Wesley, "Equip me for the war" (combat with sin).

19 No. 936, J.S.B. Monsell, "O Love divine and golden."

20 Nos. 408, W.E. Winks, "In the night our toil is fruitless"; 409, "Sow in the morn . . . "; 410, T.T. Lynch, "Oft when of God we ask" (work); 411, F.R. Havergal, "Now the sowing and the weeping" (esp. metaphors of field labour and well-digging).

21 No. 406, by Mrs. A.L. Coghill, also No. 122 in *Gospel Hymns and Sacred Songs* (New York: Biglow & Main 1875), No. 23 in *Council School Hymn Book* (London: Novello 1905). Written for Canadian newspaper in 1854, thence (unacknowledged) in Sankey's *Sacred Songs and Solos* (Julian, 1622ii).

22 Nos. 176-84, respectively: "When Thou, my righteous Judge shall come"; "Lo! he comes, with clouds descending"; "O quickly come, dread Judge of all"; "When Jesus came to earth of old" (contrasting original "weakness, and woe" with Second Coming on "great white throne," but prayer for "love" to replace "conscious fear"); cf. 179, "Great God, what do I see and hear" (W.B. Collyer): "O shield us through that last dread hour, / Thy wondrous love extending."

23 Written 1870, for services of "National Thanksgiving" in *Church Hymns* (Anglican) (Julian, 327ii). In many children's hymnals, e.g., No. 500 in *Congregational Sunday School Hymn Book* (London: Congregational Union 1881), No. 256 in *School Hymns*, ed. Clarke (London 1892), and No. 81 in *Hymns for School Use*, comp. H. Buchanan Ryley (private printing, London 1910, for Emanuel and other Dacre Foundation schools).

24 Nos. 134, 135, 160, 155, 240, 275.

25 Put conditionally as Davie concludes (*Gathered Church*, 93), that evidence neither confirms nor denies this charge against religion of Lawrence's mother, in T.S. Eliot's *After Strange Gods*. Selection for children's services (Nos. 735-75) has proportionately fewer sentimental or vapid items than in *Congregational Sunday School Hymnal* (1881), which the boy probably used.

26 "Hush! blessed are the dead" (E.H. Bickersteth) is No. 604 in the Sunday-school, and "Safely . . . " No. 606 in the adult book.

27 Davie, 95. On Congregational hymnody, Benson (457-9), contrasts *Congregational Hymns*, ed. W. Garrett Horder (London: Elliott Stock 1884), as example of the "Literary Movement" with Barrett's which "aimed to distinguish sharply hymns from sacred poems . . . preserve . . . practicable hymns . . . of Congregationalism" yet "draw freely from the Hymnody of all sections of the Church" and which, though more theologically explicit and less poetic than Horder's, "put the authorized Hymnody of Congregationalism fully abreast with that of other Churches both from a literary and musical standpoint."

28 Nos. 709, 696, 693. But section (691-709) also includes "Golden harps are sounding" (702), "Jesus, meek and gentle" (691), and "Saviour, teach me day by day" (706), all escapist or condescending. Congregational hymnal a rpt. of Benson's Presbyterian one of 1895.

29 Benson's condemnation of *English Hymn Book* for omitting items R.W. Dale (ed.) deemed sentimental, for being unchurchly and for avoiding "commonplace" implies such indulgence (Benson, 456-7).

30 Nos. 474-638; respectively Nos. 520, 522, 545, 630, 540, 555, 578.

31 Nos. 633, 515, 573.

32 Nos. 542, 610.

33 E.g., in *CH* but not Congregational hymnal: "All things bright and beautiful" (521); "Day by day, the little daisy" (524); "God is always near me" (525); "Golden harps are sounding" (543); "Here we suffer grief and pain" (589); "I want to be like Jesus" (560); F. Crosby, "If I come to Jesus" (557); "Joy bells are sounding sweetly" (612); "Little children, praise the Saviour" (546); "Little children, wake and listen" (530); "Lord, a little band and lowly" (605); "O what can little hands do" (572); Crosby, "Safe in the arms of Jesus" (593); "Shall we gather at the river" (594); "The world looks very beautiful" (569); "There is a city bright" (555); "There is a happy band" (592).

34 Nos. 171-97, esp. "Weary of earth . . . " (176); "Weary of wandering from my God" (178); Luther, "From depths of woe

I raise to thee" (184); "Rock of Ages" (191); "I lay my sins on Jesus" (194); "Jesu, Lover of my soul" (193); "Jesu, thy blood and righteousness" (196); Anne Brontë, "Oppressed with sin and woe" (186); "There is a fountain filled with blood" (174); and Calvinistic hymns by Watts, and Bonar, "Not all the blood of beasts" (171) and "Not what these hands have done" (173).

35 No. 260, by S.R. Hole (1819-87), in *AM* (1889), No. 584, headed "For a Service for Working Men."

36 Rarely included after 1900; not in *EH* (1906), but in *AM* (1904), No. 585.

37 *Essex Hall Hymnal* (London: British and Foreign Unitarian Association 1891), Preface.

38 Nos. 23, 145, 130, 245, 249, 329 (by Unitarian John Bowring). Cf. 15 texts of Watts: "Ye nations, round the earth, rejoice" (14); "Before Jehovah's awful throne" (15); "Lord of the worlds above (30); "My soul, repeat his praise" (52); "High in the heavens, eternal God" (70); "I sing the almighty power of God" (83); "O God, our help . . . " (103); "O happy soul that lives on high" (189); "My God, how endless is thy love" (20); "Awake our souls! Away our fears" (224); "My loving Master, Friend and Lord" (313); "There is a land of pure delight" (355); "Great God, whose universal sway" (415); "Jesus shall reign . . . " (422); "From all that dwell below the skies" (508). Only Nos. 70, 313, and 508 changed, but Nos. 14, 52, 70, 189, 201, 313, 355, 415, and 422 omitted from revised edn., 1902.

39 E.g. (respectively), "It came upon the midnight clear" (298); "O Love divine, that stoop'st to share" (98); "I heard the bells on Christmas day" (297); "Behold the Prince of peace" (306); "Today be joy in every heart" (300). Whittier (306) a Quaker, the rest New England Unitarian.

40 E.g., A. Norton, "Where ancient forests widely spread" (496), in which forests, "cataract's ocean-fall," and "lone mountain's silent head" are "thy temples, God of all."

41 Editors explain in 1902 that sales of 1891 edn. so far exceeded expectations that "stereo plates" had worn out.

42 In the 1891 book, the Preface says that Martineau had gone too far in demytholo-

gizing, and sections on Christ's birth, teaching and example, Lord's Supper and Easter-tide (294-324) follow those on worship, "Praise in Nature," trust in divine love and guidance, and Christian ethic, but precede those on future life, seasons, work, "Our Country," etc. In 1902, those for Christmas, Easter, Baptism, and the Lord's Supper (467-89) follow other sections listed above, and also those on times and seasons, listed separately as Winter, Spring, Summer, Harvest, and Autumn, with New Year (401-66), with clear implication of less emphasis on sacraments and more on nature. Natural times and seasons have 40 texts in 1891, sacraments and liturgical seasons the same number in each.

43 No. 463 (in 1891 edn.) has only first stanza by Wesley, remainder by John Taylor (1750-1826), and appears under "Seasons" (463-79). Remaining stanzas deal with winter, spring and summer, autumn and the passage of time, so hymns's religion is wholly naturalistic.

44 Nos. 120, 483, 330, 495, 323, 63, 170, 367, 105 (1902).

45 "Jesus, by thy simple beauty" (319) and "Jesus has lived, and we would bring" (481), both otherwise unknown, but 25 beginning with "Father" and 20 with "God" include well-known "Father again, to thy near name" (422), "Father, hear the prayer we offer" (283), "Father I know that all my life / Is portioned out for me" (69), "God bless our native land" (528), "God moves in a mysterious way" (145), "God of mercy, God of grace" (95).

46 Nos. 345, 323 (1902).

47 *Hymns of Modern Thought* (London: Houghton 1900).

48 Text from *PCH* 381.

49 E.g., "How happy . . . " (H. Wotton, pub. 1651) in *Hymns and Psalms for Secondary Schools*, ed. J. Downes (London 1911), No. 40 and in 1932 supplement to hymnal for St. Paul's Girls' School (see Ch. 15); "O brother . . . " (Whittier, 1850), in *School Hymns*, 478, *Prayers, and Hymns for the use of St. Paul's Girls' School* (London, private printing 1929), *Supplement* (in 1972 rpt.).

50 Nos. 135, 25, 172, 61, 76, 24.

51 Preface, 1; No. 190.

52 John Henry Newman, *Apologia pro vita*

sua, ed. M.J. Svaglic (Oxford: Clarendon 1967), 185.

53 Preface.

54 Routley (*PCH*, 142) treats nineteenth-century "Unitarian, Congregational and Presbyterian divines" as "New England Calvinists" producing poetically superior hymns, e.g., Sears, Holmes ("Lord of all being, throned afar," *PCH* 375), Samuel Longfellow ("I look to thee in every need," *PCH* 377), Samuel Johnson ("City of God," and "Life of Ages, richly poured," *PCH* 379, 378), John W. Chadwick ("Eternal Ruler . . . "), Frederick L. Hosmer ("We pray no more . . . for miracle", and "Thy Kingdom come, on bended knee," *PCH* 388).

55 Norton, "When ancient forests . . . "

NOTES TO CHAPTER SEVEN

1 For very different view of Victorian child-conditioning in hymns, see Tamke, *Make a Joyful Noise. . . .*, Chapters 3-4.

2 James Janeway, *A Token for Children . . . Conversions, Holy Lives and Exemplary Deaths of Several Young Children* (1672), and John Bunyan, *A Book for Boys and Girls, or Country Rhymes for Children* (1686, facsimile edn., London: Elliott Stock 1889), both discussed in Arthur P. Davis, *Isaac Watts: His Life and Works* (London: Independent Press 1943), 74-6, and Escott, 205-6. Davis finds Watts' *Divine Songs* relatively "tolerant and gentle," while Escott, citing Calvin, Jeremy Taylor, and Milton on original sin in children, thinks them unfairly judged by the "brighter light of our more humane and less sadistic times" (!).

3 *PCH*, 124.

4 Cornelia Meigs, Anne T. Eaton, Elizabeth Nesbit, Ruth H. Vigeurs, *A Critical History of Children's Literature . . .* (New York: Macmillan 1953), 72.

5 On interest in nature, see Keith Thomas, *Man and the Natural World: A History of the Modern Sensibility* (New York: Pantheon 1983), 280-5, 300-3 (English subtitle *Changing Attitudes in England, 1500-1800*).

6 Watts, *Divine Songs Attempted in Easy Language, for the Use of Children . . .* (London 1715), No. 16, "Let dogs delight . . . "; Benjamin Harris (comp.),

New England Primer (Boston ca. 1683). To Watts' 28 *DS* were usually appended 8 *Moral Songs*.

7 Ann and Jane Taylor, *Hymns for Infant Minds* (London 1809). Hymns sometimes bear Ann's marital name (Gilbert). Tamke, in "Hymns for Children: Cultural Imperialism in Victorian England," *Victorian Newsletter* 49 (1976), 18-22, n. 12, cites claim of London Sunday School Union (1903) to have issued over 2,225,000 copies of *Hymns for Infant Minds*.

8 Watts, *Hymns* II, 90, 69, 58, 3.

9 Wilbur M. Stone, *The Divine and Moral Songs of Isaac Watts* (New York 1918), cited in Davis, 81-2.

10 Watts, *Works* I, xix.

11 Samuel Johnson, "Life of Watts," in *Lives of the Poets*, ed. George Birkbeck Hill, 3 vols. (Oxford: Clarendon 1905), Vol. III, 308, of all Watts' writings for children.

12 Watts, *Works*, loc. cit.

13 E.g., *Birmingham School Board Hymn Book* (1900, 1904 as Education Committee . . .), No. 39.

14 Stanza 7, conventionally omitted (*HG* 320), perhaps for doctrinal reasons, God being absent from Hell.

15 Bunyan, 11, "Upon the Bee"
   The Bee goes out and Honey home
      doth bring;
   And some who seek that Hony [*sic*]
      find a Sting,
   Now would'st thou have the Hony and
      be free
   From stinging; in the first place kill
      the Bee.

   This Bee an Emblem truly is of Sin,
   Whose Sweet unto a many death hath
      been.

16 Janeway, Part I, Example 4, cited in Escott, 208.

17 Escott, loc. cit.

18 Cf. Bunyan's poem "Upon Apparel" (discussed in Davis, 76) with Shakespeare, Sonnet 146 and Sidney, *Astrophel and Stella*, Sonnet 5.

19 Watts, *Works* I, xx.

20 No. 9 in *March's Library of Instruction and Amusement* (London 1845); and *Divine and Moral Songs: Pictured in Colours by Mrs. Arthur Gaskin* (London, n.d.), dated 1896 in Simon House, *A Dictionary of British Book Illustrators and Caricaturists* (London: Antique Collectors' Club

1978), 314. On pre-Raphaelite illustrations of *DS*, see House, 78.

21 E.g., in *Hymns for the Chapel of Harrow School*, 3rd edn., ed. Henry Montagu Butler (London 1881), No. 31 ("The night is come, wherein we rest," by Weiss, trans. C. Winkworth), on charity to invalids, widows, orphans, etc., No. 53 ("Lo, the feast is spread today," by Dean Alford), on produce and merchandise "freely given" to be "freely shared."

22 Esmé Wingfield-Stratford, *A Victorian Tragedy* (London: Routledge 1931), 57-8.

23 Davis, 81.

24 Watts, *Works* I, xix.

25 In National Library of Scotland, bound with set of tracts, but presumably alluded to in *Questions with Answers taken from Dr. Watts' Hymns for Children, Enlarged from the London edition* . . . (Boston, MA: Sabbath School Society 1842), of which 1843 rpt., and several editions of *An Explanation of Dr. Watts' Hymns for Children, in Questions and Answers, by a Lady* (3rd edn., London 1829) in British Museum Catalogue.

26 "Almighty God . . . eye" in *Hymns Selected & Original . . . in Leeds Sunday School Union Hymn Book* (Leeds 1878); *Methodist Sunday School Hymn Book* (London: Wesleyan Methodist S.S. Union 1879); Baptist *Psalms & Hymns for School and Home* (London: Haddon 1882); *Methodist Free Church School Hymns* (London: Crombie 1888). "Happy the child . . . " in *Collection of Hymns for the Use of Methodist Sunday Schools*, ed. Joseph Benson (2nd edn., London 1816); SSU Hymn Book (Leeds, 1834); *Sacred Song Book for Children*, ed. C.H. Bateman (Edinburgh: Gall & Inglis 1843); *Children's Hosannah* (Jerrold 1858); *Leeds Sunday School Union* (1878); Methodist S.S. (1879); *Psalms . . . School and Home* and *Methodist Free Church*. "How doth . . . Busy Bee" in Quaker *Hymns for Instruction of Young Persons* (London: Darton, Harvey & Darton 1818); SSU (Leeds, 1834); Congregational SS (1881); Methodist Free Church. "I sing . . . power of God" in Methodist (1816), SSU (1834); Sacred Song (1843), Leeds SSU (1878); Congregational SS, Methodist Free, Mason's Orphanage (1883), Birmingham Board Schools (1900) hymnals. "Lord I ascribe . . . grace" in Methodist (1816); SSU (1834), Sacred Song; hymnals and Quaker *Hymns for Young Persons* (7th edn., York: Sessions 1903). "There is beyond the sky" ("Heaven and Hell") in Quaker *Young Persons* (1818); SSU (1834), Sacred Song; *Children's Hosannah* only; "Whene'er I take my walks abroad" in Quaker *Young Persons* (1818); SSU (1834); *Children's Hosannah*; Methodist Free and Quaker *Young Persons* (1903).

27 Cited in Doris Mary Armitage, *The Taylors of Ongar* (Cambridge: Heffer 1939), 173.

28 Taylors, *Hymns* . . . , authorial Preface.

29 *Hymns and Moral Songs for Use in Board Schools* (Manchester: Heywood 1878). Title symptomatic of Watts' influence.

30 "Great God" in *Sacred Song Book . . .* ; *Children's Hosannah*, (Anglican) *Church Sunday School Hymn Book* (London, 1879 originally 1868); Leeds SSU (1878), Methodist SS (1879), Congregational SS, (Baptist) Psalms & Hymns (1882), Methodist Free Church; also hymnals for [full reference Ch. 8, n32] Mason's Orphanage (1883), Birmingham Board Schools and (Quaker) Young Persons (1903). "Now that . . . " in *Hymns Selected by a Clergyman for His Schools* (London, n.d.), Leeds SSU (1878), Methodist (1879), Congregational (1881), Methodist Free and Mason's Orphanage hymnals. "There is . . . " in all but last of these, also in *Sacred Song Book*, *Children's Hosannah*, and Church SS.

31 Ann and Jane Taylor, *Original Poems for Infant Minds* (London 1804), published anon., in 12th edn. by 1815 (Armitage, 188).

32 Frances Mary Yonge, ed., *A Child's Christian Year* (London 1841), many items by Newman, Isaac Williams, and Keble (whose Preface I quote in text).

33 E.g., Addison, "When all thy mercies, O my God," "When rising from the bed of death"; Anstice, "O Lord, how happy we should be," composed shortly before his death at 28, after attaining a Double First at Oxford and becoming Professor of Classics at King's College, London.

34 Preface, *Selection of Hymns and Poetry for the Use of Infant Schools and Nurseries* (London: Home and Colonial Infant School Society 1838).

35 *Divine Songs*, No. 15, "O 'tis a lovely thing for youth / To walk Wisdom's way,

fear a lie, speak truth'' has a verse on the death of Ananias and also (st. 5): '' . . . every liar / Must have his portion in the lake / That burns with brimstone and with fire,'' (st. 6) ''Then let me always watch my lips / Lest I be struck to death and hell, / Since God a book of reckoning keeps / For every lie that children tell.'' No. 11, ''There is beyond the sky.'' No. 13, ''Why should I say 'tis yet too soon'' has threat (st. 4) God's ''dreadful anger'' might ''strike me dead upon the place,'' (st. 5) '' 'Tis dang'rous to provoke a God'' whose ''Almighty rod / Can send young sinners quick to hell.'' Use for infants by editors with enlightened intentions says much about educational climate.

36 ''Lord, teach'' by J. Rylands (1786); ''Here we . . . '' by Thomas Bilby, who ran a Training School for infant teachers, in *The Infant Teacher's Assistant* (1831-2) (Julian, 142-3).

37 Jane E. Leeson, *Hymns and Scenes from Childhood* (London: Burns 1842). So in original and Julian (669-70), but *Hymns and Songs of* . . . in *HG* 444. Cf. Butler, *The Way of All Flesh*, passim, esp. Ch. 40. Author a Roman Catholic by 1851, when she translated ''Victimae Paschali'' and publisher Burns was RC in 1848, when he published Newman's *Loss and Gain.*

38 ''Loving Shepherd'' much altered in *AM* (1875), text commonly used; modern hymnal-uses of this and ''Saviour . . . ,'' listed in *HG* 444, 632.

39 *Hymns for Children Selected with a View to Being Learned by Heart* (Oxford: Parker 1856) headed: ''To do my Duty in that State of Life to which the Lord shall . . . call me'' (anon.). ''If Any Man is seen to be Religious and Bridleth not his Tongue'' published in Newman and Froude (ed.), *Lyra Apostolica* (1836).

40 *Twenty-Six Hymns for Nursery or School* (London: Nelson 1857). Probably intended to be cut out and pinned up, as in large, double-page format, with blank backs. Only 14 hymns remain in British Library copy, which has frontispiece design round opening lines of ''Once in Royal David's city.''

41 *Hymns for Very Little Ones* (London: SPCK, Tract Committee 1866), ''written chiefly to be read to . . . *very* little children'' who, it ''has been found . . .

liked to hear them again and again, and thus unconsciously learnt them'' (Preface). Nos. I, VIII.

42 *Prayers and Hymns for Little Children, for Use in Infant Schools and Preparatory Departments* (London: Oxford University Press 1932).

NOTES TO CHAPTER EIGHT

1 Matthew Arnold, ''Forsaken Merman,'' ll. 14-17, 72-3.

2 M.G. Jones, *The Charity School Movement: A Study of Eighteenth-Century Puritanism in Action* (Cambridge University Press 1938, rpt. London: Cass 1964), 5; figure in SPCK survey, 1729 (Jones, 72).

3 ''Holy Thursday'' (c. 1784, pub. *Songs of Innocence*, 1789) taken at face-value by Jones (60), but sometimes seen as ironic, as in David V. Erdman, *Blake: Prophet Against Empire* (revised edn., New York: Doubleday 1969), 121.

4 Watts, *Works*, II, 717-41.

5 Bernard Mandeville in ''On Charity and Charity Schools'' on whose ''venom'' and fallacious argument see Jones, 43.

6 Watts, 717ff., 723.

7 Edmund Gibson, cited in ibid., 733: ''If charity schools'' give ''a more polite education, if the boys should be taught fine writing, the girls fine working, and both . . . singing, they would be too ready to value themselves upon these attainments,'' and think themselves ''above the meaner and more laborious stations. . . . ''

8 735, cf. 736: ''If you . . . put them to a trade, you give them a lasting inheritance,'' words used by Bunyan to denote way of salvation.

9 717.

10 ''Birmingham Blue-coat Charity Schools Hymn Sheets,'' in Birmingham Public Library. Hymn 1 (of 2) for 12 June 1726, sermon by Bishop of Lichfield.

11 28 April, services in St. Philip's (now Anglican Cathedral) and St. Martin's. Cf. ''watchful guardian, rob'd in Light,'' with Blake's ''wise. . . . ''

12 ''Eternal Father of Mankind,'' sung 18 October 1747; 13 May 1750; 13 April 1766.

13 From 12 May 1751 to 1766, then from 10 May 1767 to 13 October 1793.

14 20 October 1793 at St. Paul's Chapel and

St. Bartholemew's, preacher Josiah Pratt, Curate of Dowles.

15 6 October, preacher John Eyton, Vicar of Wellington, "Once more before thy Altars, Lord / the suppliant Orphan bends"; services also on 22 and 29 September, preachers a Vicar of Walsall and a Chaplain of Queen's College, Cambridge.

16 *Psalms and Hymns for Use of Chapel of Asylum for Female Orphans* (London 1801).

17 *Hymns Selected for the Use of Young Persons in a Charity School* (Dublin: William Watson 1812).

18 10 May 1812.

19 *Hymns for the Use of Chapel of Asylum for Poor Female Orphans* (Bristol 1811), Preface, which gives 1795 as foundation year.

20 Respectively "Thou God of glorious majesty" (*Coll. P.*, 58); (*OH* II, 55) "When thou, O Lord, shall stand array'd / In majesty severe"; "My waken'd soul, extend thy wings."

21 Based on a version of the *Dies irae* and intended for Advent Sunday.

22 "Father of mercies, lend thine ear," sung after sermon by Bishop of Worcester, 27 September 1840.

23 30 May 1847, at St. Philip's. Hymn No. 140 in (unnamed) hymnal: "Hear, Lord, the song of praise and prayer . . . From children, made the public care, / And taught to seek Thy face . . . ," st. 2.

24 *Sacred Songs for Home and School, Compiled for Sharp Street Ragged School* (Manchester: William Brenner 1858).

25 *Hymns for Oulton Evening School* (1858).

26 DS No. 9: "Almighty God, thy piercing eye" (6); Dorothy Thrupp, "Poor and needy though I be / God Almighty cares for me" (11); Anne and Jane Taylor, "How long sometimes a day appears" (25); author unknown, "Though in a foreign land" (96); J. Newton, "One there is above all others" (39, *OH* I, 53); unknown, "O, it is a weary life" (69); unknown, "The Gospel ship has long been sailing" (41); H.F. Lyte, "My rest is in heaven, my rest is not here" (72).

27 No. 123 (original to book); unknown, "To speak the truth is always right" (128).

28 *Dove Row Ragged School Hymn Book* (London: Partridge, ca. 1860).

29 "My English home! My English home!" (58); "Beautiful Zion . . . " (11); Jemima

Luke, "I think when I read that sweet . . . " (40).

30 *A Collection of Hymns for Children and Young Persons, Principally Designed for the Use of Charity and Sunday Schools* (London 1810). Editor's Preface admits some expressions above heads of children but claims to avoid "expression of sentiments and feelings to which . . . children in general are strangers" lest he teach them "the language of hypocrisy. . . . " Several hymns on Judgment but none on Passion.

31 *Hymns and Anthems sung in the Chapel of the Foundling Hospital* (London 1874). Translations listed as original poems by Caswall, Neale, Winkworth, etc.

32 *A Book of Prayer and Praise* compiled for use in Sir Josiah Mason's Orphanage, Erdington (Birmingham 1883). Information from Editor's Preface.

33 No. 175 by J. Buckworth (1779-1835), 84, by Mrs. Alexander, continues "Not born to high estate"; 196, anon., "Many voices seem to say"; 256, "We ask not wealth, O God, from Thee"; no author given, but in section (256-66) headed "Submission." "O Lord, in sickness and in health / To every lot resigned, / Grant me, before all worldly wealth, / A meek and thankful mind." 279, anon., "Thou must not seek for ease nor rest"; 268, anon. in section "Christian Work" (268-83) that otherwise includes well-known hymns "Sow in the morn thy seed" (Montgomery), "Work is sweet, for God has blest" (G. Thring), "A charge to keep I have" (Wesley). "Though lowly" our lot is No. 281.

34 *School Hymnal and Service-Book* compiled by G. Thorn and Randall Williams for Harrow County Boys' (Grammar) School (London: Dent 1923), 161.

35 Included in books for Uppingham School and Birmingham Board Schools discussed in Chapters 11 and 12.

36 Anon.

NOTES TO CHAPTER NINE

1 Cf. *Book of Sacred Songs* (London), Preface: "The School Boards throughout the country have, almost without exception, determined that hymns shall be sung in their schools."

2 Ernst Christian Helmreich, *Religious Ed-*

ucation in German Schools: An Historical Approach (Cambridge, MA: Harvard University Press 1959), 76, 86, 92.

3 *Psalms, Hymns and Spiritual Songs for Use of Pannal and Low Harrogate Village School* (private printing 1831), in Manchester Public Library, Preface.

4 Ibid., in Supplement.

5 *Easy Hymns for the Use of Children in National Schools* (London: SPCK, 1831).

6 *Hymns for the Use of Schools* (London: National Society 1851). Page numbers unrecorded, *mea culpa*.

7 *Hymns for the Use of Schools* (London: sold at Depository of National Society 1856).

8 Cento from Doddridge, "Lord of the Sabbath, hear our vows," printed first by Rippon (1787), then as "Prayer for the Felicity of Heaven" by National Society (1856). See Julian, 693i.

9 *National Society's Graded Hymn Book* (London, n.d.). In Bernarr Rainbow Collection, King's College, London. Latest item "For the beauty of the earth" (1864).

10 E.g., No. 20, birthday hymn to "our little playmate / For you, dear little child, we pray."

11 Supplemental, for Foreign Missions, No. 1.

12 I.e., for church seasons, e.g. "As with gladness . . . "

13 In view of Sister Mary Edward. *Hymns used by Pupils of the Sisters of Notre Dame* (Manchester: Ledsham 1883).

14 *Catholic Hymns with Holy Mass for Children* (Dublin: J. Duffy 1900). No. 53, "O Sacred Heart" and No. 63 have phrase.

15 *Hymns for Day Schools* (London: Joseph Tarn [1874]).

16 Preface.

17 151, A Minute, how soon it is flown; 222, God is so good, that He will hear; 37, God made the world, in every land; 214, God: what a great and awful word; 49, How kind in all His works and ways; 229, How long sometimes a day appears; 72, Jesus, who lives above the sky; 212, Lord, I have passed another day; 216, Lord, I would own Thy tender care; 207, My Father, I thank Thee for sleep; 213, Now condescend, Almighty King; 94, O thank the Lord, for He is kind; 227, Oh that it were my chief delight; 152, The morning hours of cheerful light; 182, The year is just going away; 164, When a foolish thought

within; 220, When daily I kneel down to pray.

18 Preface.

19 London compiler attributes No. 171 to W. Hoyle, but Julian, 1676i, gives no definite author and traces hymn to American *Young Men's Singing Book*, 1855. Nos. 140 and 172 not in Julian, but No. 172 is No. 79 in *Birmingham School Board Hymn Book* (1900), where author given as J.H. McNaughton.

20 Respectively "Beauteous scenes on earth appear" by R. Robinson (1814-87), a London compiler (Julian, 970i), and "Now pray we for our country" by American bishop A.C. Coxe, inspired by tour of English abbeys and cathedrals in 1840 (ibid., 266i).

21 "Courage . . . " by Norman MacLeod (1812-72), influential Scottish minister and Queen's Chaplain, for *Edinburgh Christian Magazine* (1857); listed in Julian 709ii as "Trust in God, and do the right." In many late Victorian and Edwardian children's collections. "Live for" (not in Julian) in *Essex Hall Hymnal* (Unitarian), 1891 but anon.

22 E.g., "Glory to thee, my God, this night" (42); "Come, let us join our cheerful songs" (22); "Hark the glad sound . . . " (59); "Christ the Lord is risen today" (20); "God moves in a mysterious way" (49); "For ever with the Lord" (37). "Awake my soul, and with the sun" (10) and "Jesus shall reign where'er the sun" (86) assigned to Wesley.

23 Nos. 2, 3, 4, 6, and 7 of the above recur frequently in Sunday-school books of this period.

24 Hardy, *Tess of the d'Urbervilles*, Chapter 4. Hymn published in *The Infant Teacher's Assistant* (1831-32), by Thomas Bilby (1794-1872) (Julian 142-3), q.v.

25 Assigned in *HG* 462 to Charlotte Elliott, in *Invalid's Hymn Book* (1834), though Julian 1675ii says pub. anon. in Kirkby Lonsdale *Songs from the Valley* (1834). Lines quoted support *HG*, which lists major hymnals using shortened text, usually "My God and Father. . . . "

26 From *Hymns for Infant Minds*.

27 "There is an Eye that never sleeps" (109); "A gentle and holy child" (3), cf. Jesus on need to become as little child to enter heaven.

NOTES TO CHAPTER TEN

1 Laqueur, 155.
2 *The Children's Hymn Book*, ed. Mrs. Carey Brock, rev. J. Ellerton, Bishop W.W. How, and A. Oxenden (London, 1881); *Congregational Sunday School Hymn Book* (1881); *Methodist Sunday School Hymn Book* (1879); (Baptist) *Psalms and Hymns for School and Home* (1882); *A Voice of Praise for Sunday School and Home* (London: London Sunday School Union 1886).
3 Thomas Hardy, Wessex Novels, esp. *Far from the Madding Crowd*, Ch. 6, *Tess of the d'Urbervilles*, Chs. 4, 5, 10, 47; Flora Thompson, *Lark Rise to Candleford* (1939), Ch. 5, passim. See also Hardy's essay "The Dorsetshire Labourer."
4 "Age of . . . " a section (72-3) in Chapter 7 of Meigs et al.'s *Critical History of Children's Literature*. Laetitia Barbauld, *Hymns in Prose for Children* (1781), scriptural paraphrases; Sarah Trimmer, *An Easy Introduction to the Knowledge of Nature* (1782) and *History of the Robins* (1786); Mary Sherwood, *History of the Fairchild Family* (3 parts, 1818-47). Meigs also discusses Hannah More's *Cheap Repository Tracts* (from 1789) and Mary Wollstonecraft ("Mrs. Mason"), *Original Stories* (1788).
5 *Hymns for Young Persons*, ed. "R.H." (London: Parker 1834), Nos. 100, 101.
6 *Collection of Hymns for . . . Methodist Sunday Schools*, ed. Joseph Benson (2nd edn.: London 1816, originally 1806); *Hymns for Children* Principally of Sunday School, ed. Rowland Hill (London 1819, originally 1790).
7 Wordsworth, *Prelude* V, 411-12.
8 *The Way of All Flesh*, Chapters 25, 40.
9 *Hymn Book for Scholars*, 15th edn. (Montreal 1837), originally London: Sunday School Union, c. 1816.
10 "Comprehensive Rippon" (1844), 493.
11 Cf. Hill, 108: "Make us lowly, meek and mild," but in Hill, 119 "Tender, merciful and mild" enjoins kindness to animals. Meaning of stock religious phrase can vary with context.
12 *Hymns for Children and Young Persons, on the Principal Truths and Duties of Religion and Morality* (London: Blanshard 1814, originally 1806), Preface.

13 See above, 7-8 and 275, n31.
14 *Hymns for the Use of Church of England Sunday Schools* (Hull 1823).
15 John Fawcett (Baptist), "Religion is the chief concern," published 1782.
16 Gordon Rattray Taylor, *The Angel-Makers: A Study in the Psychological Origins of Religious Change, 1750-1850*, rev. edn. (London: Secker and Warburg 1973, originally 1958), Ch. 3 (passim).
17 *Sabbath School Hymn Book* (London: Simpkin, Marshall; Leicester: Winks 1825), Preface.
18 "Psalms and Hymns" to be sung by the Children of St. John's Schools, Newcastle, Sunday, 27 May 1827. Most St. John's Anniversary hymn sheets 1823-32 use elevated vocabulary, but on 23 March 1828 children sang "Thou art our shepherd-Glorious God" which includes verse "Thy wisdom fixed our lowly birth" used at Pannal and Low Harrogate village school (see above, 121).
19 *Hymns . . . for the Instruction of Young Persons*, Preface (which says for Society of Friends).
20 *Selected Hymns for the Use of Young Persons* (1903), Preface.
21 Stanza 8, "His hand my guard . . . keeps me with his eye."
22 Usual version a cento from two items in *Hymns and Sacred Poems* (1742), *Hymns for Children* (1763) (*HG* 216), condemned in popular citation. Fullest available text, 8 vv. (of which st. 6 quoted), in *EH* 591, *AMR* 451.
23 Told me by a member of Hymn Society of Great Britain in 1979. On poet's father, Major Humphreys, of Norfolk, see William Alexander, Introduction to *Poems of Cecil Frances Alexander* (London: Macmillan 1896).
24 "We are . . . children poor" in Hook's *Church Sunday School Hymn Book* (Leeds Parish Church 1850), " . . . weak" in *AM* (1868), but both forms in common use (Julian, 1241ii).
25 On religious value of "home" in American revival hymnody, see Sizer, 35, 103, 112, 137, and esp. 157ff. Text, *PCH* 301.
26 *PCH* 311.
27 "Just as I am, without one plea" in Charlotte Elliott, *Invalid's Hymn Book* (1838).
28 "Just as I am, Thine own to be" Marianne Hearn, pseudonym Farningham (her birth-

place). *HG* 380, after Julian, 1647i, cites *Voice of Praise* (1887), but see Congregational Sunday School (1881), No. 427.

29 "Learned": *Church Sunday-School H.B.* (1868); *Songs of Praise for Sunday Schools* (London: Jarrold, 1870); *Presbyterian Hymnal*, Sunday School Supplement (1876); *Book of Praise for Children* (London: Hodder & Stoughton 1881); *Children's H.B.* (1881); *Congregational Sunday School H.B.* (1881); *Home and School Hymnal* (Edinburgh: Edinburgh University Press 1893).

"Popular": *Methodist Scholar's Hymn Book* (1870); *Leeds Sunday School Union H.B.* (1878); *Methodist Sunday School H.B.* (1879); *Psalms and Hymns for Home and School* (1882); *Sunday Scholar's H.B.* (London: Sunday School Union 1884); *Methodist Free Church School Hymnal* (1888); *Children's Hymns* (Methodist 1923).

"Board": *Book of Sacred Songs* (London 1873); *School Board H.B.* (Huddersfield, 1873); *Hymns & Moral Songs* (Manchester 1878); *Council School* (1905); *Hymns and Tunes for . . . Elementary Schools* (London: Novello 1908); *School H.B.* (London: Evans, 1920); *H.B. for School Children* (Leeds: Arnold 1922). I did this survey before seeing *Birmingham School Board H.B.* (1900).

30 Including Cheltenham (1864, 1890), Giggleswick (1874), Harrow (1881, 1895), Eton (1937), Rugby (1885), Wellington (1880), Winchester (1910), Worksop (1938) and *Public School H.B.* (1903, 1919), but not Bedales (1901).

31 "Lord, teach . . . " (1786), in (London) *Book of Sacred Songs* (1873) but too Calvinistic for most secular schools, e.g., st. 3: "A sinful creature I was born, / And from my birth have stray'd." By John Rylands, Baptist minister (Julian, 983ii). "Come, sing . . . ," J.J. Daniell, pub. *AM* 1868, on male and female ideals, and "It is" (W.W. How, 1872), too recent (see Julian, 279ii, 541i) for early Board Schools, but "Come, sing . . . " in Birmingham (1900).

32 "A Verse Life of Jesus" (1866), Part I (January), "The Story Wanted" commonly used after adoption in Sankey's *Sacred Songs and Solos* (1875). Part II (November), was "The Story Told" (Julian, 483ii).

33 Composed 1871, rarely used in 20th century, but title commonly cited.

34 Both in *PCH* 305.

35 *Council School H.B.* (1905), 89.

36 Added to *Paris Breviary* (1736) (Julian, 240ii).

37 American translation by Charles T. Brooks (c. 1832) of "Gott segne Sachsenland" (1815), revised Dwight in New Congregational H.B. (1859), 998. On history of this and English hymn by Hickson (1836), see *HG* 227.

38 *Songs of Praise for Sunday Schools* (London: Jarrold [1870]), price twopence.

39 Preface.

40 Usual tune "Ruth" in *Methodist School Hymnal*, 172. *Songs of Praise Enlarged* (1931), 7, has more solemn tune "Ghent."

41 Prynne said hymn not "written specially for children" but agreed to simplify st. 4 from "Through terrestrial darkness / To celestial day" to "passing darkness . . . endless day" in children's hymnals. Adult text, *AM* (1889), 194.

42 Scribbled in 1871 when fatigued by visit to a school in Birmingham, and sung to her own tune ("Hermas") when dying. Inclusion in *HG* (252) indicates twentieth-century use despite imagery.

43 "Jesus . . . " composed (1839) for her own children and posthumously published (1841) (*HG* 369). This and "I think" *PCH* 300, 301.

44 Published in *Children's H.B.* (1881) and listed by Julian as in "common use" but not in *HG*.

45 "Growing together, wheat and tares," author "unknown." Not in Julian.

46 Thomas Hornblower Gill (1819-1906), of Unitarian parentage, refused endorsement of 39 Articles necessary for Oxford entrance. Later became Anglican Evangelical. Julian notes hymns "almost exclusively used" by Nonconformists, lists 75 in 421-3, asserts influence of Watts, but calls him "really original." W.G. Horder (Congregational) thought him in 1880s best living hymnist. Gill called hymns non-theological "divine love songs" (*HG* 421). His idolatrous patriotism therefore of Puritan and Romantic origin.

47 "Archness," i.e., speaker's dual posture as child and adult. In "Suppose . . . " intention to encourage growth undercut by inane example. After completing MS, I saw Mary G. De Jong's "I Want to be like

Jesus: The Self-Defining Power of Evangelical Hymnody," *Journal of American Academy of Religion* LIV (1986), 461-93, which treats metaphors for Christ in American nineteenth-century hymnals as representing human relationships and hymn-singing as a child's rehearsal for life. Ms. De Jong, like Ms. Sizer, finds stereotypes of male dominance and female submission, but notes Christ as Lover, Friend, and Saviour, then a "Feminization of Deity" followed by a reaction toward "Masculine Christianity," with consequent images of Christ as "Captain." Finally, she notes elusive search for "Christian wholeness" (478ff.), as remarked of present-day hymnody in Chapter 16, below.

48 E.g., Leeds SSU 1834 (rev. 1862) and 1878. 1834 edn. very Calvinistic. Texts dropped in 1862 edn. emphasize child's early death and loss of parents. In 1878 edn. stress on child's "littleness," self-identification with Jesus yet sentimental distancing of Gospel events, and on nature.

49 *A New Selection of Hymns for the Use of Schools* (7th edn., Edinburgh: Oliphant 1824).

50 *The Sabbath School Minstrel* (Edinburgh: Fraser 1835). Flavour conveyed by page-headings and high proportion of Watts' darker texts. "When the last . . . " is "O for an overcoming faith" (Watts, *Hymns* I, 17) recast for Scots Paraphrases (Julian 829ii).

51 *Presbyterian Hymnal*, compiled for . . . United Presbyterian Church (Edinburgh: Elliott, 1876). On English use, see Benson, *English Hymn*, 527.

52 *Scottish Hymnal* Children's *Supplement*, Printed for the Committee (1882). No. 369, "Above the waves of earthly strife" (anon.); 384, "I love to think . . . " (anon.). Neither in Julian. Selection in adult portion of *Scottish Hymnal* (Edinburgh: Blackwood, 1885) much superior.

53 Children's Hymnal, Church of Scotland (Edinburgh: Blackwood 1885) has 89 items (200 in Supplement), excluding worst, e.g., "I'm a little pilgrim" and "Safely, safely gathered in" but including "Shall we gather at the river," "There is a happy land / Far, far away," "We are but little children weak" and "I love to think. . . . "

54 *Home and School Hymnal* (Edinburgh: Edinburgh University Press 1893). On

disputed authorship of "Take comfort, Christians, when your friends / In Jesus fall asleep" (253), see Julian, 188ii.

55 *Scottish National Hymnal for the Young* (Edinburgh, 1910). Music in tonic sol-fa suggests intended for less-educated. Information from Preface.

56 *School Praise* (London: Nisbet 1912).

57 "I've two little hands to work for Jesus" (283), anon.; No. 231 by M.A.S. Deck; neither in Julian. Selection on other topics much better.

NOTES TO CHAPTER ELEVEN

1 Gathorne-Hardy, 144.

2 Ibid., 80-8 (esp. 86), 120-1, 88-94, 207, 264-5, also Newsome, passim.

3 *Psalms, Anthems and Hymns Used in the Chapel of Rugby School* (1824); *Psalms and Hymns for the Use of . . .* (Rugby 1843); *Hymns for the Use of Rugby School* (Rugby: Lawrence 1885, originally 1876); *Hymns with Tunes for . . .* (Rugby 1906), Preface.

4 *Hymns and Paraphrases of Scripture for the use of the Grammar School, Leeds* (London: Hurst, Robinson 1826). Headmaster's Introduction.

5 Hymn 17, "O how I love thy holy word" headed "Affliction Sanctified." Apparently adapted from Watts, "O how . . . law" in *Psalms*, 119.

6 Hymn 26, headed "The narrow way."

7 Hymn 14, "My song shall bless the Lord of all." Not in Julian.

8 Hymn 13, headed "The Sower."

9 Gathorne-Hardy, 109-11.

10 "A Sermon for the Nineteenth Sunday after Trinity, October 16th, 1887, in Uppingham School Chapel" by Edward Thring, Head Master (private unpaged rpt. 1941), kindly given me by Mr. Bryan Mathews, Archivist of Uppingham School.

11 In section of *Primitive Methodist Hymn Book* (1855), discussed above, 44-45.

12 Transition is main theme of Newsome, *Godliness and Good Learning*.

13 *Hymns for use in the Chapel of Cheltenham College* (London, private printing 1890), Preface by "H.A.J." (editor).

14 Especially in "The Hotspur" (London 1933-59) and "The Magnet" (London 1929-40).

15 A version of "Ein feste Burg."

16 *Hymns for the Chapel of Harrow School,*
ed. Charles J. Vaughan (London 1855).
Julian (937ii) notes number of hymns on
death as "out of proportion in a school
collection."
17 No. 143 by Heber. 141, "Dark river of
death that is (art) flowing / Between the
bright city and me" (J. Edmeston); title of
15 unrecorded, *mea culpa*; 74, "O Thou
from whom all goodness flows" (T. Haweis
1792); 19 possibly C. Wesley "Fain would
I leave this world below" (1737, rev.); 180
unidentified.
18 *Psalms and Hymns for the Use of Clifton
College* (1863). Ridicule in Gathorne-
Hardy, 84-5, 106, but credit for lack of
class bias and introduction of science, 143,
153.
19 Cheltenham, private rpt., n.d., ed. (Bishop)
Barry. Original edn. dated in Preface to
1890 edn.
20 "The royal banner is unfurled," J. Chan-
dler (1837), rev.
21 *Hymn Book for the Use of Wellington
College* (5th edn. 1880).
22 "Who Thy mysterious Supper share" (209),
"Ye royal priests of Jesus, rise" (208);
"Bread of heaven, on Thee we feed"
(216).
23 Fullest discussion in David Newsome, *The
Parting of Friends: A Study of the
Wilberforces and Henry Manning* (London: Murray 1966), 165.
24 *Hymns and Tunes for the Use of Clifton
College* (3rd edn., 1885).
25 *Hymn-Book for the Use of Uppingham
and Sherborne Schools* (private printing
1874), with Supplement, 1892. Kind gift
of Mr. Mathews.
26 In No. 17 (1806) quotation begins with
same line as first line of Lyte's version of
Ps. 16. G. Thring, Dean of Wells,
published No. 154 in 1866.
27 *School Hymns with Tunes . . . Supplementary to Church Hymns* (London: Bell
1892).
28 Discussed on 214.
29 "Come, ever-blessed Spirit, come," taken
from "Father of all, in Whom we live"
(Bishop C. Wordsworth 1862). (Julian,
368i). On Miss Beale's feminism, see
Gathorne-Hardy, 274-5.
30 *Psalm and Hymn Book for Bedales School*
(private printing 1901).
31 Idea of Permanence and Progression, in
Coleridge's *Constitution of the Church and

State*, discussed in A. Owen Barfield, *What
Coleridge Thought* (London: Oxford University Press 1972), 168-71, 259 n49.
32 "Life of Ages . . . " and "O God, in
whom . . . ," by Unitarians Samuel
Johnson and Samuel Longfellow, both
first in *Hymns of the Spirit* (1864).
33 *Hymns for . . . Harrow School* (4th edn.
1881).
34 "O merciful and holy" (H.M. Butler, for
this hymnal): "The night is come, wherein
at last we rest" (M. Weiss, trans. C.
Winkworth); "Lo, the feast is spread
today" (H. Alford); on work, e.g., 267,
"Go, labour on: spend and be spent" (H.
Bonar, 1843), esp. Carlylean is "Speed,
speed thy work, cast sloth away" (st. 4),
but theme is missionary work; more literally, Nos. 421, "Work is sweet . . . ,"
422 "Work! for it is a noble thing"
(anon.). 391 is "Jesus! when Thou once
returnedst / From the Temple of the Lord"
(J. Bahnmeier, 1819, trans. C. Winkworth),
on Christ as model for boys.
35 "Teach me to live! 'Tis easier far to die,"
420, Ellen E. Burman (1737-61), 1862.
Sentimental esp. on Christ (387ff.) and on
Worship (400ff.).
36 William E. Purcell, *Onward Christian
Soldier: A Life of Sabine Baring-Gould*
(London: Longmans 1957), 74, contra-
dicting view of hymn as "knocked off
. . . in ten minutes at Horbury." Uncri-
tically reprinted in Ronald Pearsall, *Night's
Black Angels: The Forms and Faces of
Victorian Cruelty* (New York: McKay
1975), 33. Written for children's festival at
Horbury, Whitsun (June) 1964, about
time of hymnist's departure from Hurstpierpoint, Sussex. His "home parish,"
claimed by Purcell as Horbury, was Lew
Trenchard, Devon, where he returned as
rector in 1881. His first curacy at Horbury
from 1864, following ordination (Julian,
114i), but Purcell gives schoolteaching
career as 1857-65.
37 Written as "Hymn for the Accession"
June 20 (1873) (Julian, 1087ii).
38 *Selection . . . for . . . Preparatory
Schools* (1894) listed on page 279, n27.
Frontispiece has at head Greek text of
Matt. 5.8 ("Blessed are the pure in
heart . . . ") and at foot: Μάκαριοι οἱ
καθαρι τῆ καρδία; ὅτι αὐτοὶ τὸν Θεὸν
ὄψονται. (It is hardly right for the impure
to lay hold on the pure), found neither in

New Testament nor in early Christian Greek writings listed in Arndt-Gingrich *Lexicon*. (Information by David Campbell, translation by Gordon Shrimpton.)

39 *Psalms and Hymns for the Chapel of Marlborough College* (London: R. Clay, Sons & Taylor, private ptg.).

40 Excluding texts preoccupied with blood, death, and sentimental devotion, except "Rock of Ages" among Passion hymns including "Ride on, ride on . . . ," "Go to dark Gethsemane," "O sacred head . . . ," "Stabat mater," and "When I survey . . . ."

41 Again exceptional, but prescribed for Advent, hence applied to Judgment.

42 By John (later Bishop) Armstrong (1847). (Julian 1551ii).

43 Documented in Newsome, 61-6, 93-8, 106-9, 195-9, 201-6, 217-22, 236-8.

44 *Cantanda Carthusiana* (Godalming 1894) has 130 anthems, but only 8 hymns: "For thee, O dear, dear country," "Jesu, Thou joy of loving hearts," "O Father, who didst all things make," "O God, whose wisdom made the sky," "Onward, Christian soldiers," "O worship the King," "Saviour, blessed Saviour" and "Saviour, when in dust to Thee."

45 See Appendix A.

46 See Appendix B.

47 See Appendix C.

48 See Appendix D.

49 E.g., (Psalm), "As the hart the brooks desireth," (Watts-Wesley) "Call Jehovah thy salvation," "Captain of Israel's host . . . ," "Deck . . . " not in *Public School H.B.*

50 Otherwise, only "The head that once was crowned with thorns" still known, but "We plough the fields and scatter" not in Uppingham, Harrow (1881) or Rugby. Not all Clifton or Marlborough items noted, *mea culpa*.

51 BBC service "New Every Morning." Wesley, "Christ whose glory fills the skies."

52 Bonar, "Thy way, not mine, O Lord" (pub. 1857).

53 "Thoughts impure" in Ken's midnight hymn "My God, now I from sleep awake."

54 William B. Collyer (1812), then erroneously called "Luther's Hymn." Julian, 454-5, shows most fearsome lines, "But sinners, filled with guilty fears, / Behold His wrath prevailing; / For they shall rise, and find

their tears / And sighs are unavailing" as inserted in Cotterill's *Selection* (1819), to replace "Far over space, to distant spheres, / The lightnings are prevailing; Th'ungodly rise, and. . . . " (an instance of Evangelical internalization).

55 Gilbert Rorison (1851) intended typological sense, i.e., divine Shepherd, but schoolboys matured later than now, hence alternative reading.

56 Edward H. Plumptre (1864).

57 On eschatology of "A few more years . . . " (1844), see *HCM*, 140.

NOTES TO CHAPTER TWELVE

1 Hardy, "Men who march away" (1914), *Stories and Poems of Thomas Hardy*, ed. N.V. Meeres (London: Macmillan 1947), 173-4.

2 Robert Graves, *Goodbye to All That: An Autobiography* (London: Cape 1929). Donald Hankey, *A Student in Arms* (London: Melrose 1917). Siegfried Sassoon, *Memoirs of an Infantry Officer* (London: Faber and Faber 1930).

3 Based on 1 Tim. 6.12, 2 Tim. 4.7.

4 Jane C. Simpson (1831).

5 Julian, 1629ii, says Draper's other two texts first published by Novello, publishers of *Council School H.B.*

6 Matthew Henry, on Lev. 8.35: "We have every one of us a charge to keep, eternal God to glorify, an immortal soul to provide for, needful duty to be done, our generation to serve; and it must be our daily care to keep this charge . . . of the Lord our Master, who will shortly call us to account about it . . . Keep it, that ye die not." Alteration (1904), now standard (*PCH* 71, *HG* 1). Context in *AV* sacrificial rite, as instructed by Moses, and verse "Therefore . . . abide at the door of the tabernacle . . . seven days, and keep the charge of the Lord, that ye die not. . . . "

7 On author and hymn, published by 1860, see Julian 405ii, 1714i.

8 F.W.H. Myers, obituary in *Century Magazine XXIII* (November 1881), 62, rpt. in *George Eliot: The Critical Heritage*, ed. David Carroll (London: Routledge 1971), 36-7.

9 *Coll. P.* (1780), 326, originally *Hymns and Sacred Poems* (1742).

10 Julian says "popular piece for children

... usually ascribed to 'Miss Abby Hutchinson' " (1576i), but cites *New Sabbath School Bell* (1859) for view that music by her and words by "M." (1659ii).

11 J.G. Wallace, originally (1825) in a Unitarian hymnal as "There's not a star whose twinkling light," under heading "God seen in Nature." First " . . . not a tint . . . " in 1860 edn. of J.R. Beard's (Unitarian) *Collection of Hymns*. . . . (Julian, 1162ii).

12 *HG* 227. Julian (1566) indicates American version, ending "God save the state," more popular even in Britain.

13 1861, headed "Soldier's Hymn" (Julian, 530i).

14 Frances M. Owen (1872), wife of master at College, for Confirmation. First hymnal rpt. *Cheltenham College Hymn Book*, 1890 (Julian, 1595ii).

15 1899, headed "In Time of War" (Julian, 1612).

NOTES TO CHAPTER THIRTEEN

1 See above, 4, 15, 98 and *HCM*, 10-11, 108-11.

2 *Supplementary Hymns* to *Congregational Church Hymnal for Mill Hill School Chapel* (Bristol 1907); *St. Olave's and St. Saviour's Grammar School Hymnal* (London 1907).

3 E.g., "Let all the world in every corner sing" (27), "You that have spent the morning light" (3), "Come, O come in pious lays" (30); c.f. Ben Jonson, "I sing the Birth was born to-night" (15), John Quarles, "O King of kings, before whose throne" (68), J. Milton "Ring out, ye crystal spheres" (from "Ode on Morning of Christ's Nativity") (14).

4 See n.14, above.

5 Information from Mr. Matthews and Julian.

6 From *Thirty Hymns for Public-School Singing* (1899). Originally 1893, for Confirmation, while Skrine was Warden of Trinity College [school], Glenalmond, Perthshire (Julian, 1703i).

7 "Our fathers were high-minded men," prompted by disruption in Church of Scotland, 1843 (Julian, 473ii); "To realms beyond the sounding sea" first in *New Congregational Hymnal* (1859), as "Prayer on Behalf of Colonists." Items no longer in adult denominational collection.

8 Cf. also "Though lowly here our lot may be" (71), and "Say not the struggle nought availeth" (73), by W. Gaskell and A.H. Clough. Macdonald, "A quiet heart, submissive, meek" (1855) on "Blessed are the meek . . . " for Sunday-school collection co-edited by his brother (Julian, 708i).

9 Cf., under heading *The Nation*, "God save our native land" (Hickson) and "When wilt Thou bless the people" (Elliott).

10 Hymnal "abbreviated" from the St. Olave's hymnal (frontispiece).

11 Thomas Hughes, author of *Tom Brown's Schooldays*. See Julian, 541ii.

12 Hankey, *A Student in Arms*; *A Passing in June* (London: Longmans 1915); *The Lord of All Good Life: Jesus . . .* (London 1914), etc.

13 E.g., "Lift up your hearts" (4), "Forth in Thy name, O Lord, I go" (12), "For all the saints" (32), "Ten thousand times ten thousand" (33), "O God, our help in ages past" (34), "God moves in a mysterious way" (35), "O worship the King."

14 On Nichol (1862-1926), author of children's hymns popular in North of England, see *HG* 793.

15 See J.A.W. Bennett, *Poetry of the Passion* (Oxford: Clarendon 1982), 62-84 passim.

16 E.g., singing of "Veni Creator Spiritus" by soldiers embarking under Louis IX of France, documented in *HCM* 75, 219 n18.

17 *Methodist School Hymnal* (1911). "Who is . . . " by Frances Havergal (1877), "Hark, how the watchmen cry," C. Wesley, " . . . for the Watchnight" (1749), and *Coll. P.*, 305; Sterne, "Life is opening out before you" (1888 or after); Rev. Frederick Jackson (Baptist), for *Sunday School Hymnary* (1905); William F. Sherwin (American Baptist), pub. 1869.

18 *Edinburgh Academy Hymn-book* (Oxford: Oxford University Press 1904).

19 *A New School Hymnal*, ed. E.M. Palser (London: Harrap 1913); *Hymns for the use of Manchester Grammar School* (Manchester 1913), in John Rylands Library, Manchester.

20 "Lord, thy children guide and keep / As with feeble steps . . . ," W.W. How (1854).

21 Newsome, 26-7: "in the 1870s . . . godliness and good learning ceased to be essential concomitants. Godliness came

more and more to be associated with manliness, especially by the school known . . . as 'muscular Christian'." See also 195-8, 216ff., 235ff.

NOTES TO CHAPTER FOURTEEN

1 Carl Zuckmayer, *A Part of Myself*, trans. Richard and Clara Winston, (London: Secker and Warburg 1970), 153.

2 Ibid., 114-15.

3 Ibid., 153.

4 Milton Sager, *When a Great Tradition Modernizes* (Chicago: Chicago University Press 1972), 21.

5 "Look down, O Lord! with pitying eye," No. 441 in *Sabbath School Hymn Book* (1825), No. 449 in *Church Psalmist*, attributed to Doddridge, but phrases not in 1793 edn.

6 William Williams (1772). Variants in Julian 856i.

7 Used also for "The Church's one foundation," but original tune "Calcutta" (*EH* 547) by Heber himself (*HG* 213).

8 "Souls in heathen darkness lying" (1852). Variants and reprints listed in Julian 1069i.

9 Ps. 72, in Watts, *Psalms* and *PCH* 43.

10 "Sun of unclouded righteousness," *Coll. P.* (1780), 431. Originally 1758.

11 Michael Bruce, in *Scots Paraphrases and Congregational H.B.* (1884), 560. See Julian 188i and 1033ii.

12 "Hills . . . " first in *Hymnal Companion* (1870), 116, popular once set in *Public School Hymn Book* (1919) to "Little Cornard" (Martin Shaw) (*HG* 284).

13 No. 793 in *Baptist Church Hymnal* (1900).

14 *Church Missionary [Society] Hymn Book* (London 1899), No. 242: "We scan the years swept from us" (W.J.L. Sheppard).

15 Tamke, 131-2.

16 J.R. Watson, "The day Thou gavest," HSGBI 10:6 (1983), 144-50.

17 Stanzas 3-4 "now unacceptable to many . . . . updated in various ways, first and best in *Hymns for Church and School* [1964]" (*HG* 284).

18 John Oxenham, 1908, for London Missionary Society's "Pageant of Darkness and Light," published 1913 but first sung as hymn well after First World War (*HG* 331 lists no hymnal before 1939 save (Quaker) *Fellowship Hymn Book* (1920)

and, uncertainly, (Scottish) *Church Hymnary* (1927)).

19 Tamke, 128.

20 Hymn excerpted by W.G. Harder (ed.) from poem "A Vista," beginning "Sad heart, what shall the future bring?", for *Worship Song* (1896), used as "theme-song by League of Nations Union" and set as cantata by John Ireland, but vogue during and after First World War (HG 730). With "A loftier race . . . shall rise" cf. Shelley "Choruses from *Hellas*": "A loftier Argo cleaves the main" and cf "With flame of freedom in their souls / And light of science in their eyes" with ibid. "Heaven smiles, and faiths and empires gleam / Like wrecks of a dissolving dream." More generally, cf. "Nation with nation . . . / Inarmed shall life as comrades free" with Shelley's final protest " . . . must hate and death return? / . . . must men kill and die?" Quotations from No. 312 in *Songs of Praise Enlarged* (1931). Perry records use after *Methodist Hymn Book* (1933) only in *Congregational Praise* (1951) and *Baptist Hymn Book* (1962), confirming claim (*HG*, loc. cit.) that lyric dropped out of use owing to "humanistic" tone.

21 No. 495 in *Family Hymn Book* (London: Blackie 1864), first line unrecorded, *mea culpa*.

22 Julian 1114 quotes hymnist's MS account. Original tune "Patmos" and present one "Consecration" both by her father, Canon William Henry Havergal (d. 1870).

23 John Stuart Batts, "Fighting the Good Fight: The Victorian Hymn-Writers Take the Field," paper read to (U.S.) North-East Victorian Studies Conference, 1980.

24 First in Charles Wesley's *Character of a Methodist* (1742), then *Hymns and Sacred Poems* (1749); divided by John Wesley into Nos. 258-60 of *Coll. P.* (1780), (Nos. 266-8 in 1830), of which first hymn, 4 eight-line stanzas, altered in (English) *Methodist Hymn Book* (1933) No. 484 (cf. No 541), given in Appendix to Ch. 14. Shorter version in Appendix is selection made for *AM* (1861), thence later edns. of *AM*, *EH*, and *Public School Hymn Book*. Longer selections, e.g., 32 lines in *Congregational Praise* (1951), required by tune "From Strength to Strength" (1902).

25 E.g., *Coll. P.* 264, cf. Mk. 4.37, 39; 265, cf. Matt. 24.6-7; 266, cf. Ps. 130.1 and

esp. Jonah 2.6; 269 "David and Goliath," cf. 1 Sam. 17.23-54; 275, cf. Exod. 33.19-20, 32-3; 277, Abraham, when severely tried, cf. Gen. 22.1-19; 284, cf. 1-3 and whole narrative of Exodus.

26 *HG* 646.

27 Originally in How, *Psalms and Hymns* (1854), quotation from *AM* (1889), No. 588.

28 See 297 n36.

29 See *HCM*, 63-4. Neale's trans. (1852) rev. for *AM* (1861) hence text but not necessarily history familiar to hymnist.

30 *HG* 193 cites stanzas 1 and 4 of five from Montgomery's hymn generally used hymnals. Full text in his *Original Hymns for Public, Private and Social Devotion* (London 1853), 158, headed "Valiant for the Truth."

31 Bennett, 71-81, 99-102.

32 Tune older than text (*HG* 592).

33 In *Scottish National Hymnal for the Young*, No. 186; *chant de tribu* in Davie, *Gathered Church*, 21.

34 See *HCM*," 108-11, 222-3 n48.

35 Doddridge, *Hymns*, Nos. 84, 140.

36 No. 367, "Now let our Songs address the God of Peace" headed "For the Thanksgiving-Day for the Peace," 25 April 1749.

37 *OH* II, 64, "On the Commencement of Hostilities in America."

38 Seen in *Hymns for . . . Poor Female Orphans*, No. 86; see Julian, 123ii.

39 See above, 152-3.

40 By American Episcopal priest Arthur C. Coxe, published 1840 (Julian, 266), readily naturalized.

41 John Russell Wrexford a Unitarian exminister resigned 1831 owing to failure of voice (*HG* 439).

42 *Jubilee Hymns* (London: SPCK 1887). Nos. 2, 5 (Stone), 10, "Thousand stars in heaven are burning" (Baring-Gould); 6, "Awake, O Church of England" (Jackson Mason); 13, "English children, lift your voices" (Ellerton).

43 Cf. MacIntyre, 66-7: "Christianity, confronted with the secular life of a post-Industrial Revolution society, has found it impossible to lend meaning to that life."

44 No. 998 in *New Congregational Hymn Book* (1859), as "God save. . . . " Line on "state" added to text of C.T. Brooks (1832-5) by John S. Dwight (1844). (Julian, 1566)

45 By Samuel F. Smith (Baptist), supplied in 1832 to fit tune by Lowell Mason (*HG* 458). Quoted from (U.S.) *Congregational Hymns* (1897), 665.

46 Frederick L. Hosmer (Unitarian), 1884, for Unity Festival in Chicago, usually rev. to "my country" (Julian, 1650ii). In rpt. for John Downes' *Hymns . . . Secondary Schools* (London: Dent 1911), 91, of 3 vv. applicable to Britain, st. 2 includes "For thee our fathers . . . Upon thy holy altar / Their willing lives they laid."

47 Original, "The Present Crisis," in Lowell's *Poems* (1849), protested against war with Mexico. English selection by W.G. Horder is 16 lines out of 90, from "When a deed is done for freedom . . . " History in *HG* 585 (q.v.), both texts in *PCH* 370. For "By the light of burning heretics" Horder has more ecumenical " . . . burning martyrs."

48 "Tell them to stand up for Jesus," interpreted as Jesus in person of a slave, as speaker, Rev. D.A. Tyng (d. about 1854) had suffered for his Abolitionist views (cited in Julian, 315ii).

49 Davie, *Dissentient Voice*, 56-64, esp. 57.

50 *Hymns of Modern Thought*, 90; Henry Scott Holland, 1902, *EH* 423; Gilbert Keith Chesterton, 1906, of *EH* 592.

51 Dock strike, supported by Morris and Cardinal Manning, led to demonstrations and arrests.

52 *Hymns in Times of National Crisis* (London: Lindsey Press 1914); *In Hoc Signo: Hymns of War and Peace* (London: SPCK 1914); *Hymns Suitable for Use in Time of War*, selected by Committee on Psalmody of Church of Scotland (London: Oxford University Press 1914); *Psalms, Paraphrases, Hymns and Passages of Scripture Suitable for Use in Time of War*. Committee on Psalmody . . . Scotland (London: Oxford University Press 1914).

53 John W. Chadwick (Unitarian), 1864, re American Civil War; John G. Whittier (Quaker), 1850. Others in section: "The King, O God, his heart to Thee upraiseth" (*Yattendon Hymnal*, based on text of 1615); "When wilt thou save the people"; "Judge Eternal . . . "; "Lift thy song among . . . "; Kipling's "Recessional" and the National Anthem. N.B. also "Lord of the brave . . . " (10).

54 Alan Wilkinson, in *The Church of England and the First World War* (London: SPCK 1978), 33-5, cites A.F. Winnington-

Ingram, Bishop of London's published sermon "A Call to Arms" preached at a Territorial Army camp at a general's request as inducing men to volunteer for foreign service; his preaching on the "Holy War" to soldiers in September, 1914, and calling on the Church, "the oldest fighting regiment in Europe," to "justify its claim to be the National Church," and calling it in 1919 "national and patriotic to its core." He cites the Archbishop of York as claiming to "envy the man who is able to meet the call" and pitying one who "makes the great refusal," and Bishop Moule of Durham in 1915 on the "holiness of patriotism."

55 No. 2, "Now to heaven our prayer ascending," W.E. Hickson (1836). (Julian, 1648ii)

56 No. 8. Cf. *Hymns Adapted to the State of the Nation at This Alarming Crisis* (Hull 1804), mainly millennial hymns on "crisis" as manifesting divine wrath at United Kingdom.

57 Helmreich, 87-93.

58 Between 1870 and 1902 Education Acts, most rural and some urban schools were Church of England. Surrey and Leicestershire County Records for this period include regular church and H.M. Inspectors' reports of children learning hymn-texts along with passages of Scriptures. Cf. Wilkinson (156): "Never were such hymn-singers known" (Scott Holland) and "Boys sang in the fields. . . . The chapels were full of singing. When the . . . war came, it was singing, singing all the time" (a villager). Wilkinson adds that "Almost every soldier would know a dozen or so hymns from day or Sunday school, church or chapel," his examples (153) being "Rock of Ages," "Sun of my soul," "O God our help . . . ," "Abide with me," "Eternal Father, strong to save," and "Onward, Christian soldiers."

59 On Geoffrey Studdart-Kennedy, a chaplain-missioner called "Woodbine Willie" for distributing cigarettes, see Wilkinson, 74, 136-8, 244 (on his patriotism destroyed by war).

60 See *Collected Poems of Wilfred Owen*, ed. C. D. Lewis (London: Chatto, 1963), passim; Robert Graves, *Goodbye to All That: An Autobiography*; Vera Brittain, *A Testament of Youth* (London: Gollancz 1933) and W.B. Yeats, "Easter, 1916."

61 Cf. Ps. 51.16-17, "The sacrifices of God . . . a broken and contrite heart

. . . ." with Isa. 57.15 God dwelling on high "with him . . . of a contrite and humble spirit" and 66.2-3 on rejection of priestly animal sacrifices for one "poor and of a contrite spirit" who "trembleth at my word."

62 On source, see n64. Sir John Arkwright "The Supreme Sacrifice and Other Poems in Time of War" (London: Skeffington 1919).

63 Josiah Conder, "Bread of heaven, on Thee I feed" (1824).

64 No. 81 in *Ashford Grammar School Hymnal* (Ashford 1937).

65 *HG* 324. "Thaxted" and Vaughan Williams' "Abinger" in *Songs of Praise Enlarged*, 319.

66 First in *Motherland Song Book* (1919), set of "peaceable patriotic songs" and first a hymn in *Songs of Praise* (1925) (*HG* 764).

67 Eric James, "I vow to thee, my country," HSGBI 10:1 (1982), 1-4.

NOTES TO CHAPTER FIFTEEN

1 "What heroes thou hast bred / England, my England," G.K. Menzies, listed only in Perry (as *SP* 325).

2 *School Hymnal and Service Book for . . . Harrow County Grammar School for Boys*, pp. 56-8.

3 Ibid., pp. 52-5. "Lord of our life, and God of our salvation" by M. von Lowenstern (1644), trans. Philip Pusey (1840), then *AM* (1868), 329.

4 *Songs of Praise Enlarged* (hereafter *SPE*) (London: Oxford University Press 1931).

5 Mr. William Serjeant, Archivist, West Suffolk County Council, informs me that Palser's collection was used under title *West Suffolk County Hymnal* (2nd edn. 1915, copy dated 1920), but "must have been in much wider circulation."

6 Palser's heading for Nos. 63-73a.

7 *Hymns for the Chapel of Harrow School* (London 1927), Nos. 266-72, last being "Peace" version of National Anthem (1919), *SP* 187, st. 2 on United Kingdom as "One realm of races four. . . . Home of the brave and free . . . nurse of chivalry," and st. 3 on the Commonwealth as "Kinsfolk in love and birth, / From utmost ends of earth, / God save us all. / Bid strife and hatred cease . . . hope and joy increase; / Spread universal peace. . . . "

8 *Cheltenham Ladies' College Hymnal* (Ox-

ford: Oxford University Press 1919). Information re school services by Miss Cleary and Mrs. Johnson, the School Librarians. Parents must agree to Anglican instruction.

9 *Prayers and Hymns for the Use of St. Paul's Girls' School* (London, private printing 1929; rpt. 1972).

10 Helen Waddell, *Medieval Latin Lyrics* (London: Constable 1933), 163-5. See *HCM*, 93-4.

11 *Worksop College Hymn Book* (London: Novello 1938).

12 "Almighty Father of all things that be" (1908), Canon Ernest E. Dugmore (1900), for industrial exhibition (Julian, 1630ii).

13 No. 63 in *SPE*, to which Joyce Anstruther (1901-53) assigned copyright, therefore probably designated text. Her novel used for wartime film *Mrs. Miniver*, idealizing middle-class rural life.

14 Originally in *Hymns for Our Lord's Resurrection* (1746); N.B. st. 4: "Till all his foes submit," st. 5: "And take his servants up / To their eternal home."

15 De la Mare (1873-1956) published verse from 1902 to 1933.

16 Originally Isa. 2.4, but Micah 4.3 better known. From poem "A Vista" in *New and Old* (1880), first sung as hymn 1896, then theme song of League of Nations Union (*HG* 730). Author (1840-93), well-known essayist and literary journalist.

17 *Hymns for the Use of Wakefield Girls' High School* (London: Oxford University Press 1933).

18 Composed in 1840 by John Stuart Blackie, classics professor at Aberdeen and Edinburgh universities. Martineau's editorial to *Hymns of Praise and Prayer* (1874) (see *HCM*, 4-5, says "more and more" modern texts "do but touch" on scriptural passage before passing to significance for inner life.

19 *Hymns for Use in Schools* (Leicester Education Committee 1927); *Prayers and Hymns* . . . (Leicester County Education Committee 1928), hymn-numbers identical; *Wulfruna: Wolverhampton School Hymnal* (Wolverhampton Education Committee, [1932]); *Hymns for Junior Schools* (1935), and *Oxford Book of School Worship* (1936), both (London: Oxford University Press).

20 1920, identical rpt. 1960.

21 *Songs of Praise for Children*, eds. P.

Dearmer, R. Vaughan Williams, M. Shaw (London: Oxford University Press 1929), v-vi.

22 "Where the flag of Britain flies" by Frederick A. Jackson, Baptist minister, for *Sunday School Hymnary* (1905) (Julian, 1610i).

23 On Evans and Arnold hymnals, see 295, n. 29.

24 "Lord of all . . . " (*SPE* 565), *Junior Schools* 73, not in *Oxford . . . Worship*.

25 Routley "once saw Briggs' royalty sheet . . . the size of a small hearth rug" (letter, 20 March 1980).

26 *SPE* 567; *Junior Schools*, 74; Leicester books, 147.

27 *English School Hymn Book*, eds. Alfred H. Body, Desmond MacMahon (London: University of London Press 1939), in 12th rpt. by 1967.

28 Nos. 3, 116; 80, 77; 94, 90; 48, 149; 169, 15 (*SPE* 53). In last, earth, "With garlands," and sea with "field" shining as "silver shield" say their "beauties are but for a day"; likewise sun whose "chariot" rolls on "amber and gold" wheels, and moon say their "days of light are numbered"; if God's beauties thus "gild the span / Of ruined earth and sinful man, / How glorious" the "mansion" where the "redeemed" dwell with Him.

29 Nos. 218, 209, 220, 83.

30 Nos. 102, 21 ("Abroad the regal banners fly"), 128, 144.

31 Leicester 153, 142, 76, 91, 115, 160, 102, 174, 60, 155, 129, 152, 101; Wulfruna 102, 100, 37, 41, 118, 162, 107, 54, 60, 130, 176, 59, 122.

32 Nos. 157, 151, 152; 6, 78; 25, 87; 130.

33 English *SHB*: 147, 2; 58, 72; 144; 125, 109. Leicester: 192, 41; 103, 81; 51; 11, 183.

34 English: 165, 127, 59; Wulfruna 15, 33, 39.

35 In *Hymns and Human Life*, Routley miscounts as 52.

36 Leicester: 206, 8, 10, 144, 188, 12. Wulfruna: 131, 132, 88, 104, 75, 123. English: 18, 35, 42, 16, 138, 113. Junior: 89, 99, 14, 102, 97, 25.

37 Leicester: 177, 4; 79, 125, 106; 140, 139; 100, 97; 141, 182. Wulfruna: 62, 117; -; 155, 171; 97, 148; 48, 49; 98, 67. Junior: 139, 4; -; 128, 131; 62, 77; 92, 93; 29, 142.

38 "We're little, tiny pilgrims" (8), "We, O God, are—" (9) not in Julian, who lists

similar title by G. Slack (1899) (703ii); "Little birds are singing" (7) untraced; "Little beams of rosy light" (18) by Fanny Crosby (1869).

39 *Methodist School Hymnal* (London: Wesleyan Methodist Sunday School Department 1923), "Children's Hymns" section.

40 "I thank . . . " not in Julian, but in Perry, copyright J.W. Butcher; "Lord . . . ," by Canon Thomas A. Stowell (1875); "Singing . . . " not in Julian or Perry, hence secular; No. 8, "Holy Spirit, hear us" by William Parker (Baptist, ca. 1880); " 'Tis not to ask for gifts alone" (listed by Perry only in *Methodist H.B.*, 1933), by Mary Olivant, b. 1852; "We are starting on a journey," (30), permission of James Littlewood, unlisted in Julian or Perry; "Coming, coming, yes they are" (3), permission of J.W. MacGill, again unlisted.

41 *School Hymn Book of the Methodist Church* (London: Methodist Youth Dept. [1949-50]), seen in private collection of Mr. Everson Whittall, Preston, Lancs. Dated on internal evidence, and discussed in *Making Melody* (same publishers 1950).

42 For Industrial Christian Fellowship, 1921 (*PCH* 455), but Perry lists only in SP.

43 *School Worship* (London: Independent Press 1926).

44 *Scottish Church Hymnary for the Young* (London: Oxford University Press 1928).

45 *Scottish School Hymnary* (London: Oxford University Press 1959).

46 *Hymns for Catholic Schools*, comp. E.J. Cross, for Catholic Teachers' Federation (London: Burns and Oates, n.d., 1961 rpt. with Appendix of 24 items added to original 80, by request of teachers).

47 Sister Mary Edward, who gave original date as 1941; Bennett, 184.

48 "Dear Little One, how sweet Thou art" (1849).

49 No. 20, "God of mercy and compassion," by Edmund Vaughan (1854). See Julian 1720ii.

50 *Enthusiasm*, 521-30, 592-3. Bennett (181-2) compares the images in "Rock of Ages" to those in medieval poems, but calls Evangelical hymns "near to being egocentric rather than Christocentric." The converse is true of those compiled by Cross.

NOTES TO CHAPTER SIXTEEN

1 *Odes of Solomon*, discussed in my *HCM*, 20-9.

2 *HCM*, 56-7.

3 Ibid., 68; *PCH*, 58.

4 *HCM*, 56-7, 65, 71-2; Bennett, 3, 67, 71-2, and above, 152.

5 *HCM*, 38, 43-5, 60.

6 Ibid., 90, 220 n32, on Newman, *Mission of the Benedictine Order* (London: Young 1923, orig. 1858), 55ff.

7 *HCM*, 100-5, 107-10.

8 Tennyson, *In Memoriam*, LVI, 12.

9 Thomas, 152, 17-18, 36.

10 Cited ibid., 158-61; Cowper, *The Task* (1785), VI, 220-600 *passim*; Gilbert White, *The Natural History and Antiquities of Selborne* (1789).

11 Carol Doran (music) and Thomas H. Troeger (lyrics), *New Hymns for the Lectionary: To Glorify the Maker's Name*, I (of three), Nos. 1-52 (New York: Oxford University Press 1986).

12 Bob Dufford, SJ, "Be not afraid" (1975), based on Isa. 43.2-3; Lk. 6.20ff., No. 8 in *Glory and Praise: Songs for Christian Assembly*, I (Phoenix: North American Liturgy Resources 1977).

13 *100 Hymns for Today*: A Supplement to Hymns Ancient and Modern (London: Clowes, Melody Edn. 1969), Nos. 28, 52.

14 Published 1969, rpt. as No. 182 in *More Hymns for Today*: Second Supplement to Hymns Ancient and Modern (London: Clowes 1980). Cf. Wren, "Lord Christ, the Father's mighty Son," No. 53 in *100 Hymns for Today*.

15 Doran and Troeger, Nos. 11-12.

16 Sung during Hymn Society of America Conference, Toronto, July 1986.

17 Set to John Wilson's tune "Lauds" (originally for Montgomery's "Songs of Praise the angels sang"), published under Wren's title (Carol Stream, IL: Hope Publishing Co. 1979).

18 *Hymns for Church and School* (4th edn. of *Public School H.B.*) with introductory essay by Erik Routley (Henley: Gresham Books 1964). Of 31 schools replying (24 boys' or mixed, 7 girls'), 5 use this, 8 *AMR*, 6 *SP*, 6 name *Church Hymnary*, *Methodist H.B.* or *EH* or (2) own hymnal, or (1) *In Every Corner Sing* (Nelson), for

total of 25. From 1870 to 1940, 4 used *AM*, 11 *Public School H.B.*, 2 *EH*, 2 *Church Hymnary*, 1 *Methodist H. B.* and 6 their own, total of 22. 6 schools using *AMR* also use *100 Hymns for Today*.

19 Information re Bristol G.S. (1971-2) mainly from Mr. Keith Howard, now Head at Queen Mary's School, Walsall; supplemented by Mr. John Mackay and Mr. G.J. Weaver.

20 Letters from Mr. John Grayson (Wolverhampton), and Mr. A.N. Fairbairn (Leicestershire), 9 and 10 January 1980.

21 Mr. Derek Burrell, then Headmaster, letter 2 June 1981, and during my visit that year to Truro School.

22 Information from Dr. R. Stuart Louden, member of Church Hymnary Revision Committee (letter, 15 May 1980).

23 D.S. Brewer, *Traditional Stories and Their Meanings* (London: English Association 1983, unpaged), Section VI: "Those few candidates who answered . . . were almost all convinced that Aesop was the author of one of the books of the Bible" (referring to Cambridge English Tripos, 1982).

24 Rev. F.S. Pritchard, in 1981.

25 *100 Hymns for Today*, Nos. 89, 86; John Hick (ed.), *The Myth of God Incarnate* (London: SCM Press 1977), esp. 8, 173-6 (Hick); 53-4, 57-9 (Michael Goulder); 140-1 (Don Cupitt).

26 *100 Hymns for Today*, No. 5.

27 Ibid., No. 13.

28 Ibid., No. 33. Mr. Burrell informs me that author attended Truro School.

29 Ibid., No. 42. Cf. Dante, *Paradiso*, Canto XX, and 2 Sam. 6.14.

30 Concluding line of "Among School Children": "How can we know the dancer from the dance." *Collected Poems of W.B. Yeats* (London: Macmillan 1963), 242-5.

31 *Odes of Solomon* 11.8-10.

32 Text, literal translation, and discussion in my *HCM*, 78-80; translators listed in Julian, 1214-15 and *HG* 881, except for recent free translation by J.W. Grant, "Holy Spirit, font of light" which renders quoted lines as "All that gives to us our worth, / all that benefits the earth, / you bring to maturity," a naturalistic image.

33 Samuel Beckett, *Endgame*; Eliot, "Waste Land," 384.

SELECT BIBLIOGRAPHY

Limited to works cited first-hand in notes; standard literary works mentioned only if quoted or referred to in detail.

WORKS OF REFERENCE

Holy Bible, The. Authorized Version 1611
House, Simon. *A Dictionary of British Book Illustrators and Caricaturists.* London: Antique Collectors' Club 1978
Julian, John, ed. *A Dictionary of Hymnology.* 2nd edn. 1907, rpt. New York: Dover Publications 1957
Perry, David W. *Hymns and Tunes Indexed by First Lines.* London: Hymn Society of Great Britain and Ireland and Royal School of Church Music 1980
Routley, Erik. *An English-Speaking Hymnal Guide.* Collegeville: Liturgical Press 1979

HYMNS AND LITURGICAL VERSE KNOWN BY AUTHOR AND COLLECTOR

Agg, John, ed. *A Collection of Hymns for Public Worship.* Evesham 1795
Bridges, Robert. *The Yattendon Hymnal.* Eds. Robert Bridges and H. Ellis Woolridge. Oxford: Oxford University Press 1899
Burder, George (comp.). *A Collection of Hymns from Various Authors, Intended as a Supplement to Dr. Watts' "Psalms and Hymns."* London 1784. 14th edn. 1810

Cotterill, Thomas. *A Selection of Psalms and Hymns for Public and Private Use, Adapted to the Services of the Church of England*. 1st through 6th edns. Newcastle, Staffs 1810-15. 8th edn. Sheffield, printed for edition by J. Montgomery 1819. 9th edn., 1820 ("Cotterill's Selection").

Cowper, William. *Olney Hymns*. See Newton, John.

Denham, David. *The Saints' Melody*. 1837. Rpt. London 1870

Doddridge, Philip. *Hymns Founded Upon Various Texts in the Scriptures*. Ed. Job Orton. 1755. Rpt. London 1793

Gadsby's Hymns. Ed. John Gadsby. Manchester 1853. Originally *A Selection of Hymns for Public Worship*, ed. William Gadsby. Manchester 1814

Greene, R.L. (ed., introd.). *Early English Carols*. 2nd edn. Oxford: Clarendon 1977

Heber, Reginald. *Hymns Written and Adapted to the Weekly Church Services of the Year*. London: Murray 1827

Irons, Joseph. *Zion's Hymns, intended as a Supplement to Dr. Watts' "Psalms and Hymns," for Use of . . . Congregation at Grove Chapel, Camberwell*. 3rd edn. London 1825 (originally 1816)

Keble. *Christian Year*. See entry under General Literary Works

Leeson, Jane Elizabeth. *Hymns and Scenes from Childhood*. London: Burns 1842

Lynch, Thomas Toke. *The Rivulet: A Contribution to Sacred Song*. London 1855

Martineau, James E. *Hymns of Praise and Prayer*. London: Longmans 1874

Newton, John and Cowper, William. *Olney Hymns*. 3 vols. London 1843, single-volume edn. (originally 1792)

Reynolds, William J. *A Joyful Sound: Christian Hymnody*. New York: Holt, Rinehart and Winston 1978

Rippon, John. *A Selection of Hymns from the Best Authors Intended as an Appendix to Dr. Watts' "Psalms and Hymns."* London 1787

—. *Selection of Hymns for the Use of Baptist Congregations Intended as a Supplement to . . .* ("Comprehensive Rippon"). London: Haddon 1844

Routley, Erik, ed. *A Panorama of Christian Hymnody*. Collegeville: Liturgical Press 1979. Parallel text hymns, arranged by period and language, with introductory essays

Sankey, Ira D. See Gospel Songs.

Smart, Christopher. *Hymns for the Amusement of Children*. Dublin: W. Strater and J. Williams 1772

Spurgeon, Charles Haddon, ed. *Our Own Hymn Book: A Collection of Psalms and Hymns for Public, Social and Private Worship*. London: Passmore and Alabaster 1869

Taylor, Ann and Jane. *Hymns for Infant Minds*. 37th edn. London 1846 (originally 1809)

Troeger, Thomas H., and Carol Doran. *New Hymns for the Lectionary: To Glorify the Maker's Name*, Vol. I (of three). New York: Oxford University Press 1986

Watts, Isaac. *Hymns and Spiritual Songs*. 3 vols. London 1707, 1709

—. *Psalms of David Imitated*. London 1719

Wesley, Charles and John. *Hymns and Sacred Poems*. London 1739

—. *Hymns and Spiritual Songs Intended for the Use of Real Christians of All Denominations*. London 1762 (originally 1753)

Wesley, John, ed. *A Collection of Hymns for the Use of People Called Methodists*. 1780. Vol. 7 in *Works of John Wesley*, eds. Franz Hildebrandt, Oliver A. Beckerlegge and James Dale. Oxford: Clarendon 1983

—. *A Collection of Hymns for People Called Methodists*. Rev. edn., with Supplement. London: Wesleyan Conference Office 1830

Wither, George. *Hymns and Songs of the Church*. London: J.R. Smith 1856 (originally 1623)

HYMNS AND SERVICE BOOKS (FOR ADULT WORSHIP)

Baptist Church Hymnal: Hymns, Chants and Anthems. London: Psalms and Hymns Trust 1900

Choice Selection of Hymns and Spiritual Songs for . . . Prayer, Conference and Camp Meetings, A. Windsor, VT 1827

Church [of Scotland] Hymnary. Rev. edn. London: Oxford University Press 1928

Church Hymns. London: SPCK 1871

Church Missionary Hymn Book. London: Church Missionary Society 1899

Church Psalmist or Psalms and Hymns for the Public, Social and Private Use of Evangelical Christians. Philadelphia 1847 (originally New York 1843)

Collection of Hymns adapted to Public Worship [Baptist], A. Eds. John Ash and Caleb Evans. Bristol 1769

Collection of Hymns and Anthems Used in St. Andrew's Chapel Aberdeen [Episcopal Church of Scotland], A. 16th edn. Aberdeen 1836

Collection of Hymns for Camp Meetings, Revivals, etc., for the Use of Primitive Methodists, A. Hugh Bourne. Bemersley 1841. Bound in with *Large Hymn Book* [q.v.]

Collection of Hymns for People Called Methodists. 1780. See Wesley, John.

Collection of Hymns for Public Worship, A. 1795. See Agg, John.

Collection of Hymns from Several Authors with . . . Translations from the German Hymn Book of the Ancient Moravian Brethren, A. London 1741

Collection of Hymns from Various Authors, A. See Burder, George.
Collection of Hymns of the Children of God [Moravian], A. Ed. John
   Gambold. London 1754
Congregational Church Hymnal. Ed. George Barrett. London: Congrega-
   tional Union 1884
Hymnal for Use in Congregational Churches. Eds. Louis F. Benson and
   William Gilchrist. Boston: Pilgrim Press 1897 [Rpt. of *Presbyterian
   Hymnal*, Philadelphia 1895]
English Hymn Book, The. Ed. R.W. Dale. London: Hamilton, Adams;
   Birmingham: Hudson 1874 [Congregational]
English Hymnal, The. Eds. Percy Dearmer and Ralph Vaughan Williams.
   London: Humphrey Milford and A.R. Mowbray 1906 [Anglican]
Essex Hall Hymnal. London: British and Foreign Unitarian Association
   1891
—. Rev. edn. 1902 [Unitarian]
Glory and Praise: Songs for Christian Assembly. Phoenix: North American
   Liturgy Resources 1977
Gospel Hymns and Sacred Songs. Comps. P.P. Bliss and I. Sankey. New
   York: Biglow and Main 1875
Gospel Hymns Consolidated. Toronto: Copp, Clark and Co. 1883
Hymn-Book Annotated, The. Toronto: Oxford University Press 1939
   [Anglican]
Hymnal Companion to Book of Common Prayer. Ed. Edward H.
   Bickersteth. London 1870: rev. edn. (1878) rpt. Longmans 1919
Hymnary, The. Toronto: United Church of Canada Publishing House 1930
*Hymns Ancient and Modern, for Use in Services of the Church, with
   Accompanying Tunes*. London: Clowes 1861, 1875, 1889, 1904, 1906-22
   (*AM*) [Anglican]
Hymns Ancient and Modern Revised. London: Clowes 1950
*Hymns for the London Mission (1874) by the Compilers of "Hymns
   Ancient and Modern."* London: Clowes 1874
Hymns of the Protestant Episcopal Church. Philadelphia: Hooker 1845
*Hymns Selected from Most Approved Authors for Use of Trinity Church,
   Boston*. Boston: Munroe, Francis, Parker 1808 [Episcopal]
Large Hymn Book for the Use of Primitive Methodists, The. Bemersley,
   1825, rpt. 1841
Methodist Hymn Book [Canada]. London 1904. Methodist New Connexion
   and Methodist Church of Canada 1874
Methodist Hymn Book. London: Methodist Conference Office 1933
*More Hymns for Today: Second Supplement to Hymns Ancient and
   Modern*. London: Clowes 1980
New Congregational Hymn Book. London: Congregational Union 1859

Olney Hymns. See Newton, J.

100 [One Hundred] Hymns for Today: A Supplement to Hymns Ancient and Modern. London: Clowes, Melody edn. 1969

Our Own Hymn Book [Baptist]. See Spurgeon, C.H.

People's Hymnal, The. Comp. R.F. Littledale. London: J. Maters 1867 [Anglican]

Plymouth Collection of Hymns and Tunes. Comp. Henry W. Beecher. New York: Barnes 1855

Presbyterian Hymnal with Sunday School Supplement. Comp. by Committee of United Presbyterian Church. Edinburgh: A. Elliott 1876

Primitive Methodist Hymn Book. Ed. John Flesher. London: R. Davies 1854

Primitive Methodist Hymnal. Ed. George Booth. London: E. Dalton 1887

Psalms, Hymns and Passages of Scripture for Christian Worship ["The Leeds Hymn Book"]. London: Partridge and Oakey 1853

Rivulet, The. See Lynch, T.T.

Sacred Songs and Solos. 1873. Thereafter English title of *Gospel Hymns and Sacred Songs*.

Scottish Church Hymnary. Edinburgh 1898

Selection of Hymns . . . intended as an Appendix (Supplement) to Dr. Watts' . . . , A. (Rippon's "Selection" and "Comprehensive Rippon"). See Rippon, J.

Selection of Psalms and Hymns . . . , A. See Cotterill, T.

Small Hymn Book [Primitive Methodist]. 1809, rpt. 1841 bound with Large *HB* [q.v.]

Songs of Praise. Eds. Percy Dearmer, Ralph Vaughan Williams, and Martin Shaw. London: Oxford University Press 1925 [Anglican]

Songs of Praise Enlarged. Ed. G.W. Briggs. London: Oxford University Press 1931

Village Hymns for Social Worship: Designed as a Supplement to the Psalms and Hymns of Dr. Watts. Ed. Asahel Nettleton. New York: Sands 1840

HYMN BOOKS: SPECIALIZED

Domestic Praise: A Selection of Hymns appropriate to Family Worship. Manchester: H. Whitmore 1850

Evensong [The]: A Selection of Hymns and Chants for Family Worship arranged for four voices by W.H. Birch. London n.d.

Family Hymn Book. London: Blackie 1864

Hundred Hymns Selected by the Readers of "Sunday at Home" as the Best in the English Language, A. London: Religious Tract Society 1888

Hymns Adapted to the State of the Nation at This Alarming Crisis: Intended

Chiefly to be Used on the Days Appointed for General Fasting and Humiliation. Hull: W. Crossley 1804

Hymns for Public Worship for Use of Working Men's Christian Association. Omega Place, St. John's Wood, London: private circulation 1872

Hymns in Time of National Crisis. London: Lindsey Press 1914

Hymns of Modern Thought. London: Houghton 1900

Hymns Suitable for Use in Time of War. Select Committee on Psalmody, Church of Scotland. Oxford: Oxford University Press 1914

In Hoc Signo: Hymnal of War and Peace. London: SPCK 1914

Jubilee Hymns. London: SPCK 1887

Odes of Solomon. Trans. James Hamilton Charlesworth. Oxford: Clarendon 1973

Psalms, Hymns, Paraphrases and Passages of Scripture Suitable for Use in time of War. Select Committee on Psalmody of Church of Scotland. Oxford University Press 1914

Sailor's Hymn Book, The. Comp. under British and Foreign Sailors' Society. London: Ward 1850

A Selection of Hymns Adapted to the Devotions of the Closet, Family and Social Circle. Ed. Archibald Alexander. New York: Leavitt 1831

Soldier's Book of Hymns, The. Comp. "C.H.M.," an Officer. Devonport 1863

Soldier's Hymn Book, The. Comp. and pub. Aldershot Mission Hall and Soldiers' Institute 1869

Victorian Hymns: English Sacred Songs of Fifty Years. London: Kegan Paul 1887

Yattendon Hymnal, 1899. See Bridges, R.

HYMNALS FOR CHILDREN AND SCHOOLS

Ashford Grammar School Hymnal. Ashford: Headley Bros. 1937

Baptist Sabbath School Hymn Book. London: Simpkin and Marshall; Loughborough: Winks and Son 1825

Birmingham Blue-Coat Charity Schools Hymn-Sheets 1724-1847. Unpublished. Birmingham Public Library

Birmingham School Board Hymn Book. Birmingham: School Board 1900. Republished as *Birmingham Education Committee . . .* 1903

Book of Praise for Children, A. London: Hodder and Stoughton 1881

Book of Prayer and Praise Compiled for Use in Sir Josiah Mason's Orphanage. Birmingham: Erdington 1883

Book of Sacred Songs for [London] School Board Schools. London 1873

Cantanda Carthusiana [Charterhouse School]. Godalming: W.B. Stedman 1894

Catholic Hymns with Holy Mass for Children. Dublin: Duffy [1900]

Cheltenham Ladies' College Hymnal. Oxford: Oxford University Press 1919

Children's Hosannah, The: The Penny Sunday-School Book, Selected by a Committee of Sunday School Teachers. London: Jarrold and Sons [1858]

Children's Hymn Book, The. Eds. Mrs. Brock Carey. Rev. John Ellerton [Bishop] W.W. How, A. Oxenden. London 1881

Child's Christian Year, The. Ed. Frances M. Yonge. London 1841

Church Sunday School Hymn Book with Liturgy. London 1879 (originally 1868)

Church Sunday School Hymn Book (Infant Class ed.). London: Church of England Sunday School Institute 1880 (originally 1868)

Clifton College Hymn Book. See *Psalms and Hymns for . . . Clifton . . .*

Collection of Hymns for Children and Young Persons Principally Designed for Use of Charity and Sunday Schools: Published for Benefit of Walworth Charity and Sunday Schools, A. London 1810

Collection of Hymns for the use of Methodist Sunday Schools, A. Ed. Joseph Benson. 2nd edn. London: Blanchard 1816 (originally 1808)

Congregational Sunday-School Hymn Book. London: Congregational Union 1881

Council School Hymn Book. London: Novello 1905

Dove Row Ragged School Hymn Book. London: Partridge 1860 (?)

Easy Hymns for use in National Schools. London: SPCK 1831

English School Hymn Book. Eds. Alfred H. Body and Desmond MacMahon. London: University of London Press 1939

Eton College Hymn Book. London: Oxford University Press 1937

Explanation of Dr. Watts' Hymns for Children, in Questions and Answers, An. See Cottle, Mrs.

Psalms and Hymns for use of Chapel of Asylum for Female Orphans. London 1801 (originally 1775)

Hymn Book for Scholars. 15th edn. Montreal 1837 (originally London: Sunday School Union ca. 1816)

Book for School Children. Leeds: Arnold 1922

HyLeeds: Arnold 1922

Hymn Book for the Use of Wellington College. 5th edn. 1880

Hymn Book in Use at Emanuel School. Comp. H.B. Ryley. London: Philip and Tacey 1910

Hymns and Anthems Sung in the Chapel of the Foundling Hospital. London: Swift 1874

Hymns and Moral Songs for Use in Board Schools. Manchester: Heywood, for City of Manchester School Board 1878

Hymns and Paraphrases of Scripture for Use of the Grammar School, Leeds. London: Hurst, Robinson 1826

Hymns and Psalms for Secondary Schools. Selected and Arranged by John

N. Downes. London: Dent 1911

Hymns and Psalms for Secondary Schools. Selected and Arranged by John N. Downes. London: Dent 1911

Hymns for Catholic Schools. Comp. E.J. Cross. London: Burns and Oates [1941]; rpt. 1961

Hymns for the Chapel of Harrow School. 1st edn., ed. C.J. Vaughan, Harrow: Crossley and Clarke 1855; 4th ed., rev. and enlarged edn., ed. H.M. Butler, Harrow: J.C. Wilbee 1881; 5th edn., Harrow: Wilbee 1895

Hymns for Children and Young Persons on the Privileges, Truths and Duties of Religion and Morality. Ed. Joseph Benson. London: Blanshard 1814 (originally 1806)

Hymns for Children, Principally [of a] Sunday School. Comp. and composed Rowland Hill. London 1819

Hymns for Children, Selected with a view to being Learned by Heart. Oxford: Parker 1856

Hymns for Church and School (4th edn. of *Public School Hymn Book*). Henley: Gresham Books 1964

Hymns for Day Schools. London: Joseph Tarn 1874

Hymns for Junior Schools. London: Oxford University Press 1935

Hymns for Oulton Evening School. 2nd edn. 1858 [no place or publisher given in British Library]

Hymns for Use in Schools. Leicester: Leicester Education Committee 1927

Hymns for Use of the Chapel of the Asylum for Poor Female Orphans. Bristol 1811

Hymns for Use of Church of England Sunday Schools. Hull 1823

Hymns . . . for Use of Manchester Grammar School. Manchester 1913 (originally 1905)

Hymns for the Use of National Schools. London: National Society 1851

Hymns for the Use of [National] Schools. Sold at Depository of National Society London [1857]

Hymns for the Use of Young Persons [Society of Friends]. 7th edn. York: Sessions 1903

Hymns for Very Little Ones. London: SPCK [Tract Committee] 1866

Hymns for Young Persons. Ed. R.H. London: Parker 1834

Hymns Selected and Originally . . . Intended [for] . . . Devotional Exercises of Children and Teachers in the Leeds Sunday School Union. Leeds: Heaton 1834

Hymns Selected by a Clergyman for the Use of His Schools. London: Hamilton, Adams, n.d. [post-1827]

Hymns Selected for the Use of Young Persons in a Charity School. Dublin: Watson 1812

Hymns Selected from Various Authors and Chiefly Intended for the

Instruction of Young Persons. London: Darton, Harvey 1818

Hymns Used by Pupils of Sisters of Notre Dame. Manchester: Ledsham 1883

Leeds Sunday School Union Hymn Book. Originally 1833; rev. edn. Leeds 1878

Methodist Free Church: School Hymns. London: Crombie 1888

Methodist Scholar's Hymn Book. London: Wesleyan Conference Office 1870

Methodist School Hymnal. London: Wesleyan Methodist Sunday School Department 1911

Methodist School Hymnal. London: Wesleyan Methodist Sunday School Department 1923

Methodist Sunday School Hymn Book. London: Wesleyan Methodist Sunday School Union 1879

National Society's Graded Hymn Book. London: National Society n.d.

New Children's Hymnal [Church of Scotland]. Edinburgh: Blackwood 1885

New School Hymnal, A. Ed. E.M. Palser. London: Harrap 1913

New Selection of Hymns for the Use of Schools, A. 7th edn. Edinburgh: Oliphant 1824

One Hundred Hymns for Schools. London: Oxford University Press 1956

One Hundred Hymns for Special and Schoolroom Services, Cottage Meetings, Family Worship, and Private Devotion. Ed. "lay member," dedicated to E.R. Eardley-Wilmot, Rector, All Souls, Marylebone. London: Rivingtons 1861

Oxford Book of School Worship. London: Oxford University Press 1936

Prayers and Hymns for Little Children for Use in Infant Schools and Preparatory Departments. London: Oxford University Press 1932

Prayers and Hymns for Use in Schools. Abridged edn. of *Songs of Praise* with a few additional hymns. Leicester: Leicestershire Education Committee 1928

Prayers and Hymns for the Use of St. Paul's Girls' School. London: private printing 1929

Psalm and Hymn Book for Bedales School. 1901

Psalms and Hymns for the Use of Clifton College. 1st edn., ed. J. Percival 1863; 3rd edn., ed. J.M. Wilson 1885

Psalms, Anthems and Hymns Used in the Chapel of Rugby School. Rugby: Rowell and Sons 1824

Psalms and Hymns Used in the Chapel of Rugby School. Rugby: Rowell 1835; rpt. 1843

Psalms and Hymns for the Use of the Congregation of Rugby School Chapel. Rugby 1859

Hymns for the Use of Rugby School. Rugby 1885

Hymns with Tunes for the Use of Rugby School. Rugby 1906

Psalms, Hymns and Spiritual Songs for the Use of Pannal and Low Harrogate Village School. Private printing 1831

Psalms and Hymns for the Chapel of Marlborough College. London: R. Clay, Sons and Taylor, private printing 1878

Psalms and Hymns for School and Home. London: Haddon 1882. [Baptist]

Psalms and Hymns for Use of Chapel of Asylum for Female Orphans. Rev. and enlarged edn., London 1801

"Psalms and Hymns" to be Sung by Children of St. John's Schools, Newcastle. 1823-32

Public School Hymn Book. Ed. Committee of Headmasters' Conference. London: Novello 1904, 1920, 1950. For 1964 edn. see *Hymns for Church and School*

Public School Hymn Book, Companion to. See Furneaux, W.

Rugby School (all edns.). See *Psalms, Anthems and Hymns*.

Sabbath School Hymn Book. See Baptist

Sabbath School Minstrel. Edinburgh: Fraser 1835

Sacred Song Book for Children. Comp. C.H. Bateman. Edinburgh: Gall and Inglis 1843

Sacred Songs for Home and School Compiled for Sharp Street Ragged School, Manchester. Manchester: W. Bremmer 1858

St. Olave's [Grammar School] Hymnal. Comp. W.G. Rushbrooke. Surbiton: J. Philpott 1907

School Board Hymn Book. Huddersfield: G. Whitehead 1873

School Hymn Book, The. London: Evans 1920; rpt. 1960

School Hymn Book of the Methodist Church. London: Methodist Youth Department [1949-50]

School Hymnal and Service Book. Comps. George Thorn and Randall Williams, Harrow County Boys' School. London: Dent 1923

School Hymns with Tunes . . . Supplementary to "Church Hymns." Ed. Dorothea Beale. London: Bell 1892. [Cheltenham Ladies' College]

School Praise: A Hymn Book for the Young. London: J. Nisbet 1912

School Worship. London: Independent Press 1926

Scottish Church Hymnary for the Young. London: Oxford University Press 1928

Scottish Hymnal Supplement [for Children]. Private printing for Hymn Committee of Church of Scotland 1882

Scottish National Hymnal for the Young. Glasgow: C. Glass 1910. Rev. from 1899 hymnal of Scottish National Sabbath School Union, Glasgow Foundry Boys' Society and Glasgow Boys' Brigade

Scottish School Hymnary. London: Oxford University Press 1959

Selection of Hymns and Poetry for the Use of Infant Schools and Nurseries, A. London: Suter 1838

Selected Hymns for Use of Young Persons. 7th edn. Comp. John Ford. York: W. Sessions [Society of Friends] 1903

Selection of Hymns Not Found in 'Hymns Ancient and Modern' For Use in Preparatory Schools, A. Winchester: private printing 1894

Songs of Praise for Sunday School Children. Sel. by Committee of Sunday School Teachers. London: Jarrold [1870]

Songs of Praise for Children. Eds. P. Dearmer, R. Vaughan Williams, and M. Shaw. London: Oxford University Press 1929

Supplementary Hymns for Use in Mill Hill School Chapel. Comp. "MacC., J.D." Private printing, Bristol 1907

Twenty-Six Hymns for Nursery or School. London: Nelson 1857

Voice of Praise for Sunday School and Home, A. London: London Sunday School Union 1886

Hymns for the Use of Wakefield Girls' High School. London: Oxford University Press 1933

Winchester College Hymn Book. Rev. edn. London: Oxford University Press 1928 (originally 1910)

Worksop College Hymn Book. London: Novello 1938

Wulfruna: the Wolverhampton School Hymnal. Comp. T.F. Kinloch Wolverhampton: Wolverhampton Education Committee 1932

LITERARY WORKS (INCLUDING AUTOBIOGRAPHIES AND LETTERS)

Alexander, Cecil Frances. *Poems of Cecil Frances Alexander*. Ed. William Alexander. London: Macmillan 1896

Arnold, Matthew. "Forsaken Merman, The." 1849

Augustine, Saint. *Confessions*

Austen, Jane. *Emma*. London 1816

Beckett, Samuel. *Endgame*. Trans. by author from *Fin de partie* and *Acte sans paroles*. London: Faber 1958

Blake, William. *Songs of Innocence*. London 1789

—. *Songs of Experience*. London 1794

Brittain, Vera. *A Testament of Youth*. London: Gollancz 1933

Brontë, E. *Wuthering Heights*. London 1847

Bunyan, John. *A Book for Boys and Girls, or Country Rhymes for Children*. 1686, facsimile edn. London: Elliott Stock 1889

Butler, Samuel. *The Way of All Flesh*. London: Grant Richards 1903

Carroll, Lewis. See Dodgson

Chaucer, Geoffrey. *Prologue to Canterbury Tales*

Clemens, Samuel ("Mark Twain"). *Adventures of Huckleberry Finn*. New York: Harper 1884

Coleridge, Samuel Taylor. *Christabel*. 1816

—. "Frost at Midnight." 1798

Cowper, William. *The Task* in *Poems by William Cowper*. 2 vols. London: Johnson 1800. Vol. 2 (originally 1785)

Dickens, Charles. *Bleak House*. 1853

—. *David Copperfield*. 1850

—. *Dombey and Son*. 1848

—. *Great Expectations*. 1860

Dodgson, Charles Lutwidge ("Lewis Carroll"). (1) *Alice in Wonderland*. 1865. (2) *Alice Through the Looking-Glass*. 1871

Eliot, George. See Evans.

Eliot, Thomas Stearns. *Waste Land, The*. New York: Boni and Liveright 1922; Richmond: Hogarth Press 1923

Evans, Mary Ann ("George Eliot"). *Middlemarch*. London 1871. Harmondsworth: Penguin 1965

—. *Adam Bede*. London 1859

Gaskell, Elizabeth. *Mary Barton*. London 1848

—. *North and South*. London 1854-5

Hardy, Thomas. *Far From the Madding Crowd*. London: Macmillan 1974 (originally 1874)

—. *Stories and Poems of Thomas Hardy*. Ed. N.V. Meeres. London: Macmillan 1947

—. *Tess of the d'Urbervilles: A Pure Woman*. London: Macmillan 1891

Harris, Benjamin (comp.). *New England Primer*. Boston, MA: ca. 1683

Hopkins, G.M. *Letters of Gerard Manley Hopkins*. Ed. C.C. Abbott. 3 vols. London: Oxford University Press 1935.

Janeway, James. *A Token for Children . . . Conversions, Holy Lives and Exemplary Deaths of Several Young Children*. Edinburgh 1672

Keble, John. *The Christian Year: Thoughts in Verse for Sundays and Holydays Throughout the Year*. London: Oxford University Press 1914 (originally 1827)

Lewis, C.S. *Surprised by Joy*. London: Bles 1955

—. *They Stand Together: Letters of C.S. Lewis to Arthur Greeves, 1914-63*. Ed. Walter Hooper. London: Collins 1979

Lyte, Henry Francis. *Poems, Chiefly Religious*. London: Nisbet and March 1833

—. *Poetical Works*. Ed. John Appleyard. London: Elliott Stock 1907

Milton, John. *Comus: A Masque*. 1634

—. *Paradise Lost*. 1674

—. *Poetical Works*. Oxford: Oxford University Press 1904

Newman, John Henry. *Apologia pro Vita sua*. Ed. M.J. Svaglic. Oxford: Clarendon 1967 (originally 1864)

—. *Loss and Gain*. London: Burns 1848

Owen, Wilfred. "At a Calvary Near the Ancre" in *Collected Poems of*

Wilfred Owen. Ed. Cecil Day Lewis. London: Chatto and Windus 1963

Russell, Bertrand. *Autobiography of.* 3 vols. Toronto: McClelland and Stewart 1967-9

Sassoon, Siegfried. *Memoirs of an Infantry Officer.* London: Faber and Faber 1930

Shakespeare, William. "Sonnet 146"

[Shaw, C.]. *When I Was a Child: Memories of an Old Potter.* London: Methuen 1903; rpt. Wakefield: S.R. Publishers 1969

Sidney, Sir Philip. *Astrophel and Stella.* Sonnet 5

Taylor, Ann and Jane. *Original Poems for Infant Minds.* London 1804

Tennyson, Alfred. *In Memoriam.* London 1850

Thackeray, William Makepeace. *Vanity Fair: A Novel without a Hero.* London: Bradley and Evans 1848. Macmillan edn. 1911; rpt. Toronto: Macmillan 1969

Thompson, Flora. *Lark Rise to Candleford.* London: Oxford University Press 1939

Waddell, Helen (trans. & ed.). *Medieval Latin Lyrics.* 4th edn. London: Constable 1933. Parallel Latin-English texts (originally 1929)

Watts, Isaac. *Divine Songs . . . Attempted in Easy Language For Children (with Moral Songs).* London 1715

—. *Divine and Moral Songs.* London: March's Library of Instruction and Amusement No. 9 [1845]

—. *Divine and Moral Songs: Pictured in Colours by Mrs. Arthur Gaskin.* London 1896

—. *Works of the Reverend and Learned Isaac Watts, D.D.* Ed. George Burder. 6 vols. London: J. Barfield 1810

Wesley, John. Journal in *Works of John Wesley.* 14 vols. London: Methodist Conference 1872; rpt. Grand Rapids: Zondervan 1958-9

White, William Hale ("Mark Rutherford"). *The Revolution in Tanner's Lane.* 8th edn. London: T. Fisher Unwin 1890

Wordsworth, William. *Lyrical Ballads.* Preface. London 1802 edn.

—. "Ode on Intimations of Immortality from Recollections of Early Childhood" in *Poems of 1807.* London

—. *The Prelude, or Growth of a Poet's Mind.* 1805, 1850. Parallel text edn., ed. J.C. Maxwell. Harmondsworth: Penguin 1971

Zuckmayer, Carl. *A Part of Myself.* Trans. Richard and Clara Winston. London: Secker and Warburg 1970

BOOKS, CRITICAL, HISTORICAL OR THEOLOGICAL

Adey, Lionel. *Hymns and the Christian "Myth."* Vancouver: University of British Columbia Press 1986

Anstruther, Ian. *The Scandal of the Andover Workhouse*. London: Bles 1973

Ariès, Philippe. *Centuries of Childhood (L'Enfant et la vie familiale sous l'Ancien Regime)*. Trans. R. Baldick. London: Cape 1962

Armitage, Doris Mary. *The Taylors of Ongar*. Cambridge: Heffer 1939

Barfield, Arthur Owen. *History in English Words*. 1926. 3rd edn. Grand Rapids: Eerdmans 1967

—. *The Rediscovery of Meaning and Other Essays*. Middletown, CT: Wesleyan University Press 1977

—. *What Coleridge Thought*. Middletown: Wesleyan University Press 1971. London: Oxford University Press 1972

Bailey, Albert Edward. *The Gospel in English Hymns: Backgrounds and Interpretations*. New York: Scribners 1950

Bennett, Ian. *Poetry of the Passion*. Oxford: Clarendon 1982

Benson, Louis F. *The English Hymn: Its Development and Use*. 1915, rpt., Richmond, VA.: John Knox Press 1962

Booth, Charles. *Life and Labour of People in London*, 7 vols. London: Macmillan 1902

Bowen, Desmond. *The Idea of the Victorian Church*. Montreal: McGill University Press 1968

Brewer, Derek Stanley. *Traditional Stories and Their Meanings*. London: English Association 1983

Brown, Ford K. *Fathers of the Victorians: The Age of Wilberforce*. Cambridge: Cambridge University Press 1961

Cecil, Lord Edward Christian David. *The Stricken Deer: or the Life of Cowper*, 2nd edn. London: Constable 1933 (originally 1929)

Chadwick, Owen. *The Victorian Church*, 2 vols. London: A. and C. Black 1966

Clarke, W.K. Lowther. *One Hundred Years of Hymns Ancient and Modern*. London: William Clowes 1960

Colquhoun, Frank. *Hymns That Live: Their Meaning and Message*. London: Hodder and Stoughton 1980

[Cottle, Mrs.]. *An Explanation of Dr. Watts' Hymns for Children, in Questions and Answers by a Lady*, 3rd edn. London 1829

Coveney, Peter. *Poor Monkey* (U.S. title *The Image of Childhood in Victorian Fiction*). London: Rockliff 1957

Currie, Robert. *Methodism Divided: A Study in the Sociology of Ecumenicalism*. London: Faber 1968

Davie, Donald. *Dissentient Voice*. Notre Dame: Notre Dame University Press 1982

—. *A Gathered Church: The Literature of the English Dissenting Interest 1700-1930*. London: Routledge and Kegan Paul 1978

Davies, Horton. *Worship and Theology in England*, 5 vols. Princeton: Princeton University Press 1961-75

Davis, A.P. *Isaac Watts: His Life and Works*. London: Independent Press 1943

Elliott-Binns, L.E. *Religion in the Victorian Era*. London: Lutterworth Press 1946

Erdman, David V. *Blake: Prophet Against Empire*. Rev. edn., New York: Doubleday 1969

Escott, Harry. *Isaac Watts: Hymnographer. A Study of the Beginnings, Development and Philosophy of the English Hymn*. London: Independent Press 1962

[Evans, Mary Ann]. *George Eliot: The Critical Heritage*. Ed. David Carroll. London: Routledge 1971

Furneaux, William. *A Companion to the Public School Hymn Book*. London: Novello 1904

Fussell, Paul. *The Great War and Modern Memory*. New York: Oxford University Press 1975

Gathorne-Hardy, Jonathan. *The Public-School Phenomenon*. 1977, rpt. Harmondsworth: Penguin 1979 (originally Hodder and Stoughton 1977)

Graves, Robert. *Goodbye to All That: An Autobiography*. London: Cape 1929

Hankey, Donald. *The Lord of All Good Life: Jesus and the Weakness of His Church*. London: Longmans 1914

—. *A Passing in June*. London: Longmans 1915

—. *A Student in Arms*. London: Melrose 1917

Harrison, J.F.C. *The Second Coming: Popular Millenarianism 1780-1850*. London: Routledge and Kegan Paul 1979

Helmreich, Ernst Christian. *Religious Education in German Schools: An Historical Approach*. Cambridge, MA: Harvard University Press 1959

Hobsbawm, E.J., and George Rude. *Captain Swing*. London: Lawrence and Wishart 1969

Johnson, Samuel. "Life of Watts," in *Lives of the Poets*, III. Ed. George Birkbeck Hill. Oxford: Clarendon 1905

Joinville, Jean de. *Chronicles of the Crusades*. London: Bell and Daldy 1865

Jones, Mary G. *The Charity School Movement: A Study of Eighteenth-Century Puritanism in Action*. Cambridge University Press 1938. Rpt. London: Cass 1964

Keble, John. *Sermons Academical and Occasional*. Oxford: Parker 1848. Bound in with *Christian Year* (Oxford University Press)

Kendall, Holiday Bickerstaffe. *The Origin and History of Primitive Methodism*, 2 vols. London: E. Dalton n.d.

Kierkegaard, Søren. *Purity of Heart Is to Will One Thing*, trans. Douglas V. Steere. New York: Harper and Row 1948

King, Rev. James. *Anglican Hymnody: Being an Account of 325 Standard Hymns of the Highest Merit According to the Verdict of the Whole Anglican Church*. London: Hatchard 1885

Knox, Ronald A. *Enthusiasm: A Chapter in the History of Religion*, 2nd edn. Oxford: Clarendon 1962 (originally 1950)

Laqueur, Thomas W. *Religion and Respectability: Sunday Schools and Working Class Culture 1780-1850*. New Haven: Yale University Press 1976

Lewalski, Barbara Kiefer. *Protestant Poetics and Seventeenth-Century Lyrics*. Princeton: Princeton University Press 1979

Longmate, Norman. *The Workhouse*. London: Temple Smith 1974

Lowther, Clarke. See Clarke.

MacIntyre, Alasdair. *Secularization and Moral Change*. London: Oxford University 1967

McLeod, Hugh. *Class and Religion in the Late-Victorian City*. London: Croom Helm 1974

Manning, Bernard Lord. *The Hymns of Wesley and Watts: Five Informal Papers*. London: Epworth Press 1942

Marshall, Madeleine Ford, and Janet Todd. *English Congregational Hymns in the Eighteenth-Century*. Lexington: Kentucky University Press 1982

Meigs, Cornelia, with Anne Thaxter Eaton, Elizabeth Nesbitt, and Ruth Hill Viguers. *A Critical History of Children's Literature*. New York: Macmillan 1953

Newman, J.H. *The Mission of the Benedictine Order*. 1858, rpt. London: Young 1923

Newsome, David. *Godliness and Good Learning: Four Studies on a Victorian Ideal*. London: Murray 1961

—. *The Parting of Friends: A Study of the Wilberforces and Henry Manning*. London: Murray 1966

[Newton, John] "Omicron." *Twenty-Six Letters on Religious Subjects*. London: Oliver 1774

Padover, Saul K. *Karl Marx: An Intimate Biography*. New York: New American Library 1980

Pearsall, Ronald. *Night's Black Angels: The Forms and Faces of Victorian Cruelty*. New York: McKay 1975

Purcell, William. *Onward Christian Soldier: A Life of Sabine Baring-Gould*. London: Longmans 1957

Questions with Answers taken from Dr. Watts' Hymns for Children [1838 ed. alluded to in . . .]. Boston, MA: Sabbath School Society 1842. See also Mrs. Cottle.

Rattenbury, John Ernest. *The Evangelical Doctrines of Charles Wesley's Hymns*. London: Epworth Press 1941

—. *Wesley's Legacy to the World*. London: Epworth Press 1928

Ritson, Joseph. *The Romance of Primitive Methodism*. London: Dalton 1909

Routley, Erik. *Hymns and Human Life*, 2nd edn. London: Murray 1959

—. *Christian Hymns Observed*. London: Mowbray 1983

Sager, Milton. *When a Great Tradition Modernizes*. Chicago: Chicago University Press 1972

Shücking, Levin C. *The Puritan Family*. Trans. Brian Battershaw. New York: Shocken Books 1970

Semmel, Bernard. *The Methodist Revolution*. New York: Basic Books 1973

Sizer, Sandra S. *Gospel Hymns and Social Religion: The Rhetoric of Nineteenth-Century Revivalism*. Philadelphia: Temple University Press 1978

Strachey, Lytton. *Eminent Victorians*, 2nd edn. London: Chatto 1921

Tamke, Susan. *Make a Joyful Noise unto the Lord: Hymns as a Reflection of Victorian Social Attitudes*. Columbus: Ohio University Press 1978

Taylor, Gordon Rattray. *The Angel-Makers: A Study in the Psychological Origins of Religious Change 1750-1850*. London: Heinemann 1958, rev. edn. Secker and Warburg 1973

Tennyson, Georg B. *Victorian Devotional Poetry: The Tractarian Mode*. Cambridge, MA: Harvard University Press 1981

Thomas, Gilbert. *William Cowper and the Eighteenth Century*. London: Allen and Unwin 1948 edn. (originally 1935)

Thomas, Keith. *Man and the Natural World: A History of the Modern Sensibility*. New York: Pantheon 1983

Thompson, Edward Palmer. *The Making of the English Working Class*. New York: Pantheon Books, and London: Gollancz 1964.

Toynbee, Arnold. *Arnold Toynbee: A Selection*. Ed. W.F. Tomlin. London: Oxford University Press 1978

Wearmouth, Robert F. *Methodism and the Working-Class Movements of England, 1800-50*. London: Epworth Press 1937

Werner, Julia Stewart. *The Primitive Methodist Connexion: Its Background and Early History*. Madison: University of Wisconsin Press 1984

Wilkinson, Alan. *The Church of England and the First World War*. London: SPCK 1978

Willey, Basil. *Nineteenth-Century Studies: Coleridge to Matthew Arnold*. London: Chatto 1949

Wingfield-Stratford, Esme. *A Victorian Tragedy*. London: Routledge 1931

ARTICLES

De Jong, Mary G. "I Want to Be Like Jesus: The Self-Defining Power of Evangelical Hymnody." *Journal of American Academy of Religion* LIV (1986): 461-93

Drain, Susan. "An 'Incomprehensible Innovation': The Application of Copyright Law to Hymn Publishing in the Church of England 1860-80." *Publishing History* 15 (1984): 65-90

Encyclopedia Britannica, 14th edn., "Slavery." 1972

James, David L. "Hightower's Name: A Possible Source." *American Notes and Queries* 13 (1959): 4-5

Tamke, Susan J. "Hymns for Children: Cultural Imperialism in Victorian England." *Victorian Newsletter* 49 (1976): 18-22

NAME AND SUBJECT INDEX

Working Men's Christian Association, hymns, 51
Wreford, John Russell, 209
Wren, Brian, 246, 248

Yonge, Charlotte M.: *Child's Christian Year*, 107, 142

Yattendon Hymnal. See Bridges, R.

Zinzendorf, Nicholas von, Count, 6
Zuckmayer, Carl, 196-7, 215

INDEX OF FIRST LINES AND TITLES
(Includes only items quoted or discussed)